BECOMING LA RAZA

RHETORIC AND **DEMOCRATIC** DELIBERATION
VOLUME 34

EDITED BY CHERYL GLENN AND STEPHEN BROWNE
THE PENNSYLVANIA STATE UNIVERSITY

Co-founding Editor: J. Michael Hogan

EDITORIAL BOARD:

Robert Asen (University of Wisconsin–Madison)
Debra Hawhee (The Pennsylvania State University)
J. Michael Hogan (The Pennsylvania State University)
Peter Levine (Tufts University)
Steven J. Mailloux (Loyola Marymount University)
Krista Ratcliffe (Marquette University)
Karen Tracy (University of Colorado, Boulder)
Kirt Wilson (The Pennsylvania State University)
David Zarefsky (Northwestern University)

Rhetoric and Democratic Deliberation focuses on the interplay of public discourse, politics, and democratic action. Engaging with diverse theoretical, cultural, and critical perspectives, books published in this series offer fresh perspectives on rhetoric as it relates to education, social movements, and governments throughout the world.

A complete list of books in this series is located at the back of this volume.

BECOMING LA RAZA

NEGOTIATING RACE IN THE CHICAN@ MOVEMENT(S)

JOSÉ G. IZAGUIRRE III

The Pennsylvania State University Press | University Park, Pennsylvania

This volume is published with the generous support of the Center for Democratic Deliberation at the Pennsylvania State University.

Library of Congress Cataloging-in-Publication Data

Names: Izaguirre, José G., III, author.
Title: Becoming la raza : negotiating race in the Chican@ movement(s) / José G. Izaguirre III.
Other titles: Rhetoric and democratic deliberation ; v. 34.
Description: University Park, Pennsylvania : The Pennsylvania State University Press, [2024] | Series: Rhetoric and democratic deliberation ; volume 34 | Includes bibliographical references and index.
Summary: "Provides a rhetorical history of the Chicana/o movement by examining pivotal movement texts of the mid- to late-1960s, showing the variety and multiplicity of the movement as it gained traction during an intense period of the Cold War"—Provided by publisher.
Identifiers: LCCN 2024035085 | ISBN 9780271098753 (hardback)
Subjects: LCSH: Chicano movement—History. | Mexican Americans—Politics and government—20th century. | Mexican Americans—Race identity. | Rhetoric—Political aspects. | United States—Race relations—History—20th century.
Classification: LCC E184.M5 I93 2024 | DDC 305.868/72073—dc23/eng/20240807
LC record available at https://lccn.loc.gov/2024035085

Copyright © 2024 José G. Izaguirre III
All rights reserved
Printed in the United States of America
Published by The Pennsylvania State University Press, University Park, PA 16802–1003

The Pennsylvania State University Press is a member of the Association of University Presses.

It is the policy of The Pennsylvania State University Press to use acid-free paper. Publications on uncoated stock satisfy the minimum requirements of American National Standard for Information Sciences—Permanence of Paper for Printed Library Material, ANSI Z39.48–1992.

For the first time in the history of the United States . . . there is a powerful current of opinion that places under judgment the very values and beliefs on which Anglo-American civilization has been built. Is that not unprecedented?
—Octavio Paz, *The Labyrinth of Solitude*

CONTENTS

List of Illustrations | ix

Preface | xiii

Acknowledgments | xix

Introduction | 1

1 A De/Colonial Aesthetic: Whiteness and Mexican American Politics (1848–1965) | 25

2 A Poetics of Apathy: The Farmworkers' Movement and El Plan de Delano (1966) | 42

3 A Poetics of Ambivalence: "I Am Joaquin" and the Year of La Raza (1967) | 68

4 A Poetics of Relationality: The Invention of a Global Raza (1968) | 105

5 A Poetics Otherwise: (Re)Bordering Mexican American Politics (1969) | 122

6 A Poetics of Deferral: La Raza, Ruben Salazar, and a Global Violence (1970) | 147

Conclusion | 181

Notes | 195

Bibliography | 215

Index | 237

ILLUSTRATIONS

1. Cover of the photobook *Basta! La Historia de Nuestra Lucha*, 1966 | 52

2. Luis Valdez and portion of "El Plan de Delano" from *Basta! La Historia de Nuestra Lucha*, 1966 | 55

3. Activists and portion of "El Plan de Delano" from *Basta! La Historia de Nuestra Lucha*, 1966 | 56

4. Activist yelling into megaphone from *Basta! La Historia de Nuestra Lucha*, 1966 | 59

5. Politicians and a portion of "El Plan de Delano" from *Basta! La Historia de Nuestra Lucha*, 1966 | 60

6. Agribusiness representatives and a portion of "El Plan de Delano" from *Basta! La Historia de Nuestra Lucha*, 1966 | 61

7. Portion of English text of "El Plan de Delano," 1966 | 62

8. Brief history of the National Farm Workers Association from *Basta! La Historia de Nuestra Lucha*, 1966 | 63

9. The last two pages of *Basta!* 1966 | 64

10. Portion of "I Am Joaquin" by Rodolfo "Corky" Gonzales, published in *La Raza*, 1967 | 76

11. Portion of "I Am Joaquin" by Rodolfo "Corky" Gonzales, published in *La Raza*, 1967 | 77

12. "Plan de La Raza," published in *La Raza*, 1967 | 80

13. Portion of "I Am Joaquin" by Rodolfo "Corky" Gonzales in scripted font, 1967 | 84

14. Portion of "I Am Joaquin" by Rodolfo "Corky" Gonzales, published by El Gallo Press, 1967 | 86

15. The Program of El Plan Espiritual de Aztlán, published in *El Gallo*, 1969 | 130

16. The Prologue of El Plan Espiritual de Aztlán by Alurista, published in *La Verdad*, 1969 | 133

17. The Prologue of El Plan Espiritual de Aztlán by Alurista, published in *El Gallo*, 1969 | 135

18. The Prologue of El Plan Espiritual de Aztlán by Alurista and a portion of brief synopsis of the Chican@ Youth Liberation Conference, published in *Bronce*, 1969 | 138

19. Portion of brief synopsis of the Chican@ Youth Liberation Conference, published in *Bronce*, 1969 | 139

20. English translation of the Program of El Plan Espiritual de Aztlán and the Prologue by Alurista, published in *El Grito del Norte*, 1969 | 141

21. Spanish translation of the Program of El Plan Espiritual de Aztlán and the Prologue by Alurista, published in *El Grito del Norte*, 1969 | 142

22. Collage of photographs taken during the Chican@ Moratorium, published in *La Raza*, 1970 | 160

23. Cover of the special issue of *La Raza* on the Chican@ Moratorium, 1970 | 163

24. Photograph of man and child at the Chican@ Moratorium, published in *La Raza*, 1970 | 165

25. Photographs of marchers at the Chican@ Moratorium, published in *La Raza*, 1970 | 166

26. Photograph of bride and groom at the Chican@ Moratorium, published in *La Raza*, 1970 | 167

27. Photographs of police at the Chican@ Moratorium, published in *La Raza*, 1970 | 170

28. Photographs of police outside the Silver Dollar Café, published in *La Raza*, 1970 | 171

29. Photographs of police engaging with Chican@s at Chican@ Moratorium, published in *La Raza*, 1970 | 174

30. Scene at the Chican@ Moratorium, published in *La Raza*, 1970 | 176

31. Back cover of the special issue of *La Raza*, 1970 | 179

PREFACE

It might be odd to say that I feel as if I have been destined to write this book, but, in some ways, it is difficult to set aside that feeling because of how strongly I felt I *needed* to write it. My parents were both Mexican American migrant workers who traveled throughout the Southeast and Midwest in the late 1960s and into the 1980s. They picked a range of fruits and vegetables, including melons, watermelons, onions, and oranges. Throughout their youth Gloria and José (or "Jr.") traveled for about six months out of the year to pick produce, barely having enough time to complete grade levels, much less make lasting friendships. Letting the seasons guide their work schedules, their homes were both here and nowhere. In fact, so busy were their travel schedules and so disparate from each other's that it was only through a felicitous set of circumstances that my parents even met. Spending his last year of high school at "home" in a small town in Texas (Mercedes), my father inquired about the young woman living next door to his grandmother in the next town (Weslaco)—my mother. After two years of distance dating and while my mother was working in Ohio, my father drove from his hometown in Texas to ask for my mother's hand in marriage. The rest, as they say, is "history."

Except that it isn't. In fact, saying so dismisses not only their past but the futures they energized, subjecting to deletion the hardships associated with their decision to leave strenuous but stable work in the fields to even consider a life outside of migrant labor. It erases the near-death experience that visited a sleepless father working two jobs while trying to earn a bachelor's degree, sets aside the pregnancy that enfeebled a young mother relying on a four-year-old son to make her peanut butter sandwiches, and makes light of the loneliness of living 350 miles away from the closest family while my father finished college. And this is without even making mention of the immigration from Mexico that started it all, the life lived in the "borderlands" of Texas, the entrepreneurial spirit and the endurance that made living in the United States possible at all. Naming these stories as "history" dehistoricizes their story; cheapens it; voids it of meaning for those that lived through it.

And yet, it would also be a mistake to presume that this "history" is just like that of every other Mexican American in the United States, or even that of every migrant worker. In fact, while I have certainly met others with similar stories, rarely have I ever encountered an *equivalent* one, if only because I rarely meet anyone with the last name Izaguirre! Although the fact that within the span of three generations, a family of migrant workers saw their first PhD and university professor join their lineage might be construed as (un)exceptional to some, it is my view that an appreciation and expectation of heterogeneity and difference also allows for and invites the creation of a special community among those that *happen* to share similar experiences, whether that be in the fields of migratory labor or not. Anticipating heterogeneity encourages community formation without denying the specificity of any one of its parts. Differences, in other words, form the grounds and supply the conditions for the political work that all of us benefit from. Without variation, we lose ourselves and each other.

Personally speaking, I escaped field work, but my parents' histories and herstories constitute my scholarly senses while I work in my own field of rhetorical studies. Through rehearsal and recollection, their history has inescapably become my own, and it informs not only the content of my inquiries but my positionality with respect to it—the faint sense that I am someone looking from the outside in. Their past struggles form an inescapable part of the identity I perform and experience daily as a scholar, even while I might not wear the same sunbaked skin. Yet when I began my research into Mexican American politics in the United States, I noticed a surprising lack of involvement from my family in what might have seemed a ready-made opportunity for them to be involved in their own self-determination. Their work in the fields certainly overlapped with el movimiento, but rather than take to the streets, they stayed and worked. When I asked my father about their lack of involvement in la causa, he said that in the 1970s they had heard of a "César Chávez" but, at the time, they hadn't thought too much of him. It seems that my family wasn't "moved" by any kind of social movement, and they don't seem to have regretted it. To them, it appears, Chávez and the broader movement's history mattered very little. And, growing up, Mexican American politics mattered very little to me too.

Now, this book does not necessarily supply an explanation for my family history's lack of convergence with the energy of Chican@ movement(s). Nor do I offer some rationale for why my family never really cared to be politically active despite sharing in a desire for self-determination. Although there is a place for that kind of research, ethnographic and even auto-ethnographic, I do not perform it here. Rather, this book really stems from a compelling interest to understand a phenomenon that I would not have otherwise known had I not been exposed to it during my graduate studies in communication. It was while I was at the University of Illinois that I first began to seriously consider the nature of Mexican American grassroots politics, culturally resonant public communication, and the wide range of activist participation among those that shared in what had defined my family's life in the United States. I discuss this more in the Introduction, but as I devoured this rhetorical history I was struck by two aspects of my journey's beginning: first, that the vantage point of elder white men, notable scholars John C. Hammerback and Richard J. Jensen, formed the basis for understanding mid-twentieth century Mexican American rhetorics, and second, that their vantage point, however generative, seemed to suggest that 1960s Mexican American rhetorics followed a predictable path from a discrete and definable "culture" to their final communicative forms. The second of these features, which I found to be the most unsettling given my own sense of distance from those events and my family's lack of political involvement, seemed to be undergirded and energized by the premise "Mexican American rhetorics are defined by an inherent Mexicanness." And, while I could not identify it at the time, the first feature seemed to be due to an overwhelming whiteness that rhetorical studies has endured and is now attempting to correct in earnest. In the two decades between the publication date of germinal essays on Mexican American rhetorics and when I entered graduate school, the central theoretical apparatus regarding the rhetorical rationale of Mexican Americans, the Chican@ movement, or its activists had gone nearly unquestioned and reinforced by editors of major publication outlets. Mexican Americans were, in essence, located firmly in a "field," rendered stuck in an inventional circle of "Mexicanness." The more provocative moments in Mexican American rhetorical history were explained by a simple linear procedure.

This book, consequently, tries to crack a scholarly imposition that would relegate Mexican American rhetorical invention to a presupposed historical or cultural foundation and, instead, suggests other resources and consequences for Mexican American rhetoric(s) as they were formulated and publicized in the 1960s. In some ways, this book provides a fresh accounting of a phenomenon that came to be known as the Chican@ movement(s). It tracks the variety of political energies undergirding this phenomenon at its inception and tries to offer a new point of reference for understanding how different Mexican Americans across the Southwest responded to it. In other ways, the book retraces a familiar story and simply tries to offer a different angle from which to view it. Both, I believe, are necessary to the rhetorical histories we write, for, in doing so, we multiply the histories that *can* be written.

Rhetorical study, after all, entails the interrogation of how things are made to "matter" (to borrow from the late Thomas Farrell), and for my family, Chican@ movement politics mattered less than their own concerns. But that didn't make my father and mother any less "Mexican American," nor does it manifest a failure in Chican@ movement rhetorics circulating during the mid-1960s and beyond. What I hope my project sparks is simply an interest in discerning just how multiple el movimiento was, and a guide for capturing the plethora of responses to Chican@ movement activism, whether that would have been acceptance, rejection, or apathy.

In the end, I am certainly trying to fill a historical lacuna in my own personal life with this book, but I'm also hoping to have written a book that might, at the least, begin to supply a framework for understanding the variety of interests that overlapped, clashed, and paralleled one another without requiring their intersection during a brief period in the vast history of Mexican American politics in the United States. While some might presume a more "accurate" rhetorical history could be told by interviewing my grandparents, uncles, aunts, or parents, tracking labor history, or even searching through the ephemeral and incomplete archive my paternal grandfather left behind, I think a curiosity compelled by an indirect connection also provides a meaningful stance from which to view Chican@ movement history. If anything, it makes the presumption of difference even easier to sustain, since I have no other alternative but to view it as an outsider—someone different—looking in toward a phenomenon that is already distant from me in time. This book presumes that Chican@ movement(s) were persuasive in diverse ways at various times or, stated another way, that *different* Chican@ texts made *different* things matter at *different* times while urging the formation of a new Mexican American community—La Raza. If my own experience is any indication, the lived experiences of Mexican Americans are varied, multiple, and divergent.

Even so, this book also puts into focus one of the more pivotal constructs that animates variations in and of Latinx politics—coloniality—that can also be seen in my family's history in the migrant work that required their whole attention. There were certainly personal constraints that prevented my family from participating in la causa, but it would be disingenuous and tragic to pin their apathy solely on their shoulders. Let's be clear on this point: there is a cost to political action. Taking seriously that there are, beyond personal decisions, external, violent pressures that *impose* particular outlooks on culture, language, and what might be deserved or expected in this life, this book attempts to showcase the interanimation of rhetorical work and a colonial impulse in operation when my parents were laboring in the United States during the second half of the twentieth century—and that is still at work in the lives of many who are viewed and treated as part of a so-called "invasion." This book hopes to show that Mexican American politics cannot be contained by a singular god-term like "history." Inventing ways of living life together is the result of ordinary men and women struggling and succeeding at "making things matter." This book simply tries to tell a part of that story, and, in doing so, makes an appeal for more inquiry into this crucial and eventful time in Mexican American politics.

ACKNOWLEDGMENTS

Since I began this journey nearly a decade ago, I have found that the company I keep matters more than the path I take. My partner and best friend, Liz, deserves the highest honor I can give, since she's also the greatest gift I have ever received. At no other time has that been truer than during the journey to publish this book. Rather than wait for the end, I thought it more fitting to place her at the top (verbally *and* visually) of these acknowledgments. This book is as much a product of her prodding and listening ears as it is a work of my hands. I couldn't have done it, nor would I ever have wanted to, without her.

Many mentors and colleagues too have, at one point or another, served as conversation partners, incisive readers, curious scholars, and champions during the writing of this book. I will, unfortunately, probably leave some off this list of recognition, and for that I already feel remorseful. Still, I would feel worse not even trying to express my appreciations, and so here goes!

Colleagues at the University of Texas at Austin have been a constant stream of support. Mark Longaker read the draft a few times, each time reading my unnecessarily dense prose with care. Davida Charney too asked incisive questions that compelled me to solidify my own scholarly identity—a feature of her scholarly generosity that I'm sure many of us within her circle of influence have both felt and appreciated. Her comments encouraged me to be the best scholarly version of myself. The Department of Communication Studies at UT also provided a place to share my ideas. To the weekly writing group composed of members of the Rhetoric Society of America student chapter (RSA@UT-Austin), I owe special thanks. Kimber Harrison, Jamie Bezotte, Nathaniel Repay, and Abigail Burns, bright and talented emerging scholars of rhetoric, made various chapters you will read in this book better. Two special people in my home Department of Rhetoric and Writing, Holly Schwadron and Sara Casselberry, were invaluable in getting this project off the ground. Without their diligence, this project would have not received the institutional support it called for. Many thanks to you.

Important on this journey too were scholarly communities outside of Texas. Drs. Sara McKinnon, Allison Prasch, Rob Asen, Jennell Johnson, Rob

Howard, Anirban Baishya, the Department of Communication Arts at the University of Wisconsin–Madison, as well as its graduate students, invited me to speak on my book project and supplied productive conversations that made the latter portions of the book better. I also want to thank Mario García and the rest of the Sal Castro Memorial Conference crew, a group of community activists, scholars, and partners invested in histories of Mexican American politics that listened and probed my work in what might be the last Memorial Conference in Santa Barbara, California. What a delight to spend a few days discussing each other's work and encouraging each other to continue to insist that Mexican American histories be part of our scholarly conversations. Interlocutors have also emerged from unanticipated places. I want to thank Kelly Happe and Barbara Biesecker for their intellectual spurring, and my new home, the Department of Communication at the University of Colorado Boulder, who have been incredibly affirming and supportive. Special thanks also go to Ralph Cintron, who is from my hometown of Mercedes, Texas, and graduated from Mercedes High School like myself. His written prose is one I've looked to for inspiration and his sophisticated use of language to describe the politics of everyday people has been a reminder that the things we write about, regardless of how "lofty" or not they might be viewed, gain special significance when we write about them with reverence and curiosity.

Much like everyone else's writing in the last five years, my writing also felt the weight of the COVID-19 pandemic, and because of this I have to admit that my nonscholarly company has been just as important to the writing of this book as has been the academy. For nearly two decades Jeremy and Lyndsi Parker have been faithful friends who have refused to stop believing in me and my contributions. Dustin and Jodie, as well as Thomas and Lorissa, were people I could just be "me" around, which was crucial for my sanity as I started a new job that had very few options for social gatherings. Similarly, a group text involving a mix of PhDs and professionals helped me maintain perspective on life through many, many memes. I am thankful for them.

As with most projects of significance, this book could not have been possible without material supports in the form of labor, finances, and time. I would not have been able to complete this book project without a College Research Fellowship from the College of Liberal Arts, nor would I have been able to take research trips without a Summer Research Fellowship. I also want to acknowledge the Office of the Vice President for Research, Scholarship and Creative Endeavors of the University of Texas at Austin for funding for this book project. These generous awards were pivotal to completing the book manuscript and were awarded by my previous institution, the University of Texas at Austin. Archivists, librarians, and library assistants across the country provided invaluable labor in creating scans, helping secure permissions, finding archival materials, and the like. Molly Hart has been amazing, working with me on multiple projects, including this one. Xaviera Flores, too, just a delight to work with, looking out for me and for communities typically left out of the conversation of academic work. I want to mention Kristen Chinery and Dawn Lawson at Wayne State University, Sara Conner and Tim Noakes at San Diego State University, Laura R. Senturia at the Denver Public Library, Carla Alvarez at the Benson Library at the University of Texas at Austin, and archivists at the University of Texas-Rio Grande Valley. Without this material support, this book would have been impossible.

I also need to thank the activists who are and continue to be invested in Chican@ movement history. Some have since passed away, while others continue to be involved in la causa in new ways. Tessa Koning-Martinez, daughter of Elizabeth "Betita" Martinez, believed in the project right away. Alurista also gladly gave support, as did Joe Razo, editor of *La Raza*. Richard Saiz and Carlos LeGerrette both gave insight into the publication of *La Verdad* and were willing to give their support to someone they had never met before but who wanted to include them in this project. Lea Ybarra shared information via email, Félix Gutierrez answered an email sent at the last minute(!), and the Gonzales family graciously allowed me to reproduce portions of Rodolfo "Corky" Gonzales's "I Am Joaquin" in this book. Though they certainly did not need to grant permission to an unknown scholar living in Texas, Charlotte Gonzales especially was receptive, generous with her time, and sympathetic to the struggles Mexican Americans face. I am, in no uncertain terms, grateful for her and the Gonzales family's support.

Finally, my extended family have been so supportive of my work, even when it has at times provoked sharp disagreements. My parents always ask how my writing is going, even when this history did not intersect with their own. My siblings called attention away from writing when it was necessary. My in-laws too have been accepting of the work I do. While I don't get to see them all as much as I would like, they have never rejected me. That deserves some credit!

Special thanks too go to Archna Patel and Josie DiNovo, as well as Alex Ramos, Catherine Osborne, and the entire production team at The Pennsylvania State University Press who have worked to make this book a better product. Starting this process during a pandemic certainly did not make for the best conditions to start a publication relationship. Yet Archna and Josie have been incredibly patient with me as a first-time author, reading drafts and taking time to explain the publication process to someone as dense as me. Josie, who I think has been part of this project the longest, has also been a joy to work with as I navigated the tedious task of producing a final form of the manuscript and acquiring all necessary permissions. And, as for the reviewers of this book, the project is better because of their care. At a time when we all worried about COVID tests, online teaching, and simply bearing the burdens provoked by a global pandemic, generous scholars read this manuscript and offered to make it better. I hope it makes them proud.

To my children, Rebekah and Eleanor. As they have grown up, they have probed more and more into what I do, what my research accomplishes, what it means for me and for them. Never have they complained about my research trips. Neither have they ever questioned whether the work was worth it. Instead, they have wondered aloud what race means, how it shapes social relations, why it does so, questioned its legacies, and, ultimately, asked how and why race has mattered for Mexican Americans. Perhaps most important, they have reflected on what it means for them to share in a Mexican American legacy. In short, they've learned to appreciate what it is to think and live rhetorically in a shared world. And that is one of their many gifts to me.

INTRODUCTION

On March 10, 1968, the widely acclaimed "presidente" of Mexican American activism[1] César Chávez appealed to a crowd of nearly ten thousand people to sustain their commitment to nonviolent activism. Still striving in a wage strike that was then in its third year, activists were fatigued and frustrated. Agribusiness giant Giumarra Vineyard Corporations stoked those frustrations to a boiling point by fervently, and in some cases violently, resisting the movement in and out of the fields.[2] Some activists viewed violence as a pragmatic solution to Giumarra's counter-resistance, and, in response to this growing sentiment, Chávez stopped eating. Doing so created an opportunity to spotlight this violent turn and, at the same time, encouraged activists to stay true to the nonviolent "destiny" they had circulated in the 1966 El Plan de Delano.[3] Nonviolence had been integral to the farm workers' resistance since it began in 1965, but, most important, nonviolence had worked. Contracts between the National Farm Workers Association (NFWA) and growers had been signed. Wages, however meager, were increased. Most important, "campesinos" gained bargaining power. Although showing signs of fragility at this crucial juncture, self-representation had been achieved. Why abandon nonviolence now?

Not all activists agreed, however, with Chávez's assessment of the potency and appropriateness of nonviolence for Mexican American politics. At a February 1968 symposium held during Chávez's fast for nonviolence at the University of California, Los Angeles, Mexican American activists defended violent, societal upheaval—political revolution—as a necessary response to a pervasive *and* systemic whiteness repressing Mexican Americans not only in California's fields but everywhere. Reies López Tijerina, who was on appeal bond for his participation in the shoot-out with police at Tierra Amarilla, New Mexico, in 1967, pronounced the emergence of a new consciousness taking hold among Mexican Americans. Violence was part and parcel of that awakening, and, in his mind, violence was a timely addition to the ways in which Mexican Americans operated as political activists: "The violence in New Mexico was the moment of awakening of La Raza. . . . I myself am not a violent man. I don't believe in outright violence. But in dealing with our government, we find it urgent and natural to make our demands in a different way from 30 to 40 years ago."[4] Luis Valdez, who had been part of Chávez's efforts in California only two years prior as a coauthor of El Plan de Delano and as the director of Teatro Campesino, lambasted the racial repression instituted by "gabachos" (i.e., Anglos). Valdez made clear that nothing less than political revolution was an acceptable strategy for Mexican Americans to deploy: "It's time for a new Mexican revolution. . . . And which Chicanos are going to lead the next revolution? The ones in the belly of the shark! Nosotros! We're going to lead that revolution!"[5] Self-representation through nonviolence might have been a "destiny" for some, but others cast doubt on its efficacy. If political gains were to follow Mexican Americans into the next decade, violence could not be dismissed out of hand.

There are at least two ways that past and current rhetorical scholarship interested in Mexican American politics might help us explain this apparent friction brewing over the question of non/violence, both of which respect the multifaceted and deeply cultural communicative acts of the Chican@ movement phenomenon taking shape in the later 1960s. We might, for example, take this moment to be indicative of a clash in personalities. César Chávez, on the one hand, believed nonviolence to be a moral and religious imperative for activist work,[6] and he and his partners believed that nonviolence was the best strategic play for the farmworkers despite the intensified resistance.[7] His fast for nonviolence in the face of violence levied against him and the organization he cocreated with Dolores Huerta displayed how far he was willing to go to insist upon nonviolence and how influential he was in sustaining it in the farmworkers' movement. Those present at the symposium, on the other hand, seemed ready to accept violence as an appropriate "alternative," and, with the newly made hero Tijerina in attendance,[8] violence only gained greater appeal for the ways it brought Mexican American political visions to life. Attributing this felt disagreement over non/violence to personal preferences or personalities roots whatever discourse(s) encouraged their acceptance in agents and their actions,[9] and it ensures taking into account how a "Mexican American" culture, broadly defined, played a role in shaping the rhetorical decision-making of movement leaders. An individuated approach to this moment in 1968, in other words, is underwritten by the belief that agents shape the rhetorical landscape in which they participate, and we can assess and affirm rhetorical choices by directing attention to the ways in which these actors parlayed their personal experiences, cultural praxis, and/or political affinities into these choices.

We could, in addition, approach this rhetorical dissonance as indicative of a misalignment in ideological perspectives constituting Mexican American politics, as Mariscal does when he locates Chávez within a movement filled with alternative, competing political orientations all coinciding in el movimiento of the latter part of the twentieth century.[10] Focusing on vocabularies or "ideographs" threading line(s) of arguments together,[11] an ideological approach broadens the scope beyond single individuals and encourages a systemic interrogation of activist rhetorics—including the communities that adhere to and around them—all resonating together as a whole. The ideology of the NFWA and its activists, since its inception, had been relatively conservative, and in this moment in 1968, at least ideologically speaking, advocates of nonviolence evinced this traditional bent in earnest.[12] Ana Raquel Minian details how the organization often projected their membership as "an idealized figure of the physically disciplined resident/laborer deserving rights,"[13] with whom many in and outside of the farmworkers' movement identified.[14] Rejecting violence, then, was a logical and fitting choice for those associated with and persuaded by the farmworkers' movement. For others, violence channeled an assertiveness linked to direct-action politics that those within and outside of Mexican American politics promoted. Alaniz and Cornish capture this perspective when, reflecting on movement activism, they assert that "nonviolence can be an extremely effective *tactic* in the face of overwhelming force, but as a *principle* it is reactionary."[15] More than simply reacting to their circumstances, Mexican American activists had also begun their own organizations across the United States, published their own newspapers, and actively worked to mobilize communities to meet their own needs. Tolerating and even calling for violence, then, simply represented an insistence on maintaining the right to choose the self-determination already guiding activist work in the late 1960s. An ideological analysis surfaces rationales for both frictions and solidarity within a large movement with many different actors, and it allows scholars to ground rhetorical choices within a relatively stable network of ideas while still affirming some flexibility between the way that specific rhetorical choices might be communicated. This firm flexibility captured in the ideological approach, incidentally, fits the "cultural" angle as well, since it invites a coherence that is situated specifically in Mexican American symbols and histories.

Although agential and ideological approaches to Mexican American rhetorics of the 1960s account for robust scholarly examinations, both lack adequate ways of dealing with the variation and variability of Mexican American politics in the middle of the twentieth century. For, while we can certainly recognize the effectivity of singular actors in Mexican American politics in the twentieth century, a multiplicity of agents both named and unnamed came together to form a new political scene. These same activists, all with their own purposes and discrete rhetorical capacities, contoured a Mexican American movement over space-time, building and elaborating upon past discourse(s) as they negotiated new and emerging context(s). At times, too, Mexican American texts were products of multiple actors, which complicates attempts to identify relevant rhetors. Though certainly useful and even necessary, an emphasis on singular actors inadvertently flattens a Mexican American movement that was as stochastic as it was upheld by popular individuals. Similarly, an ideological perspective certainly recognizes a common rationale for the diversity of appeals constituting Mexican American politics, but an ideological perspective risks abstracting communication from a highly energetic context and reducing rhetorical choices to singular, totalizing motives. While a rhetor might be carried along by ideological commitments, even positing ultimate terminologies such as "nonviolence," "La Raza," or "nationalism" as formative vocabularies for activist work, there is an indeterminacy that persists in all rhetorical discourse. This indeterminacy stems from rhetoric's interconnectedness to multiple, overlapping spheres of influence—including personal experience(s). An ideological perspective, though generative for injecting a degree of predictability into otherwise unpredictable rhetorical discourse and for including a cultural appreciation specific to "Mexican American" rhetoric, nonetheless erases the response-ability of Mexican American communicative acts at the same time that it might appear to elucidate defining features.

There is, however, another way to apprehend not only the tensions between Mexican American rhetorics but the solidarity constituting Mexican American politics that, on the one hand, refuses firm grounding in persons, organizations, or even ideological orientations and, on the other, invites a robust appreciation of the ways in which tumultuous contexts, both internal and external, informed the production of Mexican American suasive discourse(s). Taking seriously the *aesthetic* features of discourse, we can pivot our rhetorical analysis of Mexican American political discourse(s) in the latter 1960s from singular rationales and gain an analytical footing that both affirms individuated interventions while also amplifying the multiplicity of rhetorical forms that might appear in response to the multifaceted influence of context(s). An aesthetic appreciation, moreover, allows us to bring together examinations of the rhetorical features of a text with a formative and equally aesthetic element baked into political dynamics in the United States since its inception—race. Although at times more latent than salient, an appreciation of the ways in which race and racial identity were integral to inventions of "Chican@" movement discourse reveals a fluid, evolving, multifaceted, and flexible Mexican American politics that cohered in the middle of the twentieth century.[16] Returning to our opening rhetorical problem of 1968, it is important to remember that between 1965 and 1967, there was a growing yet variable racial interest among Chican@ movement activists and a palpable rhetorical investment in representing Mexican American politics racially—most notably, though not exclusively, through the moniker "La Raza." Luis Valdez referred to the farmworkers' movement as a "murmuring" of La Raza giving way to "revolution" in 1966.[17] In 1967, Rodolfo "Corky" Gonzales published and circulated the (in)famous "I Am Joaquin: An Epic Poem," a text seemingly pushing for a racial—and at times problematic—view of Mexican American history.[18] And, by the fall of 1968, activists Elizabeth "Betita" Sutherland and Beverly Axelrod did not hide the racial emphasis of El Grito del Norte. In this newspaper proclaiming the "Cry of the North," the editors made clear their intention "to advance the cause of justice for poor people and to preserve the rich cultural heritage of La Raza."[19] By the time we witness the complicated coherence of Chican@ movement activists surfacing in 1968, racial concerns were more, not less, pressing. Some activists had rallied around a sharp racial conflict with "gringos," while others, like Chávez, made clear an intention to partner with institutional whiteness.[20] This moment in 1968 reveals how, in addition to being personally motivated and ideologically rich, Chican@ movement discourse was rife with racially derived dissonances and harmony, stasis on the question of racial representation, and dis/agreement concerning the racial cast of Mexican American politics.

The breadth of variations and differentiations in Mexican American politics in the mid- to late 1960s, to be sure, has been noted and explained by various scholars across the disciplinary landscape. During the early years of Chican@ movement(s), which, for the purposes of this book, began in 1965 with the farmworkers' movement,[21] there were public frictions and divergences, as well as strong coherences between and among activists and their preferred modes of Mexican American politics. Chávez's strategic (and for others disappointing) disagreements with the more "radically" prone has been documented,[22] as have been the tensions among the other three "horsemen" Rodolfo "Corky" Gonzales, Reies López Tijerina, and José

Angel Gutierrez.[23] So too have contributions from and fractures in Chicana feminism occurring later in the 1970s been unearthed and "retrofitted" to provide rich accounts of the breadth and depth of Chican@ movement activism both before and after the 1971 Conferencia de las Mujeres.[24] The unique contributions of activists such as Anna Nieto-Gomez, Lucy Moreno, Francisca Flores, Julia Luna Mount, Enriqueta Longeaux y Vasquez, the writers involved with *Hijas de Cuauhtémoc*, and Chicana participants in the East LA Blowouts like Vicky Castro have been shown to be not only parallel but pivotal to evolutions in Chican@ movement(s). Moreover, the wide range of organizations differing in objectives, goals, and ideologies constituting "the" movement as the years progressed have recently been reaffirmed.[25] These studies are admirable in their breadth and, indeed, necessary, since they showcase the diversity of political proposals and ideological pledges constituting Chican@ movement(s) and the exclusive praxis these multiple arms eventually espoused (e.g., cultural nationalism). Nevertheless, the racial negotiations underpinning Chican@ movement discourse in "Plans," chapbooks, newspapers, marches, and speeches, and the ways that racially derived claims informed evolutions in Chican@ movement(s) over spacetime, have yet to be examined for their augmentation and diversification of Mexican American politics. Contentions over whether or not to be violent or nonviolent, whether to accept or reject political revolutions, how to implement nationalism, and even how to dodge the draft, though certainly pragmatically motivated, also hinged on the formation of a racial identity that aligned or otherwise reinforced these decisions among Mexican Americans coming together in new ways. There were, in addition to these Chican@ activist interventions, racially forming consequences linked to the political context(s) activists encountered and constituted with each intervention, ramifications that were both internal and external to Chican@ movement(s). Chican@ movement activists and their communicative acts, in short, were consistently guided and energized by racial concerns.

This book, *Becoming La Raza: Negotiating Race in the Chican@ Movement(s)*, is a rhetorical history that elaborates upon the premise that race was a crucial, consequential, and constitutive feature of Chican@ Movement(s) and, consequently, was one of its *defining* features. In addition to ideology, culture, and political orientation, this project shows how various activists, writers, and leaders of grassroots organizations were also guided in their communicative praxis by a negotiation of racial identity amid and in response to multiple violent circumstances undersigned by systemic and sedimented whiteness. This book, thus, joins many in the field of rhetorical studies and beyond that have set their sights on exposing the impact of and offering a corrective to an overwhelming whiteness in the discipline.[26] Yet while there are certainly scholarly motivations for a book that centers race in Chican@ movement rhetorical histories, this book also supplies additional reasons for why banning conversations about race *in* history in the United States is neither optimal nor desirable.[27] This book highlights how, whether from "above" or "below," race is an inescapable, material(izing) trope whose enduring legacies inform the ways in which not-white communities survive.[28] Race is no more unavoidable than, to borrow Matthew Houdek's language, "breathing" and, perhaps for this reason alone, cannot be set aside.[29] Moreover, in following how race and non/violence follow one another over time throughout Chican@ movement histories, this book joins in the circulation of critical reminders to "refuse" to abandon these conversations because, for many of us, our histories have been and continue to be horrifically, if not always visibly, marked by violence.[30] As Ersula Ore reminds us, the terrorization of not-white lives is, in many respects, central to the performance of US citizenship,[31] which means that to "refuse to forget" is to insist on not only the ever elusive "social change" but also the possibilities of an entirely different political and just spatio-temporal order.[32] This book, though certainly examining a movement that might be viewed as sufficiently covered, reinforces the premise that to chronicle US history in its various manifestations necessitates the composition of a racial history. The two are inextricably linked, and, as I will show in this rhetorical history, race was a formidable influence in the contours of Chican@ movement(s).

At the same time, this book does not simply inject more voices into Chican@ movement history—as necessary a project as that is. Rather, to continue with this aural metaphor, this book *amplifies* some familiar and not so familiar voices as I trace the racial impulses within Chican@ movement(s). That is, I take seriously the way that Chican@ movement discourse(s) also compelled responses from other Chican@ activists. I will say more about my choice of sources for this rhetorical history shortly, but a quick note for now. Chican@ movement discourse(s), whether racially concerned or not, were not *obeyed*, even if they were taken up later. But, to trace this influence *within* Chican@ movement discourse(s), I need to address one of the more prohibitive points of view preventing scholars from seeing such intra-movement influence. Readers must grapple with how a scholarly obsession with "new" is itself a form of silencing under the guise of "progress" that keeps us from listening intently to the voices that we have. For this, I have focused on fragments of communication we can generally call "texts" and, while I might certainly include "new" texts in the analysis, their newness is not what defines their inclusion nor what grants them rhetorical significance. This book is an attempt *to see* the racial consequences of Chican@ movement rhetorical work,[33] whether that be in communication that has yet to be uncovered or in communicative acts that, while familiar, have not (yet) been deemed racially compelling. In short, this book promises a reading of Chican@ movement texts that has, thus far in rhetorical scholarship, not been accomplished. In doing so, it proposes a history that takes seriously the breadth of rhetorical practices converging and clashing to form "Chican@ Movement(s)."

Inventing Rhetorical Histories of Chican@ Movement(s):
Racial Rhetorical Criticism in De/Colonial Mode

Becoming La Raza supplies a Chican@ movement rhetorical history that examines Chican@ texts published and circulated shortly after the emergence of the farmworkers' movement in California. This book takes part in a plethora of scholarly histories demonstrating dis/continuities in "the" Chican@ movement of the 1960s, 1970s, and 1980s. These history projects support the "long" thesis of the Chican@ movement posited by Chican@ studies scholars,[34] by highlighting activists, organization, and ideologies over the span of decades if not centuries.[35] Scholars contributing to this expansive sense of "Chican@ movement" include Rudy Acuña, Ernesto Chávez, Ernesto Vigil, Juan Gómez-Quiñones, and Irene Vasquez.[36] More recent scholars, such as Dionne Espinoza, Maylei Blackwell, Marc Rodriguez, and Stacey Sowards, too, have all recognized the breadth of Chican@ activism over a long(er) period of time by supplying or advocating for studies that trace Chican@ politics over decades.[37] What has come to be known as el movimiento was not only a punctiliar phenomenon spanning a couple of decades; it was, as these studies and Paz's comment in the epigraph attest, enduring.

Nevertheless, approaches that adhere to a "long" perspective, inadvertently or not, appear to presume that movement vocabularies, figures, and styles solidified as soon as they were invented. Studies taking *too* long of a perspective gloss over the multiple negotiations made by activists as Chican@ movement activism proliferated across the United States. In the parlance of rhetorical studies, longer histories risk neglecting the contingencies of Chican@ movement activism and the kairotic pressures informing the invention of movement discourse(s). In contrast to these studies with timespans equaling a decade or more, I take seriously the processual quality of communication and supply a "short(ened)" history of discourses constituting the movement's racial politics during the early years of its emergence, 1965–1970. I do so to apprehend how Chican@ movement discourse(s) negotiated racial interests in response to a variety of contextual factors occurring concurrently during these years: the accumulation and congregation of Mexican American activists who possessed discrete values, perspectives and political leanings, the proliferation of activists across different spaces in the United States (for example, from California to New Mexico to Texas), and the weight of the Cold War increasingly impacting not-white persons and Mexican Americans in particular in disproportionate ways throughout the Viet Nam War. Each chapter contributes to the composition of a rhetorical history that takes racial dynamics into account without presuming that Chican@ movement discourse(s) were enduring, stable, or necessarily visible all at once. By using a shorter periodization to bound the analysis of Chican@ movement(s), I propose a more associative and pluralistic vision of Chican@ movement discourse(s) that takes seriously the presence of contingencies and timeliness. Thus, it is not that this book centralizes *the* Chican@ movement or even *a* movement. This rhetorical history, rather, concerns Chican@ movement(s).

As a rhetorical history focused on discovering and explicating the racial dynamics of Chican@ movement discourse(s), this study follows the "imperative" of racial rhetorical criticism called for by Lisa Flores. Racial rhetorical criticism, she writes, is a methodology "that is reflective about and engages the persistence of racial oppression, logics, voices, and bodies and that theorizes the very production of race as rhetorical."[38] This book engages with Chican@ movement discourse(s) with an eye toward the racial dynamics energizing claims to land, nationalist politics, and creation of its popular figures of speech like La Raza and Aztlán. Yet because each chapter traces racial impulses in Chican@ movement discourse(s), the explicitness with which activists denounced whiteness, or the consequences of adopting nationalism as a political program, I view the aggregation of what came to be called "Chican@ movement(s)" as constituting a unique *racial project*. Following Omi and Winant, who define a racial project as "an interpretation, representation, or explanation of racial identities and meanings, and an effort to organize and distribute resources (economic, political, cultural) along particular racial lines,"[39] I take it that ways in which Chican@ movement discourse(s) managed racial expectations, posited racial identities, appealed to racialized histories, or projected ideals of a "Bronze people" constituted a *way of seeing* Mexican American bodies and their political actions. There was an active investment in *racializing* Mexican American politics by activists, just as there was for other racial groups around the United States leaning into establishing not-white, non-European political communities (Black Power, Red Power). At stake in the fabrication of how Chican@ movement activism was interpreted racially by those on the outside looking in were resources of all kinds, ranging from political clout to material livelihoods, and consequently this book follows Flores's call to attend to race in rhetorical criticism by treating Chican@ movement(s) as constitutive of a racial project taking shape over space-time.

The rise of the popular Chican@ movement terminology in La Raza suggests, certainly, a racial emphasis, but it would be a mistake to presume that the *use* of this language was consistent or stable among the various activists and discourse(s) that deployed it. Moreover, to take the use of the language of La Raza in 1966 as equivalent to its use in the formation of "La Raza Unida Party" in 1970 flattens the rhetorical work accomplished—or problems introduced—with each iteration and deployment. To borrow again from Omi and Winant, I take it that a multitude of Chican@ movement texts, separated by space-time, all contributed to a multi-faceted process of "racial formation," namely, the ways that "racial identities are created, lived out, transformed, and destroyed."[40] As this book's tracing reveals, racial vocabularies were deployed differently and movement discourse(s) projected racial identities in discrete, though familiar, ways. Chican@ movement texts constituted a multifaceted, multivalent, and polyphonic racial project shaped heavily by intra- and extra-movement context(s), and, in turn, different texts participated in racial forming processes in discrete ways. The racial hues present in Chican@ movement(s) were a consequence of rhetorical work. Whether implicit or explicit, this book identifies and interrogates how race was a *topos*, an energetic communicative "place" from which discourses are invented and at which they are contested,[41] and I explore how collections of various Chican@ movement texts participated in racializing Mexican Americans in the late 1960s. Taken collectively but not collapsed, each of my chapters discerns the racial formation accomplished in and through the texts under investigation.

Yet it is also important to recognize that the possibility of identifying race as a *topos* guiding Chican@ movement discourse(s) at all testifies to the formative and enduring power of coloniality in US political life. Contemporary ideas about race are, fundamentally, a *colonial* construct, a feature complicating Latinx identity in particular, and integral to building visions of "America."[42] Quijano puts it this way: "One of the fundamental axes of this model of power is the social classification of the world's population around the idea of race, a mental construction that expresses the basic experience of colonial domination and pervades the more important dimensions of global power.... The racial axis has a colonial origin and character, but it has proven to be more durable and stable than the colonialism in whose matrix it is established. Therefore, the model of power that is globally hegemonic today presupposes an element of coloniality."[43] This suggests that oppositions to and protests along a racial axis indicate an attempt to resist or otherwise unmake colonial impositions. In rhetorical studies, attempts to identify and resist colonial frameworks have shown to be a promising and productive scholarly pursuit.[44] With respect to understanding Latinx identity in particular, José Cortez and Romeo García's recent essays on "Latinx identity" and "Latinx writing" extend conceptions of what "Latinx" signifies by exposing the fictions that underlie its very (colonial) productions.[45] This scholarship, which is distinct from the "decolonizing" projects in rhetorical studies such as that called for by Michael Lechuga, Iris Ruíz, and Raúl Sánchez,[46] grapples with the comprehensiveness of colonialism's legacies, their persistence and endurance in the very architectures of knowledges in colonies and elsewhere, including how colonial relations become institutionalized vis-à-vis a "Colonial Matrix of Power" (CMP).[47]

As scholars in rhetorical studies turn toward the promises and potentials of taking coloniality into account, I propose that, in the scholarly project of racial rhetorical criticism, a recognition of a *de/colonial mode* in rhetorical discourse(s), particularly from discourse(s) typically cast as "subaltern" or "marginalized," complicates viewing de/coloniality as a monologic, univocal, or homogenous process in which "rhetoric" participates.[48] That is, the de/coloniality operationalized in rhetorical appeals cannot be viewed in binary terms but, in the words of Mignolo, should be understood as an "option(s)" generating procedure.[49] Present as a corollary of coloniality, de/coloniality refers to an analytic *and* a praxis, a means of reinventing scholarly profiles in academic spaces and a political program for "re-existence" that (re)imagines life apart from coloniality outside of and at the boundaries of coloniality's scope.[50] Driven by what Mignolo describes as "border thinking," or invention from the limits of coloniality's reaches,[51] de/coloniality, whether emerging from the ivory tower or on the streets, involves the creation of options outside of the singular universe proposed in colonial visions. If the thrust of de/coloniality resides in "nothing more than a relentless analytic effort to understand, in order to overcome, the logic of coloniality underneath the rhetoric of modernity, the structure of management and control that emerged out of the transformation of the economy in the Atlantic, and the jump in knowledge that took place both in the internal history of Europe and in between Europe and its colonies,"[52] then adopting de/coloniality as a *mode* within racial rhetorical criticism entails interrogating the multiple ways coloniality vis-à-vis race is dis/instituted at multiple scales, from individual to communities. Moreover, a de/colonial mode entails discerning how institutional arrangements ramify colonial ties and how these inform the rhetorical work of those oppressed by racially motivated subjugation. The concept of the "white racial frame," for example, has many points of contact with colonialism and is itself underwritten by it. Joe Feagin and others identify the dominance of the "white racial frame" for understanding racial dynamics in the United States.[53]

But, where Feagin and others theorize the implementation of the white racial frame both from and apart from colonial tendencies, holding onto the colonial trace(s) of a racial project allows us to see the depth to which colonial work is a de/humanizing project affecting the whole of human experience(s), including self-perceptions.[54] In this book, I propose and enact a de/colonial mode in racial rhetorical criticism that recognizes the multiplicity of ways that Chican@ movement discourse(s) negotiated white supremacy, racial classifications, and racial violence over time in various and, at times, contradictory ways. In so doing, my deployment of a de/colonial mode enables seeing the political, de/colonial possibilities present in and accomplished through Chican@ movement discourse along the axis of race while refusing to see them as homogenous, unitary, or even convergent at any one time. De/coloniality is, in short, stochastic, at times faint or blurred, but it should never be circumscribed by strict definitions of what de/coloniality "looks like." To do so would be to impose the very homogenization that coloniality compels in and through all of us invoking such a right and making such demands.

In critiquing Chican@ movement discourse(s) in a de/colonial mode, we will see how coherences within Chican@ movement(s) were created while, at the same time, witnessing how dissonances complicated solidarity pure and simple. Chican@ movement discourse(s) constituting the racial project spanned a spectrum of de/coloniality, and while we might find some of these discourses insufficiently or inadequately "de/colonial," I find Walter Mignolo's distinction between de/coloniality (a conceptual and theoretical orientation) and decolonization (a formal political process) to be a helpful way of conceptualizing how Chican@ movement discourse(s) varied in their de/colonial pushes. De/coloniality, as Mignolo defines it, refers to "long term processes involving the bureaucratic, cultural, linguistic, and psychological divesting of colonial power." The process of decolonization, on the other hand, conjures images of a "handing over the instruments of government," more institutionally dependent than de/coloniality, and more fiction than fact.[55] Decolonization as a political project was a prominent political phenomenon during the Cold War, particularly during the 1960s, and assuredly informed Chican@ rhetoric(s). But decolonization was not necessarily part of the political interests of early Chican@ movement(s) rhetoric(s) until the writing of "El Plan Espiritual de Aztlán," nor was it always a feature of Chican@ movement racial rhetorics. These features of Chican@ movement(s) suggest(s) that de/coloniality and decolonization were two related though distinct discursive projects, existing, to be sure, on a spectrum over and against coloniality but not necessarily in alignment. They certainly *can* be, but it is not required. And consequently, writing a racial rhetorical history compels understanding how de/colonial work and decolonizing work differ, where they intersect, and how each might have reinforced and/or attenuated the other throughout Chican@ movement(s). De/coloniality and decolonization were not mutually exclusive, but neither were they equivalent *rhetorical* ends. Understanding their respective rhetorical forms enriches our understanding of the complexities involved in the invention of the Chican@ movement racial project and provides what I refer to here in this book as a portrait of the de/colonial praxis of Chican@ movement(s).

The Poetics of De/Colonial Praxis: An Examination of Chican@ Movement Aesthetics

This book's racial rhetorical history proposes taking seriously the ways that Chican@ movement(s) constituted a racial project. Yet, as I have suggested, race is a consequence of both intra-movement dynamics and external pressures. Viewed in this sense, the racial identities projected in and through Chican@ movement(s) cannot be viewed simply as a product of any one activist, text, or organization. Rather, following Chican@ studies scholar Carlos Gallego, who in his study of Chican@ poetry encourages scholars to attend to the political and identificational resonance of discursive forms when examining texts asserting a "Chican@" identity, I, too, pay focused attention to "forms." Gallego argues that identity is represented in the forms language takes—read aesthetics here—just as much as in proclamations of identity or the use of cultural scripts identifying communities,[56] which means that attention to the ways in which Chican@ texts participate in racial formation must attend not only to *what* is stated but also *how* proclamations of identity are represented. Although Gallego urges this methodological shift, in part, to loosen the boundaries of what can be labeled "Chican@" discourse,[57] my interest in this book is to surface how aesthetic forms activate and empower racial formations. While I am not advocating for a split between "form" and "content" (and neither is Gallego), what Gallego offers to this book's interest in tracing the racial rhetorical work in Chican@ movement text and, in following this thread, the de/colonial praxis of Chican@ movement discourse(s), is a reconceptualization of what constitutes the "identity" forwarded in and by Chican@ texts. That is, identity posited in and through texts is as much a product of how a text appears as it is of a text's assertions, particularly when the latter corresponds (or not) with shifts in the former.

In this book, I argue that tracing the racially formative power of Chican@ movement discourse(s) invites an aesthetic appreciation so as to understand not only how identity becomes "constituted" but to apprehend how various Chican@ movement rhetorics contributed to the Chican@ movement racial project in their own ways even while coalescing through the use of similar or equivalent claims. In rhetorical communication studies, Charland's essay on "constitutive rhetoric" is, understandably, recognized as a foundational explication of the formative power of discourse for inventing communal identities.[58] This ideologically-based approach has also been applied to the study of Chican@ movement identities by Fernando Delgado, Lisa Flores, and Marouf Hasian.[59] Although productive, the "constitutive" approach is limited because it emphasizes *what* assertions are mentioned rather than *how* these assertions are *represented*. It is one thing to surface vocabularies, for example, associated with Aztlán (such as people, Chican@, Nahua, etc.) and construct identifiable attributes. It is quite another to interrogate artistic renderings of Aztlán, to examine whether accented or not, to observe that the words might be handwritten in script rather than typed. Moreover, a focus on ideology emphasizes too much a coherence over time. The aesthetic interventions associated with movement vocabularies, even when ideologically coherent, as I will show throughout this book, were racially constitutive, but they also injected movement-altering differences. The aesthetics of constitutive discourse, in addition to forming community through the power of "ideas," cannot be dismissed as mere "ornamentation" to what otherwise might have appeared as an ideological consistency.

Aesthetic appreciations, however, have yet to achieve much recognition in studies of Chican@ movement(s) or in studies of Latin@ Vernacular Discourse (LVD) more broadly. Certainly, the study of LVD "implicat[es] the decolonial; that is, the process of decolonization,"[60] but scholars of Latinx rhetorics and Chican@ movement rhetorics in particular have yet to displace the equivocation between the "rhetorical" and the "strategic," a methodological orientation that misses how race and racial formation are sites operating in the realm of aesthetics—how bodies, communities, and actions are made to *appear* and be *seen* in political life. Although recent work, such as Darrel Wanzer-Serrano's study of the Young Lords Organization (YLO), showcases how generative a de/colonial approach to Latin@ rhetorics can be, his analysis of the YLO's "decolonial praxis" highlights the instrumentality of the YLO's rhetoric by forwarding the "delinking" processes attached to their politics.[61] As he sums up his work, "I do not intend this book to be a philosophical project on decoloniality. I seek, instead, to enrich our understandings of *how* activists perform epistemic disobedience and enact delinking through a critical engagement of the Young Lords' grassroots rhetoric and political action."[62] The YLO's rhetoric is racial insofar as it is also constitutive of a strategic reframing of their political nationalism within the US political landscape.[63]

However, by examining the aesthetics of Chican@ movement rhetorics, I highlight the importance of aesthetics to the formation—and unmaking—of regimes of racial representation in public life.[64] While I survey how this emerged in Mexican American politics in chapter 1, for now, I want to stress that racial representation(s) and their undoing converge at the level of the aesthetic. As Omi and Winant explain:

> While acknowledging the inherent instability and socially constructed characteristics of race, we argue that there is a crucial *corporeal* dimension to the race-concept. Race is *ocular* in an irreducible way. Human bodies are visually read, understood, and narrated by means of symbolic meanings and associations. Phenotypic differences are not necessarily seen or understood in the same consistent manner across time and place, but they are nevertheless operating in specific social settings. Not because of any biologically based or essential differences among human beings across such phonemic variables as 'color' or 'hair texture,' but because such sociohistorical practices as conquest and enslavement classified human bodies for purposes of domination—and because these same distinctions therefore became important for resistance to domination as well—racial phenotypes such as black and white have been constructed and encoded through the language of race. We define this process as *racialization*—the extension of racial meaning to a previously racially unclassified relationship, social practice, or group.[65]

Racial formation, Omi and Winant suggest, is a result of aesthetic (that is, rhetorical) interventions and corroborates with political complexes that are themselves subject to aesthetic (re)formulation(s).[66]

Yet, since racial rhetorical projects hinge on times and spaces,[67] it would be inappropriate to characterize these interventions as a "style." For Robert Hariman, a "style" can be and often is associated with a particular politics, a "repertoire" that has, at least conventionally, ossified through antecedent and established use.[68] Moreover, I cannot categorize these racializing interventions as fundamental features of "Chicano/a" identity. For, to do so, I risk essentializing an identity that gained political significance at a particular moment in time. My study unpacks the racial implications of many interventions, such as uses of English and Spanish language codes, illustrations, figures of speech, textual layouts, the location and placement of images on pages, media, and photographic reproductions. That is, I am interested not only in how these aesthetic decisions might have been part of an overall "strategy" of Mexican American politics (such as serving cultural nationalist ends). All of these interventions might have been, certainly, part of broader "strategies" and constitutive of a praxis with both explicit and unstated political and ideological objectives. García lands on the term "ethos" to describe what I am referring to here as "praxis."[69] Although we use different terms, we both attempt to take into account how practices, more than simply theories, ideas, or culture, were pivotal to how movement activists enacted their politics. I use the term "praxis" here because I want to note how the racial rhetorics of Chican@ movement(s) were contingent and productive communicative acts and surfaced in response to a variety of overlapping pressures, unforeseen situations, and emergent obstacles. Whether or not these racially consequential discourse(s) were pragmatically defined or wrapped up in explicit denouncements of whiteness and/or Blackness, the apprehension of a Chican@ movement racial project and its de/colonial force, I propose, lies in interrogating the aesthetics of Chican@ discourse(s) as they appeared and evolved over time.

Given the variety of aesthetic decisions comprising Chican@ movement discourse(s), I propose a conceptual frame for understanding the constellation of aesthetic features I identify in each of my case studies. Taken collectively, a term that captures an appreciation of the association between aesthetic features, their practical ramifications, and political commitments in rhetorical studies that I use for each chapter's conceptual framing is *poetics*. These intersections captured in the terminology of poetics are explored in classical sources,[70] yet scholars such as Jacques Rancière and Walter Mignolo have highlighted the politics of poetic processes resisting and remaking dominant, hegemonic controls.[71] Within Chican@ studies, attention to ways that social experiences such as colonialism or life in the borderlands have resulted in particular communicative patterns in Mexican American communities has given way to the illumination of what scholars have termed a "Chican@ poetics."[72] And, in a project dedicated to tackling how poetics empower de/colonial disruptions, particularly those along the axis of race and gender, micha cárdenas explicates the trans of color poetics that delineate the ways that trans persons navigate violence at multiple scales.[73]

I should be clear that in proposing a "poetics" for the language forms, figures, visualizations, signs, and symbols in my case studies, I do not mean to identify an "intention" or to somehow suggest that I have isolated "the" poetics of Chican@ movement rhetorics or even those belonging to a single activist-author. Although this project is influenced, in some ways, by Mikhail Bakhtin, this poetic interest is not a Bakhtinian sort of isolation.[74] Rather, what I mean to do in applying the term "poetics" for each chapter is to try to organize the aesthetic moves present in the text(s) under examination, capture a feature of the racial implications of its aesthetic interventions, and distinguish the contribution of each text to the Chican@ movement racial project evolving in the late 1960s. Furthermore, in using the terminology of poetics to capture the aesthetics present in Chican@ movement text(s), I mean to identify the intersections between context, identity, and politics that Chican@ rhetorics exemplified and highlight potential overlaps between interests guiding the fields of Chican@ studies, rhetorical studies, and politics that are normally un(der)explored.

Still, one might wonder what kind of *rhetoric* this book presupposes or offers, since my focus on aesthetics might suggest a "form" and "content" split that cannot actually be sustained. A consensus, to be sure, exists among scholars, namely that separating "form" from "substance" misses the appeal of form and the persuasiveness of the "surfaces" of discourse.[75] However, what I propose in this book is a more integrative appreciation of Chican@ "forms" and "contents," a perspective that takes the aesthetics of Chican@ discourse as constitutive of and crucial to the racial claims that galvanized Mexican Americans in the United States in the late 1960s. Historically, we have seen how race has been subject to and influenced by aesthetic (re)creations like the Negritude movement in the Antilles or muralistas in Mexico, and yet with respect to Chican@ movement discourse and its rhetorical features, namely, its figures, exploitations of generic conventions, play with language codes, or photographic representations, aesthetics have been either underappreciated or treated as a dismissible aspect of Chican@ movement discourse(s). This is regrettable. This book, however, highlights the interconnectedness between the "form" and "content," not by disentangling them but by showcasing the racial force of their integration in Chican@ discourse(s). Attending closely to the aesthetics of Chican@ movement rhetorics, thus, makes manifest various permutations of de/colonial praxis pervading Chican@ movement(s) in the mid- to late 1960s. The aesthetic investments I trace in the book typified how activists tried altering the racial "terms of the conversation" of US coloniality not simply by changing the content of their rhetorical work but also by attending to the forms of Mexican American politics in inessential ways.[76] Each of my case studies, which I preview below, identifies and analyzes the racial implications of the aesthetic work present in and through Chican@ movement(s).

Sources and Chapters

To write this racial rhetorical history, I turn to texts contributing to the (re)negotiation, (re)invention, and (re)circulation of Mexican American racial identity, all published and circulated at different times and in spaces. In many ways, Chican@ movement(s) can be understood as *textual* phenomena, among the many consequences of the "mimeograph revolution"[77] that witnessed publications from multiple marginalized communities displacing whiteness in favor of other forms of identification.[78] The formation of a Chicano Press Association (CPA) supported the proliferation and quick spread of vocabularies, ideologies, political orientation, and, yes, aesthetic choices. It should come as no surprise then that the years in which Chican@ movement(s) gained significant traction also saw an expansion of Chican@ print spaces, empowering growth and, at the same time, introducing frictions between and among Chican@ activists who responded to antecedent discourse(s). We might view this textual affiliation as a sort of connective tissue stitching together both consonant and competing political visions constituting Chican@ movement(s).[79] Texts published by Chican@ organizations and activists, thus, accreted to produce what I consider to be Chican@ movement discourse(s), and, in keeping with the racial rhetorical history proposed in this book, attending to the rhetorics comprising Chican@ movement discourse(s) in its multiple formats and modes supplies a rich archive for tracing evolutions in the Chican@ movement(s)' racial project.

To trace evolutions in the Chican@ movement(s)' racial project, particularly between 1965 and 1970, I consider spatial influences. Consequently, I trace Chican@ movement discourse(s) and their racializing consequences as they spread and spanned the Southwest United States, a region that proved to be an important aspect of the (re)invention of the myth of "Aztlán." Since Aztlán was believed, or better stated, *claimed* to be located in the Southwest, I have chosen to examine Chican@ movement texts germane to this physical area within the time frame of the late 1960s. I begin in California, move eastward to land in Colorado and New Mexico, before returning to California when nationalist notions of Aztlán were beginning to ossify and inform institutional moves in Chican@ movement(s). I take into account these geographical constraints and pressures as I trace evolutions in Chican@ movement discourse(s),[80] but, at the same time, I note how Chican@ movement discourse(s) stitched the Southwest together, an important *aesthetic* move in the Chican@ racial project. The texts I examine in this study, thus, provide a window into the geographical spaces within which Chican@ movement activists tried to amplify and circulate a racialized political identity.

Similarly, in keeping with the processual approach here, I attend to temporal constraints associated with each text as well. That is, I situate my texts within their energetic and, at times, repressive context(s), so as to take seriously the contingency of Chican@ rhetorical racial formation(s). Beginning as I do with the farmworkers' movement in California, I then follow the publication of Chican@ movement discourse(s) *through* time so as to identify the racial dynamics embedded and exemplified within Chican@ movement texts. This is an important, if not crucial feature of this book, since it contrasts largely with rhetorical histories presented by the two prominent voices of Chican@ movement histories in rhetorical studies and those following their path: John C. Hammerback and Richard J. Jensen. These two, more than any other rhetorical historians, have not only seemingly drowned out contemporary studies of Mexican American rhetorics, particularly Chican@ movement rhetorics, but have even been allowed to dominate conversations regarding the writing of Mexican American rhetorical histories and those of other "ethnic minorities."[81] The importance of their work, of course, cannot be discounted, if only because, as Michelle Holling makes clear, their work promoted the voice(s) of Mexican Americans as worthy of study from the vantage point of public address.[82] In making claims about Mexican American and/or Chican@ movement discourse more generally, however, their form of rhetorical historical scholarship has generally presumed a stable substratum, such as culture or personal biography, as its grounds and security. In so doing, they flatten the temporal elements of Chican@ movement discourse(s) and, in turn, reduce their kairotic potentials. This kind of analysis suggests that Chican@ movement rhetorics could only have appeared one way—a product of culture and/or minority status. Attending to time and its processual unfolding encourages an appreciation of this contingency.

Moreover, what their scholarship has by and large lacked is a robust distinction between what Michel-Rolph Trouillot describes as process(es) and narrative(s) of history. Events, situations, and chronologies of historical time are not equivalent to the stories told about those historical processes.[83] Hammerback and Jensen's work certainly represents an appreciation of historical processes (and other scholars favoring a more "public address" perspective on Mexican American discourse),[84] but their work does not always interrogate the tensions between process and narration or, in some cases, take seriously their distinctions.[85] In contrast, what I do in this book is hold in tension how these Chican@ texts have conventionally been "read" and ask how *else* we might understand the suasiveness of these texts in light of the contingencies that informed them. The introduction of a de/colonial mode in racial rhetorical criticism is but one way that I tackle this analytical reorientation.

This study, thus, takes seriously publication dates of Chican@ movement texts, and, in so doing, I grapple with the internal and external dynamics to which each text responds. Doing so encourages a revisitation of familiar Chican@ rhetorics to identify how their contexts shaped their final forms and the writing of a rhetorical history that recognizes both the ossification and flexibilities of Chican@ movement rhetorics as movement dynamics accreted and movement discourse(s) accumulated in spaces like the Chicano Press Association. In other words, this book, more than previous Chican@ movement rhetorical histories, underscores that there were few if any *predeterminations* of Chican@ movement discourse(s)—whether those be history, ideology, or the all-encompassing "culture."[86] Following this aim for a more situated look at Chican@ movement rhetorics, this book is presented in the form of a chronology, which, I think, allows for an appreciation of actors, events, organizations, and global happenings without being beholden to them.

And, while this chronological presentation might appear to undermine the de/colonial mode in its imposition of a linearity,[87] I should be clear that the aim of this book is not to propose a temporal frame or even a periodization for Chican@ movement(s) *per se* as much as it is to appreciate and showcase a processual unfolding of Chican@ movement discourse(s) during its most energetic and explosive activity. The chronological presentation facilitates this book's processual examination and, at the same time, follows the contextual complications informing Chican@ movement(s) as their context(s) shifted or changed. I do this, too, by noting the unique contributions and/or alterations present in *reproductions* of texts. The manifesto "El Plan Espiritual de Aztlán" was published in 1969 and marks an important turn in Chican@ movement(s) that I pick up in chapter 6. Yet there are crucial aesthetic distinctions between reproductions in *El Gallo, La Voz,* and *El Grito del Norte* that cannot be ignored or simply regarded as ornamental for a movement negotiating what it meant to take part in "nationalism." Coupled with the contextual shifting also seen in the ways in which the Viet Nam War became increasingly baked into Chican@ movement discourse, when a text was published *mattered,* as did the publication venue, and the aesthetic distinctions each of these contextual features offered. As I will show throughout the book, there were notable impacts in the shape of the Chican@ racial project that followed or paralleled changes in context(s), whether that be the intensification of the Viet Nam War or a new print space. In following a more chronological approach, I show how the Chican@ movement racial project evolved and changed over time.

Although some might anticipate a case study in the first chapter, I begin instead with the conclusion of the Mexican American War in the nineteenth century. As a way to illustrate the insights that a de/colonial mode might introduce to the practice of racial rhetorical criticism I perform in the rest of the book, I first provide a rhetorical history tracking with typical long-range histories of Mexican American politics in the United States in order to illuminate its colonial impulses. Yet while this might appear like a step away from the short(ened) history I claim to offer in the rest of the book, this first chapter, in enacting a de/colonial mode in racial rhetorical criticism, draws out how whiteness was established as a public aesthetic for the newly colonized Mexican Americans in and through colonial impulses. Employing what Christa Olson and Debra Hawhee term a "pan-historiographical" approach, I describe how the racial project(s) to which Mexican Americans have been subjected since the nineteenth century, following the conclusion of the Mexican American War, represent an aesthetic investment associated with the force of US coloniality. I highlight how multiple institutions have, since the Treaty of Guadalupe, participated in the racial formation of Mexican Americans vis-à-vis aesthetic impositions. Yet this chapter also surfaces resistance to aesthetic repressions in print spaces and proposes a frame for understanding how textual aesthetics serve as a site in which to oppose and offer competing racial projects. In short, this first chapter highlights how a de/colonial mode in racial rhetorical criticism enriches our understanding of context in (racial) rhetorical histories.

Chapter 2 provides the first of my case studies and begins where the Chican@ movement is said to have begun: the farmworkers' movement in the San Joaquin Valley in California. The farmworkers' movement articulated their activism in racial terms in their manifesto, the Plan de Delano, and its forceful declarations were instrumental to framing the publicity of a nascent movement. However, in this chapter, I examine a photobook published at the end of the year in which they publicized their strike via a pilgrimage to Sacramento. This photobook, which was a reproduction of the Plan de Delano, provides an intriguing entry point in this racial rhetorical history not because it published a familiar document but because it seemingly attenuated the racial rhetorical work of the original Plan de Delano published only months before the photobook. Through what I call a *poetics of apathy*, this photobook's aesthetic interventions attempted to deescalate some of the emotional tenors associated with the racializing force of the original manifesto, and it compelled viewing Chican@ movement(s) as compatible with systemic whiteness. Although holding onto aspects of the racial work present in the original publications of Plan de Delano, the publication in the form of a photobook introduced friction to the de/colonial praxis of Chican@ movement(s). From the start, we see the Chican@ movement racial project taking deliberate but no less unanticipated turns.

In chapter 3 I move on to Denver, Colorado to take on one of the most familiar and problematic texts in the Chican@ movement(s): "I Am Joaquin: An Epic Poem." While scholars have largely been content to render it a product of Gonzales's personal ideology or simply as "propaganda," I highlight what I call a *poetics of ambivalence* guiding the aesthetics of the original publication from 1967. Exploring the Rodolfo "Corky" Gonzales Papers held at the Denver Public Library, observing various drafts of the poem, and comparing the publication of the original poem to other reproductions of it, I find that the poem's 1967 form certainly encouraged taking it as an assertion of facts. Yet after my examinations of the poem's aesthetics, I show how it was itself energized by an increasing appeal to disrupting a racial homogeneity among Mexican Americans, not necessarily through imperatives but through a more subjective mood. While not neglecting its problematic features, I highlight how the poem did more than simply rehearse ideology or incite political fervor. On the contrary, the poem harnessed and amplified a kind of racial middling advanced in and among Mexican American activists at the end of the 1960s. Taking this temporal connection into account is crucial for understanding how "I Am Joaquin" participated in shifting the de/colonial praxis of Chican@ movement(s) after the farmworkers' movement.

Chapter 4 supplies a transition point of sorts in my tracing of the racial project comprising Chican@ movement(s), since it takes into account the growth of Chican@ movement(s) and the increasing appeal of the moniker La Raza to identify its activism. After the El Paso Conference in 1967, yet prior to the Denver Youth Conference in 1969, a period of accumulation and expansion of notions of La Raza converged with an increased interest in global concerns. Spearheaded by Chicana activists invested in representing Mexican American as constitutive of a global "Raza," political reimaginings suffused by the intersections of international and domestic happenings took off in the Southwest in New Mexico. In this chapter, I propose that a *poetics of relationality* stimulated aesthetic moves in the newly formed newspaper *El Grito del Norte* in New Mexico. In the heart of the Southwest, a cadre of activists, led by feminist Chicanas, inspired attention to the Raza on the "north" side of the US-Mexico border and, at the same time, encouraged viewing Mexican Americans as a *globally* important racial community.

Chapter 5 traces the emergence of nationalism in Chican@ politics, one of the more defining and complicating features in Chican@ movement(s). After the Chican@ Youth Liberation Conference in 1969, movement activists advocated for an explicit turn toward decolonization. This move, I argue, emerged not simply in the adoption of a particular ideology or the mythical figure of Aztlán. Instead, activists negotiated the consequences and appeal of adopting nationalism espoused in the newly scripted El Plan Espiritual de Aztlán. Tracing various reproductions of the Plan in spaces across the Southwest United States, I show how newspapers parlayed what I refer to as a *poetics otherwise* to construct the nationalism, in various ways, of El Plan Espiritual de Aztlán. And, furthermore, I show how the aesthetics of these reproductions of the Plan exemplified and ameliorated the internal fractures in Chican@ movement(s) taking place along the axis of gender. The aesthetic moves circulated in reproductions of El Plan Espiritual de Aztlán shifted the de/colonial praxis of Chican@ movement(s) by offering a push away from de/coloniality to a more aggressive decolonizing impulse.

Chapter 6 takes on one of the more latent but not entirely visible issues present in Chican@ movement(s) throughout: the question of non/violence. In some ways, this chapter tries, both in returning to California and putting into focus non/violence, to showcase the extent to which Chican@ movement discourse(s) evolved throughout the span of five years. To do this, the chapter interrogates the discourse associated with the one of the most (in)famous events in Chican@ movement historiography that has seemingly been neglected by scholars of rhetoric, namely, the August 29, 1970, Chicano Moratorium. Occurring after the turn to nationalism, Chicano moratoriums complicated the Chican@ movement(s)' racial project but, at the same time, offered a unique intervention by spotlighting the imposition of violence against Chican@ bodies at multiple scales—local, national, global. Analyzing a special issue of *La Raza* magazine produced in the wake of the violence that concluded the Chicano Moratorium on August 29, I highlight how its photographs demonstrated vividly the incommensurability between whiteness politics and the political community of La Raza through what I call a *poetics of deferral*. Analyzing how the activist magazine *La Raza* operationalized this poetics aesthetically, I demonstrate how Chican@ activists not only highlighted the "truth" of what happened at the demonstration that ended in violence; the magazine showed vividly through photographic evidence how Chican@ movement politics promoted a de/colonial love that whiteness could not snuff out.

The last chapter concludes the work. But rather than only review the major arguments of each chapter, I have also chosen to locate the poetics witnessed between 1965 and 1970 by surveying the emergence of what I call a *poetics of mimesis* in the post-Chicano Moratorium Chican@ movement(s)' racial project. Focusing on the beginnings of the 1970s, I note how Chican@ movement discourse(s) continued to adjust to external and internal movement pressures and how the Chicano Moratorium typified a touchstone in the evolution of Chican@ movement discourse(s). However, I also use this shift in the 1970s to highlight some intractable challenges in Latinx racial formation more broadly, since much of what we see in the 1970s continues to operate today in the form of the more positively oriented "Hispanic Serving Institution" or discriminatory bans of "critical race theory." While race might appear to be a flexible discourse, the rhetorical shifts witnessed in the 1970s Chican@ movement(s)' racial project suggest that racially oriented discourses, regardless of how de/colonial they might be, remain stuck in an inventional circle that pulls political choices toward a center firmly within coloniality's grasp. Yet, as I hope to show, without an investment in racial rhetorical criticism, the limitations of racial formation and alternative political projects outside of race remain hidden.

I

A DE/COLONIAL AESTHETIC: WHITENESS AND MEXICAN AMERICAN POLITICS (1848–1965)

Viewing Chican@ movement(s) as a racial project, as I do in this rhetorical history, entails putting into view processes of racial formation (since "race" is not necessarily a "thing") and the communicative procedures through which race has been made to appear (since rhetoric operates in the realm of appearance). Consequently, what I hope to do in this chapter is prepare the groundwork for the racial rhetorical criticism I perform in my case studies by enacting a de/colonial mode on racial rhetorics preceding the 1960s. The de/colonial mode I propose as a way to recognize the "de/coloniality" present in vernacular discourse(s) must also be applied to *contexts* for, in doing so, it becomes possible to recognize the negotiation of alternative and competing racial projects within and against which Chican@ movement(s) for example operated, each of which were and are consequences of coloniality. The de/colonial work we witness in Chican@ movement discourse(s) evinced an appreciation and use of a variety of linguistic, Indigenous, religious, and corporeal signs typically associated with being "not-white" or "not-Black" that, at the same time, had been targeted for purging from the public sphere. These signs, as I will show, comprised an *aesthetic*, all of which were not "essential" to Chican@ identity nor fundamentally "positive" or "negative." These aesthetic features, on the contrary, were rhetorically relevant in and through de/coloniality and, viewed in this sense, significant for racially formative processes. To assert and interrogate Chican@ movement(s) as racial project, thus, cannot be separated from the colonial alternatives that preceded or operated concurrently, and it is through the adoption of a de/colonial mode that these and responses to them come into focus.

The conclusion of the Mexican American War in 1848 is an appropriate place to start this inquiry into the multiple ways that coloniality spurred the emergence and form(s) of racial projects imposing whiteness on Mexican

Americans. As Laura Gómez explains, the conclusion of the Mexican American War was part of a convergence of moments "that resulted in the formation of Mexican Americans as a racial group in the United States," and that ultimately "proved central to the larger process of restructuring the American racial order in a key period stretching from the war to the turn of the twentieth century."[1] A colonial drive, she argues, was a fundamental aspect of this US takeover of Mexican land,[2] and, from this vantage point, we can see how the conclusion of the Mexican American War both enabled and furthered the expansion of what Joe Feagin and others refer to as a "white racial frame" for understanding the social and political positionality of these new (Mexican) American citizens.[3] The white racial frame is, he writes, a "broad and persisting set of racial stereotypes, prejudices, ideologies, images, interpretations and narratives, emotions, reactions to language accents, as well as racialized inclinations to discriminate."[4] The Mexican American War, though certainly not representing an "origin" of the systemic racism faced by Mexican Americans in the United States, is nonetheless a catalytic event for understanding their racialization and, for the purposes of this book, illuminates antecedent racial projects informing the contours of the Chican@ movement(s)' racial project by virtue of their insistence and renewal.

Although I recognize that a wide historical survey ranging from the conclusion of the Mexican American War in 1848 to the year the farmworkers' movement broke out in 1965 will gloss over the contingencies that I claim were integral to the shape of Chican@ movement(s) (see Introduction), I follow the provocations of rhetorical studies scholars Debra Hawhee and Christa Olson, who advocate for the use of pan-historiography as an illuminating analytic for rhetorical inquiries. Broad diachronic histories, they explain, offer an opportunity to put into view the "residual accumulation of *topoi*, beliefs, and strategic practices" that "narrow" histories might miss in their granularity.[5] My interest in the development and evolution of the Chican@ movement as racial project, as well as its relationship to de/coloniality, race, and social movement actions, suggests that a pan-historiographical approach is a productive way to trace racially formative processes solidifying the preferred political aesthetics among Mexican Americans and follow antecedent racial projects operating as Chican@ movement(s) gained traction in the mid-1960s. In the pan-history I provide in this chapter, I do not simply affirm that whiteness was imposed on and repressed Mexican American politics. In addition to underlining the pervasive and oppressive presence of whiteness, I aim to sketch how whiteness was established as the preferred and preeminent political *aesthetic* for Mexican Americans choosing to stay and flourish in the United States, how institutional and systemic violences reinforced this aesthetic as a site of rhetorical invention for Mexican American communities, and how print media afforded unique opportunities for interposing alternative racial formative processes. This history, consequently, begins with a colonial event, a historical moment that established the racial terms of engagement for Mexican Americans in the United States: the Mexican American War.

Concluding the Mexican American War, Establishing Whiteness as an Aesthetic

In 1848, the United States concluded its conflict with Mexico and took an additional step toward finalizing its ideological project, "manifest destiny," in one fell swoop by acquiring the Northwest regions of Mexico (and its citizens) in the Treaty of Guadalupe.[6] The exhibition of military might was integral to US nation-building in the nineteenth century.[7] This demonstration of physical, imperial force, however, also exposed the racist orientations toward indigeneity and not-white others baked into US nationalism.[8] President James K. Polk, since his first inaugural address in 1845, had consistently portrayed the United States' Mexican neighbor in an aggressive posture, ready to "invade" the recent acquisition of the Republic of Texas. Finally, in 1846, after Mexican troops attacked and killed US service members stationed near the Nueces River to "protect" the United States from Mexico's apparent aggression, Polk announced that "after reiterated menaces, Mexico has passed the boundary of the United States, has invaded our territory and shed American blood upon the American soil. She has proclaimed that hostilities have commenced, and that the two nations are now at war. As war exists, and, notwithstanding all our efforts to avoid it, exists by the act of Mexico herself, we are called upon by every consideration of duty and patriotism to vindicate with decision the honor, the rights, and the interests of our country."[9] Robert Ivie argues that Polk's rhetoric ultimately invented a binary between the United States and Mexico along the axis of rationality, with Mexico assuming the role of irrational actor unable and unwilling to engage with a rational US federal government simply trying to forestall war.[10] In other words, Polk harnessed rationality as a means through which to justify US actions against Mexico and set up a clear contrast between these sovereign states. The only *logical* response to a presupposed Mexican aggression, thus, was war.

This moment, however, created a spectacle that projected US (inter)nationalist ambitions and racial priorities before a watching world,[11] which an isolation of "rationality" pure and simple misses.[12] Polk's discourse racializes Mexico through war language, establishing them as worthy of violent retribution even prior to their acting, not simply because they have defied "logic" but because they are not-white.[13] Such a posture exemplifies what Nelson Maldonado-Torres characterizes as a "paradigm of war," a political stance taken up by colonial powers against the "other" that presumes a state of antagonism between colonizer and colonized.[14] Yet while this moment might have resembled the work of colonizers, the Mexican American War demonstrated an extraordinary example of colonization. As Walter Mignolo explains, this event fortified colonial difference from within rather than from without its borders—the more common route of taking over persons and places.[15] The United States expanded its borders by recasting Mexico as a "menacing" nation, a characterization that, in reality, masked Mexico's lack of preparedness to defend itself against a neighbor whose ambition was cast as a divine right.[16] Despite projecting a veneer of advancing freedom and agency for the newly acquired subjects,[17] the war's conclusion transformed Mexicans into "Mexican Americans." Or, as one author succinctly writes, it converted Mexican Americans into "strangers in their own land."[18]

The racial formation begun in the Mexican American War was scripted into the Treaty of Guadalupe of 1848, in which the United States inscribed its new subjects within the entrenched racial project of "citizenship." The category of citizenship interjected legal white/not-white classifications in the social life of the new colony. As Quijano notes, it is ultimately the "racial axis" and its "colonial origin and character" that has "proven to be more durable and stable than the colonialism in whose matrix it is established. Therefore, the model of power that is globally hegemonic today presupposes an element of coloniality."[19] Although some scholars have understood citizenship as more "ascriptive,"[20] others have theorized citizenship as more "performative."[21] This suggests that while it might have appeared as an objective legal measure for determining political freedoms,[22] when viewed from a rhetorical vantage point, the advantages of citizenship might be better understood as hinging on the *demonstration* of whiteness rather than being earned through a fixed singular designation.[23] Consequently, Mexican American bodies—marked visually through signifiers such as skin tone, cultural praxis, and language, all of which signaled not-whiteness—justified inclusion in US political life by remaking bodily cues.[24] In other words, Mexicans participated in their own racial formation at the same time that they were also subjected to racial classifications.

Of course, it is not as though this negotiation began in 1848. Mexico had its own operative racial hierarchies shaping social and economic standings that preceded those in the United States,[25] which Laura Gómez explains also informed racialization of Mexican Americans in the regions taken over by the United States after the Mexican American War.[26] Iberian colonialism in Latin America had established social systems informed by race and gender that were not discarded even after political revolutions. Constitutive of power relations in Latin America, race was sustained as a defining feature of political arrangements.[27] The imposition of racial hierarchies fomented anti-Black, anti-Indigenous, and sexual controls not unlike that witnessed in the United States.[28] Following the Mexican American War, however, racial projects associated with habitation in the United States located Mexican Americans socially and politically, and whiteness and its signifiers were placed at the top of the social and political hierarchies—a praxis that continues to plague Latinx Americans today.[29] Concretized in and through citizenship, promises of political agencies were inextricably linked not simply to classifications of whiteness but also to the generation of its appeal. Gómez sums up the contradiction this way: "Mexicans' collective naturalization in 1848 promoted a *legal* definition of Mexicans as 'white.' Tension around Mexican Americans' racial status arose because this legal whiteness contradicted the *social* definition of Mexicans as non-white."[30]

The establishment of white supremacy and the inferiority of not-whiteness, consequently, was a *rhetorical* racial project, one taking place in public and political settings—where *aesthetic* actions take on a formative force. Language(s), tropes, and vocabularies associated with both white and not-white racial identities, though arbitrarily assigned,[31] were rhetorical resources used to invent political sovereignty in the colony. Wealthy Mexicans living in California (Californios), for example, fashioned their own political identities according to established standards of (not-)whiteness associated with citizenship.[32] Arguing that they were unlike lower caste persons (such as "cholos"), they appealed to their *visual* resemblances to those of lighter colored skin to maintain political standing.[33] In so doing, Mexican American rhetors baked white supremacist logics into their justifications, which, consequently, vindicated the supremacy of whiteness over Indigenous cultures, the transcendence of a white citizenship as an ultimate identity, and the inherent inferiority of others (indios and mestizos). This rhetorical work, though taking multiple forms across various spaces, entrenched a way of seeing the bodily forms of Mexican Americans—an aesthetic process.

Although some Mexican American rhetors might have been sensitive to the consequences of their rhetorical appeals for indigenous communities within the colony,[34] the selection of whiteness and deflection of not-whiteness (re)entrenched the legitimacy of signifying whiteness to acquire and enjoy political rights. These affirmations of whiteness might have been personally advantageous for those that deployed them, but their political ramifications were significant for the colonized in that it institutionalized a standard *poetics*, a "locus of enunciation" in the words of Mignolo,[35] or an acceptable re-presentational praxis through which political rights were expected to be articulated, shaped, and introduced into public spaces by and for Mexican Americans.[36] The deployment and legitimation of whiteness in contentions over political standings furthered acceptable inventional resources, which, I suggest, circumscribed the aesthetic work of later Mexican Americans. Quijano's explanation of the internalizing consequences of European colonization corroborates how a racial imposition becomes constitutive of a rhetorical imagination for political participation: "It is not only a matter of the subordination of the other cultures to the European, in an external relation; we have also to do with a colonization of the other cultures, albeit in different intensities and depths. This relationship consists, in the first place, of a colonization of the imagination of the dominated; that is, it acts in the interior of that imagination, in a sense, it is a part of it."[37] If Mexican Americans hoped to enjoy citizenship status, then forming their responses or claims according to standards that amplified whiteness and dislocated signs of their not-whiteness was paramount—even if the consequences left them with blood-stained hands.[38]

That Mexican citizens could signify whiteness at all demonstrates how citizenship ultimately hinged on *aesthetic* formulations that could be legitimized and affirmed by others as "white." Mexican American rhetors could not necessarily alter physicality associated with not-whiteness such as hair color, skin tone, or the shapes of eyes and mouths, but in leveraging the arbitrariness of "race" rhetors (re)invented white signifiers, particularly in spaces that issued judgments on acceptability, inclusion, and privilege. Henry Louis Gates's comments on the ways that race arbitrarily signifies rather than acting as a concrete referent are apt here for explaining the ways that race becomes not something *objective* but *tropic*. "Race," he explains, "has become a trope of ultimate, irreducible difference between cultures, linguistic groups, or adherents of specific belief systems which—more often than not—also have fundamentally opposed economic interests. Race is the ultimate trope of difference because it is so very arbitrary in its application."[39]

Mexican Americans, in short, (re)projected *appearances* of whiteness. Whiteness was subject to a political *stratagem* in this sense, subject to (re)invention as much as it might have been treated as a standard of judgment.[40] Mexican Americans were not "white" or "not-white" only on the basis of law, whether *de jure* or *de facto*. Mexican Americans were white on the basis of *rhetorical* work; aesthetic imagination; political display.

These rhetorical decisions to adopt or otherwise affirm public demonstrations of whiteness reified acceptable aesthetics that, in the end, fortified the accomplishment of the colonial project—white US citizenship—in the newly acquired colony. Indeed, deploying an aesthetic, effectively or not, institutionalizes its appeal in and for public spaces.[41] Cisneros explains that the negative consequence of adopting white signifiers was that the resultant rhetorics were "easily co-opted by entrenched exclusive logics of citizenship."[42] Mexican American rhetorics, performed in public and for political effect(s), ultimately secured the superiority of whiteness in the colony and capacitated the purge of signifiers "othered" by colonial expectations. Exclusion spread, in this sense, through "symbolic" means, not only in what was being claimed but also in how rights were asserted. While some actors might have tried to negotiate whiteness and not-whiteness in less harmful ways, whiteness ultimately emerged as the political identity *par excellence* for political agency among Mexican Americans.[43]

Coloniality in the Southwest: Institutionalizing Whiteness Through Violence

The establishment of a colonial relationship between the United States and Mexican American "citizens," although itself an act of violence, also created violent conditions for enforcing these racial(ized) political aesthetics. Duany, Feagin, and Cobas remark on the inherent violence of racialization: "Sometimes the ideologies in particular interpretive frames have unintended and beneficial consequences. But racialization is incapable of generating decency, compassion, or progress of any human group. It has been evil through and throughout its operations since the seventeenth century. Why does it persist? The white racial frame and its associated racial hierarchy serve the interests of U.S. white elites splendidly, and they have the resources to support and propagate this frame. As part of the racial frame, common sense makes injustice appear inevitable."[44] Nelson Maldonado-Torres calls these conditions fortifying colonial relationships "coloniality," and it is "coloniality" that describes how colonial powers enact a multi-pronged, comprehensive effort to sustain the power differential initiated by the originating colonial event. Making a distinction between the event of colonization and the institutionalization of colonial control (i.e., coloniality), Maldonado-Torres explains that "coloniality survives colonialism. It is maintained alive in books, in the criteria for academic performance, in cultural patterns, in common sense, in the self-image of peoples, in aspirations of self, and so many other aspects of our modern experience."[45] From the vantage point of race, coloniality entails the decimation of the "difference" between colonized and colonizer, marking residual signifiers that dilute the "superior" (white) status imported by colonial powers for destruction and erasure in the colony. Walter Mignolo, drawing from the work of Aníbal Quijano, argues that it is through the CMP that colonial relationships and political life in the colony are established. The CMP, he explains, consists of "domains" through which colonial power is asserted, "spheres of management and control" that dictate the terms of acceptable forms of living life in the colony.[46]

Coloniality, I propose here, requires and invites a multiplicity of racial projects through which to impose racial standards, hierarchies, and relations within the colony, all of which ensure the survival of coloniality after colonization. Institutions, both formal and informal, energize and anchor this effort to establish coloniality's racial terms and their role in governance.[47] In what follows, I highlight various racial projects accomplished by institutions in the United States on Mexican Americans. Via violent negation (the ascription not-white)[48] these institutions marked signs among Mexican Americans such as skin tone, language codes, names, bloodlines, even "work ethic,"[49] and, in turn, forced Mexican Americans to learn how to negotiate or resist the imposition of whiteness in their day to day lives.[50] While some Mexican Americans might have been able to (re)invent their political agencies in some circumstances to escape discrimination by appealing to other political categories such as "nationality,"[51] institutions ultimately asserted violence over the bodies and minds of Mexican Americans by churning them through varying racial projects, each attempting to purge them of a "not-white" aesthetic or accept them as devoid of them.

A Labor of Violence

One institution issuing violence against Mexican Americans was the labor paradigm undergirding US capitalism. Subjected to strenuous manual labor, low wages, and a lack of opportunities for social mobility, Mexican Americans experienced acutely one of the cruelest features of coloniality's racial projects, namely, that only white labor was paid labor.[52] Although there were certainly aspects of an antecedent Mexican labor system that were discriminatory (such as paternalism in California), legal enforcements of capitalism introduced by Anglo citizens moving into the West established free-wage systems that were ruthless to not-white persons.[53] During the growth of the agricultural industry in the Southwest in the nineteenth and twentieth centuries, Mexican Americans nonetheless filled depleted white labor pools,[54] and, in the economic boom fueled by World War II, the federal government established channels for maintaining cheap Mexican American labor through the bracero program until its termination in 1964.[55] Mexican American workers were kept poor, socially vulnerable, and subject to intersectional poverty, which, following Kimberlé Crenshaw's notion of intersectionality, is made invisible at the junctures of language, culture, race, gender, and class.[56] The use of cultural labels such as "un-American," "minority," and "limited English proficient" to classify Mexican American workers identified them as a "commodity identity," which masked the racist underpinnings of the economic system into which Mexican American workers were integrated yet kept them bounded within its system at the same time.[57]

Casting Mexican Americans as not-white justified low wages and the negation of employment opportunities, and Mexican American women in particular bore the brunt of this kind of intersectional oppression.[58] Mexican Americans were labeled "peons" within the labor context, disposable and replaceable, and, consequently, were a population in need of proactive management through repatriation and exclusion despite their crucial roles in buttressing the US economy.[59] Although there were socially conscious individuals who tried to intervene and re-racialize Mexican American identity during the early twentieth century (such as Paul Taylor and Dorothea Lange), the not-white labor of Mexican Americans was effectively less valuable than that coming from white workers.[60]

Correspondingly, Mexican Americans often dwelled in isolated spaces that could not be escaped through any "opportunities" the government might offer them.[61] Mexican Americans flocking to and living in barrios, a kind of slum, at the turn of the twentieth century could not afford to live anywhere else given their exceptionally low wages. Mirandé calls this process "barrioization," which, he explains, is the "virtual elimination of the Mexican from the social and political life of the community at large; through isolation Chicanos become invisible, if not nonexistent."[62] Some, of course, chose to live in these close-knit cultural pockets for their own cultural survival, since doing so also furnished opportunities to participate in community building activities. While living in these social enclaves, Mexican Americans attended church services together or enjoyed Mexican food in community restaurants. This concentrated form of community living might have preserved and allowed Mexican Americans to maintain cultural elements treated publicly as not-white, but housing choices were also limited by prejudices that confined them to these private spaces.[63] Sociologist Jody Vallejo, however, has shown how social (and spatial) mobilities, at times, entailed adopting and parlaying signifiers of whiteness (including English language mastery), and by deploying these signifiers successfully, as we saw with Californios, some were empowered to cross over racially construed economic boundaries with greater ease. Vallejo acknowledges in her study of the Mexican American middle class that whiteness is not a necessary condition for social mobility, but she admits that social mobility perhaps increases the appeal of whiteness among those that have experienced financial success: "Some Mexican Americans might be able to cross boundaries with whites and disappear into the established white population.... Who is better poised to do so than those who have entered the middle class? Middle-class Mexican Americans might be a harbinger of this pattern."[64] Institutionally, the spread and enforcement of US capitalism embedded Mexican Americans in social precarity and displayed the repression of race-induced poverty.[65] Escape happened only in and through whiteness.

Epistemic Violence

Mexican Americans also experienced epistemic violence from US educational institutions that reinforced the inferiority of not-white signifiers and the superiority of Anglo culture(s). A recognition of the sinister role educational institutions play in perpetuating oppressive social norms, values, and ideology, of course, is not new.[66] For Mexican Americans in the United States, education served as a potent site through which epistemological control could be diffused efficiently and signs of "Mexicanness" dislodged from their supposed "American" identity. Circumscribing the limits of knowledge and public expression, US educational institutions were the locus from which knowledge could be issued (that is, they were Eurocentric). At the same time, they were the home of the appropriate rhetorics through which knowledge and recognition could be accessed (that is, whiteness). Mexican Americans were expected to learn English, forced into trade school, and required to "Americanize," and Mexican American persons that were unable or unwilling to do so were deemed intellectually deficient on account of these racially indexing significations.[67]

For Mexican American women, in particular, education and the trajectory that it promised were used as a means by which to execute severe racial projects. Women, more than men, were forced to negotiate a complicated and double-edged relationship with the institution, since young girls were often forced to quit school and support the family's well-being through work.[68] Moreover, women who were unable to speak English could not participate in decision-making for their children, and Mexican American girls and women were sometimes subjected to forced sterilizations on account of a perceived mental inferiority linked to their racial background.[69] Nevertheless, as Emma Pérez has shown, women were also critical actors in resisting the decimation of cultural symbols enforced by educational institutions. A "decolonial imaginary," a concept Pérez uses to describe how the enforcement of colonial rule is resisted in a variety of mundane spaces,[70] was enacted by women who labored to stem the tide of "Americanization" in their daily lives. Women formed clubs and organizations through which they could influence the education of their children,[71] and some in the early twentieth century, such as Carolina Munguía, advocated for increased educational opportunities for both children and women.[72] Education might have been an invasive racial project through which gendered violence was applied to Mexican American bodies, but it was also a context that catalyzed unique and creative forms of resistance among those disciplined by it.

The 1947 *Mendez v. Westminster* case in California was a pivot point in the execution of the racial project imposed on Mexican Americans in educational spaces. The case ended the segregation of Mexican American students from white students in schools,[73] creating the appearance of a promise of equality upheld by activists even while facing resistance from white communities.[74] Up until then, Mexican Americans were simply an "educational problem" that was best dealt with by segregating them from the dominant Anglo community,[75] and securing the inferiority of not-white, Mexican signs through both "additive" and "subtractive" measures intended to assimilate them.[76] Though certainly not a linear process,[77] sanctioned integration in public schools, in essence, legalized "Americanization" of Mexican Americans in ways that coincided and supported a curriculum guided by a complex of Cold War nationalism and whiteness.[78] Educational institutions, thus, performed a double erasure with respect to the aesthetics of Mexican American public life: they homogenized Mexican Americans as a singular group of not-white, inferior bodies, and they infused Mexican Americans with whiteness by teaching them to divest themselves of their not-whiteness. In educational spaces in particular, Mexican Americans were taught to "forget" their not-whiteness and learn how to be white Americans.

Re-presentational Violence

Stuart Hall's media theory suggests that "media" exist as a (racially) identifying institution,[79] an assemblage of persons, organizations, and governmental agencies that interpellates audiences through a robust discursive "suturing."[80] Although Hall's assessments of the racism undergirding media and its representations link it to ideology in particular,[81] as an institution (re)producing and circulating representations, mediated images of identity are potent forces influencing identity formation(s) among those hailed by them. Kimberlé Crenshaw's own theory of intersectionality includes an "exploration of the problem of representational intersectionality—in particular, how the production of images of women of color and the contestations over those images tend to ignore the intersectional interests of women of color,"[82] which suggests that representations are not simply supports for racial violence but their very enactment. This mediation is, however, uneven, indeterminate, and, perhaps better stated, disparate, as recent scholarship has pointed out. This unevenness has resulted in a recent turn away from simply interrogating "representations" of Latinx communities to critical inquiries over the political economical processes dictating systemic issues like access, decision-making, and power dynamics.[83]

Nevertheless, racialization, Arlene Dávila suggests, is integral to the ways media institutions operate, entailing "issues of racial diversity, representation, and parity," and, in the 1960s, Mexican Americans challenged egregious racial stereotypes directly.[84] Indeed, as seen with Mexican American laborers, attributes perceived to be "un-American" were caricatured and leveraged in advertisements and film for monetary gain in ways that drew mostly understated criticism prior to the 1960s.[85] By the 1960s, however, there was a growing awareness of misrepresentations that were also racializing Mexican Americans, and these motivated direct actions such as the East LA Blowouts in 1968 in California.[86] Media scholar Chon Noriega notes that caricatures like the "Frito Bandito" campaign by Frito-Lay and the use of Emiliano Zapata by Elgin Company (a watchmaker) in the late 1960s were predicated on particular tropes construing Mexican Americans as gatekeepers of and, in turn, hindrances to the Western Frontier.[87] Representation, which might have appeared to be merely a superficial concern, was materially consequential. Noriega adroitly connects institutional mullings, like the Kerner Report, to the ways in which Chican@ activists responded to representational grievances. If the government seemed to admit that racialization at the level of media representation was materially consequential, then contests over representation were not, in fact, superficial: "What the [Kerner] report did, in effect, was to place racial discrimination and growing social unrest squarely within the context of a mediated nation, while linking problematic discourse (stereotypes) not to mass communication per se but to employment within its related industries."[88] Those involved in the entertainment industry, like musicians for example, responded to pressures to conform to whiteness by removing signs of not-whiteness through various "de-ethnicizing" procedures such as changing last names.[89] Media representations, to be sure, might have appeared secondary to more "substantial" concerns, but their racial project motivated racist ideas about what made a "Mexican."[90]

Extra-Legal Violence

Finally, Mexican Americans were also subjected to various forms of extra-legal repression for their apparent performances of not-whiteness. Policies, as Rancière points out, violate equality and circumscribe acceptable political forms by positioning subjects into unequal social arrangements,[91] but it is through institutionalized police forces that policies of inequality are enforced in practice and in public. For Mexican Americans living in the Southwest, extra-legal violence battered Mexican American bodies for manifestations of not-whiteness and performances of its potential for political power.[92] These violent acts entailed mob violence, which resulted in the typically unrecognized lynching of Mexican Americans,[93] but it also involved, in the words of Mirandé, the institutionalization of double standards of justice and criminality—"Gringo Justice"[94]—that enabled their continuation. The Texas Rangers were one such executor of this kind of "justice." The Rangers, who were in practice defenders of Eurocentric ideals,[95] terrorized Mexican Americans along the Texas-Mexican border.[96] Shortly after the writing of "El Plan de San Diego" in 1915 by disenfranchised Mexican Americans, for example, Texas Rangers infused their "law-keeping" in the region with racial prejudices. Mexican American bodies, revolutionaries or not, were potential targets for punishment. This targeted racial policing formed a direct contrast to the revolutionaries, who, while proclaiming revolution, did not tap so easily into racism to amplify their claims against the political order.[97] Similarly, the Texas Rangers were a traumatizing force for those living in the borderlands, as Gloria Anzaldúa references in her recollection of life in the Rio Grande Valley.[98] The reign of terror by the Texas Rangers continued into the middle of the twentieth century as well. In Crystal City, Texas, shortly after the city's leadership flipped from Anglo to Mexican American in the early 1960s, the Texas Rangers were present once more to preserve the social order that had apparently been undermined by the acquisition of political power by Mexican Americans—the majority population.[99]

Moving westward, violence continued to follow Mexican Americans onto public streets. In California, the infamous Zoot Suit Riots of the 1940s represents one of the more prominent racial conflicts involving Mexican Americans in the twentieth century. Viewing the ruffled pants, bright colors, and long coats of young Mexican Americans' style as threatening, servicemen and police officers alike attacked Mexican American youth for their apparently delinquent behavior made manifest through clothing. Although Octavio Paz perhaps places too much stress on the psychology of Mexican Americans typified in the pachuco's dress,[100] that their flamboyant clothing was believed to expose the character of Mexican Americans illustrates the racial underpinning subjecting them to policing and the response(s) of those spectating (including Eleanor Roosevelt).[101] Stripping pachucos' pants and revealing their nakedness as retribution for their stylistic choices, white servicemen made a spectacle of their warring with Mexican Americans over performances of a perceived not-whiteness. Even the terms used to refer to these incidents, such as "riots" and "Zoot-suit" rather than the preferred term of Mexican Americans who dressed that way ("pachuco") exemplifies how power is asserted and invoked in the manner in which these incidents are talked about publicly.[102] After World War II and into the heart of the Cold War, the Los Angeles Police Department (LAPD) continued to intertwine criminality, subversive behavior, and racial prejudice into an assault on bodies marked as not-white (Mexican Americans, African Americans, etc.). The LAPD handled not-white offenders brutally, and undercover surveillance programs identified Mexican American groups like the Brown Berets as criminal organizations.[103] As I argue in chapter 6, as resistance to the Viet Nam War intensified, police brutality targeting Mexican Americans bore an astonishing resemblance to this Cold War conflict. Extra-legal violence became its own racial project, as it targeted the bodies of Mexican Americans for discipline with ferocity and in public.

Contesting Colonial Aesthetics: Mexican Americans and Print Media

Mexican American men and women experienced multiple forms of racial violence in the United States, as institutions imposed colonial orderings—coloniality—among them across space and time. Each of these institutions enacted its own racial project, characterized by different modes, vocabularies, physical violations, and tropes, while yet enforcing coloniality's sanctioned political expectations. Multiple institutions established patterns of control by marking signs vis-à-vis negation, as "not-white," which limited, though not entirely erased, the appropriate aesthetics in and for public affairs. This violence was, fundamentally, a rhetorical violence, not in the crude sense of *symbolic* violence but in the sense that punishments of not-white signs de-legitimized particular rhetorical resources activating or otherwise enhancing Mexican American political life—denying a place for the "de-" in de/coloniality. Institutions advanced "exceptionalist" ideals that were also racist expectations for all "American" citizens,[104] promoted "American" symbols for articulating and inventing political agencies, and, at the same time, punished re-presentations that failed to align with the whiteness required of "American" citizenship.

Print spaces, however, supplied sites for exploring and cultivating de/coloniality and in so doing encouraged the remaking of the relationship between whiteness and Mexican Americans. Spanish language newspapers published in the United States during the nineteenth century were spaces in which challenges to the superiority of whiteness could be circulated widely and the effects of coloniality contested in public forums. American Studies scholar Gabriel Meléndez explains that "print culture in Mexican origin communities in the Southwest remained an expression of opposition to Anglo-American political, social, and cultural hegemony in the Southwest after 1848. And the volume of that resistance is impressive. From 1880 to 1935 more than 190 newspapers were founded in over thirty communities in New Mexico, Colorado, Arizona, and Texas."[105] These newspapers covered national and international events in English and Spanish, and they supplied creative opportunities for Mexican Americans that could, in turn, spur others to *reimagine* their political identities.[106] The newspaper *El Clamor Público* in Los Angeles (1855) is one of the most notable and well-researched examples of these,[107] but there were others scattered across the Southwest, such as *El Ciudadaño* in El Paso (1899) and *El Mosquito* in New Mexico (1899). On the one hand, newspapers (even Spanish language newspapers) were yet more ways through which Anglo America asserted control over newly acquired citizens. After all, these newspapers could not ignore US-related news and viewpoints. On the other hand, Spanish language newspapers provided channels through which Mexican Americans resisted racial violences expressed corporeally (including in lynchings) and symbolically.[108] These print spaces, even prior to the activism of the 1960s, were yet spaces in which rhetorical imaginations excluding whiteness were fomented and preserved by Mexican Americans.

Of course, even these spaces satiated demands of whiteness, appeasing "coloniality" even in resistance.[109] In fact, obliging standards of whiteness was an incessant struggle among Mexican American political organizations advocating on behalf of Mexican American communities. Some political organizations, like the League of United Latin American Citizens (LULAC), called for assimilative tactics that heightened the political rights of Mexican Americans through a representational praxis premised on illuminating how whiteness was a coincident, if not constitutive, feature of Mexican American identity in the United States.[110] These organizations enforced the acceptance of whiteness as an integral aesthetic for their political subjectivization, all the while attempting to weaken the institutional erasure of their not-whiteness in official channels, such as the courts, and in their own daily lives.[111] Claiming and adopting whiteness was integral to the work of some Mexican American organizations, and there was hope that such exhibitions would generate equal political status.[112] Just as in the early Southwest, whiteness continued to dominate strategies for establishing, asserting, and articulating political rights within the colony.

After World War II, however, decolonization waves in Africa, Asia, and the Americas,[113] energies from domestic movements like the Civil Rights Movement, and international conferences condemning colonially derived racism encouraged reimaginations of political identities.[114] In print spaces harnessed by politically minded Mexican Americans, a firm commitment to articulations of not-whiteness emerged in unique ways as activists joined in social movement(s).[115] Articulating a kind of political "emancipation" using alternative languages other than English (Spanish, Nahuatl), local knowledge(s) and myths (Aztlán), and non-Protestant religious practices (Catholic) that were purged by institutional violence(s), Chican@ newspapers, pamphlets, and magazines (re)invented political identities that disrupted their predetermined social positions and articulated emancipation, in the words of Rancière, along the axis of race.[116] In other words, in Chican@ print spaces we see attempts to *invent* a racial project reimagining Mexican American politics outside of the entrenched and violently enforced (colonial) whiteness. Taken together, print spaces converged to enable the formation of what has come to be known as the "Chicano Movement."

Yet even as Chican@ movement discourses published in these print spaces were influencing and energizing Mexican American politics in the United States, their emergence coincided with the intensification of the United States' aggressive stance in Viet Nam in the mid-1960s. With a heightened sense of urgency stemming from the draft and the perceived disproportionate casualty rates of Mexican Americans in the war, activists scrutinized the supposed inviolability and apparent viability of a whiteness aesthetic for attenuating the effects of racially motivated violence felt at home and abroad. This shift was most visible in the rise of the moniker(s) "Chicana/o" to describe the Mexican American politics of those born in the United States, yet having ties to Mexico. The Spanish term "Chicano," initially used by anthropologist José Limón to describe Mexican Americans who had rejected their Mexican culture after migrating to the United States,[117] emerged as a pregnant term with political aspirations. The term was constitutive of "[una] ideal genérico que impera en nuestro compromiso social y que enciende toda esperanza utópica por conquistar, finalmente, la marginación continua ye la angustia polongada" ("[a] general ideal that prevails in our social compromises and that ignites our utopic hopes to conquer, finally, continual marginalization and prolonged anguish").[118] At the turn of the decade, Chican@ movement activists viewed themselves as both the Viet Nam War's subjects of execution and its objects of destruction. Their experience, thus, was unique and furnished an indispensable perspective on the consequences of US-derived colonial violence(s).[119] The shape of the Chican@ movement racial project, consequently, not only followed activists or even the circulation of Chican@ movement discourse(s). The Viet Nam War, too, informed the contours of the racial project, as it competed and challenged the force of this Cold War manifestation.

In the 1960s, a profoundly energetic Mexican American activism surged and, along with it, the fabrication of an alternative racial project that encouraged the (re)invention of Mexican American racial politics. Beginning with the farmworkers' movement in California, Chican@ movement activists churned out multiple ways of re-presenting Mexican American politics, its relationship to systemic whiteness, and the racial violence with which Mexican Americans grappled in the United States. Worked out aesthetically, an array of poetics gave form to an alternative racial project beginning to take shape in and through a new form of Mexican American politics: Chican@ movement(s).

2

A POETICS OF APATHY: THE FARMWORKERS' MOVEMENT AND EL PLAN DE DELANO (1966)

The proclamation that farm workers in California catalyzed a "social movement in fact" had a range. Although the farmworkers' movement certainly participated and, in some ways, led the way in reinventing the image of the Mexican (American) farmworker in the United States in the 1960s, there was a corresponding conservatism undergirding the NFWA's "causa" that prevented it from becoming, as some have described, "leftist." Ana Raquel Minian documents, for example, how recasting sexual liberation as an "Anglo" form of sexuality was central to the farmworkers' reinvention of stereotypes casting them as sexual deviants.[1] Similarly, prior to the 1970s, the farmworkers' movement leaned into a discourse of nativism that perpetuated racist discourse pinning the depression of farmworker wages on immigrant workers.[2] So strong and enduring was the conservative pull in the farmworkers' movement that Matt Garcia, who offers a compelling history of the way that César Chávez energized the movement's decline in the 1980s, summarizes the movement's diminution as a manifestation of taking "defeat from the jaws of victory." This decline occurred, he argues, because of a persistent refusal to adjust the movement's strategic moves in light of new, evolved circumstances—the 1960s were, after all, different from the 1980s.[3] Yolanda Alaniz and Megan Cornish issue a biting assessment of the way that this conservatism undermined the movement's work and trajectory: "The Union's political timidity weakened its ability to withstand conservative pressure from the labor bureaucracy and the Democratic Party."[4]

I begin my study of the Chican@ movement(s)' racial project with the farmworkers' movement. I do so because of the racial significance of its manifesto, the Plan de Delano, and its subsequent reach, both in terms of its content *and* its form in later texts like the Plan de La Raza (1967) and the Plan de Santa Barbara (1969).[5] The Plan de Delano, which circulated during a peregrinación, a pilgrimage, from Delano to Sacramento in 1966, corroborated Luis Valdez's assessment of the racial import of the farmworkers' activism in the 1960s. In his eyes, the farmworkers' movement was all about breaking La Raza free of a racist hegemony in the United States that manifested in multiple forms: "We are the repelled by the human disintegration of peoples and cultures as they fall apart in this Great Gringo Melting Pot, and determined that this will not happen to us. But there will always be *raza* in this country. There are millions more where we came from, across the thousand miles of common border between Mexico and the United States. For millions of farm workers, from the Mexicans and Philippinos [sic] of the West to the Afro-Americans of the South, the United States has come to a social, political, and cultural impasse."[6] The Plan de Delano announced that a not-white social movement composed of campesinos had begun, and that this racial(ized) community, like other oppressed communities in the United States, was now reimagining its politics. "The strength of the poor is also in union," it pronounced. "We know that the poverty of the Mexican or Filipino worker in California is the same as that of all farm workers across the country, the Negroes, and poor whites, the Puerto Ricans, Japanese, and Arabians; in short, all of the races that comprise the oppressed minorities of the United States."[7] In the mid- to late 1960s, racial motivations inspired movement activists to join the NFWA and follow Chávez. Young activists are believed to have followed Chávez because he looked like them and their family members.[8] Valdez goes so far as to say of Chávez that, "although he sometimes reminds one of Benito Juarez, Cesar is our first real *Mexican-American* leader" (italics Valdez's).[9] In the Plan de Delano, we find a public acknowledgment that it was along the axis of race that the farmworkers derived validation as a "social movement."

Yet I also start with how the farmworkers' movement other rhetorical forces beyond "culture," "religion" or "ethnicity" informed the contours of its racially forming discourse(s), and, in turn, the de/colonial strength(s) of the manifesto. Chávez himself, for example, refused the language of La Raza within the NFWA, claiming that its use amounted to an anti-Gringo racism.[10] To ascribe this view to the influence of "culture" or "ethnicity" would, aptly, seem inadequate. Nevertheless, the ways in which the prevailing conservatism in the farmworkers' movement I noted above informed the composition of the farmworkers' manifesto has received very little interest from scholars across the disciplinary landscape, much less in rhetorical studies. Certainly, this conservatism was not enough to separate the farmworkers' movement from broader Chican@ movement(s).[11] As Minian remarks, "The only Chicana/o group for which club activists showed any respect was the United Farm Workers. This is surprising given that from the 1960s to the early 1970s the UFW called for increasing restriction on foreign migration."[12] But, when race and its relationship to the construction of Latinx identity is of central concern, it possesses and poses its own problematics in public communication because of Latin America's complex racial (and racist) history.[13]

Racial identities in the United States, moreover, have been complicated by the racialization of Mexican Americans, as Flores succinctly states: "Quite simply, Mexicans within the United States have troubled racial categories from the very beginning."[14] Race, Stacey Sowards shows in her analysis of Dolores Huerta's stratagem of "haciendo caras," complicates rhetorical agencies, contouring discourse in a multitude of unpredictable but no less effective ways.[15] Similarly, Natalia Molina argues persuasively that race is entirely relational, hinging on the creation, maintenance, and disruptions of linkages between racial groups through what she terms "racial scripts."[16] Racial formation, in other words, is uneven, subject to reinterpretation, reinvigoration, and reinvention in contexts that are themselves variable. Indeterminacy suffuses racial rhetorics, however ossified they might appear, and, if race is acknowledged in the Plan de Delano at all, the racial formation it accomplished cannot be presumed to be either singular or stable. Though certainly signaling assertion vis-à-vis the language of a "Plan," the racialization encouraged by the Plan must nonetheless be viewed more as a *proposal* and interrogated with that in mind.

In this study tracing the contours of the Chican@ movement(s)' racial project and following their de/colonial praxis between 1965 and 1970, an exploration of the complications involved in racial negotiation is accomplished not by presuming a secure racial line between the farmworkers' movement and subsequent Chican@ movement activism but by, instead, discerning how the farmworkers' movement negotiated racial dynamics after the initial circulation of the Plan de Delano; after victories for higher wages had been achieved; after the movement gained national attention. This chapter, consequently, interrogates how a conservatism embedded within the farmworkers' movement's activism inflected the racial formation made possible in and through the Plan de Delano by attending closely to its visualization after the peregrinación. By the end of 1966, the same year as the peregrinación, a reproduction of the farmworkers' manifesto published as a photobook, *Basta! La Historia de Nuestra Lucha* (Enough! The tale of our struggle), remade the racial work of the Plan de Delano through visual rhetorical means. As I have written elsewhere, the racially forming power of the Plan de Delano was as much a consequence of visual rhetoric as it was a product of verbal rhetorical choices. Although *Basta!* also contained the Plan's verbal rhetoric (at least partially), an examination of the often-overlooked and taken-for-granted aesthetics of this reproduction of the Plan de Delano reveals that visual rhetorical entailments, though certainly not voiding the racial characterization espoused by the Plan's verbal rhetoric, reconfigured its racializing impulse(s). Giving form to what I refer to in this chapter as a *poetics of apathy*, this photographic reproduction of the Plan de Delano reinvented its racial attachments by splitting and splicing the text throughout its pages, stitching it back together with photographs from, primarily, the pilgrimage, and forwarding singular images of farmworkers and white power players. Through aesthetic choices, this reproduction refined and redefined the racial identity of "los campesinos" and their relationship to systemic whiteness. This reproduction of the Plan de Delano might have yet forwarded the "ideology, philosophy, and direction for the forward march of the Chicano [sic] movement"[17] and retraced some prior de/colonial commitments. An analysis of this reproduction's aesthetics, nevertheless, demonstrates how by the end of 1965, the farmworkers' movement celebrated the year's successes by exploding its own iconic text.

Visualizing the Farmworkers' Movement: (Re)Racializing Farmworkers in the United States

Visual representations of farmworkers, their living and working conditions, and even their personal characters had become a site of intense public scrutiny in the early 1960s in ways that paralleled and diverted from previous patterns. Historian of photography Steven Street, who chronicles this contest of competing images of California farm labor, writes that its history "unfolds as an extended parable of the American West and an epic subplot in photographic history. It has roots stretching back to the earliest forms of exploratory visual representation at the beginning of the Spanish frontier in North America . . . and it embraces a wide spectrum of artistic expression and personalities."[18] The plethora of photographic exposés that appeared in the wake of CBS's *Harvest of Shame* in 1960, such as *Death of the Valley* by Dorothea Lange and partner Pirkle Jones, and M. F. K. Fisher and Max Yavno's *The Story of Wine in California*, consequently, were not necessarily new in their foci. Social documentary exposés, like Lange and Taylor's *An American Exodus* in the 1940s, had shed light on the particular struggles with which farm workers grappled. But what made Edward R. Murrow's televised presentation distinct was the prominent, if still understated, role race played in framing migrant farm work as a travesty. *Harvest of Shame* initiated a "new era in the visual story of California's farm workers," a fresh chapter in the narrative of farm laborers in the United States that made their plight difficult to deny by the public and politicians alike.[19] Most important, the video documentation furnished by *Harvest of Shame*, though not explicitly naming racism as a factor, nonetheless *implied* a racial prejudice in its emphasis on Black migrants and their supplying of "unfree labour."[20] Murrow, appearing to remark on the racial tinge of the presentation, summarized the plights of migrant workers from a white person's point of view: "We used to own our slaves. Now we just rent them."

Photographer-activists, however, played a crucial role in sparking a moral outrage over the plights of farmworkers in the 1960s, although they did so at their own peril. Industry giants such as DiGiorgio fired back at activists with lawsuits and retaliative threats. As these socially conscious image-makers became invested in exposing the ills that farm workers experienced in California's supposed idyll, they formalized their efforts by joining organizations such as the National Farm Labor Union, the Agricultural Workers Organizing Committee, and the Congress of Industrial Organizations. Photographers publicized these organizations' claims in local newspapers courageous enough to publish them. They circulated images of the consequences of farmworkers' low wages, their dilapidated housing, and the safety hazards and unsanitary working conditions of their jobs. George Ballis, prior to working with the NFWA, was sued for his photographs exposing deplorable working conditions ignored by DiGiorgio. Unsurprisingly, DiGiorgio sued, and Ballis wasted time and energy simply dealing with the headaches that the lawsuit brought.[21] By the mid-1960s, farmworkers and their working conditions were no longer invisible, nor were they relegated to the periphery of American social life. The harm experienced by farm laborers, particularly migrant laborers, was portrayed as a disgraceful scourge in the United States,[22] and agribusiness lost more and more control over how farmworkers were portrayed to the public.

Despite the increased visualization of the industry-imposed poverty farmworkers experienced, colonially derived racial logics underpinning Mexican and Mexican American farm labor conditions were left unchallenged and underexposed. That stoop labor in particular, for example, was used to test the racial fitness of Mexican Americans received little attention.[23] Moreover, up until 1964, Public Law 78 (PL 78), too, reinforced the precarious position of Mexican laborers in the United States. PL 78 was adopted as an adjusted iteration of the bracero program,[24] a governmental concession that allowed "importing" Mexican nationals to perform farm work while also setting parameters for their employ.[25] Public (re)presentations like *Harvest of Shame* and *The Slaves We Rent*, however, framed "foreign" workers—"Mexican Braceros" as well as workers coming from the "Caribbean"—as contributing to this American problem. These workers, it was claimed, were responsible for depressing the "wage scale" of the "domestic migrant."[26] Xenophobic attitudes, a corresponding disregard for the working and living conditions of Mexican workers, and a pernicious lack of oversight and regulations were part and parcel of the bracero's experience working in the United States, which paralleled the reality of Black and white migrant workers traveling throughout the southeastern United States in *Harvest of Shame* but was ignored.[27] These "braceros" were, instead, (re)presented *in opposition* to "domestic" workers and as part of the problem to be solved.

In 1965, however, after the expiration of PL 78, a growing collective of farm workers, politicians, and activists participating in the Civil Rights Movement in the South coalesced in their intervention on behalf of Mexican American farm workers in particular.[28] On September 16, 1965, the commemorative date of Mexican independence from France, the Mexican American–led National Farm Workers Association (NFWA) joined the Filipino-directed Agricultural Workers Organizing Committee (AWOC) in a wage strike. Photographers were crucial to the strike's success, and by winter's time the NFWA was actively cultivating relationships with photographers, hiring and deploying them to augment the publicity of their strike.[29] George Ballis, a former Marine turned photographer-activist, put to use his social sensibilities and the training he received from Dorothea Lange to help.[30] At the time of his entry into the farmworkers' movement, Ballis was still a photographer for the *Valley Labor Citizen*, where he had already been chronicling the effects of the bracero program on labor pools, as well as working with SNCC in Alabama. Yet as the strike progressed into 1966, photographers such as Ballis and Jon Lewis were pivotal not only in publicizing the farmworkers' strike but also in transforming racial perceptions that pegged farmworkers as lazy, undignified, and weak. Richard Street, commenting on Lewis's contributions in particular, explains that his personal aesthetic was decidedly "positive." Lewis, Street continues, "was not there to benumb and exacerbate suffering through exploitive voyeurism generated according to a mass media timetable.... [Lewis] was not there to provide spectatorial gratification."[31] Concerned about photographic representations, the movement's leadership folded into their protest a campaign that aimed not only at making farmworkers public but also remaking their identity as whole—a precursor of the Chican@ photographic emerging in earnest at the turn of the decade (see chapter 6).[32]

This turn to photographers certainly added an additional media outlet for the farmworkers' struggle similar to that found in the Civil Rights Movement,[33] but it also exemplified the visual rhetorical sensibilities of activists involved in the farmworkers' activism. Visual appeal was crucial to the farmworkers' mobilization and the invention of a public identity, for, as Gunckel argues, "[h]ow community was articulated and visually represented to multiple audiences is inextricably linked with the broader struggle over media representations within the Chicano movement."[34] Shortly after the union's birth, for example, President César Chávez asked his brother Richard to come up with an "emblem for the Union, a flag that people could see," which would encapsulate the NFWA's identity for those inside and outside the union. Richard drew up the now famous black eagle, attending to reproducibility among activists just as much as cultural representation in his design: the rigid shape of the eagle made it easy for sewers to reproduce on fabrics by hand.[35] In 1966, photographs from the movement's activism were reproduced and circulated widely in multiple venues: Eugene Nelson's *Huelga: The First Hundred Days of the Great Delano Grape Strike*; *The Grape Strike*, published by the National Advisory Committee on Farm Labor, and *Basta! La Historia de Nuestra Lucha*. Both *The Grape Strike* and *Basta!* featured Ballis's photographs, and within a year of the beginning of the wage strike, visual depictions of farmworker activism in California were reaching many in and outside of California, circulating information about the strike, and contesting mischaracterizations of the farmworkers participating in the movement. Affirming the claims of the Plan de Delano, the photographs corroborated the emergence of the "social movement" but, most important, it was in these visual rhetorical appeals that the racial tenor of the farmworkers' activism could be affirmed, cultivated, and made to matter.

Remaking the Plan de Delano, Injecting Apathy into Racialization

Though each of these books chronicling the farmworkers' strike contained images, only one of these included the Plan de Delano: Ballis's *Basta!* The photobook, published by the Farm Worker Press after the pilgrimage, was advertised for purchase in the newspaper affiliate *El Malcriado: The Voice of the Farm Worker.* Bill Esher, the editor, even sent a copy to Senator Robert F. Kennedy. Kennedy, who had been one of the more prominent sympathizers of the farmworkers' struggle and participated in the Migratory Labor Senate Subcommittee meetings in California prior to the peregrinación,[36] praised *Basta!* highly: "I think you did an excellent job in portraying both the problems of these people and their spirited desire for change."[37] In a December issue of *El Malcriado*, editors compared the work to Edward Steichen's *Family of Man*, a publication from the mid-1950s that claimed to offer a "camera testament, a drama of the Grand Canyon of humanity, an epic woven of fun, mystery and holiness" through a representation of the "master piece of God"—the human "face."[38] Ballis, who, as part of his working practice, took time to get to know his photographic subjects rather than simply objectify them,[39] might not have shared the universalist sentiment of Steichen's *Family of Man*, but his photographs in *Basta!* nonetheless shared in its humanist orientation. Using a 21-mm camera, Ballis often took close-up shots of his subjects, which, in turn, supported his belief that through exposure social change was possible.[40] The photographs published in the photobook, thus, were pivotal to showing the "face" of the farmworkers' movement and to advocacy on their behalf.

While Steichen's work might have been global in scope, culturally diffuse, intertextual, and temporally expansive, *Basta!* anchored its photographic representation(s) in a single event: the pilgrimage to Sacramento. Leveraging the remediating power of photography and the expectations of an exposé, Ballis's photographs put forth an "immediate" representation of the farmworkers' activism through the "peregrinación."[41] However, it was the Plan de Delano that glued together the photographs of the pilgrimage, its activists, and its apparent focus on their "journey." Doing so, of course, was unnecessary. One might imagine that memorializing the pilgrimage *photographically* could have been accomplished without the Plan. After all, in the same way that the Plan might have re-presented the farmworkers and their peregrinación, so too did the photographs in *Basta!* amplify the voice(s) of the movement, showcase the faces of its activists, and advance compelling photographs embodying the Plan's pronouncements. American film critic and award-winning author James Agee's statements on the weakness of words to *embody* a message appear to explain the rhetorical rationale for emphasizing visuals in *Basta!*: "Words cannot embody; they can only describe. But a certain kind of artist, whom we will distinguish from others as a poet rather than a prose writer, despises this fact about words or his medium, and continually brings words as near as he can to an illusion of embodiment."[42] Given how prominently the images feature, in contrast to the language of the Plan de

Delano, very little, if anything, would have been lost by letting the images, sans Plan, "speak" for themselves.

The inclusion of the Plan de Delano in the photobook, however, adjusts the rhetoric of the photobook *and* the rhetoric of the Plan. We have in this publication a combination of verbal and visual rhetoric, a single "textual event,"[43] and, consequently, the rhetorical features of this reproduction of the Plan de Delano, which is to say its racially forming potency, differed from prior reproductions. Indeed, I propose that the apparent memorialization of the moment through a photobook reconfigures the pathos of the Plan de Delano.[44] The photobook, in celebrating the farmworkers' activism as past tense, reworks its present significance, making still what is otherwise dynamic through photographic representations. And it is this reconfiguration that marks the contribution of this reproduction of the Plan de Delano in *Basta!* to the racial contours of the Chican@ movement(s)' racial project—apathy. As scholars in rhetorical studies have argued, apathy is not to be viewed merely as the absence of pathos, or the lack of emotional intensity, as much as it is its remaking. That is, apathy entails (rhetorical) choice(s): decisions to care less about something and, perhaps, care more about something else. Emotions, after all, are not a zero-sum game, and neither is apathy inert. As Alan Gross's study of emotion's "shadow history" suggests, viewing apathy merely as the absence of emotional rigor—a rhetorical achievement in itself—derails efforts to see the political possibilities it might provoke.[45] Apathy, in short, is not so much the removal of a melody but a change of key. And, in this photobook, the Plan de Delano takes on a different racial tenor not by erasing race but by, instead, taking whatever racial attachments the text spurred and recasting them in different terms.

According to Nathaniel Rivers, it is precisely the politics of apathy, the ways in which feelings are reconfigured for reconsidering how we live life together, that we should take note of in our assessments of an apparent *lack* of concern. For, in so doing, we see the invention of new possibilities that prior pathetic orientations might obscure or foreclose.[46] An analysis of the text's aesthetics reveal an attempt to (re)channel the racial ramifications of the Plan de Delano's verbal rhetoric and reinvest it in something less concrete—the pilgrimage. This retuning of the racial attachments retraces the conservatism of the farmworkers' movement, showcasing the apprehensive tendency in the farmworkers' movement toward controlling the "image" of the farmworkers. But it also does much more. As I will show, there were also racial ramifications wedded to this reconfiguration, one of which was the dissolution of racial friction between "el campesino" and systemic whiteness. The farmworkers had initiated a movement, even a *social* movement, and the scores of photographs in *Basta!* depicting farmworkers, in some cases recognizable figures such as Luis Valdez, evinced how farmworkers rather than outsiders (like the SNCC activists) sustained their own activism. Here lies, I suggest, the de/colonial significance of the Plan de Delano in the photobook: it forwards a change to the European "zero-point" epistemology and decenters whiteness from the farmworkers' activism. And yet the photobook's aesthetic, which entailed fragmenting the Plan's text, splicing together the remaining slivers, and gluing it together with photographs of the farmworkers' activism—in some cases taking the text out of order—nonetheless still adjusts the range of de/colonial possibilities this publication affords. No longer a Plan aesthetically, the aesthetics of the photobook looked to uplift the racial claims the Plan made and, instead, reposition farm worker activism less as racial struggle and more as transcendent cause, a battle with no boundaries, and, consequently, amenable to all.

(Re)Narrating the Struggle of El Campesino: A Poetics of Apathy

The (a)pathetic retuning of the Plan de Delano begins in the photobook's initial page following the cover (fig. 1). The cover page includes a photograph with the obligatory title text, but the combination of text and image forecasts the ways in which the photobook's aesthetic transforms the racial force of the Plan de Delano's verbal rhetoric in this reproduction. The first image of the photobook, a black-and-white close-up image of an activist named Jorge Zaragosa, is blown up to take up half of the entire cover page. The photograph sits opposite the title, its subtitle, and the book's credits to George Ballis *and* the Plan de Delano. These texts are overlaid on a black background, which at once accentuates the title of the photobook and augments the resonance between visual and verbal rhetorics in the photobook. The clarity and size of the image of Zaragosa on the cover suggests a photographic emphasis, despite the appearance of text and photograph together. Clearly in view are Zaragosa's bandanna with the stitched NFWA eagle on a white circle, his worn dark-toned skin, head tilted and mouth agape as if prepared or preparing to speak. In this depiction, Zaragosa appears composed, contemplative, reflective, demure even, and coupling this posture with his direct gaze toward the text on the page, the image suggests that this "tale" or "historia" is not history at all, but, more provocatively, a *memory*. It is a

Fig. 1. The cover page of the photobook *Basta! La Historia de Nuestra Lucha*, depicting Zaragosa. Digitized from The Nettie Lee Benson Latin American Collection, The University of Texas Libraries. Images from *Basta! La Historia de Nuestra Lucha* and *El Plan de Delano* are used with permission of the United Farm Workers of America. For more information about the United Farm Workers, please visit www.ufw.org.

recollection issuing from Zaragosa himself, the image suggests, and viewers have arrived precisely at the moment at which Zaragosa shares it.

Framing Zaragosa as the source of the historia, however, also reduces his significance to the contents of the photobook. His apparent gaze away from the viewer and toward the text on the right side of the page at once decenters his significance to the tale and positions him as a replaceable agent in this particular history. The page contains no reference to Zaragosa personally, leaving it up to readers to determine the identity of the activist, which, for community members, might (or might not) have been evident. Yet Zaragosa's posture and fixed attention on the text reinforces his own insignificance to this tale. Taken together, this depiction of the activist de-emphasizes Zaragosa's personal contributions and suggests that his role is not to advance the struggle or even to publicize the Plan's objectives. Instead, his role is, quite simply, to (re)state *a* tale.

While this reduction of Zaragosa's role might be taken merely as a personal slight, given that the movement promoted solidarity and community identity, as the first campesino (re)presented in the photobook, Zaragosa stands synecdochally for the "our" purported by the text's title and, consequently, puts in stark relief the aesthetic reconfiguration of the Plan de Delano to come. The blown-up image of Zaragosa certainly suggests an emphasis on his agency and role in the publicized struggle, but forwarding this particular image of a calm and collected activist highlights the attempt to reconfigure the vigor associated with the farmworkers' manifesto by suggesting that the Plan de Delano exemplifies the work of singular individuals divorced from a community, and that the Plan de Delano is less an assertion and more of a recollection. The Plan de Delano, however, was not a text produced by only one individual, nor did it re-present any one singular individual's desires or plans. Hammerback and Jensen, for their part, overstate Chávez's importance to the *writing* of the Plan de Delano in their retelling of his "rhetorical career," although we might certainly credit Chávez with the general theme of the peregrinación that is privileged in *Basta!*[47] As Chávez himself recalled to Jacques Levy, "We assigned Luis Valdez to write our plan, and I gave him some of the topics. Then I made some modifications, and after a few corrections by the executive board, we went to the strikers, who approved it."[48] The Plan de Delano was representative of a community's demands and concerns, and its authorship exemplified a communal, coalitional energy sustaining the farmworkers' movement. Moreover, the Plan de Delano was written as a way of providing an ignorant public with topoi, topics of conversation, to discuss the farmworkers' struggle in California, and not only to serve as an object to be mulled over. Highlighting a nameless campesino, whose posture and gaze reflects poised contemplation, reframes the Plan de Delano more as a private document than a public-facing one.

Similarly, relocating the Plan within a tale displays the photobook's rhetorical movement toward transcendence, which, in turn, circumscribes its pronouncements and the racial distinctions it compelled. As Burke explains, "The stimulus towards transcendence, or symbolic bridging and merging, arises from the many kinds of conflict among values implicit in a going social concern. Such conflicts are heightened to a point of crisis, necessitating scrupulous choices between acceptance and rejection of the authoritative symbols, in proportion as a given order of rights and purposes attains efficient bureaucratic embodiment."[49] Re-presenting the Plan as part of a broader historia transformed the Plan from the imperative mood to the indicative and, in so doing, dissolved the conflicts represented in and through the Plan, both verbally and through the genre of a "plan."[50] The campesina/o no longer makes demands, nor does s/he protest; campesina/os, instead, reminisce. Memories, to be sure, can be a powerful means of speaking back to power (such as testimonios),[51] and memories contain affective attachments.[52] Personal memories, moreover, as scholar Dana Cloud has argued, can become manifest in a "null persona," a consequent limitation of rhetorical agency because of the weight of a borne trauma.[53] Memories, simply stated, are rhetorical constructions both in their consequences and causes. Consequently, memories have community-forming power, a product of the ways in which certain memories are made to matter and communities are encouraged to forget certain others.[54] In presenting the Plan de Delano within the context of a tale, the photobook imposes an inventive restriction on what *can* and what *should be* stated—a direct contrast to the agency that the Plan de Delano energized—and it reorients the pathos of the Plan de Delano to a "causa" less restricted to a particular time and place. This move to transcendence delimits the kairotic potentials of photobook and the Plan de Delano, since timely discourse relies on the negotiation of options in the moment.[55] Both texts, the photobook *and* the Plan de Delano, tragically lose relevance. Unbound by time, both are texts without a future and an end. The photobook, in short, promises a reinvention of the racial discourse of the farmworkers' manifesto by freeing the movement's struggle from the "scramble of the Barnyard," from clashes, disagreements, conflicts, and, later in the photobook, racism.[56]

The racial apathy previewed by the cover continues throughout the photobook, as combinations of Ballis's photographs and text from the manifesto appear in tandem to tell the historia of the farmworkers' movement. The photobook's attempt to reconfigure the Plan as a narration of the campesina/os' struggle creates a representative gap between the Plan de Delano and the farmworkers. This gap certainly existed prior to the photobook, as signifieds are never tied inextricably to their signs. Homi Bhabha's interrogations of the relationship between narrations and the nations they invent, however, are relevant for understanding this reproduction of the Plan de Delano. Ballis's photographs, coupled with the text, give the appearance of a narration of the farmworkers' movement. But this narration claiming to depict campesina/os is ultimately fictitious, a fabrication that posits a singular voice erasing differentiations in the movement, and, consequently, augments the gap always and already present. In the photobook's attempt to close the gap between the sign (the photobook) and signified (the campesina/os) through the telling of a tale that apparently united them, the photobook instead widens

Fig. 2. Photograph of Luiz Valdez and a portion of text from "El Plan de Delano" in *Basta! La Historia de Nuestra Lucha*, 1966. Digitized from The Nettie Lee Benson Latin American Collection, The University of Texas Libraries. Images from *Basta! La Historia de Nuestra Lucha* and *El Plan de Delano* are used with permission of the United Farm Workers of America. For more information about the United Farm Workers, please visit www.ufw.org.

the chasm.[57] Consider these two images (fig. 2 and 3), both of which depict farmworker(s) speaking words from the Plan. The image of Luis Valdez is the only photograph with a caption. It indicates that the photograph depicts his "reading" the text of the Plan: "Luis Valdez lee el Plan de Delano, durante un mitin de campesinos / Luis Valdez reads the Plan of Delano at a farm workers rally." Viewed historically, including the text of the Plan with this image of Valdez "reading" the text suggests a coherence between the photobook's photographic representations and the Plan de Delano that augments its representations.

However, viewed aesthetically, the coupling of this image and caption defuses the racial energy of the Plan de Delano purported by their coupling. The image, though apparently representing a reading of the Plan de Delano, is nonetheless abstracted from a specific context in which the reading was performed, and the insertion of a terse caption presented in the third person creates even further separation between the performance and the text of the Plan de Delano included on the page. The temporal contradiction, a

Fig. 3. Photograph of activists and a portion of the text from "El Plan de Delano" in *Basta! La Historia de Nuestra Lucha*, 1966. Digitized from The Nettie Lee Benson Latin American Collection, The University of Texas Libraries. Images from *Basta! La Historia de Nuestra Lucha* and *El Plan de Delano* are used with permission of the United Farm Workers of America. For more information about the United Farm Workers, please visit www.ufw.org.

consequence of the aesthetic of these pages, casts a racializing shadow upon Valdez. Valdez, like Zaragosa, gazes directly at the Plan's text on the right side of the page and yet, with mouth slightly open, is never "heard" reading the text. Like Zaragosa, Valdez is composed and demure. His role as dramatist is erased, positioning him more as ventriloquist than performative leader in the farmworkers' movement.[58]

This representation curtails Valdez's agency and, consequently, suggests that the Plan is more domesticating than liberatory. Rather than recording all of Valdez's words or noting the compelling aspects of his delivery, all of which would have been catalyzed and reinforced by the verbal rhetoric of the Plan, the photograph and caption frame Valdez as *merely* reading the text of the Plan like an actor in a broader play in which he is not the director. Correspondingly, the rhetorical potency of the Plan de Delano, as a suasive text, no longer arouses, energizes, or mobilizes for a present struggle. Instead, the Plan de Delano pacifies and, in turn, resonates with the racial trope of the docile farmworker.[59] But because Valdez's agency is yet present—he is presented as reading the text, after all—the Plan de Delano still activates. It still calls and compels action, yet it does so less for a "social movement." Rather, the Plan de Delano invites contemplation, reflection, and personal devotion. Although Valdez had personally recalled, in his article in *Ramparts* in July, the myriad of ways in which the farmworkers' activism had burst through a bloody history and a flurry of present and past conflicts, all of which the Plan de Delano noted too, here he is presented as an effectively silent though still present supporter.

A similar reinvention of farmworker agency occurs on a page appearing later in the photobook. Reproduced below, the page includes photographs of less prominent farmworkers and verbiage from the Plan's second proposition. In both images on this page, there are depictions of farmworkers apparently engaged in conversation(s) and performing public speech(es). Campesinos address counterparts both inside and outside buildings, and in both situations—though drastically different, in that one photograph appears to capture a picket (the left) while the opposite photo presents a meeting (the right)—strong deliveries characterize the bodily postures of speakers. Listeners appear spellbound. Once again, for both photographs, the text of the speech is the Plan de Delano. A single statement, in English and Spanish, supplies the captions for these photographs and purports to exemplify verbally the image(s) of the farm workers.

The use of a singular statement to caption the photographs, however, drastically undercuts the energy and agency of the campesinos displayed in each image. Photographs, on the one hand, appear to depict the content of the Plan. They show how "se acabaron los años cuando el campesino no decía ni hacía nada para levantarse / the years are gone when the farm worker said nothing and did nothing to help himself." Supporting the validity of the Plan's verbal claims, photographs highlight how in picket lines or in meeting houses, farmworkers are taking ownership of their struggle and relying upon themselves to activate one another in this wage strike. On the other hand, including a partial quote of the second proposition gestures toward the refiguration of the Plan's racial politics in the photobook. Using the second proposition, one of the most conservative statements in the Plan due to its appeal to governmental authorities, affirms, quite thinly, the actions depicted by the photographs. The Plan, in essence, is used to reinforce a restraint on the farmworkers' activism, effectively circumscribing the agency of the farmworkers depicted, not by discarding it but by reshuffling it toward a collaboration with the politicians called out in the Plan de Delano. The Plan de Delano, as caption for these photographs, recasts the division between the farmworkers and politicians that marks the entire second proposition and, instead, appears to promote political collaboration. Including more of the proposition covering US politics heightens the contrast between the full Plan de Delano and this excerpted version. Politicians, the Plan de Delano stated,

> saw the obvious effects of an unjust system, starvation wages, contractors, day hauls, forced migration, sickness, illiteracy, camps and sub-human living conditions, and acted as if they were irremediable causes. The farm worker has been abandoned to his own fate—without representation, without power—subject to mercy and caprice of the rancher. We are tired of words, of betrayals, of indifference. To the politicians we say that the years are gone when the farm worker said nothing and did nothing to help himself. From this movement shall spring leaders who shall understand us, lead us, be faithful to us, and we shall elect them to represent us. WE SHALL BE HEARD.[60]

These moments of farmworker deliberations exemplify a democratic move, to be sure, but one that is wholly coherent with the US political system. Distancing the farmworkers from the division presupposed in the second point of the Plan de Delano, the combination of verbal and visual rhetoric suggests that this division has been transcended—identifying one with the other.[61]

This pathetic reorientation of the Plan de Delano surfaces sharply when we contrast these images to the photograph on the next page. This image is a full spread of an activist mid-yell (fig. 4), which in and of itself might appear to reinforce the original pathos of the Plan de Delano. Nonetheless, the absence of the manifesto's text on this page is notable—a curious move considering the prevalence of the Plan de Delano in the photobook. Yet, when contrasting this image with the prior photographs of activists, that this photograph contains no caption heightens the repurposing of the Plan de Delano's racial energy. The image of the activist mid-yell, in contrast to the images of Valdez and Zaragosa, certainly captures a different energy. Refusing the Plan de Delano a place *alongside* this photograph, however, evinces a separation that sustains the preeminence of campesina/os in the photobook while de-emphasizing the Plan de Delano. Though having the potential of underlining the racial agency present in the Plan de Delano in this photograph, the photobook locates the racial militance of the farmworkers' movement firmly within acceptable political actions in the United States and even grants a degree of respectability to farmworkers "yelling" for their rights.

Fig. 4. Photograph of an activist yelling into a megaphone in *Basta! La Historia de Nuestra Lucha*, 1966. Digitized from The Nettie Lee Benson Latin American Collection, The University of Texas Libraries. Images from *Basta! La Historia de Nuestra Lucha* and *El Plan de Delano* are used with permission of the United Farm Workers of America. For more information about the United Farm Workers, please visit www.ufw.org.

The photobook, instead, relocates that pathos away from the Plan de Delano, reinforcing the split via absence.

Critical to the formulation of a poetics of apathy was the aesthetic fragmentation of the Plan's text. Breaking away from prior reproductions, all of which reproduced the text in full, at times without images interspersed throughout the text,[62] this reproduction in the photobook consistently splices text and image together, suggesting coherence without actually *showing* it. This fragmentation of the Plan de Delano disrupts its propositional features, undercutting the imperative force of the pronouncements and the movement objectives they forward. Rather than consistency, the Plan's fragmentation signals dissonance and, in so doing, reconfigures the racial force of the Plan's declarations.

The effects of this textual splicing on the racial identity of campesina/os is most poignant when putting into view its images depicting whiteness (figs. 5 and 6). Although a systemic, institutional(ized) whiteness undergirded the intersectional oppression facing campesina/os in California, pages discussing the opposition farmworkers faced included photographs of white

Nuestros sueldos y condiciones de trabajo han sido determinados desde arriba, porque demasiados legisladores irresponsables, quienes pudieran habernos ayudado, han apoyado a los rancheros en su argumento de que la miseria del campesino es un "caso especial".

Our wages and working conditions have been determined from above, because irresponsible legislators who could have helped us, have supported the rancher's argument that the plight of the Farm Worker was a "special case".

Fig. 5. Photographs of politicians and a portion of text from "El Plan de Delano" in *Basta! La Historia de Nuestra Lucha*, 1966. Digitized from The Nettie Lee Benson Latin American Collection, The University of Texas Libraries. Images from *Basta! La Historia de Nuestra Lucha* and *El Plan de Delano* are used with permission of the United Farm Workers of America. For more information about the United Farm Workers, please visit www.ufw.org.

individuals, suggesting that racial opposition derived from individual actors. The Plan's text, which identifies and speaks to "opponents," is reinforced by photographs of white individuals across different institutions. From governmental representatives, to growers, to ranchers, photographs apply a "face" to those opposing the farmworkers in California, once again highlighting the struggle in which farmworkers were engaged.

These photographic representations of "opponents" toed the line distinguishing supports for de/coloniality. On the one hand, official portraits of Congressmen Sisk and Hagen (misspelled in the photobook) contrast sharply with photographs of the farm workers in "action" in the preceding pages. The Plan's text, which claimed a lack of representational coherence between the farmworkers and their "Representatives," appears to be reinforced by the dissonance between their representations. Farmworkers are somewhat active, while these officials lack energy. These men were "irresponsible legislators," the Plan asserted, "who could have helped us, [but]

Fig. 6. Photographs of agribusiness representatives and a portion of text from "El Plan de Delano" in *Basta! La Historia de Nuestra Lucha*, 1966. Digitized from The Nettie Lee Benson Latin American Collection, The University of Texas Libraries. Images from *Basta! La Historia de Nuestra Lucha* and *El Plan de Delano* are used with permission of the United Farm Workers of America. For more information about the United Farm Workers, please visit www.ufw.org.

have supported the rancher's argument that the plight of the Farm Worker was a 'special case.'" Whereas farmworkers were pictured working, mobilizing, speaking, and listening, these Representatives appear unmoved and unmovable—an indictment pronounced in and by the Plan.

On the other hand, photographs showing two men and a woman outside or otherwise in a field where campesina/os might have worked undermines the systemic and institutional(ized) whiteness energizing the farmworkers' oppression. Each photograph, positioned here as portraits, suggests that these "opponents" operate independently of one another, each confined to their respective locations, which, in turn, suggests that whatever "opponents" farmworkers face were not related in any way but just as "special" as their own representational dilemmas. Reinforced by the fragmentation of the Plan's text, the aesthetic representation of photographs acidifies the bulwark of systemic whiteness and, correspondingly, reduces the racial incommensurability between campesina/os and agribusiness. Farmworkers might have experienced racial discrimination, but, these photographs suggest, it occurred not because of the system but on account of a few actors operating singularly on their own.

Coupling fragments of the Plan with individual portraits dismantles the revolutionary expectations issuing from the manifesto's generic form. The genre of the Plan, which hinged on systemic rejection and presupposed revolution, was accompanied by an aesthetic saturation of demands and grievances listed all at once, a stylistic choice that heightened the Plan's affective energies.[63] Sustained in the pamphlet and in other reproductions of the Plan de Delano in *El Malcriado* that maintain the listing aesthetic, the affective intensity of the Plan disappears when the text is split, spliced, and reduced to atoms (contrast, for example, with fig. 7). Dismantling the Plan's generic form, the photobook's isolation of white actors and the obliterations of its propositions smooth out racial edges while yet sustaining them. Though certainly not completely eradicating the racial energies, these aesthetic choices nonetheless blunted them without denying them outright. Pathos was shifted, not disavowed. The last two pages of the photobook, a page with text followed

Fig. 7. Portion of English text of "El Plan de Delano," 1966. Farm Worker Movement Documentation Project, UC San Diego Library. Images from *Basta! La Historia de Nuestra Lucha* and *El Plan de Delano* are used with permission of the United Farm Workers of America. For more information about the United Farm Workers, please visit www.ufw.org.

by a photograph of farmworkers marching, accentuate the poetics of apathy implemented in the aesthetics of this reproduction. The last two pages of the photobook include a brief "history" of the wage strike and the NFWA followed by an image of marchers (figs. 8 and 9). The photobook's penultimate page, titled "The National Farm Workers Association," details the union's origin, the state of the strike in 1966, and some of the victories earned during that year (such as the contract signed with Schenley Corporation). The photobook's final image, a full-page photograph, depicts marchers, all of whom can be presumed to be affiliated with the farmworkers due to their dress, the one visible picket sign reading "Don't Mourn—Organize (Joe Hill)," and their darker-toned skin and black hair. With their backs turned toward the camera, they appear to be "exiting" the historia of the publication. The summary of the NFWA's activity and the image of the farmworkers continuing their march each provide a fitting conclusion to the book. Each suggests a continuation of the tale of the farmworkers' struggle even after this conclusion.

Nevertheless, these final pages stress the photobook's apathetic turn. The brief history included here at the conclusion of the document neglects to

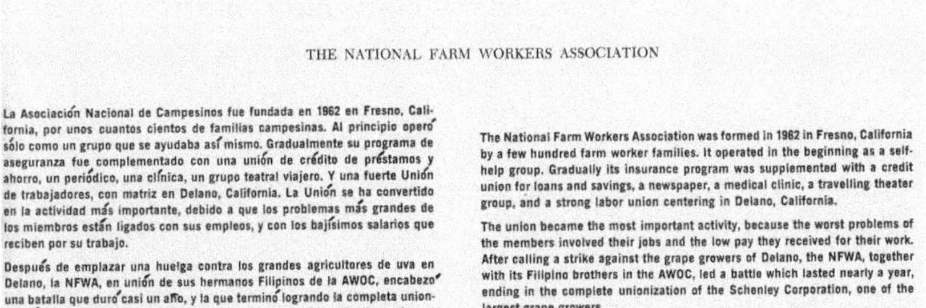

THE NATIONAL FARM WORKERS ASSOCIATION

La Asociación Nacional de Campesinos fue fundada en 1962 en Fresno, California, por unos cuantos cientos de familias campesinas. Al principio operó sólo como un grupo que se ayudaba así mismo. Gradualmente su programa de aseguranza fue complementado con una unión de crédito de préstamos y ahorro, un periódico, una clínica, un grupo teatral viajero. Y una fuerte Unión de trabajadores, con matriz en Delano, California. La Unión se ha convertido en la actividad más importante, debido a que los problemas más grandes de los miembros están ligados con sus empleos, y con los bajísimos salarios que reciben por su trabajo.

Después de emplazar una huelga contra los grandes agricultores de uva en Delano, la NFWA, en unión de sus hermanos Filipinos de la AWOC, encabezó una batalla que duró casi un año, y la que terminó logrando la completa unionización de la Schenley Corporation, una de las empresas agricultoras de uva más grandes que existen en el país.

Después de afiliarse a la AFL-CIO a mediados de 1966, la NFWA ganó unas importantes elecciones en la DiGiorgio Corporation, la segunda más grande empresa agricultora de fruta y legumbres de California. El modelo del contrato que se firmó con la empresa Schenley, se puso como ejemplo de lo que se puede lograr en la DiGiorgio.

Al extenderse la NFWA a través de todo el suroeste de los Estados Unidos, se vió claro que ésta era la Unión que podría organizar a los campesinos americanos; hasta ahora los trabajadores más mal pagados.

Usted puede indagar qué es lo que NFWA puede hacer por usted, y qué puede hacer usted por ella — poniéndose en contacto con sus representantes locales, o bien escribiendo a César Chávez a la siguiente dirección: P.O. Box 130, Delano, Calif.

The National Farm Workers Association was formed in 1962 in Fresno, California by a few hundred farm worker families. It operated in the beginning as a self-help group. Gradually its insurance program was supplemented with a credit union for loans and savings, a newspaper, a medical clinic, a travelling theater group, and a strong labor union centering in Delano, California.

The union became the most important activity, because the worst problems of the members involved their jobs and the low pay they received for their work. After calling a strike against the grape growers of Delano, the NFWA, together with its Filipino brothers in the AWOC, led a battle which lasted nearly a year, ending in the complete unionization of the Schenley Corporation, one of the largest grape growers.

The NFWA, after becoming an AFL-CIO affiliate late in 1966, won an important election at the DiGiorgio Corporation, California's second largest grower of fruits and vegetables. The model Schenley Contract was held as an example of what could happen at DiGiorgio.

As the NFWA spread through the whole Southwest of the United States, it became clear that this was the union that would organize America's farm workers, until now the lowest paid employment available.

You can find out what the NFWA can do for you — and what you can do for the NFWA — by contacting your local representative or by writing Cesar Chavez, Delano, California.

Fig. 8. Brief history of the National Farm Workers Association from *Basta! La Historia de Nuestra Lucha*, 1966. Images from *Basta! La Historia de Nuestra Lucha* and *El Plan de Delano* are used with permission of the United Farm Workers of America. For more information about the United Farm Workers, please visit www.ufw.org.

Fig. 9. The last two pages of *Basta!*, depicting marchers. Images from *Basta! La Historia de Nuestra Lucha* and *El Plan de Delano* are used with permission of the United Farm Workers of America. For more information about the United Farm Workers, please visit www.ufw.org.

mention the Mexican American origin of the NFWA. Nor does the publication make reference to the "raza" comprised of campesina/os. These terms and references were part and parcel of El Plan de Delano, and this brief history sets that aside even while referring to farmworkers as "campesinos." The photobook reduces the racial resonance of the term "campesinos" by softening the racial connection between Mexican Americans and the plethora of racial groups posited by the Plan de Delano in proposition five: "We know that the poverty of the Mexican or Filipino worker in California is the same as that of all farm workers across the country, the Negroes and poor whites, the Puerto Ricans, Japanese, and Arabians; in short, all of the races that comprise the oppressed minorities of the United States." The Spanish translation of the epilogue might have gestured toward the NFWA's racial presence, making reference to the "Filipino brothers / hermanos Filipinos," but at the same time its avoidance of the term "raza" diminishes the Mexican American racial distinction. As Molina and colleagues assert, "Race is not legible or significant outside of a relational context. From this perspective, race does not define the characteristics of a person; instead, it is better understood as the space and connections between people that structure and regulate their association. To inhabit, claim, or be ascribed a particular racialized identity or grouping is to be located in an assemblage of historical and contemporary relationships."[64] In this reproduction, the photobook avoids the explicit racial connection energizing the solidarity between campesina/os and other "races" in the United States.

The final image, too, reworks the racial presence invoked by the Plan de Delano. The shot of marchers, each of whom seems to possess the phenotype of a "campesina/o," suggests that these are not-white workers and, quite possibly, not-Black workers—a subtle yet real racial erasure to follow in the later years of Chican@ movement(s). Although there were certainly white and Black activists involved in the movement, the perspective from behind the farmworkers makes a definitive conclusion about the racial composition of these marchers difficult, although this representation does appear to reinforce the masculinist emphasis of the farmworkers' movement. The photograph, rather than highlighting the emergence of La Raza articulated by Valdez,[65] suggests that it is not the racial presence that matters in this historia. Without seeing the faces of the marchers, viewers cannot say for sure who the subjects in the photograph are, nor can a racial presence be discerned.

At the same time, there is a whitewashing in this image that, though subtle, reaffirms the push to transcend the racial clash implied by the Plan de Delano. The whitewashing comes from the signs hoisted by the marchers. Sitting in the middle of the page, the one visible picket sign towers over every one of the marchers. The sign includes the (in)famous statement by labor martyr Joseph Hillstrom, known as Joe Hill: "Don't Mourn, Organize!" Its positioning on the page casts a defining shadow over what appears to be a depiction of the farmworkers' peregrinación. Yet corridos, readings of the Plan de Delano, and banners showcasing the Virgin of Guadalupe, which were prominent during the farmworkers' march, are not shown. Of course, one reason for this absence might be that Ballis's photograph is representing not the peregrinación itself but another of the farmworkers' marches. However, even if the photograph does not depict the peregrinación in particular, this image of farmworkers would have nonetheless been connected to the peregrinación enthymematically. This connection suggests that Joe Hill's quotation, which in this photograph acts as a "caption" for the event, substitutes the voice of a white Swedish-born labor activist for those of other farmworker activists such as Dolores Huerta, César Chávez, Epifanio Camacho, and Luis Valdez. Including this picket sign with Joe Hill's phrase reconstitutes a white presence where it otherwise would have seemed less than definitive, and, among a sea of nameless farmworkers, it is the name that Ballis's photograph suggests matters most. The peregrinación, in short, is not a march for La Raza. It is a march compatible with, and perhaps representative of, whiteness. What matters, the photobook suggests in this closing, is not a not-white identity but a broader, more inclusive politics.

Conclusion

The composition of the Plan de Delano initiated a generic trajectory of "Plans" for Chican@ movement(s), each of which built off priorities implicated if not stated outright by that of the farmworkers. The Plan de Delano was reproduced once more after this in Luis Valdez and Stan Steiner's 1972 volume *Aztlan: An Anthology of Mexican American Literature*, which underscores how crucial this particular text was not only to the farmworkers' movement in California but also to the broader movement in Mexican American politics for which the San Joaquin Valley was an additional seedbed of activist energy. As the racial identity of Mexican Americans became increasingly part of the deliberations to improve social plights, El Plan de Delano in particular highlighted how a racial identity was integral to the oppression that farm workers faced in California and to their solutions.

Nevertheless, as this chapter highlights, the de/colonial sensibilities undergirding the invention of a racial identity in El Plan de Delano was not consistent with each of its reproductions, nor was the Plan's projection of a racial image of the farmworkers uniform after its original publication. Although a racial identity was certainly present in *Basta! La Historia de Nuestra Lucha*, a poetics of apathy subtending the aesthetics of the photobook remade the racial dynamics of the Plan. Photographs, which might have suggested a realist re-presentation of the farmworkers' activism, coupled with the splitting and splicing of the Plan de Delano, softened the racial conflict that the original text proposed. Compounded by the framing of the photobook as a "tale," the Plan de Delano suggested a racial energy, but in a different key. The aesthetic decisions witnessed in the photobook might have been praised, both by those associated with the movement (such as the staff at *El Malcriado*) and outside sympathizers (including RFK). However, attention to the aesthetics of this reproduction of the Plan surfaces its political and, in turn, its racializing distinction.

These aesthetic adjustments to the Plan had profound ramifications for its racial appeal, but it also clearly shows the contingency of the Chican@

movement(s)' racial project and, at the same time, the diversity of de/coloniality at this point in 1966. The photobook's aesthetic reconfigurations appeared to transcend the racial assertiveness of the Plan de Delano qua Plan. The fracturing of its verbal rhetoric, the splitting of propositions, the pairing of photographs, the isolation of whiteness, and the evasion of racial language reinvented its racially infused claims. Viewed solely from the angle of racial diminishment, the *Tale of Our Struggle* might have suggested a lack of de/coloniality. However, the prominence of race in this reproduction, though certainly remade, nonetheless positions this text as a de/colonial production. Although the insertion of ambivalence and amplification of transcendence of the conflict between campesina/os and institutional whiteness might have been diminished, there was yet racial difference in this memorialization. Though more oblique than in the original publication, the photobook was nonetheless still about the agency of campesina/os. That there were multiple approaches to the establishment of a not-white, non-Black racial identity does not necessarily mean the lack of a de/colonial sensibility. In fact, as Rancière makes clear, it is dissensus and disagreement that are crucial for a truly democratic movement, as the multitude of voices contribute to and sustain the excess of words pivotal to the demonstration of equality between political actors.[66] In this chapter, the negotiation of racial energy demonstrates how farmworker activists grappled with their success. Although whiteness was still represented as a problem with which to deal, the photobook suggested yet another way of resolving its sting. This decision might have frustrated the de/colonial sensibility of some of the movement's activists—particularly Luis Valdez—but in 1966, there appears to have been a notable racial plasticity and, consequently, a desire to be on the spectrum of de/coloniality without adopting it wholeheartedly. Indeed, the poetics of apathy present in this production did not represent a denial of de/colonial politics in Chican@ movement(s).

Even so, as Chican@ movement(s) gained traction, and racial representation continued to dominate conversations at the highest level of government, rhetorical sensibilities seemed to point toward becoming entrenched in the assertion of an anti-white racial identity and a full disavowal of systemic whiteness. The farmworkers' movement contributed to this rhetorical development, despite its apparent attempt to reinvent racial claims in ways that corroborated with whiteness. As institutions continued to both make racial identities central to political representation and yet inconsequential to their decisions, Mexican American activists adjusted aesthetic choices in ways that established a racial politics that worked for rather than against them.

3

A POETICS OF AMBIVALENCE: "I AM JOAQUIN" AND THE YEAR OF LA RAZA (1967)

The farmworkers ignited a firestorm of political energy that reverberated beyond California's state lines. As Mariscal observes, partnership with the National Farm Workers Association (NFWA) "functioned as an affective link and practical training ground" for a plethora of activists with different ideological and political interests,[1] and, when we trace the influence of farmworker tactics outside of California, we see how marches, for example, became part and parcel of Mexican American activism. Chávez, too, noted the inspiration felt by those participating in the farmworkers' march: "The people who took part in the strike and the march have something more than their material interest going for them.... For instance, some of the younger guys are saying, 'Where do you think's [sic] going to be the next strike.'"[2] In Texas, farmworkers in the Rio Grande Valley joined the NFWA and initiated their own strike, and mere months later, they marched to Austin, Texas—one of the largest demonstrations by farm workers ever to occur in the Lone Star State.[3] Even Reies López Tijerina, a fiery fundamentalist preacher dubbed "King Tiger," led his organization La Alianza Federal de Mercedes—later La Alianza Federal de Pueblos Libres (Free States)—on a march to the capital city of Santa Fe from Albuquerque. Tijerina remarked on how these antecedent protests shifted the rhetorical terrain: "In our day, politicians won't listen until the people come out with some kind of spectacular march or demonstration.... We feel we're on the right track now."[4] If the Plan de Delano's pronouncements of a movement "spreading like flames across a dry plain" were yet in doubt at the end of 1966, the activism stemming from an affinity with and for the farmworkers' movement suggested that at the very least their "flames" were appealing and adaptable.

This activism, however, as I discussed in chapter 2, was racially *forming*, and, while their circulation of "Plan de Delano" in *Basta!* might have adjusted its de/colonial potentials, activists moving on from the farmworkers held on to the racial energy that their activism catalyzed. For activists like Elizabeth "Betita" Sutherland, the racial "awakening" that the farmworkers' movement appeared to support gave her an opportunity to witness how her not-white *and* not-Black racial identity *did* matter.[5] Nevertheless, most scholars underappreciate the ways in which the racial work accomplished by the farmworkers' clashed with and reinforced subsequent Chican@ movement discourse(s). Most prefer to view political leanings, ideology, generational difference, and even personal preference as the fundamental cause(s) of these racial tensions between the farmworkers and later Chican@ movement rhetorics.[6] Communication scholars have re-entrenched this division, however incidental and unintended. Fernando Delgado, who observes that the farmworkers' movement failed to support the more "radical" claims of Chican@ movement activists, such as claims regarding urban life that placed racial discriminations front and center, writes, "Chicano leaders filled that void by focusing the Chicano citizenry on the perceived oppressive Anglo state that exercised authority arbitrarily to control and degrade Chicanos."[7] It was *race*, I argue, that both joined and distinguished Chican@ movement discourse(s) from one another and, in turn, shaped the Chican@ movement(s)' racial project into the 1970s. The independent newspaper *La Raza*, whose visual rhetoric will be the subject of analysis in chapter 6, exemplifies the negotiation of these burgeoning racial tensions most vividly in its 1967 "Christmas" issue. Across the top of that issue's cover, editors included the question "What Will You Do for La Raza in 1968?," and subsequent stories, too, included cautions against bowing to "Gringo" interests.[8] Even so, the issue also included a profile of the strike in Delano and called for increased support of the farmworkers by folding them into La Raza: "Help La Raza. Come and walk the picket line with the farm workers here in Los Angeles."[9] The issue did not "call out" farmworkers for their apparent apathy toward racial conflict. Race, instead, was cast as a point of coherence in spite of the apparent dissonances that might have also existed along those same lines. This racial connection might have made César Chávez bristle, though even he might not have denied help administered solely on the basis of race.

My brief rehearsal of the influence of the farmworkers' movement on Chican@ movement(s)' activism appearing after 1965 might not seem all that groundbreaking. After all, no one denies connections between the farmworkers and later activists, nor do scholars rebut claims that the farmworkers' movement evinced a more conservative political agenda than that following in its wake. Scholars rarely, however, trace shifts or modifications in the Chican@ movement's racial project accumulating in its touchstone texts at this time. Extrapolating forward and backward, when scholars have looked at 1967 within the timeline of Chican@ movement activism, they have understood rhetorics surfacing during this year as a sign of decisive shifts taking place, a "radical," "ideological," or, in rhetorical parlance, a tropological departure from activism preceding it. If we take on a more "radical" text published in 1967, Rodolfo "Corky" Gonzales's "I Am Joaquin: An Epic Poem," we see less of a decisive shift than Chican@ studies and rhetorical scholars have previously proposed. Though recognized as one of the most provocative expressions of "protest poetry,"[10] Gonzales's "I Am Joaquin" represents a pivot point, assertive to be sure, but not a sharp turn away from the farm workers nor the birth of something purely revolutionary. Rather, we see *variation* introduced into the de/colonial praxis of a burgeoning Mexican American politics. The Chican@ racial project taking shape in the 1960s was both informed by and an elaboration of antecedent discourse, changing course and trajectory as more voices added their contributions to Chican@ movement(s).

To see the racially forming rhetoric in "I Am Joaquin," however, we need to observe not simply the verbal claims proffered by the text—its disavowals of Anglo/Gringo systems, appeals to Mexican revolutionary histories, or apparent threats of violence. We need to pay attention to its visual features too—its superficial installations; the refigurations of its verbal texts; its proposals for a way of seeing Chican@ politics—namely, its aesthetics. In observing the aesthetic investments in "I Am Joaquin," we see a much more subtle emphasis that sustained a resonance with more racially accommodating rhetorics while, at the same time, advocating for their stretching. The publication of "I Am Joaquin," as I show below, did not so much offer a *departure* from the racial formation accomplished by the farmworkers' movement as much as a *divergence*, a split sharing in the de/colonial impulses of the farmworkers but nonetheless showcasing a different political pathos. Gonzales's "I Am Joaquin" might not have paralleled the farmworkers' Plan de Delano, but neither did it oppose it.

Although "I Am Joaquin" has been studied variously and, perhaps for some, exhaustively, this chapter proposes an aesthetic interrogation of its assertions and apparently "propagandistic" professions[11]—a de/colonial mode of racial rhetorical criticism. In proposing this alternative way of reading this text, the analysis of the publication's aesthetic reveals a sustained commitment to a racial middling that I will refer to as a *poetics of ambivalence*. Ambivalence, according to the *OED*, captures a mix of oppositions—emotional, psychological, attitudinal—all present and informing each other at the same time. Most important, a leveraged ambivalence destroys the rigid political categories that locate bodies into circumscribed political and supposedly untraversable positions within a polis.[12] In this chapter, I argue that an aesthetic appreciation of the poem, particularly its imagery, textual layouts, and equal adherence to English and Spanish language codes, reveals a multidimensional racial compromise that, on the one hand, resisted attempts by the federal government to limit the racial categories into which Mexican Americans might fit by insisting on a racial middling and, on the other, exemplified a growing racial sensibility taking place in the wake of the farmworkers' movement. If, as Kenneth Burke argued, the creation of a form promises a satisfaction of expectations,[13] Gonzales's "I Am Joaquin" both met and altered expectations aesthetically. In 1967, the Chican@ movement(s)' racial project was evolving, and "I Am Joaquin" captured and forwarded these changes in ways that branched from the farmworkers in 1966 yet also forwarded political possibilities for a racial solidarity among an increasing number of Chican@ activists.

Rodolfo "Corky" Gonzales and the Growing Appeal of Ambivalence

If, as Moore and Guzman asserted in 1966, "winds of change" were perceptible among Mexican Americans,[14] 1967 augured a proposal for the direction of that change: revolution. There was, perhaps, no more formative event in Chican@ movement activism in 1967 than the Tierra Amarilla takeover by Reies López Tijerina and La Alianza Federal de Mercedes. Others have recounted this history, so I need not do it here.[15] Instead, I want to highlight its aesthetic and, in turn, rhetorical significance for the Chican@ racial project. Tijerina's "rhetorical world," as Hammerback and Jensen argue, was millenarian or "revolutionary" in its political orientation,[16] and Chican@ studies scholar Ignacio García claims that it was at that takeover at Tierra Amarilla on June 5, 1967, that La Alianza moved on from mere "rhetorical rejections of the liberal agenda" to enact a "real split with traditional politics."[17] Lee Bebout, in commenting on this moment's impact on the "mythohistorical" interventions of Chican@ movement discourse(s), observes that the "raid transformed Tijerina into a living embodiment of the revolutionary/bandido trope" that Chican@ activists had become and were increasingly becoming accustomed to forwarding as a symbol of their imagined nationalist identity.[18] Tijerina's interventions supplied Chican@ movement politics with "the seizing of historical agency to refashion the world and the ways in which experience is ordered."[19] In other words, moments such as this provided not merely a *strategic* mode to follow but an *aesthetic* intervention, a way of sensing and making sense of the present and possible futures.

Nevertheless, it is necessary to split the rhetorical uptake of La Alianza's raid with its more formal features, a distinction that Josue David Cisneros articulates clearly in his examination of this moment. While historical assessments of this event observe a decisive turn in Tijerina's politics, an aesthetic appreciation suggests a more subtle rhetorical veering in his raid. Forwarding this event as an enactment of "border rhetoric," Cisneros offers a compelling argument for viewing this moment not merely as *separatist* but as *straddling*. Interrogating its performative aspects, Cisneros argues that

> as it did with its other expressions of activism, the Alianza straddled, stretched, and traversed this border between constructive rhetoric and revolution. The courthouse raid did not abrogate 'ideas' but, in contrast, was enacted with a clear message in mind, a message of citizenship at that (a citizens' arrest). On one hand, the Alianza took up arms against the state government and thus performed a paradigmatic act of revolution, and its rhetoric of ethnic separatism and nationalism supported this interpretation. However, the group members also framed the courthouse raid as an expression of their citizenship rights as U.S. Americans.[20]

This moment in Chican@ movement history, viewed aesthetically, was not quite as "revolutionary" as it has traditionally been interpreted to be. Indeed, in claiming that the Southwest belonged to the "Indo-Hispano" in accordance with the Royal Laws of the Indies, we might say that Tijerina and La Alianza's arguments might have been *more conservative* than those of the farmworkers, if only because they appealed to a return to a colonial history much earlier than Mexican Independence Day.[21] This is not to say that Tijerina's actions did not contain revolutionary features, or to claim that they were not politically jarring. Nor do I mean to suggest that an aesthetic appreciation of Tijerina's raid somehow voids it of political force. On the contrary, it is precisely an aesthetic appreciation that recognizes how the "border rhetoric" enacted on June 5, 1967, included "revolutionary" and "conventional" registers, both of which informed its racial significance and empowered its broad appeal.

I have begun with Tijerina's raid to set the stage for Corky Gonzales's "I Am Joaquin," a text that, interpreted by some as having the force of a divine fiat in its capacity to create a "community" much like Tijerina's raid,[22] straddled similar boundaries, though certainly not in the same way. Although Tijerina and Gonzales are often glued together as *rhetorical* partners vis-à-vis their parallel "revolutionary" discourse(s)—Gonzales's organization the Crusade for Justice had, incidentally, declared unwavering support for Tijerina and La Alianza as well[23]—I propose that ambivalence both linked and dissociated their contributions to the evolving Chican@ movement(s)' racial project in 1967.[24] Alfred Arteaga argues that Chican@ movement discourse(s) are inescapably marked by hybridity, since much of Chicana/os' lived experiences have been defined by the shifting of borders: as "the border figures the Chicano in cultural difference, so Indianness figures the Chicano in racial difference. For while Chicano subjectivity comes about because of Anglo-American conquest of Northern Mexico, the Chicano body comes about because of mestizaje."[25] Gloria Anzaldúa, most notably, has underlined this "borderland" experience,[26] but so too has José Saldívar in his isolation of a Chican@ poetics.[27] Although Arteaga also appears to limit the extent to which Gonzales's poem parlayed this "hybridity,"[28] Belgrad, too, proposes that Chican@ discourses supply strong, confident assertions of identity (whether ethnic, racial, or nationalist) that belie negotiations of various dialectics of exclusion and inclusion at different scales.[29] Indeed, if Gonzales's "I Am Joaquin" was to be a satisfactory symbol for readers, to borrow terminology from Burke once more, its appeal largely depended on its capacity to adequately represent an experience.[30] And we find that "I Am Joaquin" did not merely impose one but, rather, captured belonging and exclusion growing in earnest among young Mexican Americans. Gonzales's poem, explains Muñoz, "filled a vacuum" that gave them a historical resource through which to retrieve the (not-white) culture they felt they had lost on account of needing to learn and perform whiteness.[31]

Thus, while some scholars have tried to pin a kind of rhetorical straddling in Gonzales's "I Am Joaquin" on notions of "mestizaje,"[32] even this turn is not quite as rigid as it appears. Like Tijerina, for example, Gonzales promoted turns to history as a corrective to the imposition of Anglo ideals when he wrote his popular play *The Revolutionist*. One of the more powerful statements in the play comes from one of José Jaramillo's sons, Carlos, who conveys his feelings toward the impact of an Americanizing education on Mexican American subjectivity: "You go to school, they tear out your guts and start brainwashing you with good old American bleach that don't change your name or your color, just makes you think you're equal to die or pay taxes. Then when you go to work, they make a robot out of you and sterilize you, and then all you can have are brainwashed kids. Papá knows there is something wrong with this system, but all he has to fight with is that rifle, and maybe that's the only way. It's our battle now."[33] Certainly we might take this character's statements as indicative of a firm "revolutionary" stance held by Gonzales. However, even this language does not *require* such a reading, especially when considering how Gonzales's political tendencies resembled the conventional electoral political scheme he learned while working for LBJ's Great Society (see chapter 5).[34] Ambivalence rather than assertion seems to have been part of Gonzales's rhetoric, a move that created resonances with but did not mirror Tijerina's rhetoric in New Mexico. An examination of aesthetic choices in texts surfaces the diversity of contributions to an evolving yet increasingly appealing Chican@ movement racial project. Energized by a growing impetus to blend and integrate racial categories into which Mexican Americans were typically placed, Gonzales's "I Am Joaquin" tapped into an increasingly appealing reconfiguration of a Mexican American racial politics.

The political significance of "I Am Joaquin" comes into sharper focus when we see it within the context of not only Tijerina's raid but also in conjunction with the response of the Lyndon B. Johnson (LBJ) administration to an increasingly public Mexican American dissatisfaction with conventional politics. Indeed, four days after La Alianza's raid, the federal government's racial project, namely locating Mexican Americans firmly within a whiteness aesthetic, appeared with renewed energy.[35] On June 9, 1967, LBJ named Vicente T. Ximenes to a dual appointment as the chair of the newly created Inter-Agency Committee on Mexican American Affairs (IACMAA) and as a commissioner in the Equal Employment Opportunity Commission (EEOC). This appointment highlighted the Johnson administration's efforts to try to satisfy Mexican American disaffection with the lack of Mexican American representation in its leadership. Yet, as he expressed to aide Harry McPherson, it also corroborated with his interest in keeping the "trash" (i.e., Mexican American activism) "out of the White House!"[36] Even so, when observing LBJ's characterizations of Ximenes in his remarks at the latter's appointment, the aesthetic investment of seating a "Mexican American" on the EEOC becomes clear. LBJ did not merely choose Ximenes to represent Mexican Americans, but, rather, he leveraged this moment to laud the ways in which Mexican Americans had benefited from his Great Society initiatives.[37] LBJ praised Ximenes as a "distinguished public servant, a teacher, a war hero, a leader of the Mexican-American community,"[38] language that underscores how Ximenes's appointment was a way to encourage acceptance of a (racial) status quo—a feature of Mexican American political agendas.[39] Moreover,

LBJ remarked, "We have come here today to honor Vicente T. Ximenes. But, we have come here also to reaffirm an ideal that I think all of those present in this room share: the ideal of full opportunity for every citizen in the United States of America. Mr. Ximenes's life is a very vivid story of what we call American opportunity." By elevating Ximenes to the highest political position ever held by a Mexican American and making this moment more about *his* Great Society,[40] LBJ tipped his racially motivated hand. This moment was about fomenting whiteness as a preferred aesthetic and clearly identifying "Mexican American" politics as a contrasting political form. The rhetorical work accomplished by the LBJ administration drew clear lines of demarcation for what constituted "Mexican" and "American" politics among activists.

Although we could read Gonzales's "I Am Joaquin" as a statement that ignores the LBJ administration, particularly since it does not name either the president or the administration, I suggest that an aesthetic appreciation highlights how the poem's racialization challenged the presumptions undergirding the racial project LBJ's appointment of Ximenes sought to reinforce. LBJ's remarks at the appointment, after all, presumed assimilation, a racializing process that, to be sure, presumes whiteness as a "default" racial goal.[41] However, the logic of assimilation also presumes the presence of discrete and opposing racial categories that, at the level of the individual, are mutually exclusive. Viewing the appointment of Ximenes in this sense, LBJ positioned Mexican Americans as *either* Mexican or American, but not both.

Gonzales's poem, however, from early in its publication history, participated in disrupting the appearances of separation, clean breaks, and discrete racial identities. An English-Spanish version of "I Am Joaquin: An Epic Poem," for example, was advertised early on, announced as early as July 1967 in the Crusade for Justice newspaper *El Gallo: La Voz de La Justicia*. Subsequent issues continued to advertise it as a stand-alone pamphlet, but student organizations across the United States eventually got hold of this text and reproduced it in their own venues.[42] One of these reproductions (figs. 10 and 11) appeared in an issue of the newspaper *La Raza* in California in September 16, 1967, and while editors shortened it considerably, the aesthetics of the text suggest the disruption to discrete racial categories spurred by "I Am Joaquin." The editors described the popular circulation of "I Am Joaquin" as if it were part of a live tradition speaking to many at the current moment: "The version that came to our hands was being passed from hand to hand on a 3rd carbon copy." They added that the poem was "fast becoming a legend in the Southwest ... read aloud and recited in bars and cantinas of the lower Rio Grande Valley." Although *La Raza* was based in California, that they

Fig. 10. Portion of "I Am Joaquin" by Rodolfo "Corky" Gonzales as printed in *La Raza*, 1967. Courtesy of the UCLA Chicano Studies Research Center. Permission to reproduce images from *La Raza* granted courtesy of Joe Razo and Félix F. Gutierrez. Permission to reproduce portions of "I Am Joaquin" granted by the Gonzales family.

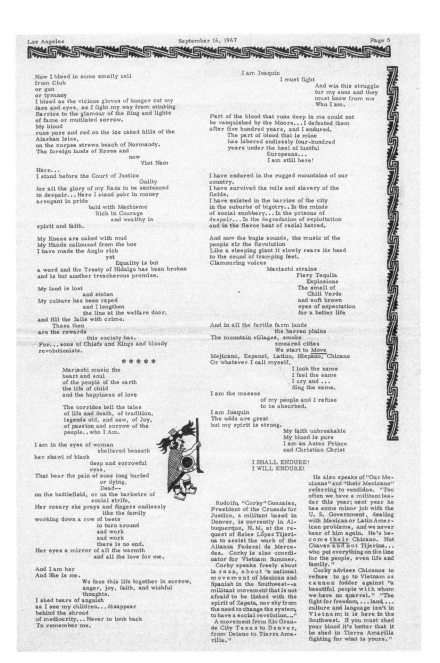

Fig. 11. Portion of "I Am Joaquin" by Rodolfo "Corky" Gonzales as printed in *La Raza*, 1967. Courtesy of the UCLA Chicano Studies Research Center. Permission to reproduce images from *La Raza* granted courtesy of Joe Razo and Félix F. Gutierrez. Permission to reproduce portions of "I Am Joaquin" granted by the Gonzales family.

refer to a region in the southernmost parts of Texas as the source of their own copy heightens the reach of "I Am Joaquin" in such a short amount of time. This poem traveled, and it traveled fast.

We would be, given conventional ways of reading this poem, tempted to see this reproduction of "I Am Joaquin" simply as an "abridged" version of the original. And yet even glancing at the poem's appearance suggests a commitment to reproducing more than simply its verbiage. For example, although this reproduction in *La Raza* avoids the Spanish-coded version of Gonzales's publication altogether, it nonetheless included portions of the poem embedding Spanish language portions within the English-coded text, such as the line "El Grito de Dolores, Que Mueran los Gauchopines y Que Viva La Virgen de Guadalupe." This line, which appears in Gonzales's version too, re-presents a disarming ambivalence toward English as a preeminent political language.[43] Inserting the Spanish-coded proper names, including the "revolutionary shout," amid a sea of English text introduces a disruption of the contact between these language codes that at once challenges commitments to the Mexican heritage alluded to in the text and admits a US presence—not unlike the farm workers Plan de Delano.[44] The illustrations, too, suggest more than "ornament." They allude to excised portions of "I Am Joaquin" that infuse an indigenous aesthetic—and its potential exclusions—to an otherwise all-English-coded poem by, metaphorically and materially on the page, occupying the center of the poem. This reproduction of "I Am Joaquin" might have included language from the poem, but the reproduction's aesthetic, the apparent negotiations of oppositions within the reproduction, suggests a commitment to the poem that went beyond simply deciding which words to include.

These aesthetic features heighten the presence of racial currents among Chican@ activists surfacing in earnest only months after "I Am Joaquin" began circulating widely in the summer of 1967. Once more, the appointment of Ximenes is important to consider when recognizing the growing appeal of an attempt to "straddle" predetermined racial categories set up for Mexican American politics. Speaking for Johnson at a press conference on September 18, 1967, Ximenes announced a meeting for October at the University of Texas in El Paso that would focus on Mexican American issues.[45] Ximenes issued invitations to at least one thousand Mexican American leaders; some leaders, however, were not included, such as Reies López Tijerina, and others refused to attend, such as George I. Sánchez, César Chávez, and Ernesto Galarza. Sánchez is said to have reacted with following quip: "I cannot accept the El Paso Conference as a sort of 'consolation prize,' with all due respect to the White House."[46] Activists believed that this meeting organized by the federal government was part of an elaborate juego (game) mocking Mexican Americans with ever-changing rules on how to achieve political recognition.[47] Furthermore, they argued, this meeting would only include "their" (that is, the federal government's) Chican@s or, more derogatively, the "Tio Tacos" and "Tio Tomas" figures that had bowed to expectations of whiteness.[48] Activists, thus, prepared a takeover of sorts for the hearings.[49] Activists from across the Southwest descended on the hearings,[50] and as they gathered to protest the meeting,[51] they claimed that it did not reflect the true "voice" of the Mexican American community. Putting together a makeshift para-conference that they dubbed "La Raza Unida Conference," activists voiced objectives for Mexican American politics from that point forward that distanced their activism from the federal government's expectations.

Critical to the formulation of their future objectives was their scripting in a text titled "Plan de La Raza Unida." Articulating an explicit *racial* resonance in their objectives (that is, invoking "raza"), activists detailed their political goals in their publication of the Plan in *La Raza* on November 15, 1967 (fig. 12). Scripted in English and Spanish, the Plan introduced its objectives by asserting that "On this historic day, October 28, 1967, La Raza Unida organized in El Paso, Texas, proclaims the time of subjugation, exploitation adn [sic] abuse of human rights of La Raza in the United States is hereby ended forever."[52] Moreover, the Plan declared, its writers wanted to "reaffirm a dedication to our heritage, a bilingual culture and assert our right to be members of La Raza Unida anywhere, anytime and in any job." That this "Plan" entailed photographs from the conference as well as verbal text underscores the aesthetic and, in turn, racial investments prepared for the Plan de La Raza's circulation. Indeed, the language of the text, too, reinforces this racial representation of the event: "We accept the framework of constitutional democracy and freedom within which to establish our own independent organizations among our own people in pursuit of justice and equality and redress of grievances. La Raza Unida pledges to join with all our courageous people organizing in the fields and in the barrios. We commit ourselves to La Raza, at whatever cost." But this reproduction of the Plan de La Raza Unida is a piece of visual rhetoric too. Splitting English and Spanish codes, as well as the bolded reference to "Chicano Power," underlines the politics enacted both within and through this Plan. Certainly, George Sánchez's summation of Chican@s being "betwixt and between" might seem appropriate here to describe the racial crafting of this document,[53] but, aesthetically speaking, the publication of the Plan de La

Los Angeles November 15, 1967 Page 5

PLAN DE LA RAZA UNIDA

On this historic day, October 28, 1967, La Raza Unida organized in El Paso, Texas, proclaims the time of subjugation, exploitation adn abuse of human rights of La Raza in the United States is hereby ended forever.

La Raza Unida affirms the magnificence of La Raza, the greatness of our heritage, our language, our traditions, our contributions to humanity and our culture. We have demonstrated and proven and again affirm our loyalty to the Constitutional Democracy of the United States of America and to the religious and cultural traditions we all share.

We accept the framework of constitutional democracy and freedom within which to establish our own independent organizations among our own people in pursuit of justice and equality and redress of grievances. La Raza Unida pledges to join with all our courageous people organizing in the fields and in the barrios. We commit ourselves to La Raza, at whatever cost.

chicano power

Photos: Felix Gutierrez

With this committment we pledge our support in:
1. The right to organize community and labor groups in our own style.
2. The guarantee of training and placement in employment in all levels.
3. The guarantee of special emphasis on education at all levels geared to our people with strong financial grants to individuals.
4. The guarantee of decent, safe and sanitary housing without relocation from one's community.
5. We demand equal representation at all levels of appointive boards and agencies and the end to exploitative gerrymandering.
6. We demand the strong enforcement of all sections of the Treaty of Guadalupe Hidalgo particularly the sections dealing with land grants and bi-lingual guarantees.
7. We are outraged by and demand an end to police harassment, discrimination and brutality inflicted on La Raza and an end tp the kangaroo court system known as juvenile hall. We demand constitutional protection and guarantees in all courts of the United States.
8. We reaffirm a dedication to our heritage, a bilingual culture and assert our right to be members of La Raza Unida anywhere, anytime and in any job.

En este día histórico, 28 de Octubre de 1967, La Raza Unida organizada en El Paso, Texas, proclama que el tiempo de la sujección, amansamiento, explotación y abuso de los derechos humanos de La Raza es los Estados Unidos ha de terminar para siempre.

La Rasa Unida, afirma la magnificencia de La Raza, la grandeza de nuestra herencia, nuestra historia, nuestro idioma, nuestras tradiciones a la humanidad y nuestra cultura. Nosotros hemos demonstrado y comprobado, y de nuevo afirmamos nuestra lealtad a los principios de la Democracia Constitucional de los Estados Unidos de Norteamerica y a las tradiciones comunes en lo religioso y cultural.

Nosotros aceptamos el marco de la Democracia Constitucional y la libertad, dentro de las cuales vamos a establecer nuestras propias organizaciones independientes en la búsqueda de la igualdad y la justicia social. La Raza Unida se compromete a juntarse con toda nuestra gente que con valentia organizar en los campos y en los barrios. Nos comprometemos, por la presente, a La Raza, a lo que cueste.

También prometemos nuestro apoyo a lo siguiente:
1. El derecho a organizarnos en uniones y comunidades es nuestro propio estilo.
2. La garantía de entrenamiento y empleo en todos los niveles.
3. La garantía de programas educacionales especiales para nuestra gente y de becas individuales.
4. La garantía de casas decentes y sanitarias sin tener que moverse de nuestras propias comunidades.
5. Demandamos representación adecuada en mesas de la practica explotadora del gerrymandering.
6. Demandamos el enforzamiento completo del Tratado de Guadalupe Hidalgo, especialmente en cuanto a las mercedes de tierras y al bilingualismo.
7. Demandamos la terminación a los abusos, discriminación y brutalidad de la policía en contra de La Raza y al sistema de "Kangaroo Court" en el trato a nuestros jovenes. Demandamos protecciones y garantias constitucionales en todas las cortes de la nación.
8. Reafirmamos nuestra dedicación a nuestra herencia, nuestra cultura bi-lingue y afirmamos nuestro derecho a ser miembros de La Raza Unida en cualquier lugar y ocasión y en cualquier empleo.

Fig. 12. "Plan de La Raza," published in *La Raza*, 1967. Courtesy of UCLA Chicano Research Center. Permission to reproduce images from *La Raza* granted courtesy of Joe Razo and Félix F. Gutierrez.

Raza Unida projected a racial ambivalence that embraced oppositions, contradictions, and conflicts within the "Chicano" by illustrating it physically on the page. Forging a middle path that included a "bilingual culture," the Plan de La Raza Unida pronounced a racial identity that was neither one nor the other but simply: *La Raza*.

This racial middling purported in the Plan de La Raza, though seemingly a simple projection of "mestizaje," infused an alternative perspective into the Chican@ movement racial project initiated by the farmworkers' movement. When compared and contrasted to the rhetorical efforts of the farm workers, there is a resonance and divergence in the Plan de La Raza that cannot be overlooked. On the one hand, the appeal to US political values such as constitutional democracy locates this version of Mexican American politics within the confines of US coloniality. Paralleling the conservative moves of the farmworkers' movement rhetoric, it appears to accept the "promise" of US democracy without questioning its viability. On the other hand, whereas the farmworkers might have ventured a bit too far to the right, this Plan de La Raza also forwarded a not-white political agenda much more earnestly. The appeal to bilingualism and its uncontained practice makes clear a commitment to de-purifying the US political aesthetic and breaking sanctioned political categories. Though perhaps accepting the terms of US coloniality, the Plan de La Raza Unida nonetheless pledged to enact them with a different accent, a rhetorical gesture that erupted coloniality's supposed solidity. If there were "white" and "Mexican" racial categories, the Plan de La Raza Unida implied that possibilities of a *both/and* rather than an *either/or*.

Isolating ambivalence both among Chican@ activists and, as I show below, within the pages of "I Am Joaquin," of course, cannot (and should not) obscure its inflexibilities. That is, even if there are more middling aesthetic threads suturing the verbal claims of "I Am Joaquin"—and Chican@ activism more broadly—together, this does not mean that these rhetorical commitments were any less exclusive or restrictive. In fact, as Cisneros's analysis of Tijerina's "border rhetoric" makes clear, the negotiation of contradictions also entails reifying the oppositions that constitute it.[54] In Tijerina's case, the raid demonstrated a commitment to both (white) citizenship and separatism in order to justify claims to land. In a similar way, the ambivalence witnessed in Chican@ movement activism in 1967 illuminated racial polarities—whiteness and not-whiteness—as much as it might have avoided making claim to one or the other. Gallego, whose interest in "Chicana/o subjectivity" differs somewhat from this book's goal, also observes the ways in which the tensions embedded within the poem are ultimately sources prohibiting escape out of the hierarchical status quo. Noting the "nationalist" underpinnings of "I Am Joaquin," Gallego writes that "despite its reliance on the rhetoric of difference and otherness, ["I Am Joaquin"] ends up producing an ontologically static notion of Chicana/o subjectivity, one that easily lends itself to a nationalist agenda, but also to ideological misappropriation."[55] Indeed, it is the very tensions found in "I Am Joaquin" that re-entrenched the "kinship" discourse supporting sexism and homophobia in later Chican@ movement discourse(s).[56] While "I Am Joaquin" might have spurred a blurring of racial categories, the aesthetics of the poem also reinscribed borders of belonging and exclusion by re-presenting and making the poles involved in the conflict appealing.

In what follows, I provide a reading of Gonzales's "I Am Joaquin" that attends to the aesthetics of its initial publication(s) in 1967. Although this focus on 1967 is enough to distinguish this chapter's examinations,[57] combining this isolation of initial publications with an aesthetic appreciation also undermines the largely reductive conclusions coming from literary-minded scholars. Gonzales's "I Am Joaquin," Bruce-Novoa concludes succinctly, represents a "versified statement of the Crusade for Justice's ideology."[58] Literary scholar José E. Limón perhaps offers the harshest critique based on his reading, taking issue with what he perceives to be an "abstract" aesthetic underlying its nationalist vocabularies: "Under its rhetoric, the poem, in its nationalistic abstractive language, frees itself from a compelling poetic imagistic rendering of class relations, from an artistic articulation of the ideologemes of such relations. It is, of course, the poem's very lack of historical particularity that makes this second articulation impossible ... [and] fails to poetically address the *lived* experiences of social domination of the greater Mexican people" (italics in original).[59] The deficiencies identified by these scholars might be right, particularly in light of the flat equivocations between the text's language and Gonzales's boxing career that sympathizers like Stan Steiner proposed.[60] The connections between "I Am Joaquin," his organization, and cultural nationalism are, to be sure, quite tight. The poem's strengths and weaknesses might appear to live and die with Gonzales—the poet without whom there can be no revolution.[61]

As I have argued above, however, the racial formation accomplished in the poem parlayed the "bilingual(ism)" and appeal of "constitutional democracy" characterizing an energetic Chican@ movement activism in 1967. This two-handed politics undergirded the emergence of "La Raza," and it typified a *response* to the rhetorical work of the LBJ administration that was attempting to contain Mexican American politics. Gonzales's "I Am Joaquin" also entered into that political fray and, in analyzing the aesthetics of the poem, its visualizations, layouts, and figures of speech, we see how its aesthetics underscored a racial turn that, on the one hand, conflicted with the racialization of the farmworkers' movement and, on the other hand, elaborated upon it. For, while some have viewed its reliance on Mexican history as a primary feature of its purpose, Gonzales appears to have given the historical element less importance than what the text was supposed to *do*—inspire.[62] Indeed, the aesthetics of "I Am Joaquin" visualized yet more variations in Chican@ movement de/colonial praxis.

"I Am Joaquin" and a Poetics of Ambivalence

The poetics of ambivalence exemplified in the aesthetics of "I Am Joaquin" appears in two of its structural features. The first is temporal, the second linguistic. Both issue an understated attack upon notions of progressivity baked into the racial hierarchy the poem presumes exists in the United States.[63] The repetition of "Yo Soy / I Am" throughout the poem, even in sections chronicling Joaquin's supposed past, evinces an ambivalence toward time and, in doing so, resists the conventional transformation of the protagonist driven by the forward motion of the plot.[64] At the same time, this resistance to "transformation" contests the "assimilation" insisted upon by the LBJ administration.[65] The poem's triadic organization, which is initiated by a description of "present" circumstances (lines 1–37), followed by a rehearsal of a "past" filled with violence and rebellion (lines 38–317), and concluded with a revisitation of "present" political energies (lines 318–501), suggests that political power is located in sustaining tensions between past and present rather than viewing the "future" as the only means of fulfillment. There is no "assimilation" in this epic, for the aesthetics of "I Am Joaquin" refuse to allow the protagonist to progress to such arbitrary, telic processes.

In addition to temporal ambivalence, a linguistic ambivalence to English and Spanish language codes similar to what we saw in the publication of the Plan de La Raza Unida exists throughout the poem (fig. 13). These two languages always appear together on a single page. English, the language racialized as a means to upward mobility vis-à-vis Americanization

I AM JOAQUIN	YO SOY JOAQUIN
BY RODOLFO GONZALES	
I am Joaquin,	Yo soy Joaquin,
Lost in a world of confusion,	Perdido en un mundo de confusion
Caught up in a whirl of an Anglo society,	Enganchado en el remolino de una Sociedad angloamericana,
Confused by the rules,	Confundido por las reglas,
Scorned by attitudes,	Despreciado por las actitudes,
Suppressed by manipulations,	Sofocado por manipulaciones,
And destroyed by modern society.	Y destrozado por la sociedad moderna.
My fathers have lost the economic battle and won the struggle of cultural survival.	Mis padres perdieron la batalla economica y conquistaron la lucha de sobreviviente cultural.
And now!	Y ahora!
I must choose Between the paradox of Victory of the spirit, despite physical hunger Or to exist in the grasp of American social neurosis, sterilization of the soul and a full stomach.	Yo tengo que escojer Entremedias de la paradoja de, Triunfo del espiritu, a despecho de hambre fisico O existir en la empuñada del neurosis social americano, esterilización de la alma Y una panza llena.
Yes,	Si,
I have come a long way to nowhere,	Vine de muy lejos a ninguna parte,
Unwillingly dragged by that monstrous, technical, industrial giant called Progress and Anglo success . . .	desinclinadamente arrastrado por ese gigante, monstruo, técnico, industrial llamado Progreso Y exito angloamericano . . .
I look at myself.	Me miro yo mismo.
I watch my brothers.	Observo a mis hermanos.
I shed tears of sorrow.	Lloro lágrimas de desgracia.
I sow seeds of hate.	Siembro semillas de odio.
I withdraw to the safety within the Circle of life . . . MY OWN PEOPLE	Me retiro a la seguridad dentro de el Circulo de vida . . . MI GENTE
I am Cuahtemoc,	Yo soy Cuahtemoc,
Proud and Noble Leader of men,	Majestuoso y Noble Guia de hombres
King of an empire, civilized beyond the dreams of the Gauchupin Cortez, Who also is the blood, the image of myself.	Rey de un imperio, civilizado incomparablemente a los sueños del Gauchupin Cortez, Quien igualmente es la sangre, el imagen de yo mismo.

1

Fig. 13. Portion of "I Am Joaquin" by Rodolfo "Corky" Gonzales in a scripted font, 1967. Note the handwritten appearance and the near equivalence between sides. The English and Spanish codes are nearly indistinguishable from one another. Rodolfo "Corky" Gonzales Papers (Box 3, Folder 41). Courtesy of the Denver Public Library. Permission to reproduce portions of "I Am Joaquin" granted by the Gonzales family.

(see chapter 1), and Spanish, the language purged in educational spaces, both occupy the public face of the poem, encountering readers as they pick up Gonzales's text. This ambivalence toward language codes, represented by their parallel placement on the page, though a consistent element of the poem's reproduction since it began circulating in 1967, has nonetheless been completely ignored by Chican@ historians, much less rhetorical scholars. This consistent presentation of English and Spanish language codes, I suggest, makes it a constitutive aspect of the poem's rhetorical force. Even in reproductions of the poem after 1967, each stanza is matched line by line in Spanish and English, and in some cases, word for word when terms are not translated (such as with proper names). English and Spanish language(s) are portrayed evenly, such that it would be difficult to distinguish "translation" from "source" or to claim that one language advances Mexican American politics and the other restricts it. Figures 13 and 14 highlight how different 1967 publications nonetheless reproduced this linguistic equivalence.

Although this inclusion of English and Spanish codes in both reproductions might appear as a consistent gesture toward English or Spanish literate readers (which it might yet be), I suggest that the communicative equivalence represented by these reproductions demonstrates a commitment to a linguistic ambivalence paralleling and, perhaps, informing the commitment to "bilingualism" asserted by the Plan de La Raza Unida in the late 1960s. To be sure, there were certainly communicative challenges related to readership that Chican@ movement newspapers took into account. The NFWA, for example, published *El Malcriado: The Voice of the Farm Workers* and its Spanish counterpart *El Malcriado: La Voz del Campesino* concurrently as a way to accommodate its linguistically diverse readership.[66] Nevertheless, these publications separated English and Spanish renderings of their newsletter, a practice that continued into the 1980s when the NFWA began publishing a magazine titled *Food and Justice* alongside *El Malcriado*. In "I Am Joaquin," placing each language in a parallel or equivalent relationship on the same page heightens an ambivalence toward either that positions the emergent Chican@ community as neither fully, comprised of contradictory racial signifiers, and, at the same time, liberated from predetermined molds that located Mexican Americans as either "Mexican" or "American." Resonating with the proclamations made at La Raza Unida Conference, Gonzales's "I Am Joaquin" inhabits the space(s) in-between linguistic communities, drawing from multiple subjectivities informed by language-use, and empowered by processes of racial formation, forwarding and privileging differences not as separate entities but as one and the same.[67]

I AM JOAQUIN   YO SOY JOAQUIN

By

Rodolfo Gonzales

I am Joaquin,
Lost in a world of confusion,
Caught up in a whirl of an
    gringo society,
Confused by the rules,
Scorned by attitudes,
Suppressed by manipulations,
And destroyed by modern society.
My fathers
    have lost the economic battle
and won
    the struggle of cultural survival.
And now!
    I must choose
        Between
    the paradox of
Victory of the spirit,
    despite physical hunger
        Or
    to exist in the grasp
of American social neurosis,
sterilization of the soul
and a full stomach.
	Yo soy Joaquín.
	Perdido en un mundo de confusión
	Enganchado en el remolino de una
	    Sociedad gringa
	Confundido por las reglas,
	Despreciado por las actitudes,
	Sofocado por manipulaciones,
	Y destrozado por la sociedad moderna.
	Mis padres
	    perdieron la batalla económica
	Y conquistaron
	    la lucha de supervivencia cultural.
	Y ahora!
	    Yo tengo que escojer
	        En medio
	    de la paradoja de,
	Triunfo del espíritu,
	    a despecho de hambre físico
	        O
	    existir en la empuñada
	del neurosis social americano,
	esterilización del alma
	Y un estómago repleto

Yes,
I have come a long way to nowhere,
Unwillingly dragged by that
    monstrous, technical
    industrial giant called
        Progress
and Anglo success . . .
    I look at myself.
    I watch my brothers.
    I shed tears of sorrow.
    I sow seeds of hate.
    I withdraw to the safety within the
Circle of life . . .
        MY OWN PEOPLE
	Sí,
	Vine de muy, lejos a ninguna parte,
	desinclinadamente arrastrado por ese
	    gigante, monstruoso, técnico, e
	    industrial llamado
	        Progreso
	Y exito angloamericano . . .
	    Me miro yo mismo.
	    Observo a mis hermanos.
	    Lloro lágrimas de desgracia.
	    Siembro semillas de odio.
	    Me retiro a la seguridad dentro el
	Círculo de vida . . .
	        MI RAZA

I am Cuauhtémoc,
Proud and Noble
    Leader of men,
King of an empire,
civilized beyond the dreams
    of the Gachupín Cortéz,
	Yo soy Cuauhtémoc.
	Majestuoso y Noble
	    Guía de hombres
	Rey de un imperio, civilizado
	incomparablemente a los sueños
	    del Gachupín Cortéz,

three

Fig. 14. Portion of "I Am Joaquin" by Rodolfo "Corky" Gonzales, published by El Gallo Press, 1967. Rodolfo "Corky" Gonzales Papers, Box 3, Folder 41. Courtesy of the Denver Public Library. Permission to reproduce portions of "I Am Joaquin" granted by the Gonzales family.

An Ambivalent Present

Turning to the aesthetics of poem's text, the opening lines verbalize the middling substrate upon which a burgeoning Chican@ racial politics is based. The text makes this racial orientation clear by highlighting how its emergence was *in response* to an aggressive whiteness. Lines 1–8 read:

> I am Joaquin
> Lost in a world of confusion,
> Caught up in a whirl of an
>   gringo/[Anglo] society,
> Confused by the rules,
> Scorned by attitudes
> Suppressed by manipulations,
> And destroyed by modern society.

Using racial indicators to characterize the encounter with systemic whiteness (note that Gonzales uses gringo/Anglo in different versions of the 1967 text), the poem asserts that the obliteration of spatial and temporal awareness induced by "gringo/Anglo" society has resulted in multiple forms of psychological repression. Coordinated by the verb "lost" in line 2, each adjective (caught up, confused, scorned, suppressed, etc.) is re-presented linearly, exhibiting the rigidity of the processes effecting Joaquin's "lost" state. US coloniality operates, the poem suggests, forcefully, and with a predetermined goal of obliteration. Each adjective characterizing Joaquin's "lostness" intensifies as the stanza reaches its inevitable conclusion—the destruction of the individual.

Although the poem begins with an adjective of ambiguity, which could just as easily capture a self-imposed loss ("I got lost"), whiteness is the center of a visual chiasmus. Racial conflict forms the crux of Joaquin's experience(s) in "modern society." Following colonization in a European mode, whiteness becomes established as the identity par excellence,[68] and, as I argued in chapter 1, whiteness is baked *systemically* into US political life through its institutions. Mexican American politics had, up to that point, adopted oppositions between white/not-white as two separate and distinct options and, in some cases, advocating for the acceptance of whiteness and the negation of the latter. One either chose whiteness vis-à-vis assimilation or chose to accept its opposite. The imposition of these two categories, however, is a form of racial(izing) violence: insistent; unrelenting; limiting. Racial distinctions, the poem claims, (in)form Joaquin's present subjectivity and are the root of whatever confusion Joaquin faces. Having to *choose* between an either/or option is a disorienting and destructive force.

The poem, however, transitions toward illuminating the political productiveness of sustaining racial tensions and refusing to view any racial categories as mutually exclusive options. As Bruce-Novoa remarks, the (racial) violence(s) depicted here is productive, as it creates a "response to the threat in the form of the work of art as a new object."[69] In 1967, the turn toward racial ambivalence spurred political energy, and, while nascent, appears here in "I Am Joaquin." The text visualizes this appeal to a racial tension through the use of ellipses. Ellipses, which syntactically function to signal omission, assert a visual presence while at the same time indexing absence,[70] and in the conclusion of this first "present" section, ellipses surface the importance of ambivalence to Mexican American politics:

> Yes,
> I have come a long way to nowhere,
> Unwillingly dragged by that
>   monstrous, technical
>   industrial giant called
>   Progress
> and Anglo success . . .
>   I look at myself.
>   I watch my brothers.
>   I shed tears of sorrow.
>   I sow seeds of hate.
> I withdraw to the safety within the
> Circle of life . . .
>   MY OWN PEOPLE (lines 24–37).

Through the repetitive use of the "I," the poem locates Joaquin primarily between "Anglo success" and "MY OWN PEOPLE." Having been mangled by the "monstrous, technical / industrial giant called / Progress / and Anglo success" and had "hate" and "sorrow" interposed between him and his "people" (or "gente," as the Spanish states), Joaquin wraps back around to the "circle of life"—a structural contrast with the linearity of "progress" in the opening stanza. This spatial reorientation is bolstered by the broken columns of the stanza, which illuminate once more how the "return" breaks the rigidity imposed by the "industrial giant."

Chican@ studies scholar Bruce-Novoa interprets line 37 as indicative of Gonzales's appeal to retreat toward a Mexican heritage for identificational relief,[71] yet a look at the poem's draft history sheds light on the way that ellipses complicate this identificational return aesthetically. An early draft of the poem's third stanza found in the Rodolfo "Corky" Gonzales Papers at the Denver Public Library suggests that ellipses were a stylistic intervention gesturing toward the indeterminacy of the racial realization the stanza implies. Ellipses interject interruptions into the racialization accomplished by "Gringo" society vis-à-vis "Progress." In the earlier draft, the interruptive function of the ellipses is clearer:

> YES, I HAVE COME ALONG [SIC] WAY TO NOWHERE... UNWILLINGLY DRAGGED BY THE MONSTROUS, TECHNICAL, INDUSTRIAL GIANT OF PROGRESS AND ANGLO SUCCESS... I LOOK AT MYSELF... I WATCH MY BROTHERS... I SHED TEARS OF SORROW, I SOW SEEDS OF HATE... AND I WITHDRAW TO THE SAFETY WITHIN THE CIRCLE OF LIFE... MY OWN PEOPLE...[72]

Reproducing the published version once more below, we can see how the passage shifts to using both page space and ellipses to *visually* accentuate this racializing interruption. This shift to page space heightens the visibility of the ellipses and their racial complications:

> Yes,
> I have come a long way to nowhere,
> Unwillingly dragged by that
>   monstrous, technical
>   industrial giant called
>   Progress
> and Anglo success . . .
>   I look at myself.
>   I watch my brothers.
>   I shed tears of sorrow.
>   I sow seeds of hate.
> I withdraw to the safety within the
> Circle of life . . .
>   MY OWN PEOPLE (lines 24–37).

The text's play with physical space and ellipses interjects tensions into the racializing processes imposed by "Gringo society," and they track with the sentiments present at the La Raza Unida Conference. If there were young Mexican Americans looking for a return to a heritage that had been lost,[73] ellipses in this segment indicate that the disconnect between them and their "past" meant that any *appeal* to Mexican history was not a clean return. Nor was the retreat final. Ellipses suggested it could never be, since ellipses also create a separation between "Joaquin" and "Mi Raza." At the same time, these ellipses highlight the racial ambiguities energizing Chican@ activists in the late 1960s. The capitalization of "MY OWN PEOPLE" suggests that "seeds of hate" at the center of the chiasmus could yet be transformed into a strong, visceral energy uniting Mexican Americans in the present.[74] Textual and tonal homologies created by the "MY/MI" suggests a bringing together of Mexican Americans of all linguistic capacities,[75] and, aligning with Gonzales's search for a new political mode (e.g., nationalism),[76] the oral/aural similarities heightens the heterogeneity of the political community brought together by the poem. Ellipses mark the text's invitation for a new form of politics that rejects rigid racial categories splitting political community formation and, instead, invites a productive racial ambivalence, one in which Joaquin and anyone else seemingly affected by the "industrial giant" could commune.

An Ambivalent Past

In the "past" section of the poem, its aesthetics surface ambivalence in a way that is less explicit but no less visible than in the "present" section. In this section of the poem, Gonzales supplies an ekphrastic vision of the rejection of racial categories by accumulating Latin@ American and indigenous monikers representing Mexican American politics during and after the event of colonialism. As rhetorical figure, accumulation describes how rhetors amplify a single "message" or "theme." Accumulation furnishes a powerful means of "piling up" without the obligation to refine, explain, or elaborate upon a theme itself.[77] This suggests that its appeal lies just as much in its performative aspect(s) as in the idea(s) it might compound. As a figure, accumulation buttresses, reinforces, fortifies, foments, assures, and, rhetorically, dissipates doubt by sheer inertia. Yet accumulation also demonstrates a *lack* of commitment to any one of its vocabularies, serving as a kind of reduction as well. Less is said in saying more and, consequently, accumulation also serves as a means of dilution. It exemplifies a firm commitment to dissolving the relative importance of the language put into its service. The racial(ized) identity monikers in the poem, thus, are re-presented here not simply because they might "represent" a pre-existent community or because they showcase something essential and nonnegotiable. Rather, from an aesthetic point of view, their accumulation throughout the section ignites a rhetorical explosive that insists readers see Mexican Americans as anything *but* European, Anglo, "American,"[78] Mexican even. Through the figure of accumulation, the imposition of rigid racial classes, labels, and signs is dislocated from Mexican American politics and the individual worth of any single modifier rendered less important through their conjunction with many others.

Within the rehearsal of colonial violence (from Iberian colonialism to the revolution led by Benito Juarez, lines 38–156), Joaquin disappears amid an accumulation of "historical" identities spanning a nearly five-hundred-year history. Each of the identities Gonzales re-presents in this history are drawn from spaces in the Americas spanning from pre-Columbian Mexico to the northern portions of Mexico acquired by the United States after 1848. Although there are certainly questions that could be raised about the history that Gonzales both includes and leaves out (as other scholars have noted),[79] it is not the "content" or historical accuracy that I take up here. Instead, I want to note how accumulation shatters the historical narration of "American" history. Names, for example, are not anglicized as they are presented in English and Spanish languages (for example, Cuauhtemoc, Chichimecas, Hidalgo, Matamoros, Guerrero). Moreover, in the iteration of "I Am Joaquin" including artwork by Yermo Vasquez appearing within a year of the original publication, accent markings cuing pronunciations visually were included in the English and Spanish versions, an aesthetic move demonstrating the permeability of the English and Spanish dividing line physically separating each of the codes. The accumulation of indigenous names, places, and things forwards a history *otherwise* through an abundance of symbols, which together form a repository that extend beyond granular approaches and tokenized foci (that is, Joaquin).[80]

Consequently, the past section makes emphatic a narratival ambivalence that undermines the "purity" of the histories that follow. As Omi and Winant observe, the creation of essential meanings about phenotypic features through process of meaning-making, such as narratives, are one way through which racial formation occurs.[81] This suggests that retelling and/or reframing histories is a crucial element of formulating a racial identity within marginalized communities, and, in this case, the text's refusal to anglicize "ethnic" features—like names were in popular settings in the decades prior to the 1960s[82]—adulterates Anglo-centric American histories and embeds a new racializing narrative within the story of a broadly conceived América that is actually not quite as "great" or homogenous as it appears.[83] The adulteration fuses both "Mexican" and "American" histories, an intermixing that would motivate the student-led East LA Blowouts in the spring of 1968.[84] Marked by an accumulation of visual cues indicating the presence of an undeniable *other* in this history, the poem subverts the supremacy of whiteness in "American" historical narrations not simply in "content" but in form.

The text initiates this accumulation by first returning readers to Iberian colonization, and it locates Joaquin (and readers) within a colonial story that centers indigenous communities:

> I am Cuauhtémoc,
> Proud and Noble
>   Leader of men,
> King of an empire,
> civilized beyond the dreams
>   of the Gauchupín Cortéz,
> Who also is the blood,
>   the image of myself.
> I am the Maya Prince.
> I am Nezahualcoyotl,
> Great leader of the Chichimecas.
> I am the sword and flame of Cortez
>   the despot.
>   And
> I am the Eagle and Serpent of
>   the Aztec civilization (lines 38–53).

In this stanza, Joaquin deploys five indigenous names—Cuauhtémoc, Maya, Nezahualcoyotl, Chichimecas, and Aztec—in addition to Cortéz, to identify the "I" in this story, which might appear to signal their historical importance for Mexican Americans. This is true, of course, but observing their representations here at the start of the rehearsal of colonial violence, each of the names presented showcases a vibrancy (civilization), alludes to prestige (Prince), and makes manifest a political power (Eagle and Serpent) birthed outside of European conquest and, in fact, preceding colonization. In the span of thirteen lines, Gonzales's text demonstrates a mass of indigenous communities that upend the relative importance of European and white influence(s) in the Americas not unlike that accomplished by Aimé Césaire in *Discourse on Colonialism* in the 1950s.[85] The "colonized" are portrayed as active and self-determined prior to the arrival of Cortéz, "progressive" and "industrial" without the baggage they brought with them. Yet while each name individually might compel appreciation and emulation as an indigenous model of agency, it is not simply their historical referent that is rhetorically powerful. It is the sheer force of their accumulated symbolic presence that augments their adulterating force *in the present*—the adulteration of the European narrative of "progress" operative in a Cold War United States.

As the "past" section progresses, the text continues this aesthetic insistence. Noting cultural figures such as Hidalgo, la Virgen de Guadalupe, and Benito Juarez, and Mexican locations such as Matamoros, Guerrero, and Morelo, as well as a host of events important in Mexican history (such as Mexican independence in 1810), the text condenses about three hundred years of history after colonialism into about three hundred lines. The condensation creates a rhetorical inertia that positions Mexican history as rich, event*ful*, and consequential despite coloniality. To be sure, applications of violence on communities leave residual effects on political life, as the text makes clear when it describes how the "I" both participated in Hidalgo's death and in Mexico's liberation. However, through the diversity of personages, events, and locales in such a small space in the poem, this historical rehearsal showcases how ambivalence undergirds the aesthetic accumulation. Without ambivalence, accumulation fails to exist, since the end of colonial violence is *genocide* or *total assimilation*—nothing in between. Here, ambivalence pushes the text's demonstrations of violence not as a triumph but as an endurance of multiplicity. Malea Powell demonstrates something very similar in her analysis of American Indian fiction. There, the presence of ambivalence underscores the presence of multiple identities and heritages that continue to persist and, indeed, energize survivance despite violent upheaval.[86] Ambivalence might be a consequence of violence, but it is also a sign and harbinger of survival.

As the text transitions from the colonial "past" section to the "present," its insistence on enlarging the presence of non-European identity monikers across the Americas reinforces the text's narratival ambivalence begun in the previous section. Although Mexican American history in the United States typically begins with the conclusion of the Mexican American War (see chapter 1), the "present" section ignores that moment altogether and, instead, leans into an accumulation of indigenous signs. Formally introducing readers to the "historical" Joaquin Murrieta in this section (line 224)—the social "bandit" borne out of racial violence in California[87]—from whom the poem's protagonist derives his name, the text's big "reveal" is at once jarring and inconsequential. It is surprising in that the poem (re)introduces Joaquin intersubjectively through a crucial political figure in Mexican American history: "I am Joaquin. / I rode with Pancho Villa, / crude and warm. / A tornado at full strength, / nourished and inspired / by the passion and the fire / of all his earthy people." (lines 157–63). This move de-emphasizes Joaquin's importance, since the figure no longer stands on his own but only in relation to others that came after him yet precede him in the narrative.

The poem silences Joaquin's importance even more when it supplies a multisensory form of accumulation. Establishing a new historical line that eventually culminates with contemporary Mexican American activism, the text presents a kind of genealogy for Joaquin by reaching backward *and* forward in time:

> I ride with Revolutionists
>   against myself.
> I am Rural
>   Coarse and brutal,
> I am the mountain Indian,
>   superior over all.
> The thundering hoof beats are my horses.
> The chattering of machine guns
>   are death to all of me:
>   Yaqui
>   Tarahumara
>   Chamula
>   Zapotec
>   Mestizo
>   Español (lines 183–97)

The separation of indigenous names into single lines reproduces the "chattering of machine guns" at the center of the stanza (line 190), which are "death to all of [Joaquin]" (line 191). The implements of violence are clearly outlined in the stanza, and the effects of these implements are felt not only where the bullets hit the body in the text; they are also felt in the bodies of readers as they speak the poem out loud (a feature that Valdez's dramatic reading in the 1969 film captures).[88] The staccato vowel sounds /ă/ and /ĕ/ that begin each name reinforce the "machine gun" image, creating a resonance through the combination of language, sound, and visual that magnifies the perversity of racial violence experienced by Joaquin.[89] Yet this violence is productive, and while the text focuses on the singular Joaquin, the text's gesture toward multiplicity stretches Mexican American histories beyond Joaquin's personal history. These identities toward the end of the stanza sustain Joaquin's racial identity, not the other way around.

The last segment of this stanza, argues Bruce-Novoa, highlights the "popular base" to which the poem appealed. Gonzales does this, Bruce-Novoa argues, by coupling four names of "Indian" origin with broader references to "Mestizo" and "Español" identities. These lines put into view the production of the "mestizo" identity that Gonzales apparently sought to convey in the poem, and, consequently, the result is the constitution of a cultural, indigenous community formed out of "tribes not considered 'highly cultured,' compared to Aztecs and Mayans."[90] In Bruce-Novoa's estimation, these names ultimately contribute to the development of Gonzales's historical and identificational pedagogy through this poem.[91] Gonzales proposes a plethora of identities, Bruce-Novoa suggests, that readers might see in themselves and their racial heritages.

Emphasizing historical referents, however, masks the violence supported by the poem's aesthetic reliance on accumulation. For, in this representation of genealogy and violence, the poem levies its own restrictions on the bodies Joaquín might represent. The replication of indigeneity on both sides of the English and Spanish divide erases the gender-based violence constituting appeals to indigeneity that later Chicanas found necessary to correct. As Vicki Ruiz's work demonstrates, indigeneity alone did not secure Chicanas a place in el movimiento, and, thus, it was Chicanas who worked toward "(en)gendering Chicano history"[92] by showcasing how Mexican American women, too, were constitutive of this history.[93] In a similar way, Normal Alarcón reimagined indigenous personages like Malinche to revise Mexican American histories such as this one that seemed to exclude the essential contributions of women in the fight for social justice.[94] The use of accumulation, which may not explicitly denounce Chicana contributions, nonetheless creates and sustains a rhetorical inertia that only later would be recognized for its violent effects. Although Gonzales's poem might have spurred racial ambivalence vis-à-vis accumulation, it solidified its masculine force.[95]

And this restrictive, gendered element is also represented *visually* in the poem's text. In one of a few places that women are mentioned in the poem, Gonzales visualizes a rigidity in Chicana identity formation that subjects them to historical processes rather than accentuating their agency within them. In the stanza speaking of violence in Mexican history, Gonzales inserts the following identification with women in that history:

> I am
> the black shawled
> faithful women
> who die with me
> or live
> depending on the time and place (lines 207–12).

The linearity of the lines, as in previous stanzas (e.g., the stanza on the "industrial giant") installs a rigidity to what the stances already describe as reductive processes. Note that women only "live and die" to show their "faithful"-ness. Nonetheless, what is fascinating about this particular stanza is how it imposes inflexibility through a columnar figuration of the lines. Lining up the adjective "faithful" with verbs "die" and "live" erases whatever contingency the "time and place" language might invite and secures it as a nonnegotiable characterization of Chicana agency. Just like Joaquin's "love" and "wife" had been killed, so too is the "black shawled" woman cast as faceless, incapacitated, and subjected to life and death, pure and simple. She does not share in Joaquin's life, nor does she take part of in the history presented in the previous two hundred lines. There is really no agency for women, only an experience chosen for her.

An Ambivalent Present

In the last section of the poem, the text turns toward assessing contemporary experiences of racial violence (again, dismissing gender violences altogether). Spurred by reflection, Joaquin sutures the violences experienced in domestic spaces such as the "cell," "Barrios," and the "Ring" with those experienced in international contexts such as "Alaskan Isles," "Normandy," "Korea," and "Viet Nam:"

> Now
>   I bleed in some smelly cell
>   from club.
>   or gun.
>   or tyranny.
> I bleed as the vicious gloves of hunger
>   cut my face and eyes,
> as I fight my way from stinking Barrios
>   to the glamour of the Ring
>   and lights of fame

> or mutilated sorrow.
> My blood runs pure on the ice caked
> hills of the Alaskan Isles,
> on the corpse strewn beach of Normandy,
> the foreign land of Korea
>   and now
>   Viet Nam (lines 318–34).

The transition manifests a *spatio-temporal ambivalence* through the deictic "now,"[96] and it calls attention to the ways in which Mexican Americans were caught between being victims and perpetrators of a global racial violence during the intensification of the Viet Nam War in 1965. Simple clauses bring each of these spaces into a parallel relationship. The cumulative assertions— "I bleed," the second "I bleed," "I fight," and "My blood"—all highlight the invasiveness of the racial violence experienced at the individual level over time (such as in barrios), but the influence of this violence becomes more comprehensive as the text veers toward Southeast Asia. The alignment of the stanza from a vertical to a slanted representation depicts the Viet Nam War as a magnetic point where past and present violences converge. The aesthetics of the stanza underscore how "now" is the time to respond to and with Chican@ movement(s).[97]

    The spatio-temporal ambivalence, then, becomes the basis for the aesthetic accumulation in characterizations of Chican@ movement(s) operating in the late 1960s. The section leans into depicting ramifications of violence in Viet Nam for the racial formation of Mexican Americans. Recalling how the disjointed stanza of the poem's opening illustrated effects of structural violence, the broken stanza here creates a resonance between the effects of the Viet Nam War and industrialization on Mexican Americans. In this present section, the lines suggest that the confusion and incoherence spawned by the violence of the Viet Nam War is matched by energetic political movement(s):

> Here I stand
>   Before the Court of Justice
>   Guilty
> for all the glory of my Raza
>   to be sentenced to despair.
> Here I stand
>   Poor in money

> Arrogant with pride
> > Bold with Machismo
> > Rich in courage
> > > and
> > Wealthy in spirit and faith (lines 335–46).

The Viet Nam War was productive in two senses, both of which are visualized by the stanza as much as they are verbally articulated. Parallel "Here I Stand" phrases indicate two distinct but related consequences. Not only had the war resulted in a "despair" or even a "guilty" conscience for those participating, but it had also spurred the galvanization of political bodies. The Viet Nam War was a contemporary exigence, racializing Mexican Americans in new and profound ways, and also calling forth political leanings corresponding to a new kind of violence. In short, Gonzales's text suggests that the Viet Nam War had emerged as not simply a new thing to protest. It was, rather, a *formative* event that was, I suggest, fundamentally racial.

Nevertheless, while this line might suggest a contemporary emergence of boldness and productivity for all Chican@s following in the wake of the violence of the Viet Nam War (*machismo*, after all, was not dismissed out of hand by Chicanas),[98] lines following later in this section visualize a rather different political impact for women, whose solidarity was prescribed to be not with other *Chicanas* but with *Chicanos* instead. Chicanas and the violence they encountered were secondary to that of Chicanos and, the more problematic ideal, the family/familia:

> I [Joaquin] am in the eyes of woman,
> > sheltered beneath
> her shawl of black,
> > deep and sorrowful
> > eyes,
> That bear the pain of sons long buried
> > or dying,
> > Dead
> on the battlefield or on the barbwire
> > of social strife.
> Her rosary she prays and fingers
> endlessly
> > like the family
> working down a row of beets. . . . (lines 407–20).

>   Her eyes a mirror of all the warmth
> > and all the love for me,
> And I am her
> And she is me (lines 425–28).

Chicanas, in this rendering, are positioned as secondary to "Joaquín" ("I am her") and located as important only within their families. Even more fascinating, however, is how these stanzas reveal a latent recognition of fractures in Chican@ movement(s) along the axis of gender. While a linear stanza might have been appropriate here, so as to reflect the burgeoning political energy of contemporary activism, this stanza is far from secure. Even so, a *recognition* of disjointedness does not in itself ameliorate political inequality nor does it empower it—a feature of hegemony that amplifies the potency of Chicana movidas at all.[99] Although the Viet Nam War might have provided an engine for the Chican@ movement(s)' racial project, gender was secondary and rendered in masculinist terms, which further complicated an already fraught Chicana rhetorical agency.[100]

The final stanzas, however, reinforce the spatio-temporal ambivalence marking the present section of the poem. The stanzas are marked by how they accentuate the emergence of Chican@ movement(s) in the late 1960s.

>   I have endured in the rugged mountains
> >   of our country
>   I have survived the toils of slavery
> >   of the fields.
> > >   I have existed
>   in the barrios of the city,
>   in the suburbs of bigotry,
>   in the mines of social snobbery,
>   in the prisons of dejection,
>   in the muck of exploitation
>   and
>   in the fierce heat of racial hatred (lines 457–62).

And, later,

>   We start to MOVE.
> >   La Raza!

Mejicano!
　Español!
　　Latino!
　　　Hispano!
　　　　Chicano!
or whatever I call myself,
　　　　I look the same
　　　　I feel the same
　　　　I cry
　　　　　and
　　　　Sing the same (lines 480–91).

The two stanzas stylize how violence, in multiple forms and from multiple institutions, has informed the shape of Chican@ movement(s). Any one of these living situations—from the barrio to the fields—issues its own violence(s) upon those living within them, but that the poem accumulates middle-passive verbs to render their impact on Mexican American bodies showcases how these conditions induced an inertia that at once deenergized and empowered Mexican Americans. The overdetermination of oppressive forces enfeebling Mexican American politics is converted into confident assertions of identity in later lines. Rejecting the binary of "Mexican" or "American" for its politics, the use of middle-passive verbs following later surfaces the racializing power of a rhetorical middling beginning to pervade Mexican American politics and characterize the emergence of Chican@ movement(s). As the text states, "We start to MOVE," or, as the Spanish states more forcefully, "Empezamos a AVANZAR" (line 480). Integral to these manifestations of racial identity is the public eschewal of the racial categories circumscribing Mexican American politics. From the in-between space(s) of these various racial monikers, political strength shows itself anew.

And yet the effects of a systemic violence cannot be undone entirely. The ending of the stanza claiming identities undercuts most of the poem's assertions, seemingly revealing a fatigue and dissipating energy among those involved. No longer sharing in the same exclamatory stance, the final lines suggest that these monikers do not amount to much of a solution to coloniality's pressures. The poem softens the political force of contemporary Mexican American politics in the phrase "whatever I call myself" and advances a blasé attitude by repeating a subtle, unassuming phrase: "the same" or "lo mismo." Whatever name might be used to identify Mexican Americans, or however many names are pulled from historical heritage (Cuauhtémoc,

Joaquin, Cortez, Francisco Madero), none of them amount to more than becoming "the same." The effects of colonial, systemic racial violence make any not-white racial sign irrelevant, since violence consumes both the symbol and the subject's racialized body. Gonzales, like Luis Valdez, took bodily features as indicative of their belonging to a *racialized* community, or "La Raza Cosmica": "Our physical and facial features attest to or lend strong evidence to the concept of La Raza Cosmica, for those of us who have worked the fields, haunted the Barrios and drifted through our mountains[,] the many faces of our people range from Trigueño (dark), Huero, [sic] (fair)[,] negro (black). We all know or have met in every community from rural to urban areas those brothers and sisters who have faces to match their knick-names [sic]; Chino (Chinese), Negra (Black woman, an affectionate term), Huero (Blonde), Indio (Indian), Moreno (Dark)."[101] Colonial violence, Gonzales suggests, invents all racial classifications and, in this sense, considers them all as equivalent. Stated differently, racial identities are, in the end, *arbitrary* or "lo mismo."

At the same time, ambivalence indexed by the language of "the same" suggests a powerful deactivation of racial hierarchies and attendant categories. Whichever political identity Mexican Americans might assume, Gonzales suggests, cracks racial controls systematized by whiteness and imposed upon any not-white body. Activating political formations, the poem invites readers to adopt public identities forged horizontally rather than vertically. As Hannah Arendt makes clear, power is inversely proportional to violence. Where there is a lack of power, violence ensues, and where violence is absent, power can be at its most potent. This reciprocal relationship came into public view in a special way during the Viet Nam War,[102] and by stylizing the stanza diagonally then leveling off at the words "the same" or "lo mismo," the stanza makes visible the formation of a political community that cares little about sustaining categorical divisions anyway—at least in 1967. Each of these not-Anglo identities constitutes "La Raza" and form a discernible "mass" of people that are no longer "absorbed" into the "gringo/Anglo society" of the opening lines. Once more following Arendt, the construction of this communal identity called forth political power. Arendt explains this transformation in this way: "*Power* corresponds to the human ability not just to act but to act in concert. Power is never the property of an individual; it belongs to a group and remains in existence only so long as the group keeps together."[103] To Arendt's explanation I would add that racial tenors have also been a feature of reclamations of political power destroyed by racially motivated violence, even if she might not have recognized (or cared to) the consequentiality of race in her theorizations.[104] The identities in the poem, all of which empower the formation of La Raza, act in "concert," thus demonstrating power in their not-gringo "sameness." Accumulating these racial monikers together in a single space, "I Am Joaquin" constitutes, formally, Chican@ movement(s).[105] In the words of Gonzales, "I am the masses of my people and / I refuse to be absorbed" (lines 492–93).

Nevertheless, while accumulation might have been a suasive aspect of the poem's aesthetic, perhaps the appeal was *too* strong. As scholars of Chican@ movement(s) have long since recognized, assertions of confidence about cultural roots in this poem surfaced a sinister exclusivity among those persuaded by Gonzales's (re)presentations. Gonzales's survey of "heroes" lacks women and reinscribes the paternalistic views of nationalism constituting decolonizing efforts of the 1960s.[106] As the Chican@ movement(s) progressed, the figure of accumulation compelled an aggressive acceptance that resulted in rigorous attempts to make a political community that looked and organized in particular ways. Women and LGBTQ persons were discursively excluded from the community that Gonzales's poem created, and it often prevented a host of actors from offering their own contributions to the ambivalent identity that "I Am Joaquin" outlined aesthetically.[107] Furthermore, accumulation activated registers in the movement that were certainly needed and energizing, but the poem's apparent acceptance of the premises of mestizaje, which was predicated on not-white identity, entrenched anti-Black sentiments. While the poem references a mestizo identity sparingly, Gonzales's reappropriation of Vasconcelos's notion of "La Raza Cosmica" reinscribed the racial (and gendered) prejudices of the concept of the "Cosmic Race."[108] As many became persuaded by "I Am Joaquin," Chican@ activists positioned themselves with respect to its claims, defending or otherwise critiquing them. And, many were, as Cherrie Moraga makes clear, treated as inferior on account of the confidence that the poem promised.[109] With respect to sexuality, Blackness, and gender, it seems, the poem's aesthetics were persuasive to a fault.

Conclusion

In my analysis of the aesthetics of "I Am Joaquin: An Epic Poem," I have put into focus textual layouts, spacing, and figural compositions, all of which I argued made manifest what I call a *poetics of ambivalence*. In concentrating on these aesthetic features of Gonzales's text, I demonstrated how its aesthetics distinguished its participation in the Chican@ movement(s)' racial project and, at the same time, parlayed expectations of Chican@ activism brewing at this time. Although the poem certainly can be linked to and understood as a reflection of Gonzales's history and politics, it can, further, be taken as a remarkable attempt to educate many Mexican Americans about a history not typically told. To borrow more instrumental language typical of studies of social movement rhetorics, ambivalence could be viewed as a strategy for articulating and persuading communities of the value of mestizaje, nationalism, notions of raza cosmica, etc. An analysis of the poem's aesthetics, however, complicates our reception of the history and, ultimately, suggests that the "Epic" is but one aspect of a broader, though not always explicit, concern. In this chapter, I have argued that an analysis of the aesthetics of the poem demonstrates how the poem's apparent ambivalences are ultimately wrapped up in a racial project involving Mexican Americans. The aesthetics of the poem, not simply its "content," compelled political mobilization along axes that were racially defined and understood, partially, as rejections of a colonially derived whiteness and resistive of the violence(s) that enforced them. We have in "I Am Joaquin" a form of de/colonial praxis. Inventing a racial identity for Mexican Americans through ambivalence, the poem encouraged a horizontal, political reimagining outside of racial hierarchies established in a colonial United States.

And yet, between the "here" and "there" that the poem's temporality straddled, the emphasis on the Viet Nam War at the start of the "present" section foreshadowed how crucial this racializing global conflict would become in later Chican@ movement discourse(s) as the decade progressed. Gonzales, for his part, appears to have already been leaning into this racial connection between violence experienced in the United States and that experienced through their involvement in the war. At an anti-war rally in 1966, Gonzales made the case that Chican@ liberation only mattered in so far as there was also a global liberation for other not-white communities tied to it. He stated, "I have involved myself in the civil rights struggle for equal rights at home, but those rights are meaningless if they are ever attained without intellectual and meaningful responsibility to speak out and take part in the struggle for survival for entire nations, our own included."[110] Through the Viet Nam War, Gonzales invented racial solidarity between Mexican Americans in the United States with other non-European, Third-World communities experiencing similar violences. His remarks exposed the weight and reach of a US-enforced racist geopolitical system.[111] Living in the barrios was equivalent to living in a war-torn region, which, at the same time, resembled serving in a military institution that devalued brown bodies. Commenting on this racial connection in a separate address, Gonzales explained, "And that's why we're saying until we understand that liberation comes from self-determination of ourselves and that we start to use the tools—the tools of nationalism to get to our barrio brothers who are still believing that machismo means they go kill a communist because they've been jived into a political war and that its [sic] not an economic war and they're being jived about the fact that they will be accepted as long as they go get themselves killed for the gringo captain!"[112] Colonial violence in the United States and around the world might have created opportunities to construct a political community premised on racial solidarity between these nations, but this solidarity was, itself, a consequence of racial violences enacted on not-white bodies.

Gonzales's "I Am Joaquin," however, focuses less on this global emphasis than it does on "domestic" politics, and this narrow attention also closed the circle of solidarity it purported to open. Focused on portraying and amplifying Mexican American experiences in the United States, the poem's aesthetics offered a forceful assertion of identity that appeared to drown out more widespread concerns—and other voice(s). Indeed, as Chican@ movement(s) evolved, and more and more voices, particularly the voices of women, took on prominent, public roles, other poetic structures emerged, and alternative aesthetics appeared that negotiated old problematics (like racism) and new ones introduced by antecedent appeals. In the next chapter, we observe how a Chican@ newspaper in New Mexico negotiated dilemmas related to the growing Chican@ movement(s), an intensifying global conflict, and an appealing nationalist political frame. As the violence of systemic whiteness spread mercilessly around the globe, a newspaper in the heart of the Southwest, initiated and led by Chicana activists, gave form to a sensibility dedicated to new ways of articulating the Chican@ movement(s)' racial project.

4

A POETICS OF RELATIONALITY: THE INVENTION OF A GLOBAL RAZA (1968)

As I argued in the previous chapter, 1967 was a watershed year in the evolution of Mexican American politics in the late 1960s. Although "I Am Joaquin" had its undeniable impact, it was only one component of an energetic Mexican American political scene. Spectacular protests like those in El Paso, Texas, in October, 1967, created informal linkages between activists sharing in a common *sensibility* and, at the same time, induced a common *discourse* centered around new political terms such as "La Raza" and "Chicano Power." After 1967, informal interconnections between activists accreted and assumed more institutionalized forms. In 1968, only one year into its existence, La Raza published a "Yearbook" that celebrated the "wind of change blowing among Mexican-Americans," and one of the ways that change was made manifest, according to the magazine, was the creation of a collective of Chican@ print spaces referring to itself as the "Chicano Press Association" (CPA). A Chican@ underground press emerged and, in so doing, depicted a "widespread attempt, throughout the Southwest, to create our own mass media."[1] As Mexican American activism expanded, so too did venues dedicated to publicizing their experiences with oppression and to mobilizing other like-minded activists to respond. If "I Am Joaquin" was a full-throated cry for a so-called revolution, the accumulation of print venues amplified it, and, together, they gave material proof of Chican@ movement(s).

That "shout," issuing forth primarily though not exclusively from the Southwest United States,[2] increasingly tapped into a global frequency, particularly as inequities baked into the "Cold War" became nearly impossible to ignore. "Cold," after all, was a relative term, a supposed antonym to the prospects of "hot" war that seemed imminent if not immanent for those operationalizing logics of "rhetoric and power" or simply masking US imperial tendencies.[3] The chill of the Cold War was more than a draft for the "Third

World" that had, since the Bandung Conference in 1955, called attention to the racial colonial violence yet persisting after World War II.[4] Argentine philosopher Enrique Dussel contrasts sharply the experiences of the "Third World" and the "First World": "From Heraclitus to Karl von Clausewitz and Henry Kissinger, 'war is the origin of everything,' if by 'everything' one understands the order or system that world dominators control by their power and armies. We are at war—a cold war for those who wage it, a hot war for those who suffer it."[5] Indeed, the "decolonization wave" of the 1960s underscored the pervasiveness of bloodshed that accompanied liberation in a post–World War II era, while those hoping to make sense of the vestiges of colonial violence grappled with its impact on the soul of the colonized after liberation.[6] Military interventions in Latin America, particularly in Guatemala, Cuba, and the Dominican Republic, as well as the conflicts in Southeast Asia, demonstrated the "global" intensity of the Cold War,[7] and, in turn, the extent to which international superpowers had created the façade of a war bereft of a scalding touch. In January 1968, the Tet Offensive, a military operation in which Northern Vietnamese military forces lead an onslaught of attacks on Southern Vietnamese outposts, intensified a growing distaste for US military interventions propagated by a Cold War stance. Public outcry grew in response to the apparent military weakening of the United States in Southeast Asia that the Tet Offensive suggested, and media coverage, which had been relatively positive up to that point, followed suit, which further reinforced discontent over the conflict.[8]

Although "I Am Joaquin" gestured toward the global interconnection between wars abroad and those at home for Mexican Americans, Ralph Guzman concretized it when he released the results of a study suggesting that, relative to other racial groups, Mexican Americans were disproportionately dying during the Viet Nam conflict.[9] As the United States shifted its strategies during the Viet Nam War from military support to an "aggressive search and destroy" operation,[10] Black and Mexican Americans bore the brunt of that violent turn. For Mexican Americans, military service placed enormous assimilative pressure and, consequently, informed their racial formation(s). This explains why, according to Mariscal, despite "material conditions of poverty, job discrimination, and educational tracking," there was yet an "overwhelming obligation to serve and 'prove' one's loyalty according to traditional notions of nation and masculinity [which] were responsible for the relatively low number of Chicano draft resisters during the Viet Nam era."[11] Guzman's study, however, as described in *La Raza*, referred to in various Chican@ newspapers, and later published as a book, now seemed to offer, at least rhetorically speaking, "proof" that Mexican Americans were being subjected to racial violence on a global scale. This evidence, though more *sēmeion* than *tekmērion* because Guzman's data relied on tracing Spanish surnames,[12] was certainly more "refutable" than "necessary" proof (as Aristotle might say) that Mexican Americans were being targeted for death in Viet Nam (as Chican@ activists claimed). In 1968, nonetheless, participating in Chican@ movement(s) did not mean simply deciding whether or not to support Mexican Americans in the Southwest, nor did it simply entail cultural revival. The year 1968 also brought with it a need to negotiate the convergence of national and international violence seeming to follow Mexican Americans wherever they were found.

This chapter explores how this convergence of domestic and international concerns informed the Chican@ movement(s)' racial project by turning to a newspaper titled *El Grito del Norte*—The Cry of the North—and published in Española, New Mexico. This newspaper was founded by Elizabeth "Betita" Martínez (a former employee of the United Nations and activist with SNCC) and Beverly Axelrod (a lawyer turned activist), and its discourse explicitly grappled with the domestic and the international through what I call in this chapter a *poetics of relationality*. Illustrating the claims of Natalia Molina and other scholars regarding the construction of identities in Chican@ activism, the newspaper's discourse racially formed Mexican Americans "in relation not only to whiteness but also to other devalued and marginalized groups."[13] Relationality, however, risks diminishing the distinctions of the experience(s) of Mexican Americans in the United States, and, in turn, decentering Mexican American experiences—a key motive force undergirding Chican@ movement proliferation across the Southwest. This chapter, consequently, demonstrates how the newspaper broached resolving the problematic of inventing a global, inclusive "Raza" that was, at the same time, rooted in Mexican American politics in the Southwest by attending to aesthetic patterns in the newspaper's coverage. Tracing aesthetics present in *El Grito del Norte* during the first year of its publication, prior to the infusion of rhetorical energy catalyzed by the nationalism of the 1969 Chicano Youth Liberation Conference in Denver, Colorado (the "Denver Youth Conference"), I argue that through the newspaper's reliance on the aesthetic of the testimonio, its discourse maintained a focus on Mexican Americans while yet expanding its global associations with other not-white communities around the world. Examining the aesthetics of *El Grito del Norte* in 1968 in particular exposes a global turn in the de/colonial praxis beginning to surface in Chican@ movement(s) during the Viet Nam War and illuminates how Mexican

Americans negotiated these international pressures at the same time that they kept in focus domestic concerns.

Re-presenting Latinx Experience(s): On the Aesthetic(s) of Testimonio

I turn to *El Grito del Norte* in this chapter because I want to forward how two women, who would have otherwise been silenced or relegated to the background of Chican@ movement(s) during these early years, carved out their own political space(s) and paved a way for a unique rhetorical contribution even prior to the heightened energy of Chicana feminism that emerged in the 1970s. Inspired by both Cuba's revolutionary politics and Reies López Tijerina's fight for Mexican American land-grant rights in New Mexico, Martinez and Axelrod sought to inject the same "revolutionary" spirit energizing these political movements into a growing "Chicano movement."[14] The formation of a newspaper brought together local activists, who exposed the various forms of racial violence, intersectional and rendering Mexican Americans invisible in and to New Mexican communities.[15] And yet, as Dennis López explains, the general rhetorical profile of the newspaper included a global orientation, "to position La Causa within a broader frame of reference, one informed by a critical understanding of the political economy of imperialism and its grim consequences for the global working classes, including Chicanas and Chicanos."[16] In the heart of the Southwest, women were at the center of an inward and outward turn in Chican@ movement(s), a rethinking of a global and local positionality of Mexican American politics, and a recasting of an identity that was anything but limited to those living in the Southwest United States.[17]

A focus on *El Grito del Norte*, too, underlines evolutions within the de/colonial praxes of Chican@ movement(s) that the political energies of women made possible. Martinez and Axelrod joined a host of women who had historically taken on the task of cultivating and protecting Mexican American identities in public and private spaces. Even prior to the arrival of the revolutionary spirit of "I Am Joaquin,"[18] women such as Carolina Munguía and Emma Tenayuca in San Antonio, Texas, labored to improve the political statuses of Mexican American women and laborers, respectively.[19] Similarly, Dolores Huerta played an active role in voter registration drives sponsored by the Community Service Organization (CSO) even before her involvement in the National Farm Workers Association (NFWA). Huerta's organizing efforts energized the NFWA, and she played a pivotal role in amplifying the boycott's reach through an effective form of "intersectional" rhetoric that appealed to many different audiences.[20] Chicanas, as Emma Pérez writes, "are marked by a unique diasporic configuration" and, I suggest, from this positionality offer(ed) a compelling contribution to the Chican@ movement racial project during the height of Chican@ movement(s).[21] In 1968 New Mexico, Martinez, Axelrod, and other Chicana writers like Enriqueta Longeaux y Vasquez and Valentina Valdez who contributed to *El Grito del Norte* formulated a contribution to the Chican@ racial project that differed substantially from antecedent movement discourse(s) and negotiated new global concerns whose urgency was not quite as palpable before the late 1960s. And, while renewed scholarly interest in this particular newspaper and in the activism of its most public figures has underscored the uniqueness of its contribution(s) to Chican@ movement(s),[22] a recognition of the relational orientation displayed in and through the newspaper underscores the racial significance of *El Grito del Norte* to Chican@ movement(s). Presaging the Third-World feminism of women activists such as Gloria Anzaldúa, Cherríe Moraga, and others who followed in the 1970s and 1980s, *El Grito del Norte* publicized a relational notion of La Raza that included Mexican Americans and communities of color facing similar racial violence(s) across the globe.

This relationality, prominent throughout its pages, appears aesthetically in the form of a common Latinx communication genre: the testimonio. Although studies of testimonio, a form of "resistance literature,"[23] have largely focused on texts authored by or ascribed to individual subjects (such as the (in)famous *I, Rigoberta Menchú: An Indian Woman in Guatemala*), the testimonio's tight link to communal praxis,[24] its representational plasticity,[25] as well as its heightened sense of political urgency,[26] suggest that the boundaries of the testimonio can be stretched to include publications constituted by and espousing multiple voice(s) such as a newspaper.[27] Chican@ studies scholars in particular have harnessed testimonio as a kind of "methodology of the oppressed" to make visible the boundaries between exclusion/inclusion and to reconceptualize belonging in different spheres.[28] The enduring definition of testimonio, offered nearly thirty years ago by John Beverley, continues to hold as a starting point for understanding this discursive form. The testimonio, according to Beverley, is a "novel or novella-length narrative in book or pamphlet (that is, printed as opposed to acoustic) form, told in the first-person by a narrator who is also the real protagonist or witness of the events he or she recounts, and whose unit of narration is usually a 'life' or a significant life experience."[29] Although this definition of the testimonio might appear to circumscribe its particular expressions or what might "count" as testimonio, testimonio is a more communicative form than any one specific expression. Beverley connects the "origin" of the genre to a contest sponsored by the Casa de las Americas in Cuba in 1970, in which a literary prize was promised to a literary piece that "document[ed] some aspect of Latin American or Caribbean reality from a direct source."[30] Portrayed as the voice of experience from a marginalized community, within Chicanx/Mexican American Studies, the testimonio has also been harnessed to forward the histories of marginalized subjects, or, as Mario García claims, as a way to "fill in the gaps" left behind after consulting conventional sources.[31] Consequently, testimonio appears to be a crucial discursive form for understanding the range of Latinx rhetorics more broadly and Chican@ movement(s)' rhetoric in particular, since historical accounting, as well as linguistic formulation (that is, Spanish), indexes a distinctly Latinx discursive form even if it might possess a relatively conventional function (e.g., autobiography).[32]

The racially forming power of the testimonio turns precisely on its representational function(s), how it offers a representation of oppressed communities and their circumstances all at once.[33] Although we might distinguish all sorts of subversive Latin@ communicative forms such as relajo, rasquachi, and chusmería from one another functionally, we can also set these apart based on their own aesthetic characteristics. Farr's descriptions of these as verbal performances aptly capture the way that aesthetics mark each of these communicative forms: "Verbal performances can occur in formal, scheduled, public events (in which primarily males perform in most culture) or it can emerge spontaneously in every day conversations. . . . Performances of verbal art are not just interesting aesthetically but are particularly salient for the creation, re-creation, and transformation of language, culture, and society."[34] Testimonio joins communicative acts that are rhetorically potent not only for *what* is said but also *how* something is said.[35] Testimonios, irrespective of their final form(s),[36] are written as first-hand, public forms of communication *posing* as a "truthful" witness to the existence of oppressive, and oftentimes violent, conditions experienced by a marginalized community. Typified by the use of the first-person pronoun ("I"), testimonios offer a singular voice as a representation of an apparently absent polyphony,[37] and this "I" speaks from a presumed inclusion in the community about which the (apparently) singular voice communicates. Of course, this is not to say that testimonios hold no truth-value, although there are certainly some that have questioned the truthfulness of the genre, anthropologist David Stoll and ideologues alike. This representational gesture is a performative act that, rhetorically speaking, constitutes the community it purports to represent as much as it might reflect a community.[38] Nevertheless, I simply mean to affirm that testimonios, *qua* representation, "embod[y] the creativity and ingenuity of actors who hold little formal power and yet who actively reject a vision of themselves as powerless,"[39] and, given this "embodiment," ought to be considered rhetorical achievements rather than simply a channel for a message. Testimonios stretch the limits of individual and community, history and memory, privacy and publicity through their successful replications.[40]

Leveraging both the "I" / "We" relation baked into testimonio as well as its revelatory function, consequently, is crucial to fulfilling the rhetorical expectations of the testimonio, and in *El Grito del Norte*, newspaper editors set up this broad(ening) representational role by claiming that its content would emphasize circumstances repressing the community of an undefined yet specific community—La Raza. In an August 24, 1968, message titled "To Our Readers," editors claimed that *El Grito del Norte* was "an independent newspaper serving northern New Mexico. Its purpose is to advance the cause of justice for poor people and to help preserve the rich cultural heritage of La Raza in this area. It is being published because the other newspapers print only what the rich and the powerful want to see published. These newspapers have created a climate of fear among people—a fear to speak the truth."[41] These comments underlined the newspaper's commitment to exposing what had otherwise been obfuscated by a "climate of fear." These circumstances, the editors suggested, ultimately affected the community's capacity to experience justice, and, consequently, *El Grito del Norte* would focus on revealing these circumstances. Unlike other newspapers, which induced fear and, through that fear, endangered the preservation of a "rich cultural heritage of La Raza," the new publication provided a space of curative exposure.

This same message to readers, however, also heightened its focus on claiming and representing the community through an emphatic use of second-person pronouns. The newspaper aimed to publish "news from your communities, writing about your complaints and problems, printing articles about things that interest you." Though committed to exposing "truth" about an oppressive context, editors established "you" as the grounds for editorial decisions about what to include in its coverage. At the same time, this claim to "represent" readers also racialized them, folding them into the La Raza editors claimed to represent. Editors insisted that "EL GRITO NORTE will publish articles in Spanish as well as English because Spanish is part of the cultural heritage of the people and their children. It is part of the Hispano way of life." The newspaper, in one sense, was to be a typification, a re-presentation, and an amplification of a community *preceding* it. And yet, in other ways, as this reference to publications in "Spanish as well as English" suggests, the newspaper invented its own readership. Editorial decisions—aesthetic decisions—constituted and validated the "part of the Hispano way of life" it claimed to represent. In other words, the newspaper fuses aesthetic intentions with racializing impulses, much like what we saw in previous chapters. In this message to "readers," editors set the stage for its representational force by forecasting some of its aesthetic pledges. The two went hand in hand.

And yet when the editorial admitted that the newspaper would "also report about the struggle of La Raza in other parts of the United States," and that it would publish "articles about some of the important things that are happening in Mexico and Latin America," editors suggested that the newspaper's representational range included La Raza that was *outside* of New Mexico but nonetheless part of its community. Aligning with the expectations of a testimonio, a genre whose representations cannot be rigidly confined by identificational boundaries, the newspaper promised a wide girth for its representations of persons and circumstances. This rhetorical expansion, nonetheless, risked diminishing the distinctions of the experience(s) of Mexican Americans in the US, and, in turn, decentering meaningful experiences which, up to this point in Chican@ movement activism, had been an engine for undergirding its proliferation across the Southwest. The editors, however, broached resolving this apparent tension not by emphasizing content per se but through aesthetic work. They concluded their message with "VIVA LA RAZA / VIVA LA JUSTICIA / VENCEREMOS" or, in English, "LONG LIVE LA RAZA / LONG LIVE JUSTICE / WE WILL OVERCOME." Although these are certainly meaningful phrases depicting the paper's tie to Chican@ movement(s)' activism (such as the farmworkers' movement),[42] including Spanish declarations in an otherwise English coded text *after* claiming a geographical expansion for its coverage illustrates the newspaper's push to defining the community of La Raza by forms as well as content. The use of language codes, as well as the pronominal forms mentioned earlier, underscored how aesthetic moves energized the contributions of the newspaper to the Chican@ movement(s)' racial project yet taking shape in the late 1960s. The newspaper's racial pushes erupted the boundaries of La Raza.

As exemplified by the editorial at the beginning of the newspaper's print run, editors represented their coverage as a type of first-person account generated by a community of activists invested in revealing oppression in New Mexico. They offered a "grito" on behalf of "La Raza." However, editors also made clear that while the "cry" might have emanated from what had been "Northern Mexico," its representation(s) extended beyond the United States.

The newspaper spoke for La Raza irrespective of any geography as it conveyed the "truth" about the "climate of fear" prohibiting access to justice. Having surveyed newspaper stories during the first year of its publication, I highlight below how the newspaper's commitment to the testimonio aesthetic mediated the tensions induced by creating and sustaining the intersection of domestic and international concerns seemingly becoming more pressing in the late 1960s. Guided by what I refer to as a poetics of relationality, the newspaper forwarded La Raza as a global Raza and, in turn, as a capacious political category inclusive of, yet not limited to, Mexican Americans in the Southwest.

Inventing an Inclusive Raza: The Poetics of Relationality in *El Grito del Norte*

El Grito del Norte entered circulation on August 24, 1968, and, over the course of four months (the last issue of 1968 was published on December 18), the newspaper reported on various events, persons, and organizations local to New Mexico. In line with the goals of the newspaper's originators, stories frequently updated readers about Tijerina's politics and life following the occupation at Tierra Amarilla on June 5, 1967, but the newspaper also chronicled the subsequent trial, Tijerina's run for governor, and his acquittal. Outside of a focus on Tijerina, the newspaper described the racist practices of local schools, detailing how New Mexican teachers and curricular designs promoted white supremacy. Stories also exposed incidents of police brutality against youth, provided local histories of not-white voices, publicized events in the Southwest sponsored by Mexican American activists, and demystified the welfare system. The newspaper's stories, in sum, exposed the "truth" about Tijerina, illuminated a racist political climate, and surfaced how New Mexicans might intervene in local issues.

Newspaper coverage invited sympathy (and critique) from New Mexico and beyond, however, as contributors and editors reported on the activities of La Raza outside of Española, New Mexico. Letters to the editor(s) hailed from California, Colorado, Indiana, New York, and Mexico City. This wide geographic interest matched the newspaper's vast coverage outside of the Southwest. In addition to focusing on local issues that La Raza in New Mexico might face, the newspaper published a standing series titled "La Raza en las Américas." In this series, editors incorporated reports of Mexican American activists in the United States as well as stories about political events in other

Latin American nations. This particular series, as its title suggests, invented "America" not as a US-originating construct but, as recent scholarship has affirmed, as a figure informed and shaped by exchange between nations sharing a landmass—América.[43] But, whereas the focus of recent scholarship has emphasized national boundaries, histories, or cultures in their assessments of this accented "Américan" identity, the relationality embedded within the conception of "América" in *El Grito del Norte* was racial. Namely, "La Raza" functioned as a racializing term for communities in América and elsewhere. Each edition's "La Raza en las Américas" was typically composed of two to five short updates collected to give a panoramic image of La Raza at different locations. Perhaps most important, these updates often focused on highlighting the racial violences these communities experienced, which further reinforced the racializing force of the term "La Raza" as it was used in the newspaper. Taken together, these updates expanded readers' view of La Raza, its whereabouts, and its shared experiences with violence in América.

Highlighting these diverse geographies might have appeared to shift the stated focus of the editors from New Mexico, but, through the aesthetic of the testimonio, the newspaper avoided reneging on its promise to focus on local concerns. Although two of the reports in the first issue focused on Denver, Colorado and Delano, California, both of which were prominent locations due to the notoriety of Rodolfo "Corky" Gonzales and César Chávez respectively, the other two "reports" expanded the geography to "América" by including reports of violence from the Mexican federal government. The first update gestured toward testimonio, while the second affirmed it in earnest.

In the first, "Juán Sebastián Valdés" contributed a story about the student movement in Mexico, which by August 1968 was gaining steam ahead of Mexico's hosting of the International Olympic Games. Valdés detailed how the student movement "surgió como respuesta a la brutal represión policica (*sic*)" (arose as a response to brutal police repression). The violence had induced a massive demonstration of about 185,000 who, in unison, pronounced their condemnation of the federal government: "¡Muera Díaz Ordaz! ¡No queremos Olimpiadas, queremos Revolución! ¡Muera el gobierno mexicano vendido a los yánkis!" (Death to Díaz Ordaz! We do not want Olympics, we want Revolution! Death to the Mexican government sold-out to the Yankees!). This contribution, written in Spanish, suggested a first-hand account, particularly since details about the movement's demonstration at the "Palacio Nacional" (and the point of view) suggested a presence at the event. The account, nevertheless, never makes use of first-person pronouns. Similarly, whether "Juán" was a student activist participating in the protest or one of *El Grito del Norte*'s contributors is unclear, since the account does not confirm that the report comes from someone who was there. At the same time, the shift to Spanish from English among these reports suggested that a Mexican or, at least, a member of "La Raza" wrote it. The shifting of language codes and the naming of the author conveyed, at least aesthetically, a first-person testimony about the protests and the racial violence in Mexico. After all, the report claimed that the Mexican government was merely an instrument of the "Yankees." The report, for all intents and purposes, *appeared* as testimonio.

The second "report," on the other hand, claimed explicitly to be a first-hand account, and the editors included a brief introductory note on the author and the circumstances of the report. The published "report" described the work of a schoolteacher in Mexico named "Genaro Vásquez," but the form in which this communication was published in *El Grito del Norte* was a "letter to the Mexican press about his escape [from prison] and explaining the reasons for his struggle." This letter, through reproduced in English instead of Spanish, depicted a *witnessing* from a sympathizer of and partner with "campesinos" who had participated in a protest against the elite (landlords, politicians, real estate agents). Vásquez claimed to have witnessed a massacre of sixty "campesinos," been imprisoned for his involvement with them, and escaped to return and help them in "guerrilla warfare." This report, in contrast to the report from "Juán Sebastián Valdés," was featured as testimonio even while it might have been translated into English.

Putting these reports from Mexico into the same column as those covering happenings in Colorado and California expanded the geography of La Raza and Chican@ movement(s) all at once. Chican@ movement(s) extended beyond the United States, and La Raza inhabited more than simply the Southwest. Still, reducing the apparent distance between Colorado, California, New Mexico, and Mexico was an aesthetic intervention. In the case of the report from "Genaro Vásquez," while it was published in English, the characterization of protestors as "campesinos" (a Spanish term not an English one) generated a resonance with Chican@ movement(s) in the Southwest. The word "campesinos" was a racialized term invoked by the farmworkers in California.[44] These "campesinos," in Vásquez's words, stood against the government through warfare, thus resisting "the dramatic reality imposed upon us by big capitalists and feudal land owners, allies of Yankee imperialism which for many years has governed us." The testimonio in both reports, though varied in form, appeared as first-person accounts of violent circumstances. And, in both accounts, the violence is affirmed as a racist, colonial violence. Even if the Mexican federal government might have been the instrument of violence, it was nonetheless motivated by a "Yankee imperialism." Through the testimonio, the newspaper invented a broad community of La Raza, spanning the Southwest and Mexico, all of whom experienced, to varying degrees, the same racial violence.

Indeed, references to racist, colonial violence(s) in and outside the US appeared throughout the column during that first year and, in turn, grounded the connections between those "Raza" in the Southwest and those abroad. In the second issue, a testimonio from a former Catholic priest explaining violence and injustice in Guatemala invented solidarity specifically with Chican@s. The update detailed the involvement of Arthur and Marjorie Melville with the poor in Guatemala. Associated with humanitarian and liberation efforts in the nation, Arthur explained in his testimony that his commitment to help Guatemalans compelled participating in armed revolution if that was the will of Guatemalans: "If the people have to take up arms and if a priest is with the people then he too must take up arms." After failing to win the rightful redistribution of land in Guatemala from the government, the government had expelled the Melvilles and, thus, they now found themselves traveling throughout the United States sharing their story. They had even met with Chican@ activists such as Corky Gonzales. Explaining how the United Fruit Co. was a powerful corporation backed by the US government yet asserting control in Guatemala as it did in the 1950s, Melville argued for solidarity to be forged between La Raza in the Southwest and Guatemala on the basis of a shared struggle against imperialism. As he explained, "Most of them already understand the problem. I have to talk to the Anglos more than the chicanos [sic].... They need to see that the ultimate enemy of the Guatemalan people is the U.S. government." This first-hand account of US coloniality fueled a rhetorical stretching of the inclusivity of La Raza to include Guatemalans and their sympathizers. Through testimonio, the newspaper's editors invented a solidarity that was hemispheric in scope. The column, thus, reveals a commitment to generating and harnessing a testimonio aesthetic to generate a racial relationality between "La Raza en las Américas."

Testimonio facilitated expanding the global community of La Raza in other columns as well. One column, contributed by an activist whose ties to Chican@ movement(s) went deep, came from Chicana Enriqueta Longeaux y Vasquez.[45] A transplant from Denver, Colorado, she had been active in Corky Gonzales's Crusade for Justice since the mid-1960s, and in spring 1968, Gonzales asked her and her partner "Yermo" (Guillermo) to head a school for the organization in San Cristobal, New Mexico.[46] While in New Mexico, Longeaux y Vasquez joined in Martinez and Axelrod's efforts with *El*

Grito del Norte and contributed articles dedicated to mobilizing and organizing "La Raza" in the Southwest and beyond. In one of her more consistent columns throughout the newspaper's print run, "Despierten Hermanos!" ("Wake Up Brothers!"), Longeaux y Vasquez deployed a variety of aesthetic moves through which she articulated her Chicana feminism and negotiated the various problematics emerging after the nationalist turn in the late 1960s.[47] One of these aesthetic moves guiding her rhetorical contribution to the expansion of La Raza surfaced in the ways Longeaux y Vasquez appealed to her own experience(s) to urge readers to respond to her arguments. Oropeza goes so far as to assert that "by far Vasquez's greatest resource in terms of conveying a sense of urgency was her own candid, conversational style."[48] Constitutive of this "style" was the testimonio.

Forwarding her personal experiences as a basis of her appeals, Longeaux y Vasquez consistently poses her interventions as emerging from encounters with Mexican American communities and the consequences of violence(s) they experienced. In the fifth issue, for example, Longeaux y Vasquez describes personal encounters with two young men entering the draft and writes about how these conversations informed her outlook on the Viet Nam War and how La Raza should respond to it. Articulating her views in the first-person singular and plural, Longeaux y Vasquez (re)presents her reflections as a witness to the devastating power of violence on La Raza:

> What does war do to our young men? I have seen men scarred for life, in that it seems to make animals of them.... Another thing I notice is that the casualties of the minorities in this war are far larger than the population of the minorities. And I see that many Gringos seem to find all kinds of loopholes to get out of going to war. When are we going to realize that we are raising kids to fight the wars for big power? And when are we going to put a stop to this madness?[49]

Longeaux y Vasquez founds her claims about the Viet Nam War, its transformational effects and its disproportionate impact on La Raza, on personal observations. She writes as a witness to these events ("I notice," "I see") and as a participant negotiating the impacts of the Viet Nam War ("When are we"). Moving deftly between first- and second-person pronouns in her explanations, Longeaux y Vasquez represents herself *and* the community. She speaks from and for La Raza.

At the same time, the testimonio that Longeaux y Vasquez projects entails a racializing force tied to the Viet Nam War. The violence was dehumanizing, she claims, as it "ma[de] animals of" those made to fight in it. Even so, the effects of the Viet Nam War located La Raza in an antipodal relation with whiteness (Gringos) rather than the Vietnamese against whom they fought. Indeed, speaking as a member of the community, Longeaux y Vasquez suggests that the Viet Nam War induces a racial partnership that includes more than those inhabiting the Southwest. In that same November issue she writes, "And let's take a look at Guatemala and other countries. Are we going to raise our kids to go kill our brothers there too? I believe that the time has come when we must learn to stand and say 'No.'" Once more speaking from the position of the "we," Longeaux y Vasquez continues, "So, I just wonder and guess about the Vietnamese. I'll bet they are people like you and I. . . . Nuestros hijos mueren y sufren mentalmente al matar a sus hermanos y nosotros lo permitemos! Despierten y piénsenlo bien" (Our sons die and suffer mentally when they kill their brothers and we allow it! Wake up and think rightly about this). The Viet Nam War certainly had a racializing impact on Mexican Americans in the Southwest, but Longeaux y Vasquez writes not as someone focused solely on La Raza in the United States. Rather, she offers a personal testimony about the violences associated with the Viet Nam War and leverages that first-hand experience to relate La Raza to the Vietnamese and other not-Gringo communities over and against white violence. Speaking as a representative of the community, her testimonio serves as launching point for expanding La Raza *globally* and, in doing so, provides a portrait of La Raza that is unbound by US borders.

Longeaux y Vasquez's writing harnesses the aesthetic of the testimonio and, from this vantage point, encourages her readers to resist accordingly. However, her fabrication of the personal testimony did more than merely serve as "evidence" for her claims about the war. That is, she does not only leverage the Viet Nam War to persuade her readers to resist it. Through this aesthetic move, the *speaking from* the community that Longeaux y Vasquez's use of first- and second-person pronouns invents, she also stretches the inclusivity of La Raza to include other not-Mexican American communities. Through the testimonio, Longeaux y Vasquez created parallels between Mexican Americans in the United States serving in the Viet Nam War and the Vietnamese feeling its violence. The testimonio was a rhetorically salient way of invoking community within La Raza but, even more than that, the testimonio grounded her reinvention of La Raza, energizing its expansion and dissolving whatever geographic boundaries might have been suggested by the terminology of "La Raza." The testimonio, in short, was a way through which to constitute a global raza.

Containing Chican@ Movement(s): A Push Toward a Nationalist Project

If 1968 was the "Year of Decision," according to *La Raza* newspaper, 1969 was the year that Chican@ movement activists *decided*. And, as the newspaper looked ahead to new ways of activating La Raza in New Mexico, particularly through community programs, educating community members, and promoting the ideas of coop programs, *El Grito del Norte* also recognized that La Raza's future might not be so promising. The violence that many experienced across the world tempered expectations. The poet Cleofes, whose poetry was commonly published in the newspaper, voiced the sentiment and rationale for such attitudes in the first issue of 1969: "A[ñ]o de '68 / que en la historia te quedastes / te fruistes y nos dejastes / con odio en el corazon / y este nuestro país / se quedo en inflación / y todas las gentes / con muy alta tasación / pues ya estos impuestos / que se hacen y se harán / es para matar mas gente / en la tierra de Vietnam" (Year of 1968 / in history you remained / you left and left us / with hate in our hearts / and in our nation / inflation remained / and all people / with high appraisal / but with these taxes / that they make and will make / are for killing more people / in the land of Vietnam). The first issue of 1969 reinforced this dampening when it dedicated its first "La Raza en las Américas" to the Tlatelolco Massacre of October 2, 1968. In fact, *El Grito del Norte* reported on nothing else in that issue's column. Pages four and five of that issue included images of dead protestors, an illustration of a young man with chains covering his mouth, long lines of protestors with their hands up, and an image of protestors holding signs, all of which were republished from *Por Que* magazine based in Mexico City. And, while it included a brief summary of the events leading up to the massacre on October 2, likely produced by the newspaper, editors also included a testimonio republished from a French magazine, *Le Monde*, of that night and the horrors executed by Mexico's federal government. The "Año de 68" had witnessed violence and, it seems, its effects were yet felt and grappled with in 1969 by Mexican Americans in the US.

El Grito del Norte continued to expose this violence in the coming years, yet the newspaper also continued to leverage the productive power of that exposure to augment a global community. In issue five (1969), editors included a story titled "We Are Not Alone" that detailed how experiences with violence had activated and connected communities to one another. According to the story, La Raza, Black communities, Puerto Ricans, and even the Vietnamese constituted a broad political community, each of whom had experienced discrete violences perpetrated against them and had built a collective voice of resistance through that shared experience. Yet this solidarity did not come without costs. Instead, the article made clear that the resulting collectivity posed a threat that invited retaliation. As the issue stated, "One of the weapons used by the *Americano* against Puerto Ricans and other groups is to try and set them against their Black brothers. It is not hard to make people who are struggling to get some crumbs from the master's table begin to fight among themselves for those crumbs." The broad racial solidarity that *El Grito del Norte* promised and established throughout its pages challenged the homogenizing force of coloniality and, consequently, the "Americano" threatened to disrupt it. Resistance invited repression, and, by 1969, the newspaper warned against it.

This felt resistance to the promotion of a broad inclusivity, global in scope and united against the violences caused by the "Americano" in the United States and around the world surfaces the aspect of de/coloniality advanced via a poetics of relationality in *El Grito del Norte*. Though we could certainly attribute this de/colonial turn to the Chicana agents leading the rhetorical contributions of *El Grito del Norte*, since they would also be ahead of the curve in the evolution of Third-World feminism, the de/colonial efforts witnessed in the pages of *El Grito del Norte* were also a consequence of an increasing attention to the Viet Nam War in the late 1960s. Viewed from the perspective of the war, *El Grito del Norte*, more than antecedent discourses examined thus far, contributed to the Chican@ movement racial project by infusing and calling forth a polyphony and pluriversality marking de/colonial interventions.[50] Indeed, witnessed in the aesthetic of the testimonio, *El Grito del Norte* adjusted de/coloniality within Chican@ movement(s) by making it a more *visible* feature of its racial work and, in turn, projected the appearance of a global scope and significance. Although "I Am Joaquin" might have gestured to this, contributors to *El Grito del Norte* made this explicit.

Even so, it would be a mistake to say that *El Grito del Norte* was *more* de/colonial than "I Am Joaquin." The newspaper, after all, joined in Tijerina's land-grant movement and supported him despite the abuse that he appeared willing to inflict on the women in his household.[51] Furthermore, Enriqueta Longeaux y Vasquez was later dubbed a "loyalist" among Chicana feminists, as she seemed more willing to accept than resist patriarchal norms in Chican@ movement(s).[52] Although I have written elsewhere about how Longeaux y Vasquez negotiated her own Chicana feminist sensibilities,[53] it might be difficult for some to locate her and others like her firmly within de/colonial politics. However, given the communal expansions of *El Grito del Norte* to include the Vietnamese, the clear anti-whiteness posture present in contributions, and stiff resistance to US imperialism, it is equally difficult not to identify the newspaper's work as de/colonial. Most important, the emphasis on fabricating *relationality* underscores the de/colonial push of the newspaper and its attempt to promote options regarding politics and culture.[54] Indeed, in *El Grito del Norte*, we see a negotiation of de/colonial sensibilities, antecedent movement discourse(s), and racist pressures all at once. In short, we see profound rhetorical work operating at a collective level and the ways this rhetorical work worked in concert to support racial formation(s) in the late 1960s.

Perhaps unsurprisingly, in the winter of 1969 the newspaper's commitment to building solidarity between and among La Raza here and elsewhere led to more opportunities to forge connections between activists across the Southwest beyond the CPA or local organizations. In issues published in February and March of 1969, an advertisement for a conference titled the "Chicano Youth Liberation Conference" sponsored by the Crusade for Justice appeared in relatively small print. The ads promised lodging and workshops on topics such as "Social Revolution," "Culture," "the Student," and "the Campesino." The stated purpose of the conference: "The new Chicano Revolution—WHERE? HOW? WHEN?" Given the brevity and size of the advertisement, it would have been relatively easy to miss. The advertisements were less than a quarter of page, and, judging from this appearance, one might conclude that the conference's significance matched the ads' negligibility.

Of course, students of Chican@ movement history know otherwise. But what is important to recognize here is that whatever effects the Denver Youth Conference might have had, its importance was largely unpredictable at this time. And, while the exclusive registers made visible at the conference might have been predictable, the nationalism that arose was not necessarily at odds with the relationality cultivated by spaces such as *El Grito del Norte*. Instead, what we find are conflicting aesthetics that continued to be influenced by global happenings and a desire for relationality cast in a different language: decolonization. Here was a new aesthetic evolving, one that relied on bordering in a way that differed from antecedent discourse(s) such as those found in "I Am Joaquin" and *El Grito del Norte*. And it was in this (re)bordering rhetoric that Chican@ movement activists hoped to inflate the inter/national agency of La Raza once and for all—though not without cost.

5

A POETICS OTHERWISE: (RE)BORDERING MEXICAN AMERICAN POLITICS (1969)

The transformation of La Raza from a term referencing communities living in the Southwest United States into a metaphor capacious enough to encapsulate a global and diffuse community persisted in 1969. Not only was this aspect of the Chican@ movement racial project supported by the political activism surrounding it, such as that emerging in and through a "Third World Left";[1] the proliferation and accumulation of movement activists also fueled its increasing appeal. Perhaps no moment in Chican@ movement history represents the diffusion of its association and discourse more than the success of the Denver Youth Conference. An estimated 1,500 activists of various ages attended this conference sponsored by the Crusade for Justice at its headquarters El Centro de la Cruzada in Denver, Colorado. The Crusade offered free housing to anyone who could simply get there as a way to incentivize attendance, but *El Gallo* also advertised the conference as something more than a free get-together: the conference promised to fulfill the "new Chicano revolution." Labeled the "Chicano Youth Liberation Conference" (CYLC), the event brought together numerous organizations created by students and community organizers alike: United Mexican American Students (UMAS), the Brown Berets, Mexican American Youth Association (MAYA), and Mexican American Student Confederation (MASC), as well as groups that were not necessarily focused on Mexican Americans but nonetheless resonated with their pursuits, such as the Young Lords Organization from New York, the Latin American Defense Organization (LADO), the Latin American Student Organization (LASO), and the Third-World Liberation Front.[2] Promising answers to questions regarding "social revolution" and "cultural work," the conference crystallized a particular configuration of "La Raza" that positioned Mexican Americans firmly within an international struggle inclusive of many not-white communities (and white sympathizers) in the Southwest and around the world.

This chapter, by centering on 1969 and the CYLC, explores not only how nationalism emerged as a pivotal aspect of Chican@ movement(s) into the next decade but also what contribution this *rhetorical* turn to nationalism had on the Chican@ movement racial project and the antecedent global emphasis constituting the de/colonial praxis invested in by Chican@ activists. Viewed from a global vantage point, adopting nationalism aligned Chican@ movement(s) with the *tercermundismo* ("Third-Worldism") pervading Latin American politics and taken up by leftists, including Chican@s, in the United States following the Cuban Revolution in 1959.[3] Locally, however, activists were drawn to nationalism for the ways it promised political possibilities outside of and opposed to systemic whiteness.[4] Even prior to 1969, Corky Gonzales's own political thought had narrowed in on nationalism as a key to Mexican American politics, and he continued to emphasize its potentials with greater earnestness after the CYLC.[5] So strong was the push and appeal for nationalism in Chican@ movement(s) that, at least for US-based activists on the outside looking in, nationalism stood out as el movimiento's defining political form.[6] Pronouncing nationalism formally as a preferred political program of Chican@ movement(s) also seems to have shifted the de/colonial praxis by proposing a form of *decolonization* in particular, the creation of a new racial state under the leadership of Mexican Americans that was not metaphorical but physical.[7] And, for the purposes of this study of the Chican@ movement racial project, I turn to the declaration scripting this program—El Plan Espiritual de Aztlán—to understand how it exemplified the negotiation of global and local dimensions associated with parallel and oppositional racial project(s).

Yet the metaphorical status of the nation of Aztlán—its rhetorical substance—cannot be so easily disrupted or set aside. Written by a collection of activists, such as Corky Gonzales, intellectual Juan Gómez-Quiñonez, and Mexican poet/graduate student Alurista,[8] El Plan Espiritual de Aztlán and its diffuse appeal were rhetorical achievements. The writing and circulation of the Plan infused "Aztlán" with political significance for the first time,[9] and, without its reproduction, repackaging, and distribution, the nationalism El Plan espoused would have likely been rendered inert.[10] Communication scholar Fernando Delgado writes that Aztlán was "illusory and [it] remains a contestable space full of meaning and hope but ultimately without substance,"[11] a description of the Plan that surfaces how its scripting was consequential, but not in any predetermined way, earning wide appeal not by some amorphous, supernatural force but on account of a multitude of activists making the figure of Aztlán appealing.[12] "We are a Bronze People," activists wrote in the prologue to El Plan's objectives, "with a Bronze Culture. Before the world, before all of North America, before all our brothers in the Bronze Continent, We are a Nation, We are a Union of free Pueblos, We are Aztlán." Offering a gesture toward earlier Chican@ Plans, such as the "Plan de Delano" and the "Plan de La Raza," yet claiming to offer a more racialized and comprehensive figure through which to unite La Raza in and around the world, El Plan Espiritual de Aztlán suggested not necessarily a new turn in Chican@ movement(s) but an elaboration of a racial movement already gaining and continuing to gain ground. A multitude of activists across the United States invested in fulfilling its promises.

The racially and politically forming power of El Plan Espiritual de Aztlán, consequently, hinged on the negotiations of community activists grappling with its significance and the politics it apparently demanded of La Raza. As a way to draw out multiplicity of the appeal of El Plan Espiritual de Aztlán and, in doing so, surface the place of the Plan in evolving Chican@ movement(s), I focus on the aesthetic contributions of various reproductions in the Chicano Press Association (CPA) of El Plan circulated after the CYLC and how these reproductions generated a *poetics otherwise* implied by its decolonizing promise(s). Made manifest by an aesthetically derived "border rhetoric," which both disentangled Mexican American politics from the influence of the "Gringo" and created the boundaries around the proposed nation of "Aztlán," the poetics otherwise advanced in and through reproductions of the Plan buttressed racial boundaries around La Raza, their politics, and their location within an international community. Indeed, this poetics otherwise set the stage for the anti-Viet Nam War resistance witnessed in Chican@ moratoriums at the turn of the decade, when activists equivocated police brutality against Mexican Americans in the United States with the casualty rate of Mexican Americans in the Viet Nam War. El Plan Espiritual de Aztlán was a critical step in formulating future outlines of Mexican American politics as the decade came to a close. As I show in this chapter, analyzing the aesthetics marking reproductions of El Plan Espiritual de Aztlán reveals a "bordering" contribution to the Chican@ movement racial project that, at the same time, fostered exclusions movement activists, notably Chicanas, condemned. By examining reproductions of El Plan Espiritual de Aztlán, we see how Chican@ newspapers furthered these exclusions and shifted the de/colonial praxis of Chican@ movement(s) at the end of the 1960s.

Bordering Aztlán: Rhetorically Configuring the Boundaries of a Nation

In many ways, scholarship about Chican@ movement(s) is all about how Mexican American politics hinges upon experiences with and alongside "borders." As one author notes, Chican@s owe their existence to border(s)—"not just for having crossed it or having been crossed by it, but for living in the border zone between nations that the line engenders."[13] Gloria Anzaldúa's *Borderlands / La Frontera: The New Mestiza*, perhaps more than any other Chican@ text, has sutured Chican@ activism to an embodied life in the region straddling the Texas/Mexico border.[14] Indeed, the concept of a border has been deployed so prominently in studies of Chican@ movement(s) that nearly all studies offer some kind of definition of what a "Chican@" is with respect to the border separating Mexico and the United States.[15] A "Chican@," from this vantage point, is a product of borders and border histories, and Chican@ discourse a consequence not only of border "life" but the "life" of the border.[16]

From a methodological standpoint, borders have made their way into analyses as an implicit though potent form of interpretation in Chican@ movement history, namely, as a way to understand tonal differences in Mexican American activism over time and bound Chican@ movement(s) as a whole. Doing so has enabled drawing through lines yet sustaining distinctions between various groups comprising the resistant "Mexican race" from its roots in the 1920s with the Orden Hijos de America ("The Order of Sons of America") to present day Chican@ activism.[17] Fernando Delgado, in rhetorical studies, makes incisions based on ideological criteria, positing verbal "ideographs" (that is, master terms within the movement that carried ideological implications, such as "Aztlán," or "La Raza") as decisive criteria making divisions between "Chicano" activism and contemporaneous factions like the farmworkers in California.[18] Still others draw their lines between various activists according to a relationship with conservatism. César Chávez, for example, distinguished himself as "assimilationist" and "accommodating," while later activists embodied the movement's working-class or "liberal" spirit.[19] From a performative point of view, Daniel Belgrad distinguishes "Chicano" as a mobilizing term "enact[ing] a dialect between accessibility (openness to the dominant culture) and inaccessibility (the assertion of difference), which accessibility is shown to be necessary, but inaccessibility is finally insisted upon."[20] Perhaps the most enduring, influential view of bounding Chican@ movement activism is Mario García's notion of the "generation." Following

Karl Mannheim, García argues that historical moments such as World War II or the Great Depression produce common attitudes in segments of the population such that these individuals form a "political generation."[21] Distinct from the "Mexican American Generation," which was pluralistic yet committed to retaining cultural distinctives,[22] the "Chicano Generation"[23] pursued "liberation" through the articulation of "militant demands for civil rights, ethnic pride, and community empowerment."[24] Although García's "generation" lacks a means of recognizing differences within and among expressions of Chican@ politics, his work nonetheless underscores how creating boundaries partitioning Chican@ politics from other Mexican American activism in the United States has endured in the study of Chican@ movement(s).

Certainly, this scholarship highlights the productiveness of taking a border(ed) approach to understanding Chican@ discourse(s) and, in particular, suggests that rhetorical bordering was inescapable if not crucial to fashioning the nationalism scripted in El Plan Espiritual de Aztlán. To some readers, perhaps, this book's insistence on rehearsing Chican@ movement history chronologically might suggest a reliance on inventing temporal borders so as to trace how Chican@ politics twisted and turned over time. Fair enough. Yet the ways in which El Plan Espiritual de Aztlán concretized its nationalist borders cannot be reduced to any singular experience, text, or word. In 1969, the nationalism proclaimed by activists at the CYLC exemplified a turning point in the racial politics of Chican@ movement(s) that was neither determined nor necessarily foreseen. And, while the Plan Espiritual de Aztlán might have suggested an appeal to a pre-originary essence to define its borders, the creation of Aztlán was nonetheless "a complex, on-going negotiation [seeking] to authorize cultural hybridities that [were emerging] in moments of historical transformation."[25] Homi Bhabha's comments on the "location of culture" suggest that cultural forms, however they might be deployed, turn on an insistent invention that creates the features of a culture over time. The borders marking off Aztlán, thus, were not created simply by the invocation of a mythic figure. On the contrary, bordering Aztlán was accomplished vis-à-vis iterative rhetorical work as activists reinscribed and proliferated their political visions through discourse.

Indeed, rhetorical scholarship on "borders" compels viewing the borders of Aztlán as subject to rhetorical invention, impermanent, permeable, and violable,[26] and, for this reason, rewritable by those accepting or otherwise contesting their limits. This "border rhetoric," as Latinx rhetorical scholar Josue David Cisneros argues, fosters "border thinking,"[27] a feature that characterizes de/coloniality more broadly. Mignolo defines border thinking as a "thinking from dichotomous concepts rather than ordering the world in dichotomies. Border thinking, in other words, is, logically, a dichotomous locus of enunciation and, historically, is located at the borders (interiors or exteriors) of the modern/colonial world system."[28] Through a border rhetoric, Chican@ movement activists inscribed a nation in a world in which they had no part,[29] claiming a space within the world system from which they had been cast out by proposing a de/colonial option outside of and free from the purview of US whiteness. Mignolo writes, "the de-colonial option starts from narrating a silenced history, the history of the formation and transformation of the colonial matrix of power."[30] These borders racial(ized) the nationalism announced in El Plan Espiritual de Aztlán, and, through a border rhetoric, animated its decolonizing impulses. Borders were drawn in and by El Plan Espiritual de Aztlán, and, along with it, an insistence that La Raza be treated as an anti-white, anti-Black other—a "bronze" political community in the United States.

The "de/colonial option" (to borrow Mignolo's vocabulary) that border rhetorics might have compelled is sustained by aesthetic features that make distinctions visible in and through discourse. Indeed, Mignolo argues that border thinking operates "in two directions: rearticulating the interior borders linked to imperial conflicts and rearticulating the exterior borders by giving new meanings to the colonial difference." This kind of thinking, however, is expressed and made notable in and through discourse, and, I suggest, in particular by the aesthetics of that discourse that mark it discretely.[31] Commenting on Lisa Flores's explanations of the ways in which Chicana feminists constructed difference, Cisneros suggests that a border rhetoric is recognizable on the basis of aesthetic forms.[32] Although Flores's primary concern resides in highlighting how Chicanas created solidarity with others all the while sustaining their own agency and subjectivity, her remarks elucidate how Chicana difference relies on the transgression and upholding of aesthetic borders that augment a discourse's appeal. Chicana feminists, Flores writes, "combine a mix of poetry, prose, and stream of consciousness. They jump from English to Spanish to Indian to Spanglish, with no warning and no apology. The different styles and languages represent different aspects of their varied heritages, and the use of expression of different backgrounds gives voice to previously silenced groups."[33] Border rhetorics, in short, give form to the cracking of hegemonic, colonial structures and facilitate the invention of signs through which solidarity can be forged apart from and in opposition to colonial influence. Of course, this undermining of coloniality and the invention of particular kinds of community cuts both ways, since the very terms of inclusion also form the boundaries of exclusion—a result of not changing the "terms of the conversation," as Mignolo might say.[34] Through the aesthetics associated with border rhetorics, the flexibility of a border nonetheless becomes viewable and, in turn, enables challenges to colonial domination.

The borders that accreted around the political notion of "Aztlán" after the 1969 CYCL, I argue, were rhetorical achievements, accomplished by a multitude of coherent but not necessarily consistent aesthetic interventions by activists. The Plan and its nationalist program gained prominence, much like many other Chican@ movement texts, as they were reproduced and circulated by the CPA. In charting the aesthetics of reproductions of El Plan Espiritual de Aztlán, that is, the border rhetoric accompanying El Plan within the first few months following the CYLC in newspapers spanning Colorado, New Mexico, and California, we see how activists both projected El Plan's nationalist impulse while at the same time grappling with its demands. Each reproduction can and should be treated as a distinct textual event.[35] Taken together, however, reproductions gave form to and proliferated what I refer to as a *poetics otherwise*, a pattern of border rhetorics that both fueled the political project of decolonization espoused in El Plan Espiritual de Aztlán while still infusing a heterogeneity into it. Shortly after the 1969 CYLC, activists joined to argue for and represent boundaries around a new political state with Mexican Americans at the center of its political life by reproducing and circulating El Plan Espiritual de Aztlán, but this amplification of the nation was neither ossified nor simply duplicated. Aesthetic interventions buttressed Aztlán while yet promising difference(s) in the new nation.

Yet, in keeping with the nationalist impulse, the aesthetics constituting Aztlán had racial ramifications that were intimately woven together with the political program promoted in El Plan. The invention of a nation-state termed Aztlán was clustered with antecedent, racializing terminology—La Raza—specifying the community represented in and through El Plan Espiritual de Aztlán. Through it, processes of racial formation and decolonization qua political project converged. This text, in short, is important not only for the ways in which it calcified an ideology. It is crucial, too, for understanding how Mexican American activists grappled with the intersections between race and politics as a global war intensified and as more activists joined la causa, how activists pushed for togetherness while at the same time asserting diversity, and how crucial aesthetic interventions were to evolutions in the de/colonial praxis of Chican@ movement(s).

El Plan Espiritual de Aztlán: Otherwising Mexican American Politics

The bordering reinscribed through reproductions of El Plan Espiritual de Aztlán followed the script of the Plan's language. Published soon after the CYLC in *El Gallo: La Voz de la Justicia* in April 1969, the Plan was reproduced with the heading "Program of El Plan Espiritual de Aztlán," implying that the "Plan" also entailed a schematic for guiding activists after the CYLC. Three major "Puntos" followed a brief introduction, each comprising multiple subpoints. The first Punto of the program explained the concept of nationalism, while the second outlined the "Organizational Goals" of Aztlán. The third included "Actions" that members of Aztlán should pursue, such as promising to read El Plan Espiritual de Aztlán at meetings, encouraging more walkouts to revise education, etc. Finally, a concluding paragraph articulated the primary objective for composing the Plan: "liberation." Capping the Plan with the rallying cry "El Plan de Aztlán is the Plan of Liberation," the document recalled the influence of an epistemology and political history rooted in Mexico's revolution(s) and their manifestos.[36] Bolstered by a quotation from Juan Sarabia, a Mexican politician who resisted the Porfiriato in Mexico in the early twentieth century, the Plan located "Aztlán" as a "new" nation and "La Raza" as its people. The Plan invoked new political structures and practices and, in doing so, gave *form* to "Aztlán" (fig. 15).

Still, attention to the parallelism baked into the final point, "Liberation," surfaces in miniature the ways that (re)bordering rhetoric coincided with and formalized the Plan's language regarding the community birthed through its nationalist call. The final paragraph contends for the "liberation" of Aztlán along four axes, namely, "culturally, socially, economically, and politically." Strung together, each of these adverbs gestures toward the multiple institutions enforcing the colonial matrix of power which Chican@ activists resisted. Locating each of these terms in parallel relationships with one another underscores the complete freedom claimed by the Plan.[37] The point closes with yet another iteration of parallelism reinforcing this initial chain. Liberation entails controlling the "usage of our lands, the taxation of our goods, the utilization of our bodies for war, the determination of justice (reward and punishment), and the profit of our sweat," all of which justify following El Plan's script. In chaining each of these together with the plural pronoun "our" (including "the determination of justice") El Plan calls forth not only its own community but its political achievements as well. Capping this point on "Liberation" is the declarative "El Plan de Aztlán is the Plan of

The Program Of El Plan Espiritual De Aztlán

El Plan espiritual de Aztlán, sets the theme that the Chicanos (La Raza de Bronze) must use their nationalism as the key or common denominator for mass mobilization and organization. Once we are committed to the idea and philosophy of El Plan de Aztlán, we can only conclude that social, economic, cultural and political independence is the only road to total liberation from oppression, exploitation and racism. Our struggle then must be the control of our Barrios, campos, pueblos, lands, our economy, our culture, and our political life. El Plan commits all levels of Chicano society: the barrio, the campo, the ranchero, the writer, the teacher, the worker, the professional, to la Causa.

I. PUNTO PRIMERO:
   Nationalism
   Nationalism as the key to organization transcends all religious, political, class, and economic factions or boundaries. Nationalism is the common denominator that all members of La Raza canagrees upon.

II. PUNTO SEGUNDO:
   Organization Goals
   1. Unity in thought of our people concerning the barrios, the pueblo, the campo, the land, the poor, the middle class, the professional is committed to liberation of La Raza.
   2. Economy: economic control of our lives and our communities can only come about by driving the exploiter out of our communities, our pueblos, and our lands and by controlling and developing our own talents, sweat and resources. Cultural background and values which is nore materialism and embrace humanism will lend to the act of co-operative buying and distribution of resources and production to sustain an economic base for healthy growth and development. Lands rightfully ours will be fought for and defended. Land and realty ownership will be acquired by the community for the people's welfare. Economic ties of responsibility must be secured by nationalism and the Chicano defense units.
   3. Education must be relative to our people, i.e., history, culture, bilingual education, contributions, etc. Community control of our schools, our teachers, our administrators, our counselors, and our programs.

4. Institutions shall serve our people by providing the service necessary for a full life and their welfare on the basis of restitution, not beggar's crumbs. Restitution for past economic slavery, political exploitation, ethnic and cultural psychological destruction and denial of civil and human rights. Institutions in our community which do not serve the people have no place in the community. The institutions belong to the people.

5. Self defense of the community must rely on the combined strength of the people. The front line defense will come from the barrios, the campos, the pueblos, and the ranchitos. Their involvement as protectors of their people will be given respect and dignity. They in turn offer their responsibility and their lives for their people. Those who place themselves on the front for their people do so out of love and carnalismo. These institutions which are fattened by our brothers to provide employment and political pork barrels for the gringo still do so only by acts of liberation and la Causa. For the very young, there will no longer be acts of juvenile delinquency, but revolutionary acts.

6. Cultural values of our people strengthen our identity and the moral backbone of the movement. Our culture unites and educates the family of La Raza towards liberation with one heart and one mind. We must insure that our writers, poets, musicians and artists produce literature, and art that is appealing to our people and relates to our revolutionary culture. Our cultural values of life, family, and home will serve as a powerful weapon to defeat the gringo dollar value system and encourage the process of love and brotherhood.

7. Political liberation can only come through an independent action on our part, since the two party system is the same animal with two heads that feeds from the same trough. Where we are a majority we will control; where we are a minority we will represent a pressure group; Nationally, we will represent one party La Familia de La Raza.

III. PUNTO TERCERO:
   Action
   1. Awareness and distribution of el Plan Espiritual de Aztlán. Presented at every meeting, demonstration, confrontation, court house, institution, administration, church school, tree, building, car, and every place of human existance.
   2. September 16th on the birthdate of Mexican Independence, a national walkout by all Chicanos of all colleges and schools to be sustained until the complete revision of the educational system: its policy makers, administration, its curriculum, and its personnel to meet the needs of our community.
   3. Self defense against the occupying forces of the oppressors at every school, every available man, woman, and child.
   4. Community nationalization and organization of all Chicanos re: El Plan Espiritual de Aztlán.
   5. Economic program to drive the exploiter out of our communities and a welding of our peoples combined resources to control their own production through co-operative effort.
   6. Creation of an independent local, regional and national political party.

LIBERATION
A nation autonomously free, culturally, socially, economically, and politically; will make its own decisions on the usage of our lands, the taxation of our goods, the utilization of our bodies for war, the determination of justice (reward and punishment), and the profit of our sweat.

EL PLAN DE AZTLÁN
IS THE PLAN OF LIBERATION !

"THE PUBLICATION OF A REVOLUTIONARY PAPER IS EQUAL TO THE TAKING OF A CITY. THE PROCLAMATION OF A POLITICAL PLAN IS THE SAME AS THE BLOODIEST COMBAT... THEY FORM EQUAL PARTS OF A REBELLION AND ARE INHERENT IN IT. I HAVE NEVER SEEN, NOR WILL I EVER SEE A REVOLUTION, WITHOUT THE PROPAGATION OF IDEAS AS A PRELIMINARY, AND THE SHEDDING OF BLOOD, AS THE INEVITABLE MEANS, OF DECIDING THE OUTCOME." Juan Sarabia

Fig. 15. Program of El Plan Espiritual de Aztlán, published in *El Gallo*, 1969. Note the lack of Alurista's "prologue" on this page (a point I return to later). Digitized from The Nettie Lee Benson Latin American Collection, The University of Texas Libraries, JSTOR "Independent Voices" Collection.

Liberation!," a statement equating "Aztlán" with "Liberation" vis-à-vis syntactic parallelism (note the "of" in each phrase, "de" in Spanish) in which the copula acts as a joint between the two. The parallelism between English and Spanish language codes, the balancing of the genitives, and the aesthetics characterizing the final statement all highlight the importance of rhetorical work in making the text and its contents *appealing*.

Turning to the visual rhetorical appeal(s) of this publication in *El Gallo*, however, surfaces how political ramifications accompanied these aesthetic choices, the border rhetoric suffusing reproductions of El Plan Espiritual de Aztlán. There are at least two forms of visual parallelism in this reproduction of the nationalist program, one guiding the spatial arrangement of the Plan's text and the other marshaled in the photographic display at the bottom of the page. Writing about the use of space for visual effect(s), visual artist Edward Tufte explains that "[s]patial parallelism takes advantage of our notable capacity to compare and reason about multiple images that appear simultaneously within our eyespan."[38] Containing the objectives, goals, and priorities intended to guide the nation-building process, the re-presentation of the Plan's text in three columns presents a panoramic view of the entire nationalist program. In presenting the entire program in three parts, the reproduction conveys a comprehensiveness and a firm cadence through which Aztlán's community—La Raza—should accomplish the politics promised by the Plan. When read together with the Plan's verbal rhetoric, this visual representation of the Plan's "program" appears as a *complete* political paradigm without deficiencies. The program is inviolable, rigid, and immutable. In this presentation, the Plan appears self-evident, perfect even, and widely applicable to any and all.

Similarly, photos beneath the language of El Plan suggest an equivalence between Aztlán's constituents that at once advances the Plan's racially forming potency and suggests an expansive liberation along multiple identity axes. Jeanne Fahnestock's definition of visual parallelism is instructive for understanding how these photographs (and images in reproductions more generally) identify the racial and gender composition of Aztlán. She writes that visual parallelism entails the "juxtaposition of three or more images in either a vertical or horizontal row or in any array of both . . . images should exhibit roughly the same size and shape. The same color, the same background, and the same orientation in the visual field (i.e., the same viewing angle) will also enhance the impression of parallelism."[39] Including rectangular frames across all photographs, employing the same color hues, and displaying subjects in similar positions within each photograph, the line of images below the Plan's objectives forward a *uniformity* within Aztlán. This photographic visualization of the membership of Aztlán, their linearity, their "supportive" positioning on the page (that is, the photos sit underneath the program), and their even distribution across the width of the page forwards a unifying portrayal that at once identifies the boundaries of the nation-state and distinguishes its community as equivalent and equal contributors to fulfilling the nationalist program. Aztlán is composed of *one* people who act collectively as *one*—La Raza.

Yet even in this apparent presentation of equivalence the limitations and violences of Chican@ nationalism begin to surface and enact a political imposition on those the Plan might claim. La Raza, these photographs showcase, is not Black, not white, but *this* kind of "bronze," and, moreover, *this* kind of body. Although photographs depict Chicanas as subjects within Aztlán, for example, their energy and political fervor are muted. Bolstered by the statement of conservatism espoused by conference participants that Chicanas like Enriqueta Longeaux y Vasquez lamented ("It was the consensus of the group that the Chicana woman does not want to be liberated"), Chican*as* do not *exist* apart from and without actively supporting Chican*os* within the nation of Aztlán. Note, too, the Chicano at the center of the page and the subdued Chicana sitting next to him as he speaks! The border rhetoric of the reproduction cut both ways. It both reinforced the creation of the nationalist state the Plan claimed. It also erected standard(s) through which to judge the Plan's community—La Raza—and render it "appropriate" or wanting.

The newspaper *La Verdad*, founded by Carlos LeGerrette and edited by Richard Saiz, published in April 1969 not the program but Alurista's prologue. Alurista's prologue, much loftier in its language, acts as a kind of framing for reading and understanding the significance of El Plan Espiritual de Aztlán. Reproduced as the front page of the newspaper, this reproduction is far more visual than verbal and, consequently, exemplifies a different aesthetic while yet reinforcing the border rhetoric conveyed by the program (fig. 16).[40] The appearance of Alurista's poetic exposition, to be sure, might suggest simply a *preference*, a desire to introduce El Plan Espiritual de Aztlán with more appealing language rather than leaning into its more procedural elements. That can be granted. However, that *La Verdad* did not publish the program *at all* suggests a more organic or flexible approach to the founding of Aztlán than that portrayed by *El Gallo*. In the summary of the events of the conference on the fourth page, the newspaper notes as much: "Although *el plan espiritual de aztlán* is our declaration of independence, the specifics on education, politics, etc. are now being worked on and will be sent to

Fig. 16. Prologue of El Plan Espiritual de Aztlán by Alurista, published in *La Verdad*, 1969. Permission to reproduce Prologue granted by Alurista. Courtesy of Special Collections & University Archives, San Diego State University Library.

all organizations that request them."[41] The prologue, published in *El Gallo* separately from the program, certainly heightens the resonance between reproductions in *El Gallo* and *La Verdad*. While the newspaper explicitly recognizes the value of the program in this reproduction in *La Verdad*, the editorial decision to reproduce Alurista's prologue without the program highlights the presence of distinct aesthetic choices, a discrete border rhetorical praxis, suggesting different political priorities even while sustaining some form of coherence with the events in Denver.

Indeed, in addition to neglecting the publication of the program of Aztlán, this reproduction also implemented its own otherwising elements that distinguished it from that found in *El Gallo* (fig. 17). First, this reproduction of the Plan's prologue was published in Spanish only, which, as we have seen thus far, has racializing consequences as much as it might represent a linguistic accommodation for readers. Although the fusion of English/Spanish language codes had become a stylistic trend of Chican@ movement discourse by 1969, the singular use of Spanish here forwards the nationalist separation and reclaiming of the US Southwest for Mexican Americans that the turn to the myth of Aztlán (a non-translatable term) also conveyed. The linguistic choice gave the appearance that English had been disavowed entirely in Aztlán. Moreover, this reproduction in *La Verdad* employs a visual parallelism emphasizing the indigeneity of Aztlán rather than the grounding on the ideal of la familia suggested by the publication of the prologue in *El Gallo*. The lines on either side of the reproduction in *La Verdad*, comprised of a mix of faceless dancing figures, enclose the Plan's text. Though aligned with one another, each dancing figure differs from the other, and they appear as mirror images on either side of the Plan. At the center of the lines on either side of the Plan, too, are a pair of eagles facing one another that join the lines of figures. The pairing with illustration of eagles reinforces the borders of indigeneity yet also gestures toward the status of contemporary Mexican American politics (invoking as it does the UFW's eagle).

The use of symmetry and replication, as well as the signs used to comprise the border around the Plan's text, heightens the distinct racial-political aims of this reproduction. Although decolonization potentials are more latent and presumed in *El Gallo*, the disavowal of English and the inclusion of signs of indigeneity underline how this reproduction also furthered the decolonizing impulse of El Plan's nationalism. Yet in pushing firmly toward decolonization, the reproduction's visual racial politics in *La Verdad* became just as exclusionary as that purported by the use of the trope of la familia—incipiently if not fully grown. As Lourdes Alberto has argued, the

Fig. 17. Prologue of El Plan Espiritual de Aztlán by Alurista, published in *El Gallo*, 1969. Permission to reproduce Prologue granted by Alurista. Digitized from The Nettie Lee Benson Latin American Collection, The University of Texas Libraries, JSTOR "Independent Voices" Collection.

invention of indigeneity for the purposes of Chican@ nationalism might have suggested an equal political realm for all genders within Aztlán, yet it also trafficked in a palimpsest of exclusions stemming from the indigenismo undersigning it.[42] The mestizo head at the top right of the page, for example, though not explicitly gendered as in the publication of *El Gallo*, evinces how this reproduction affirms the problematic notion of mestizaje. Even while the reproduction in *La Verdad* might have elided the gendered aspects of the mestizo head by including a representation without reference to gender (compare the mestizo head at the top of the reproduction in *El Gallo*), it also appears to reinscribe the anti-white, anti-Black image associated with mestizaje's problematic history.[43] Although promising to efface the gendered aspects of El Plan and propose a more flexible nationalism in publishing the broader, more metaphysical "prologue," this re-presentation's racial emphasis nonetheless leaves unquestioned the violent potentials of decolonization that El Plan invited.

The differences between these reproductions of El Plan Espiritual de Aztlán highlight the aesthetic variations constituting the poetics otherwise found in reproductions in the CPA, formal divergences that underlined the unevenness of the Chican@ movement racial project inasmuch as a shared text pointed toward unity in Chican@ movement(s). Certainly, we could view each of these reproductions as "saying" the same thing or "constituting" the same community. Whether published in English or Spanish, reproductions conveyed similar "messages" (that is to say, the Plan). Yet, as I have shown thus far, the multiple and varied border rhetorics present in these reproductions illuminates shades in the racial politics taking hold in Chican@ movement(s) and underlines variations in the Chican@ movement(s)' racial project. The ways that each reproduction broached the border rhetoric of the "original" surfaces splits in commitments to Chican@ nationalism and negotiations of the exclusive/inclusive dialectic the push to decolonization introduced. Aesthetic variations projected political differences and, though not diverting too far from a burgeoning Chican@ nationalism, indicated disparity among the unity Aztlán might have promised.

Aesthetic divergences continued in later reproductions published in the summer of 1969, and, just as we saw in *El Gallo* and *La Verdad*, those published months after the CYLC projected alternative political visions to Chican@ nationalism while also still adhering to a poetics otherwise. The aesthetic departures in reproductions showing up in *Bronce* (or *Bronze*) and *El Grito del Norte* in June and July respectively, however, also appeared to reflect shifts along the axis of gender. Both *Bronce* and *El Grito del Norte* were edited by Chicanas, and, though adhering to promises and obligations associated with Chican@ nationalism by publishing El Plan Espiritual de Aztlán, each respective reproduction exemplified negotiations of the gender politics incited by and after the CYLC. In *Bronce*, for example, editor Lea Ybarra included two articles on Chicana activism that argued for greater appreciation of Chicanas in the movement and their contributions to the trajectory of Chican@ movement(s), both of which were published ahead of the Plan Espiritual de Aztlán (figs. 18 and 19). And, even after making these decisions, the publication of the Plan was positioned within photographs taken at the CYLC and Maria Varela's commentary, which diminished the overall importance of the language of El Plan to its political visions. *Bronce* reinforces the link between its reproduction and the CYLC by citing *El Gallo* and the CPA as the source material at the bottom right of the page. Yet, unlike the reproduction in *El Gallo*, *Bronce* excludes the program altogether in the issue and, instead, reproduces only Alurista's prologue on half of one page (see fig. 18). Bordering the prologue with Varela's commentary and a plethora of action-shot photographs of conference participants, *Bronce* suffused Aztlán with a processuality that softens the boundaries suggested by El Plan Espiritual de Aztlán. Aztlán is not simply a mythical figure; it is a social construction energized by contemporary political involvement, borne out of the contributions of membership, as much as it is an appeal to the past. The production of Aztlán's community, in sum, is currently underway, and, because of this, is yet open to more membership.

Similarly, the publication of the prologue without the program suggests that editors of this reproduction in *Bronce* preferred cultivating flexibility and liberality at the borders of Aztlán rather than pushing for its more "rigid" schematics. This aesthetic re-presentation reflected the newspaper's editorial policy: "What the objective of Bronze is to present information and ideas that reflect the direction and philosophy of the Chicano movement, while at the same time allowing each individual Mejicano and Latino to contribute to the development of the movement and its philosophy, by reading and acquiring information."[44] However, it also appears to have coincided with the burgeoning Chicana feminism that some preferred to downplay at the conference (more on this in a moment). As Lisa Flores remarks regarding the way that Chicana feminists constructed solidarity, multimodality allowed for the creation of bonds across difference as much as it might have been premised on difference. This solidarity was embodied textually not by appealing to differences or similarities in experience but rather by pushing different styles and language codes together, moves that gestured toward a more

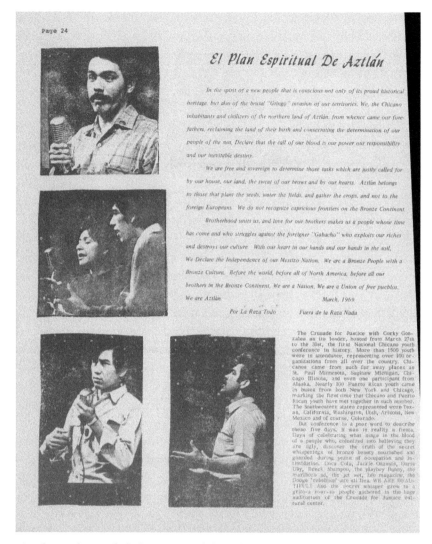

Fig. 18. Prologue of El Plan Espiritual de Aztlán by Alurista and a portion of brief synopsis of the Chican@ Youth Liberation Conference, published in *Bronce*, 1969. Digitized from The Nettie Lee Benson Latin American Collection, The University of Texas Libraries, JSTOR "Independent Voices" Collection.

expansive belonging than what participants at the CYLC decided.[45] In this reproduction, re-presentations of poetry (in the Plan), exposition (Varela's commentary), and photographs project a polyphony that escapes the exclusive capacities of the "program." Moreover, photographic presentations of Chicanas and Chicanos prepared horizontally, all shown as engaged in a

Fig. 19. Portion of brief synopsis of the Chican@ Youth Liberation Conference, published in *Bronce*, 1969. Digitized from The Nettie Lee Benson Latin American Collection, The University of Texas Libraries, JSTOR "Independent Voices" Collection.

communicative moment (listening or speaking), highlights equality between them and their contributions that went beyond that presented in *El Gallo*. Although claiming to draw from the publication of *El Gallo*, this reproduction's photographs suggest a political energy among Chicanas absent in *El Gallo*. Deploying numerical parallelism in this presentation, women appear on the top and bottom row, as do the men, and neither men nor women are depicted in a subservient position. Coupled with the exposition of the conference events by Varela, this reproduction of El Plan Espiritual de Aztlán suggests a political nationalism guided by, committed to, and a product of sustained equality between Chicanas and Chicanos. In *Bronce*, the reproduction heightens the otherness of Aztlán not by leaning into a detailed program but by forwarding a gendered liberalism premised on empowering and recognizing Chicana action(s).

In *El Grito del Norte*, however, the reproduction of the Plan Espiritual de Aztlán pushes back on this flexible nationalism by republishing both the prologue and the program—twice in the same issue. Published in July, the newspaper grappled with the consequences and implications of the CYLC openly. One of their writers, activist Enriqueta Longeaux y Vasquez, published a now (in)famous article on Chicana contributions to the nationalist project in the same issue titled "The Woman" that, she recalled later, "lost me friends and made me a target for the renowned 'Malinche' label. But, like so many of my writings, the rewards were many and this article opened centuries-old flood gates that poured forth in women's words and thoughts."[46] Explaining how she neglected to resist the conservatism stemming from the CYLC, Longeaux y Vasquez's article offered different ways in which Chicanas might act politically while still respecting the broader Chicano movement.[47] Given this gendered conservatism from one of the newspaper's prominent writers, how tightly bound the newspaper was to Reies López Tijerina's land-grant question, and Longeaux y Vasquez's close ties with the Crusade for Justice, the reproduction of both the program and the prologue of El Plan Espiritual de Aztlán emphasized a more indigenous and more rigid border rhetoric than that conveyed by *Bronce*. Appearing to reinforce the border rhetorics of El Plan Espiritual de Aztlán in ways similar to that in *El Gallo*, *El Grito del Norte* included El Plan Espiritual de Aztlán in English (fig. 20) and in Spanish (fig. 21) in word for word translations.

The publication of English and Spanish versions of El Plan Espiritual de Aztlán in this single issue both aligns with antecedent reproductions and distinguishes this newspaper's political priorities. Indeed, what marks this reproduction is how prominently English and Spanish language codes define its representations. Although a move away from separating Spanish and English language codes had begun (see chapter 3), the division in this reproduction (and in a similar way in *El Gallo*) underlined the kind of separation emphasized by El Plan Espiritual de Aztlán. Three months after the CYLC, this anti-parallel re-presentation of the text, a linguistic figure wherein equality and difference are forwarded at the same time, demonstrated a commitment to redrawing the boundaries around Aztlán. And yet, the newspaper's

El Plan Espiritual De Aztlan

In the spirit of a new people that is conscious not only of its proud historical heritage, but also of the brutal "Gringo" invasion of our territories. We, the Chicano inhabitants and civilizers of the northern land of Aztlan, from whence came our forefathers, reclaiming the land of their birth and consecrating the determination of our people of the sun, Declare that the call of our blood is our power, our responsibility, and our inevitable destiny.

We are free and sovereign to determine those tasks which are justly called for by our house, our land, the sweat of our hours and by our hearts. Aztlan belongs to those that plant the seeds, water the fields, and gather the crops, and not to the foreign Europeans. We do not recognize capricious frontiers on the Bronze Continent.

Brotherhood unites us, and love for our brothers makes us a people whose time has come and who struggles against the foreigner "Gabacho" who exploits our riches and destroys our culture. With our heart in our hands and our hands in the soil, We Declare the Independence of our Mestizo Nation. We are a Bronze People with a Bronze Culture. Before the world, before all of North America, before all our brothers in the Bronze Continent. We are a Nation. We are a Union of free pueblos. We are Aztlan.

March, 1969 (Adopted at Chicano Youth Conference, Denver, Colo.)

Aztlan, in the Nahuatl tongue of ancient Mexico, means "the lands to the north." Thus Aztlan refers to what is now known as the southwestern states of this country.

El Plan espiritual de Aztlan sets the theme that Chicanos (La Raza de Bronze) must use their nationalism as the key or common denominator for a mobilization and organization. Once we are committed to the idea and philosophy of El Plan de Aztlan, we can only conclude that social, economic, cultural and political independence is the only road to total liberation from oppression, exploitation and racism. Our struggle then must be the control of our barrios, campos, pueblos, lands, our economy, our culture, and our political life. El Plan commits all levels of Chicano society: the barrio, the campo, the ranchero, the writer, the teacher, the worker, the professional, to La Causa.

UNTO PRIMERO: Nationalism

Nationalism as the key to organization transcends all religious, political, class, and economic factions or boundaries. Nationalism is the common denominator all members of La Raza can agree upon.

PUNTO SEGUNDO: Organization Goals

1. Unity in thought of our people concerning the barrio, the pueblo, the campo, the land, the poor, the middle class, the professional is committed to liberation of La Raza.
2. Economy: economic control of our lives and our communities can only come about by driving the exploiter out of our communities, our pueblos, and our lands and by controlling and developing our own talents, sweat and resources. Cultural background and values which ignore materialism and embrace humanism will lend to the act of co-operative buying and the distribution of resources and production to sustain an economic base for healthy growth and development. Lands rightfully ours will be fought for and defended. Land and realty ownership will be acquired by the community for the people's welfare. Economic ties of responsibility must be secured by nationalism and the Chicano defense units.
Education must be relevant to our people, i.e. history, culture, bilingual education, contributions, Communal control of our schools, our teachers.

3. Institutions shall serve our people by providing the service necessary for a full life and their welfare on the basis of restitution, not handouts or beggar's crumbs. Restitution for past economic slavery, political exploitation, ethnic and cultural psychological destruction and denial of civil and human rights. Institutions in our community which do not serve the people have no place in the community. The institutions belong to the people.

4. Self defense of the community must rely on the combined strength of the people. The front line defense will come from the barrios, the campos, the pueblos, and the ranchitos. Their involvement as protectors of their people will be given respect and dignity. They in turn offer lives for their people. Those who place themselves on the front for their people do so out of love and camalismo. Those institutions which are fattened by our brothers to provide employment and political pork barrels for the gringo will do so only by acts of liberation and la Causa. For the very young there will no longer be acts of juvenile delinquency, but revolutionary acts.

5. Cultural values of our people strengthen our identity and to moral backbone of the movement. Our culture unites and educates the family of La Raza towards liberation with one heart and one mind. We must insure that our writers, poets, musicians, and artists produce literature, and art that is appealing to our people and relates to our revolutionary culture. Our cultural values of life, family, and home will serve as a powerful weapon to defeat the gringo dollar value system and encourage the process of love and brotherhood.

7. Political liberation can only come through independent action on our part, since the two party system is the same animal with two heads that feeds from the same trough. Where we are a majority we will control; where we are a minority we will represent a pressure group. Nationally, we will represent one party La Familia de La Raza.

III PUNTO TERCERO: Action

1. Awareness and distribution of el Plan Espiritual de Aztlan. Presented at every meeting, demonstration, confrontation, courthouse, initiation, administration, church school, tree, building, car, and every place of human existence.

2. September 16th on the birthdate of Mexican Independence, a national walkout by all Chicanos of all colleges and schools to be sustained until the complete revision of the educational system: its policy makers, administration, its curriculum, and its personnel to meet the needs of our community.

3. Self defense against the occupying forces of the oppressors at every school, every available man, woman, and child.

4. Community nationalization and organization of all Chicanos re: El Plan Espiritual de Aztlan.

5. Economic program to drive the exploiter out of our communities and a welding of our peoples combined resources to control their own production through co-operative effort.

6. Creation of an independent local, regional and national political party.

LIBERATION

A nation autonomously free, culturally, socially, economically and politically will make its own decisions on the usage of our lands, the taxation of our goods, the utilization of our bodies for war, the determination of justice (reward and punishment), and the profit of our sweat.

EL PLAN DE AZTLAN IS THE PLAN OF LIBERATION!

Fig. 20. English translation of the Program of El Plan Espiritual de Aztlán and the Prologue by Alurista, published in *El Grito del Norte*, 1969. Permission to reproduce Prologue granted by Alurista. Courtesy of Tessa Koning-Martinez. Digitized from The Nettie Lee Benson Latin American Collection, The University of Texas Libraries, JSTOR "Independent Voices" Collection.

El Plan Espiritual De Aztlán

EN EL ESPIRITU DE UNA RAZA QUE HA RECONOCIDO NO SOLO SU ORGULLOZA HERENCIA HISTORICA, SINO TAMBIEN LA BRUTA INVASION GRINGA DE NUESTROS TERRITORIOS, NOSOTROS LOS CHICANOS HABITANTES Y CIVILIZADORES DE LA TIERRA NORTENA DE AZTLAN, DE DONDE PROVINIERON NUESTROS ABUELOS SOLO PARA REGRESAR A SUS RAIZES Y CONSAGRAR LA DETERMINACION DE NUESTRO PUEBLO DEL SOL, DECLARAMOS QUE EL GRITO DE LA SANGRE ES NUESTRA FUERZA, NUESTRA RESPONSIBILIDAD, Y NUESTRO INEVITABLE DESTINO. SOMOS LIBRES Y SOBERANOS PARA SENALAR AQUELLAS TAREAS POR LAS CUALES GRITAN JUSTAMENTE NUESTRA CASA, NUESTRA TIERRA, EL SUDOR DE NUESTRA FRENTE Y NUESTRO CORAZON.

AZTLAN PERTENECE A LOS QUE SIEMBRAN LA SEMILLA, RIEGAN LOS CAMPOS, Y LEVANTAN LA COSECHA, Y NO AL EXTRANJERO EUROPEO. NO RECONOCEMOS FRONTERAS CAPRICHOSAS EN EL CONTINENTE DE BRONZE.

EL CARNALISMO NOS UNE Y EL AMOR HACIA NUESTROS HERMANOS NOS HACE UN PUEBLO ACENDIENTE QUE LUCHA CONTRA EL EXTRANJERO GABACHO, QUE EXPLOTA NUESTRAS RIQUEZAS Y DESTROSA NUESTRA CULTURA. CON EL CORAZON EN LA MANO Y CON LAS MANOS EN LA TIERRA, DECLARAMOS EL ESPIRITU INDEPENDIENTE DE NUESTRA NACION MESTIZA. SOMOS LA RAZA DE BRONZE CON UNA CULTURA DE BRONZE ANTE TODO EL MUNDO, ANTE NORTE AMERICA, ANTE TODOS NUESTROS HERMANOS EN EL CONTINENTE DE BRONZE, SOMOS UNA NACION, SOMOS UNA UNION DE PUEBLOS LIBRES, SOMOS, A Z T L A N.

Programa Del Plan

El plan espiritual de Aztlán desarolla el tema que el Chicano(La Raza de Bronze) debe usar su Nationalismo como la llave o denominador comun para la organizacion y mobilizaci on en masa. Ya sido cometido a la idea y filosofia del Plan de Aztlan podemos solamente concluir que la independencia social, economica, cultural y politica es el unico camino acida la liberacion total de la opresion, explotacion y el racismo. Por esto nuestra lucha debar ser por el control de nuestros Barrios, campos, pueblos, tierras, nuestra economia, neustra cultura, y nuestra vida politica. El plan compromete todos los niveles de sociedad Chicana; el barrio, el campo, el ranchero, el escritor, el maestro, al obrero, el profesional. Los compromete a la causa.

I PUNTO PRIMERO
Nationalismo: Nationalism como la llave para organizacion transcende toda region o cercos religiousos, politicos, clase, y economicos. Nationalism es el denominador con cual todos miembros de la raza pueden estar en acuerdo.

II PUNTO SEGUNDO
Proposito de Organizacion:
1. Unidad en pensamiento de nuestra gente con respecto a los barrios, el pueblo, el campo, la tierra, los pobres, la clase media, el profesional, todos comprometidos a la liberacion de La Raza.
2. Economia, control economico de nuestros vidas y nuestras comunidades solamente puede ser realidad, an echar fuera al explotador de nuestras comunidades, nuestros pueblos, y de nuestras tierras y en controlar y desarollar nuestros propios talentos, sudor y recursos. Cultura fundamental y valores que ignoran materialismo y abrazan humanismo preten el acto de comprar co-operativamente y la distribucion de recursos y production para sostener la base economica par el desarollo y crecimiento sano. Tierras justamente nuestrosjes batallers por ellas y seran defendidas. Propiedad de tierra y bienes raices seran adquiridas por la comunidad para el bienestar de la gente. Enlaces economicos de responsibilidad deben ser asegurados por el nacionalismo y las Unidades de defensa Chicana.

3. Educacion debe ser relativa a nuestra gente, i.e., historia, cultura, educacion bi-lingue, contribuciones, etc. Control comun de nuestras escuelas, nuestros maestros, nuestros administradores, nuestros consejeros, y nuestros programas.

4. Instituciones deben servir a nuestra gente supliendo los servicions necesarios para una vida llena y su bienestar en la base de restitucion no como limosna o atole con el dedo, pero restitucion por esclavitud economica, explotacion politica, destrucion psicologica de cultura etnica y la negacion de derechos humanos y civiles. Instituciones en nuestra comunidad que no estan a servicio de la gente no tienen lugar en la comunidad. Las instituciones igual que la comunidad pertenecen a la gente.

5. Defensa propia de la comunidad debe contar con las fuerzas combinadas de la gente. La defensa de la primera fila vendra de los barrios, los campos, los pueblos y los ranchitos. Su envolvimiento como amparadores de su gente tomara respeto y dignidad. Ellos en vuelta ofrecan su responsibilidad y su vida por su gente, los que se colocan en la primera fila por su gente lo hacen por amor asi ellos y por CARNALISMO. Esas instituciones que engordan con nuestros hermanos para suplir empleo y partidas de favoritismo provincial para el gringo, lo haran solamente por actos de liberacion y por la causa. Para la juventud, jamas habra actos de delincuencia juvenil, ahora seran actos de revolucion.

6. Valores Culturales de nuestra gente prestan fuerza a nuestra identidad y el fundamiento del movimiento de la Raza. Nuestra cultura une y educa la familia de La Raza asia la liberacion, con un corazon y una misma mente. Debemos asegurar que el producto de nuestros escritores, poetas, musicos y artistas sea literature y arte que despierta a nuestra gente y refiere a nuestra cultura revolucionaria. Los valores culturales de nuestra vida, familia, y hogar servirá como una arma poderosa para derrotar el sistema de del'gringo dolar'un sistema de hipocresia y comercialismo, y animará el proceso de amor y hermanidad.

7. Liberacion politica se puede obtenir solamente por nuestra acion independiente viendo que el sistema de dos cabezas que come de la misma cubeta. Donde somos la majoridad, controlaremos, donde somos la minoridad representaremos un grupo de presion; Nacionalmente representaremos un partido, La familia de La Raza.

III PUNTO TERCERO
Acion:
1. Conocimiento y distribucion del Plan Espiritual de Aztlan presentado en cada junta, demonstracion, demanda confrontacion, tribunal, institucion, administracion, iglesia, escuela, arbol edicicio, coche, y todo Lugares de existencia humana.
2. Diez y seis de septiembre, el reconocimiento de la Independencia Mejicana Una huelga estudiantil Chicana, de todo colegio y escuela, y se sostendra hasta que el sistema educativo, los hace reglas, la administracion, el plan de estudios, y el conjunto de empleados se revise completamente a servir las necesidades de la comunidad.
3. Defensa propia contra las fuerzas de los opresores en cada escuela, cada barrio, cada comunidad, y reclutar y entrenar todo hombre, mujer, y chamaco disponible.
4. Nationalismo comun y organizacion de todo chicano i.e. El Plan Espiritual de Aztlán.
5. Programa economico para char fuer a mexplotador de nuestras comunidades y la unificacion de los combinados cursos de nuestra gente para controlar su propia produccion por un esfuerzo cooperativo.
6. Creacion de un partido politico que sea independiente, en los niveles locales regionales y nacionales.

LIBERACION

Una Nacion Autonoma y libre, culturalmente, socialmente, economicamente, y politicamente; hara sus propias decisiones en el modo que se usaran nuestras tierras, la imposicion de impuestos de nuestras mercandias, la utilizacion de nuestros cuerpos para guerra, la determinacion de Justicia (regalo o castigo) y el provecho de nuestro sudor.

EL PLAN DE AZTLAN ES EL PLAN DE L I B E R A C I O N !!!

Fig. 21. Spanish translation of the Program of El Plan Espiritual de Aztlán and the Prologue by Alurista, published in *El Grito del Norte*, 1969. Permission to reproduce granted by Alurista, courtesy of Tessa Koning-Martinez, digitized from The Nettie Lee Benson Latin American Collection, The University of Texas Libraries, JSTOR "Independent Voices" Collection.

word-for-word translations of El Plan Espiritual de Aztlán showcased a lack of commitment to defining the community through *either* language code, suggesting that, instead of language, signs other than whether one spoke English or Spanish unified the nation of Aztlán. Reproducing the full program and prologue certainly exemplified an acceptance of them, but the ambivalence to language code suggested by the appearance of *reduplication* pointed to different ways of identifying La Raza. Language, in short, is not the preferred border rhetorical means.

The newspaper's treatment of the language codes, I suggest, emphasizes other visual cues besides language, and in this case, *El Grito del Norte* proposes indigeneity as the *common* feature among La Raza. Indeed, this issue frames both reproductions with signs of indigeneity across the top and bottom of the program. Much like *La Verdad*, *El Grito del Norte* leans into a border rhetoric defined by indigeneity, which, in turn, casts a frame for understanding the claims of the Plan and the identity of the community of La Raza in Aztlán. Nevertheless, this commitment to indigeneity, as well as the reproduction of the program and prologue, suggests an evasion of the question of gender in Chican@ movement(s). The turn toward indigeneity, as we saw in *La Verdad*, might have suggested a means of inclusion and exclusion that had little to do with gender. Yet as Longeaux y Vasquez's article on Chicanas in the same issue that reproduced El Plan Espiritual de Aztlán suggested, reproducing it reaffirmed a desire to side-step the question of gender for the sake of promoting coherence within Chican@ movement(s). These reproductions in *El Grito del Norte* elided the controversial, conservative statements regarding Chicanas in favor of a unity supported by a common political paradigm through which La Raza might achieve "liberation." At least at this point in Chican@ movement(s), it seems, the promises of nationalism were yet appealing and found to be worth sustaining by those that might have had less to gain by it.

A Nation in a Nation: Pushing Toward Decolonization

The appeal of El Plan Espiritual de Aztlán was the result of a collective enterprise, and not just in terms of its authorship (Alurista, Gonzales, and Juan Gómez-Quiñonez). Generated through border(ing) rhetorics exemplified in and through multiple reproductions of the text, the aesthetic appeal associated with El Plan Espiritual de Aztlán gave form to what I refer to as a *poetics otherwise*, an aesthetic exemplification of a shared yet heterogeneous decolonizing impulse. Composed in 1969 at and for the Chican@ Youth Liberation Conference (CYLC), El Plan Espiritual de Aztlán resonated and elaborated upon a de/coloniality present in prior Chican@ movement discourse(s). The Plan, in its composition, contained English and Spanish language codes, made use of indigeneity, and critiqued the oppressive influence of systemic whiteness in the United States. It offered and compelled an additional, racialized political option for Mexican Americans. And yet, as I have shown in this chapter, while El Plan Espiritual de Aztlán elaborated upon antecedent discourse(s), the claim upon the figure of "Aztlán" was associated with a distinct aesthetic—a border rhetoric—through which the text outlined its new political community. This border rhetoric was crucial to the fabrication of Aztlán and to its promise of a new racial state inhabited by La Raza. Although there was variation in the aesthetics making El Plan Espiritual de Aztlán appealing, their shared interest in establishing borders around a new political entity over and against the United States highlights the poetics suturing each together—a poetics otherwise.

A critical step in executing the assurances offered by El Plan Espiritual de Aztlán was reproducing and circulating it. Although prior studies of El Plan Espiritual de Aztlán have recognized its popularity and the spread of its nationalist ideals, scholars have been less attuned to the political negotiations evinced by variations in the aesthetic of these reproductions. This has occurred, in part, because of an overemphasis on the verbs of the Plan, a methodology abstracting the text from its publication venues and insisting on a stable "message" with each publication to ground its political significance. In contrast, this chapter has argued that an attention to the aesthetics of various reproductions spanning the US Southwest (*El Gallo*, *Bronce* [or *Bronze*], *La Verdad*, and *El Grito del Norte*) reveals political negotiations, a flexibility in commitments to the "program" of nationalism, and a sensibility to the conversations concerning gender stemming from conversations and conservations articulated at the CYLC. Though still exemplifying a poetics otherwise, each reproduction broached the nationalism publicized as integral to the "liberation" proclaimed at the CYLC differently and from distinct political stances. Utilizing aesthetic features such as visual and verbal parallelism, and spatial arrangements of images and text, newspapers injected different priorities while yet reinforcing the borders around Aztlán that El Plan announced. Certainly, each reproduction garnered and implied its terms of exclusion and inclusion. Yet presuming that each did so in the same way or that each simply replicated El Plan neglects the negotiations made by activists as they grappled with consequences of accepting Aztlán. Furthermore, this presumption assumes a stability in Chican@ movement(s)' discourse that was *visibly* not there. Despite the rigidity of the nationalism proffered in the Plan Espiritual de Aztlán, there was still much inventiveness and creativity among its advocates, and despite the popularity of El Plan, there were differences in how it was enacted and conveyed.

Of course, these presumptions, perhaps, tacitly recognize the appeal and force of the border rhetoric(s) posited in and through El Plan Espiritual de Aztlán and the nationalist politics it featured. El Plan Espiritual de Aztlán offered a decolonizing "program" for La Raza, but the decolonization Aztlán might have promised also compelled the formation of *institutions* through which to establish its objectives and goals formally. Consequently, following the (re)birth of Aztlán in Chican@ movement(s), activists began prioritizing the formation of a political party through which to bring many of their nationalist aspirations to fruition—La Raza Unida Party. José Angel Gutierrez, former president of the Mexican American Youth Organization (MAYO) in Texas, recalled how "Aztlán" motivated the desire to establish this political institution in the summer of 1969: "It was June 20, 1969, and we realized that this sweltering summer before us was to be our orientation course in community development. My wife Luz and I had returned to my hometown of Crystal City, Texas (population about 10,000), for the purpose of helping create a model city for Chicano [sic] activity. We wanted to begin Aztlan [sic]."[48] Prioritizing educational change, economic development, increased Mexican American participation in elections, and anti-Anglo control of city governments, the beginning of the La Raza Unida Party in February 1970 in Texas *materialized* the border rhetoric of the Plan by furnishing a formal institution through which to enact the decolonizing impulses promoted by nationalism. With the formation of La Raza Unida Party, activists legitimized their "nation" and, at the same time, established concrete boundaries to enclose (and foreclose) Mexican American politics. The formation of a political institution ossified the boundaries around the politics of Aztlán, and, in so doing, also hardened its borders.

The notion of a formal political party for La Raza grew in popularity and, at the next CYLC in 1970, the need for a Raza Unida Party at all levels of government comprised part of the agenda.[49] By June of 1970, Corky Gonzales emerged as the party leader in Colorado, and he advocated publicly on behalf of two La Raza Unida gubernatorial candidates.[50] Although maintaining the Plan Espiritual Aztlán as an integral piece of the party's platform,[51] La Raza Unida Party in Colorado offered another distinction to their politics: they were publicly against the Viet Nam War.[52] Although there were other issues to which La Raza Unida Party committed, in Colorado, Texas, and elsewhere, it was the intensification of the Viet Nam War and its violent effect on Mexican Americans in the United States that became increasingly part of identifying La Raza as a racial community. For, as we will see in the next chapter, there was much resonance between the violence experienced by Mexican Americans at home and that experienced in and through the Viet Nam War.

6

A POETICS OF DEFERRAL: LA RAZA, RUBEN SALAZAR, AND A GLOBAL VIOLENCE (1970)

By 1970, Chican@ activists had joined a chorus of anti-war efforts sweeping across the country calling for the United States to abandon aggression against Viet Nam. "Why must we," Rosalio Muñoz declared in 1969 at an "All Raza" conference in Albuquerque, New Mexico, "los Mexicanos, the downtrodden, the miserable, homeless, outcast, and 'un'educated go fight the wars to protect the selfish interests of our absentee landlords who stole our forefathers' land? . . . If Nixon wants war then let him send his daughters to fight for it." The formation of a national "Viet Nam Moratorium Committee" created opportunities for a broad swath of activists, socially conscious community members, and Chican@ activists to partner together in a common cause, and on October 15, 1969, a massive outpouring of anti-war sentiment flooded streets, performance centers, and universities to publicize opposition to the conflict in Southeast Asia.[1] Approximately two weeks later, on November 3, President Richard Nixon (in)famously downplayed the growing anti-war resistance in his "Silent Majority" speech, a phrase he hoped might invoke support for continued US military interventions amid an unruly citizenry.[2] A march to Washington called the "March Against Death" only weeks after Nixon's speech, however, underscored the public insistence Nixon's turn of phrase tried to dismiss.[3] Whether or not there actually was a "silent majority" was irrelevant. Anti-war sentiments had become visible, unavoidable, and public, and Chican@ activists lent their own voice(s) to an anti-war movement calling for an end to "la batalla allá," even as they continued to urge a fight against "la batalla aquí."

As I put into focus Chican@ participation in the anti-war movement appearing in earnest at the turn of the decade, this last case study explores how taking part in anti-Viet Nam War protests informed the Chican@ racial project shortly after the turn to nationalism in 1969. Up until then, Chican@

resistance to the Viet Nam War had been a relatively latent theme in Chican@ movement discourse(s). We have seen already how activists increasingly drew from Ralph Guzman's study highlighting the disproportionate rate at which young Mexican Americans were dying in the war. Also, chapter 4 demonstrated how activists writing for *El Grito del Norte* harnessed the draft to articulate a global sensibility. Anti-Viet Nam War protests mobilized many Chican@ activists across the political spectrum,[4] and Juan Gómez-Quiñonez suggests that anti-war protests signaled a convergence of a variety of different activist motivations already present in Chican@ movement(s).[5] Oropeza and others, however, also attest to the complications nationalism posed for Chican@ activism after it was introduced. Although the decision to invent "Chicano moratoriums," anti-war demonstrations that split Chican@ interests in the Viet Nam War from the broader anti-war movement, stemmed partly from feelings that the "white" anti-war movement had been excluding Chican@ contributions,[6] Oropeza cites nationalism as an external and internal point of contention complicating Chican@ movement(s) at this juncture. Chican@ moratoriums, she writes, "exposed the central political dissonance between the Chicano movement's separatist assertions and its frequently integrationist goals. Inevitably, because Chicano anti-war activism addressed a topic that had generated much protest among Americans in general, it also revealed the numerous tensions between white radicalism and Chicano nationalism. Most important, even as Chicano anti-war protest sought to foster unity within and beyond the Chicano movement, it exposed the fragility of coalition building through cultural-nationalistic appeals."[7] Stated another way, the invention of Chican@ moratoriums introduced a *racially* complicating rhetorical gesture that intensified Chican@ movement discourse(s) circulating across the Southwest. Chican@ moratoriums transformed the Viet Nam War from a circumstantial *topos* that accompanied the illumination of domestic issues to concrete evidence of a direct assault against Chican@ bodies by US institutions. The draft signified an act of genocide against Chican@s alla y aquí, here *and* there. But the creation of Chican@ moratoriums also highlighted the complications associated with totalizing figures like Aztlán and La Raza. The "bordering" discussed in chapter 5 restrained the appeal(s) of Chican@ moratoriums, even as this rhetorical configuration might have motioned toward a broader inclusivity. Resistance against the Viet Nam War was a racially forming event that informed the shape of the Chican@ racial project at the turn of the decade.

Although Chican@ historians like Rodolfo Acuña, Jorge Mariscal, Lorena Oropeza, Ernesto Chávez, Carlos Muñoz, and Juan Gómez-Quiñonez have all touched on the complications that Chican@ moratoriums posed for Chican@ movement(s), an examination of the most (in)famous of them all—the Chicano Moratorium on August 29, 1970—has been completely neglected by rhetorical studies. This absence is, perhaps, even more conspicuous when taking into account the controversial yet formative role of the August 29 moratorium's conclusion on subsequent Chican@ movement discourse(s). The Los Angeles Police Department (LAPD) squashed this demonstration by donning riot gear and, in military formations, attacking what had been, up to the assault on the activists, a peaceful demonstration. During the violence that ensued, three moratorium participants were killed: Ruben Salazar, Gilberto Diaz, and Lyn Ward. It was, however, the death of Salazar, a prominent journalist sympathizing with Chican@ movement claims, that resonated the loudest after the violence subsided,[8] and, since that time, Salazar has been hailed as a martyr despite his relative inactivity in the movement(s) prior to the moment of his death.[9] Chican@ moratoriums and the August 29 Moratorium in particular, consequently, are rich sites for rhetorical inquiry, and not only because these illuminate additional contextual resources for comprehending Chican@ movement discourse(s) outside the 1960s. Possible inquiries centering Chican@ moratoriums might also observe how they participated in place-making,[10] coalition building,[11] public controversy,[12] social movement rhetoric,[13] and embodiment,[14] all of which might illuminate the rhetorical effects of the August 29 moratorium on the contours of Chican@ activism.

This chapter offers a corrective to this neglect, but I do so to attend to shifts, alterations, and evolutions in the Chican@ movement(s)' racial project I have been tracing throughout the book. And, in this case study, I highlight how this moment in the Chican@ movement(s)' rhetorical history evinces the complexity of the racially forming power of non/violence at a point at which Chican@ movement(s)' activism had reached a point of profound energy and reach and at an event whose memory is wrapped up in the violence that ended it. The violence witnessed at the August 29 moratorium had certainly been brewing for some time, as Edward J. Escobar's study of the "dialectical" relationship between the LAPD's harassment and Chican@ movement activism illustrates.[15] Yet, after the moratorium, as the death of Ruben Salazar became pivotal to understanding how and why violence erupted at a relatively peaceful protest, US institutions (for example, the police and the media) secured a platform through which to scrutinize the racial identity of Chican@ activism. Activists were blamed for the destruction that occurred at the moratorium and, in turn, for Salazar's tragic death.

And, as if that were not enough, after yet another violent clash with the LAPD at a moratorium on September 16, 1970, the question of non/violence and its role in Chican@ movement(s) eventually ripped the moratorium committee apart.[16] The question as to whether to adopt violence or nonviolence, as I suggested in the Introduction, was a rhetorical consideration not merely in that it had pragmatic consequences, was ethically desirable for some, or was needed as a last resort in struggles against oppression.[17] Choosing either nonviolence or violence was a rhetorical decision in that it proposed an *aesthetic*; either possessed representational value for Mexican American politics amid competing aesthetic options sanctioned by US coloniality. In the wake of the fatal violence that concluded the August 29 moratorium, the place of non/violence in Chican@ movement politics became inescapably rhetorical and, in this sense, constitutive of a racial question that Chican@ activists were compelled to answer. Ignacio Chávez summarizes the purpose of the investigations into the violence witnessed at the moratorium this way: "The inquest was actually an investigation into the August 29 violence, the Mexican-American character, sheriff's department procedures, and the credibility of Chicanos and law enforcement officials. The questions asked by the county attorneys probed all aspects of the march and were thinly disguised attempts to brand the Chicano activists as radical leftists."[18] As scholars have repeatedly shown, US institutions have consistently portrayed whiteness as the standard through which to judge the criminality of not-white others.[19] And, at this point in time, as nationalist rhetorics were integrated into Chican@ movement(s) and rendered as anything but white, the non/violence witnessed at the conclusion of the moratorium was taken as a defining feature of the racial identity projected by Chican@ movement activists. The response to the question of non/violence had significant consequences for not only the trajectory of Chican@ movement politics into the 1970s but, more concretely, for identifying the parties responsible for the death of one of the most public and prominent advocates for Chican@ movement(s) in the late 1960s—Ruben Salazar.

In September 1970, a special issue of *La Raza* magazine was published that addressed the relationship between race and non/violence that the violence experienced by activists at the August 29 Chicano moratorium elevated. Although there were a wide range of articles included in the issue that addressed various topics and themes related to the August 29 moratorium, Chican@ activism, and public opinions,[20] photographs of the event were a critical component of the special issue's interventions. Although an "intersectional" approach to this chapter's rhetoric is certainly appropriate,[21] the issue supplied an array of images depicting the events before and after the violence that reinforced and elaborated on the verbal rhetorics of the issue. Indeed, the sheer number of photographs published in this essay suggests a visual rhetorical investment that, in keeping with this book's emphasis, can and should be distinguished aesthetically from its verbal rhetorics. Out of a roughly ninety-page magazine, there was at least one photograph for every page. Of course, not every page had a photograph. Some pages had one photograph, while others were full-page spreads. Other pages had more than one still image. Even so, that the number of photographs equaled at least the number of pages in the magazine highlights their importance to the rhetorical thrust of the magazine. Consequently, I examine how the special issue's visual rhetoric, comprised of photographs taken during the Chicano moratorium on August 29, 1970, and circulated in the Chicano Press Association (CPA), was sutured, framed, spliced, and arranged to highlight the multiple scales of violence—individual, national, and international—manifested at the moratorium. Indeed, the breadth and depth of the non/violence depicted in the issue's photographs heightened US coloniality's reinforcement of whiteness as preferred political aesthetic for Mexican Americans. By analyzing the aesthetics associated with the issue's photography, however, we see how this special issue of *La Raza* magazine, an instantiation of what Gunckel refers to as the Chican@ photographic, participated in the Chican@ movement(s)' racial project at the turn of the decade.

In this chapter I argue that the special issue (re)racialized Chican@ movement activists and the LAPD through careful aesthetic (re)figurations of non/violence at the moratorium. The issue, through photographic depictions, juxtaposed Chican@ movement(s) and institutional(ized) whiteness visually, pitting them as oppositional and incommensurable, as well as identifiable vis-à-vis non/violent acts. Taken together, the issue's photographs portray a nationalist variation of what I define elsewhere as a "poetics of deferral," a rhetorical agency negotiating the tensions between nonviolent action and the militancy of Chican@ identity. The issue's photographic representation of Chican@s and the LAPD underscores how the special issue's portrayals were not simply negative in their orientation, nor were they simply pictures of "what happened." That is, the issue did not only deny that Chican@ movement activism was violent, nor did it merely offer representations of the day's events that were "truer" than what had been circulated—although it certainly did this too.[22] Through juxtaposition, the issue extended a promise that Chican@ movement(s) offered an ethic for US politics that its current white structures could neither imagine nor extinguish. For, as editors depicted in the special issue, institutional whiteness was undergirded by colonial tendencies, a perverse paranoia, and, because of this colonial impulse, offered only death as its reward. If non/violence was identified *with* race, as the LAPD sought to show *after* the events of the moratorium, then the special issue identified *which* race was concretely associated with violence and which with nonviolence.

Ruben Salazar: The Man in the Middle of (In)Visible Violence

Although some activists (for example, César Chávez) certainly tried driving a wedge between la causa and the broader anti-war effort,[23] Chican@ activists from across the United States traveled to California to participate in the August 29 moratorium in East Los Angeles. The moratorium's plan included a march through East LA, to begin at Belvedere Park and end at Laguna Park (now called Ruben Salazar Park). A rally with high-profile speakers and performers was to be the march's culminating event. Rodolfo "Corky" Gonzales, who was to be one of the speakers at the rally concluding the march, described in idyllic terms the coming together of Mexican Americans from across the Southwest in an unpublished manuscript: "Greetings, abrazos, smiles. We were part of the largest gathering of demonstrating Chicanos in the Southwest and everywhere we turned there were friends, brothers, and sisters, young people, old people. We were one tremendous fiesta wrapped in rainbows of serapes, ponchos, Black flowing hair and lit up by thousands of Black, brown, and green sparkling eyes. And a countless number of voices yelling together, singing together, chanting together 'Raza Raza Raza—Chale con el draft.'"[24]

During the rally at Laguna Park, however, reports of a small disturbance at a liquor store a block away brought a police presence to the heart of the demonstration. It was at this point that the moratorium quickly turned into a bloodbath, and, despite an insistence by those on the speakers' platform that attendees resist temptations to retaliate, pandemonium ensued. Whatever idyll the march might have generated leading up to Laguna Park was quickly consumed by a violent conflict among demonstrators and the LAPD.[25]

The moratorium's violent conclusion brought intense scrutiny from news outlets, but, as Randy Ontiveros observes, the publicity painted Chican@s as the source of the violent upheaval without granting Mexican Americans a chance to give their "side" of the story.[26] The *Los Angeles Times* racialized Mexican Americans from the start, claiming that a "storm of rioting" had been initiated by aggressive Chican@ demonstrators.[27] A "disturbance slowly moved to the nearby park" where "[s]everal bottles were thrown in the direction of the police. Then more."[28] The article continued, "At the peak of the turmoil, a dozen fires burned out of control along Whittier Blvd., the main axis of the disturbance, as about 500 police and sheriff's deputies massed with riot equipment near Whittier and Atlantic Blvds."[29] Public interest in the violence at the moratorium increased as news spread that Ruben Salazar, a former journalist for the *Los Angeles Times* and the recently appointed director of the television station KMEX, had died during the violence.[30] Institutions across the country voiced interest in determining both the cause of the violence and how Salazar ended up dead. The national office of the League of United Latin American Citizens (LULAC) requested a federal investigation of Salazar's death,[31] as did Los Angeles City Councilman Thomas C. Bradley and KMEX officials. Los Angeles Sheriff Peter J. Pitchess also requested an investigation into what he believed to be "federal violations connected with the disturbance,"[32] although the federal government ultimately refused to become directly involved in investigations. The sheer magnitude of the event invited increased attention to the moratorium, and, after its conclusion in fatal violence, many more were drawn to understanding the attributes of the demonstrators, the moratorium's political commitments, and the sequence of events that led to Salazar's killing.

Due to the wide interest in Salazar's death, the coroner's office, led by Thomas T. Noguchi, scheduled an inquest hearing for September 10, 1970. The hearing was presided over by lawyer Norman Pittluck, and it included a jury, testimonies, and evidence from police officers and activists. Although conclusions reached at the inquest hearing would not be legally binding, the decision from the hearing would render the cause of death as either "accidental" or "at the hands of another"[33] and, based on this conclusion, perhaps lend directions for further legal actions.[34] In a move of atypical cooperation, the wide interest in the jury's decision led Noguchi to allow the inquest to be televised. All seven TV networks in Los Angeles came to an agreement for broadcasting the event. Some networks provided cameras at the hearing; others covered costs; still others provided Spanish translations. All networks rotated when they televised the event so as to avoid competing with one another's coverage.[35] These moves increased the publicity of the event, and each furnished public access to the details of the case for those wishing to scrutinize the moratorium and the violence that terminated it.

The inquest hearing illuminated the "facts" of the circumstances surrounding Salazar's death, and, for this reason, the hearing was crucial for both the LAPD and Chican@ movement(s) alike. The "facts" of the case, however, seem to have been settled without too much difficulty. There was and continues to be generally little controversy over what "actually" happened to Salazar on that day. Salazar was fatally shot in the head by a tear-gas projectile fired by Deputy Thomas Wilson during the mayhem that concluded the moratorium. Salazar had been waiting inside the Silver Dollar Café at 4945 East Whittier Boulevard to escape the violence occurring outside. After the violence began, police officers surrounded the café to respond to reports from an unnamed informant (Manuel Lopez) that a gunman had entered the establishment. To force the threat believed to be inside the café to exit, Deputy Wilson fired a tear-gas projectile normally reserved for breaking through solid barricades through a curtain hanging at the café's doorway. Salazar was shot (unbeknownst to police at that time) by that shell, yet officers delayed entry for a few hours to surveil outside. Police then dismissed an ambulance called out to the café, since they had not yet noticed that Salazar lay dead inside. Only after this delay did police finally locate Salazar's lifeless body lying on the floor. Although there are certainly discrepancies about what was said to whom prior to Wilson's discharge of the canister,[36] few dispute the deputy's involvement in Salazar's death, his unsanctioned firing of a Flight-Rite tear-gas projectile into the Silver Dollar, and the reasons for an active police presence outside the café. Even a recent independent review initiated by the LAPD suggests that the hearing got the "facts" of the case right.[37] The judgment of the hearing, of course, was critically important, as were the "facts" of the circumstances leading to Salazar's death. These would, presumably, be used to determine acquittals or highlight police negligence, if not criminality.

Nevertheless, testimony and evidence were not focused solely on isolating the circumstances and details about Salazar's death. When the inquest hearing began, proceedings also turned toward establishing the proposition that Chican@ demonstrators were responsible for the violence. Locating the violence of the moratorium *within* Chican@ demonstrators was a rhetorical move, a strategic shift in deliberations that could at once undermine attempts to levy moral blame on police officers for Wilson's indiscretion and, at the same time, justify the use of physical force against "riotous" Chican@ demonstrators. From the start of the hearing, testimonies from officers included how Chican@s had been looting, setting objects ablaze, and how demonstrators threw objects at police during the violence. Mexican Americans present at the hearing protested the connections between them and the violence that ensued. Some even stormed out. Joe De Anda, a teacher of Mexican American Studies at San Fernando Valley State College, loudly interjected to presiding officer Pittluck amid vocal protests at the hearing, "You are only attempting to make everyone in the country believe Chicanos are lawless and violent."[38] The death of Salazar at the moratorium, these arguments suggested, was the result of "violent" people doing "violent" things. The determination of blame for that violence on August 29 had become a public contest. The inquest hearing was not merely about determining the "cause" of Salazar's death—the objective detailing of "who," "what," "where," and "when" of his demise. The hearing had also become a racially formative conflict between Chican@s and the LAPD along the axis of non/violence.

Consequently, providing evidence that claimed to expose the events leading to Salazar's death became a way of vindicating or issuing blame on the parties involved. The LAPD submitted photographs and video of the violence taken by their own hired men to provide visual evidence that Chican@ demonstrators acted violently during the protests.[39] Photographs taken by Raul Ruiz and Joe Razo, editors of *La Raza* magazine, who had also been at the moratorium, were also submitted to the jury. Ruiz, however, was interrogated extensively about the objectivity and apparently "doctored" quality of the photographs. Requests for negatives, which Pittluck claimed were from the District Attorney, were denounced by Ruiz on account of their apparently racist motivations, "I don't understand what this line of questioning has to do with the inquest on Ruben Salazar. You did not ask for the negative of the sheriff's [photographs] and now you're putting me into this hassle of what happened to mine. Now you're starting to question my integrity, but of course I know that's because I'm a Mexicano."[40] Ruiz refused to produce negatives, claiming that he believed the photographs would be confiscated and never returned. Moreover, he added, the film had already been circulated across the Southwest and might even be as far away as Texas even as they spoke.[41] In refusing to submit negatives to closer scrutiny, Ruiz acknowledged a rhetorical potency the photographs possessed during the hearing that had very little to do with their authenticity or depictions. Photographs possessed a rhetorical energy, an inventive power, capable of being used for projecting identities and politics.

The pivotal stasis point energizing the publication and circulation of the special issue, it turned out, was not Ruben Salazar's death per se. It was, rather, the racial identity of Chican@ activists that the moratorium and the violence accompanying it appeared to project. After the hearing's jury concluded that the death of Salazar occurred not by "accident" but by the ambiguous label "at the hands of another," which acknowledged that someone killed Salazar but refused to locate accountability in any particular person, the locus of the violence of August 29, 1970, was apparently identified. For, in withholding responsibility, the verdict implicitly but firmly allocated all accountability for the violence that killed Salazar, Diaz, and Ward to the activists at the Chicano Moratorium, and rendered the LAPD's response to the "rioting" as justified, if not entirely sanctioned.

I argue here that the crux of the special issue's visual rhetorical intervention(s) was the presupposed relationship between non/violence and race that located blame for the violence that concluded the moratorium in Chican@ activists, a connection that received heightened importance on account of the investigation into Ruben Salazar's "cause of death." Indeed, this special issue parlayed the presumed relationship between whiteness and violence forwarded by media representations in news outlets—namely, that white subjects alone have the right and obligation to execute violence, while not-white bodies exist as source(s) of criminality.[42] As the issue grappled with these presupposed relationships between race and non/violence, photographs were integral to this rewriting and, in turn, the (re)projection of Chican@ politics that erupted the socio-political categorizations that such relationships purported to uphold.

(Re)Racializing Chican@ Politics: The Chican@ Photographic and Crafting La Raza

In my examination of the special issue, I interrogate the rhetorical work accomplished via use of the photographs because, following Chican@ studies scholars like Colin Gunckel, I view their use at this moment as playing a discrete role in Chican@ movement discourse(s) and the identity (racial, political, cultural, etc.) activists projected. Gunckel, a historian of Latin@ art and media, argues that the special issue of *La Raza* magazine published in September 1970 in particular is an exemplary representation of the "resistant" threads constituting the development of what he terms the "Chican@ photographic."[43] Drawing from the philosophical work of Ariella Azoulay and scholarship documenting the role of photography in Black civil rights activism,[44] Gunckel proposes that the concept of "photographic" encompasses various aspects of visual practice(s) in Chican@ movement(s), such as modes of circulation, assumptions, communality, and subjects, all of which enabled production(s) of a "Chican@" identity over time. The usefulness of the concept of the Chican@ photographic is captured by Gunckel's summary, which highlights both the broad instrumentality of the Chican@ photographic and its inventional resources: "Adopting the lens of the Chicano/a [sic] photographic allows us to account for not only how photography served as a conceptual conceit that facilitated the visualization of Chicano/a identity but also how it was instrumental to actively challenging the boundaries between media; functioned as the basis for a range of cultural production; facilitated the democratization of cultural production; rejected conventional notions of the art object; and, through the accessibility of production and circulation, facilitated the operation of Chicano/a art as a social and community-based practice."[45] The Chican@ photographic captures the thin line between visual documentation and activism in Chican@ movement(s) merging at the turn of the decade,[46] and, as Gunckel has argued in his use of the concept to interrogate the photographic practices guiding the farmworkers' newspaper *El Malcriado*, practices comprising the Chican@ photographic "facilitated the proliferation of multiple ways of conceiving identity and community" within a context of competing and allied interests.[47] Although a Chican@ photographic also reinforced and resisted gendered slants to notions of Chican@ identity, particularly in its reliance upon familia constructions,[48] in its widest sense the Chican@ photographic captures the visual rhetorical ends and means of the negotiation of identity in Chican@ movement(s).

The concept of the Chican@ photographic, thus, is useful for this study of the Chican@ racial project since it presumes that photography was not merely a neutral practice and that its productions were constitutive and consequential within specific contexts that informed their enactments. As rhetorical scholars like Cara Finnegan, Lester Olson, Ned O'Gorman, and Kevin Hamilton have argued in their respective visual studies work,[49] rhetorically tuned photographic work exists within visual cultures, and, consequently, photographs both exemplify and resist the visual culture(s) that ground their receptions.[50] These visual cultures, which guide ways of seeing photographs and apprehending their contents, contribute to what Rancière calls in his political philosophy the "distribution of the sensible."[51] That is, visual cultures both direct ways of seeing social conditions and locating bodies firmly within them in a given political community. This entrenchment of the "sensible" that visual cultures reify is precisely what enables the rhetorical formation of "icons" that Robert Hariman and John L. Lucaites identify in their work,[52] but most important, for this study, visual cultures contribute to the racial formation of bodies, as these provide a "frame" (such as the white racial frame) through which to interpret bodies.[53] Visual cultures, thus, participate in the racial formation of Latinx bodies, and, viewed in this racializing sense, energize and constrain visual rhetorics associated with a "photographic."[54] Putting into view the racial work accomplished in and through Chican@ movement(s)' photography generates insights into the ways in which a photographic grapples with these expectations—in this case, presumptions about Chican@s and non/violence. The Chican@ photographic is, I suggest, a manifestation of rhetorical *and* racial negotiations of visual cultures and the *racial* expectations they bolster.

In my examination, therefore, of the special issue's photographs, I am putting into view how this visual rhetoric engaged with and contested racial expectations stemming from the investments made by both the media *and* the police at this moment in 1970. As I argued in chapter 1, media representations projected racist stereotypes of Mexican Americans, and, as Chican@ activism became more prominent, stereotypical images endured, particularly those that might have contrasted with emerging images such as that of a cultic César Chávez.[55] Even governmental officials like Representative Henry Gonzales (D-Texas) referred to Chican@ movement discourse after the Denver Youth Conference as a manifestation of "hate speech."[56] The special issue qua Chican@ movement discourse was born out of controversy over the violence at the August 29 moratorium and, fundamentally, was rooted in a moment of violence directed against a community. How to "see" either the nonviolence or the violence of that day was the crux of the controversy and, since ways of seeing were predetermined by racist stereotypes and perceptions of criminality, locating the blame upon the not-white "rioters" spewing "hate" was all but assured. If lynching, as Ersula Ore argues, was an instantiation of violence intended to buttress the social positions of Black and White communities more generally,[57] this moment of general violence, too, was cast as a means of shielding the one (Thomas Wilson, representing the LAPD) from judgment, while judging the many (Chican@ activists) as guilty. The special issue both reveals these racist undertones and protests their validity through the visual rhetorical work it circulated.

However, this revelation was accomplished not simply by "documenting" events. The issue's aesthetic features also refigured the photographs published in the issue. Certainly, portraying "what happened" was of interest, but as I have shown so far, the "what" of the case was not that controversial. Salazar's death was concrete evidence of what happened. The primary question was *why*, and consequently aesthetic reconfigurations were a crucial aspect of answering that question. The aesthetics of the photographs conveyed racial postures, invited political reimaginations, and, at the same time, responded to the needs of those activists yet trying to make sense of their political commitments after having just experienced a full-scale attack during an otherwise peaceful protest. The aesthetics of the photographs, driven by public controversy, (re)racialized Mexican American bodies by projecting them as, fundamentally, nonviolent rather than violent.

The appeal(s) promoted by the special issue, however, did not contend for the pragmatic value of nonviolent acts, parlay religious ideals, or request support from white community members. These appeals were part and parcel of César Chávez's public call for nonviolent activism in 1968, a speech that negotiated this same problematic stemming from non/violence in the farmworkers' movement through what I have called a *poetics of deferral*. Articulating a rhetorical agency compatible with nonviolent activism and the racial consciousness of Chican@ movement(s) in the late 1960s,[58] Chávez's "Speech Breaking the Fast" exemplified a poetics of deferral through magnitude, through the implementation of Chican@ language (such as family and "men"), and in his choice to have Rev. James Drake read his speech as he recovered from a week-long fast. These were, in short, aesthetic choices that fashioned a compatibility between Chican@ ideals and nonviolent militance while, at the same time, disavowing appeals to transcendence that might have delimited the reach of his appeals. Nevertheless, accompanying Chávez's appeals was a coherence between Chican@ movement(s)' politics and systemic whiteness. Not only did Chávez choose a white man to read his address for him, each of his named supporters in the address were also white men of some (institutional) stature. Chávez's address portrayed nonviolent activism as a way to align Mexican Americans with, rather than opposed to, institutional(ized) whiteness, and, in turn, upheld its hegemony in US politics and Mexican American reliance upon it. Whatever the racial implications, these were secondary to sustaining the UFW's current programs, since these partnerships between Mexican Americans and white communities were advantageous for Chávez.

The special issue of *La Raza*, in contrast, crafted an aesthetic predicated on contrast and opposition that nonetheless exemplified a variation of the poetics of deferral Chávez had articulated two years earlier. In line with the journalistic visions of amateur photographers and editors of *La Raza* Raul Ruíz and Joe Razo,[59] the special issue's photographs re-imaged Chican@ subjects and the LAPD in an incommensurate relationship with one another. Pitting these subjects against each other provided an intersubjective rendering that explicitly highlighted the attributes of each. One of the more illustrative examples of the issue's aesthetic impulses occurs in a photomontage in the first two pages of the issue (fig. 22). The photomontage, art historian Ellen Macfarlane writes, is "in part contradictory: it condenses information for the reader even as it simultaneously seems to provide more context."[60] In this montage, the

Fig. 22. Collage of photographs taken during the Chican@ Moratorium and published in a special issue of *La Raza*, 1970. Permission to reproduce images from *La Raza* granted by Joe Razo. Courtesy of UCLA Chicano Research Center.

contradictions, condensation, and elaboration forward a contrast between the LAPD and Chican@ bodies at the moratorium. This photomontage is the most "doctored" image in the special issue, and while other photographs in the issue are also altered to a degree, the splicing together of many different scenes and its placement early in the issue suggests that it, like the table of contents that follows it, forwards a way to read the issue's visual rhetorical appeals. Cut-outs of photographs prevail in this image, which makes its fabrication clearly visible to readers of the magazine. The banner bearing the date of the moratorium—August 29—at the top center of the page acts as a kind of leading "caption" for the montage, and the presence of countless bodies of police and Chican@ demonstrators suggests that they make up the "subject(s)" of the montage more than the "event" of the moratorium itself.

Analyzing this photomontage surfaces the figure of juxtaposition giving form to the issue's photographic. Through juxtaposition, a rhetorical figure illuminating subjects via balanced contrast,[61] the issue illuminates the sharp contrast between Chican@s and the LAPD at the moratorium. Chican@ protestors appear at the center, police officers on the periphery. The faces of the protestors, which are clearly visible, invite the eyes of *La Raza*'s readers, and Chican@ men, women, and children demonstrators appear as a diverse and multigenerational political community. Police, in contrast, are masked at times and not at others, appearing nearly identical to each other, and lined up in military formations (see especially the top of fig. 22). Rarely do police officers face viewers. And yet, police face and "move" toward Chican@ bodies from the edges of the page. Police wield weapons as they do so, and at times, are shown handling demonstrators physically. Positioned at the bottom of the page is perhaps the montage's most explicit use of contrasts: an armed police officer walks with gun raised at the unarmed Ruben Salazar—who faces readers. This rendering alludes to the events at the Silver Dollar Café, which, in turn, creates a rhetorical climax for all the contrasts in the image. Juxtaposition forwards the direct clash between Chican@s and the LAPD, a confrontation that began at the moratorium and extended into the inquest hearing over Salazar's death. Chican@s and police officers, although both present, equally represented, and equally consumed by a fatal violence at the moratorium, are depicted in sharp conflict with one another.

The juxtaposition identifies both communities and their ways of living life together—their politics. Questions about the violent acts witnessed at the moratorium were, crucially, about ways in which Mexican Americans came together to voice their concerns in public. The violence terminating the Chicano Moratorium, the montage suggested, stemmed not from Chican@s—as implied by the inquest hearing—but rather because of an aggressive, militarized, and unified LAPD brutally attacking a multigenerational community of Chican@ activists. Of course, anti-war resistance was not necessarily equivalent to anti-Anglo protest, but Chicano Moratorium activists, with their use of bilingualism, claims to Aztlán, and adoption of the "Chicano" moniker, racialized their resistance to the Viet Nam War and, in turn, identified it and the LAPD within what Maldonado-Torres refers to as a "paradigm of war" guiding colonial relations.[62] The photomontage, in contrasting the LAPD with Chicano Moratorium activists rather than Chican@

movement activism more generally, positioned the LAPD as an executor of the paradigm of war guiding US involvement in Viet Nam and identified Chican@ activists with the colonized, not-white others subject to racial violence. Through juxtaposition, the issue heightens the contrast between the racial politics of the Chicano Moratorium and those of the LAPD, and, moreover, it exposed the extent to which the LAPD disciplined bodies acting publicly in "not-white" ways. The juxtaposition of (re)actions from the LAPD and Chican@ demonstrators during the moratorium exemplified a brute expulsion of not-white bodies from the political sphere and established a frame of reference from which to evaluate the rest of the special issue. The Chicano Moratorium and the LAPD were involved in an incommensurable conflict, guided by opposing but no less racially motivated politics.

Although the photomontage makes the use of juxtaposition as an aesthetic choice clear, I propose here and demonstrate below that the entire issue's photographic reproduced this aesthetic in its presentation of photographs of "live" moments. Doing so naturalized the incommensurability of its subjects by providing a seemingly "un-doctored" photographic record of events on August 29, 1970, that countered the public characterizations of Mexican Americans as violent. Yet juxtaposition also served as a crucial aesthetic for representing the political energies underpinning Chican@ nonviolence and the violence exemplified by the LAPD. Indeed, through juxtaposition, the issue also portrayed the positive elements of Chican@ politics, its ethics and modes of political friendship. Through the aesthetic of juxtaposition, the issue's photographic made manifest how de/colonial love characterized Chican@ movement activism and paranoia over the presence of not-white others in US public life as the political ethic of institutional whiteness. In so doing, the issue illuminated sources of the non/violence, the rationale of non/violence, and the political possibilities fomented by that non/violence.

Non/Violence and a Poetics of Deferral: Visualizing La Raza and Institutional Whiteness

One of the first places that this contrast between the de/colonial love undergirding Chican@ politics and the paranoia fomenting institutional(ized) whiteness appears is the issue's cover image. Circulated widely in Chican@ print spaces (e.g., *El Gallo*) and the *Los Angeles Times*, this is one of the most well-known photographs from this documentation of the Chicano Moratorium.[63] In this photograph taken outside of the Silver Dollar Café where

A POETICS OF DEFERRAL 163

Fig. 23. Cover of the special issue of *La Raza* about the Chican@ Moratorium, 1970. Permission to reproduce images from *La Raza* granted by Joe Razo. Courtesy of UCLA Chicano Research Center.

Ruben Salazar was killed, we see three sets of subjects presented linearly (fig. 23). Reading the photograph from left to right, there are two women in dresses followed by a police officer standing upright and pointing a rifle at a third group of three men at the doorway of the Silver Dollar Café. Coupling the sequencing in the photograph's subjects with the fact that the faces of both women and police officer appear directed toward the men, the image provides a track for the eyes that lead from the women to the men through the officer's weapon. In fact, so linear is the progression that the eyes of the women and the men appear to converge at the weapon itself.

The "action shot" heightens the vividness of the contrast in the photograph. Since the inquest hearing conflated the racial significance of the events at the moratorium with the death of Salazar, the photograph showcases the differences between the Chican@s and the LAPD outside the Silver Dollar Café. The image captures the policeman with his weapon pointed at Chicanos standing at the doorway despite the apparent lack of physical threat. The men at the doorway, whose presumed not-white identity is reinforced by the shadows in which they stand, appear calm and ready to receive instructions from the officer should he give it to them. The men do not cower, they do not run, nor do they bow. They stand erect, instead, and alert. The officer, in contrast, appears in motion toward them, ready to shoot, and unaffected by the cool response of the men at the doorway or the kinetic energy of the women behind him. These women, though moving toward the men like the officer, appear in a posture of warning rather than with the aggression of the officer.

Although it is difficult to assess whether these Chicanas knew the Chicanos at the doorway, that they reach out for them despite the officer's brandished weapon highlights a de/colonial love subtending their actions. Building on Fanon's experience with colonialism, Maldonado-Torres proposes that a racially inspired love undercuts the colonial impulse,[64] which, in this photograph, is clearly contrasted with the deliberate, racially inspired intent to harm depicted by the presence of the police officer. The police officer is motivated by nothing, it appears, but the weapon in front of and guiding him toward the men at the doorway. The women, however, who also move toward the men and following in the police officer's shadow, appear to both reach and recoil at the officer's aggressive movement toward the doorway. The juxtaposition of the women's actions with the singular officer showcases how their love for Chicanos insists and persists even with the horror that they appear to feel. Though recognizing the danger of the moment, Chicanas demonstrate their overwhelming *desire* for the men not by choosing violence but by choosing substitution: *their* Chicana bodies for the bodies of Chicano men waiting in the doorway. This self-less move, which contrasts sharply with the way the police officer moves to exploit the bodies of the Chicanos, highlights the way a non-sexual, affectionate love motivated by a shared experience of (racial) violence inhabits this Chicana/o interaction.[65] Yet, as if held back by the officer's presence, the women are prevented from reaching the doorway, as are their warnings to them and anyone (that is, Ruben Salazar) inside.[66]

Despite the importance of Salazar's death to the public controversy surrounding the Chicano Moratorium and the racial identity of Chican@

activists at the moratorium, it only typified one instance of the racial clash in East LA. In fact, after the cover and montage, depictions of the Silver Dollar Café disappear entirely until Raul Ruiz's article near the center of the magazine, a pivot point for the issue as a whole.[67] Although articles appearing prior to Ruiz's report make mention of Salazar's death in their explanations of the moratorium's racial(ized) resistance, such as the first article "Chicanos and the War,"[68] photographs throughout the first half or so of the magazine emphasize depicting Chican@s at the moratorium. These, much like the opening image of the cover, also project de/colonial love. In particular, images pick up on the presentation of de/colonial love by invoking the nationalist Chicano@ ideal of familia. There are certainly exclusive and repressive ideologies at work in Mexican American portrayals of familia,[69] which can readily be seen here, but what I draw attention to in these photographs (figs. 24, 25, and 26) is their highly circumscribed quality, dependent almost exclusively on establishing a racial identity for Chican@ activists that challenged the alleged identification stemming from the inquest hearings—the rhetorical

Fig. 24. Photograph of man and child at the Chican@ Moratorium, published in the special issue of *La Raza*, 1970. Permission to reproduce images from *La Raza* granted by Joe Razo. Courtesy of UCLA Chicano Research Center.

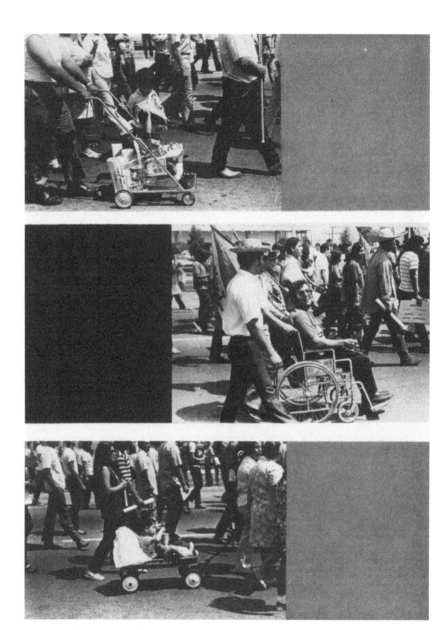

Fig. 25. Photograph of marchers at the Chican@ Moratorium, published in the special issue of *La Raza*, 1970. Permission to reproduce images from *La Raza* granted by Joe Razo. Courtesy of UCLA Chicano Research Center.

Fig. 26. Photograph of bride and groom at the Chican@ Moratorium, published in the special issue of *La Raza*, 1970. Permission to reproduce images from *La Raza* granted by Joe Razo. Courtesy of UCLA Chicano Research Center.

problem the special issue set out to resolve. The photographs in the special issue emphasized the presentation of Chican@ subjects as an intergenerational, nonviolent political community unlike the LAPD.

In these photographs, demonstrators appear in harmony with one another, not as a mass of indistinguishable actors. Chican@ activists appear self-determined, exemplifying the characteristics of the community posited and upheld by "El Plan Espiritual de Aztlán."[70] They are a distinct community operating on their own terms and in clear contrast to the expectations set up by newspapers and the publicity of the inquest hearings. The full-page spread of a beaming bride and groom who joined the event after their wedding ceremony reinforces the generational and communally focused ethic of these demonstrators. This gathering in East LA, these photographs suggest, was not characterized by violent actions but rather by a concern for and advocacy on behalf of others and each other's future(s); the moratorium was, from its inception, a nonviolent, public demonstration; it could not, therefore, also be a cause of violent turbulence capable of ending lives.

Photographs highlighted the spread of and preference for nonviolence among Chican@ activists, which had been growing in the 1970s even among those who, like Reies López Tijerina, were the fieriest of activists.[71] The photographs of these Chican@ demonstrators, however, also contrasted sharply with another Chican@ movement activist calling for the acceptance of nonviolence—César Chávez. The issue's photographs depicted Chican@ movement nonviolent activism at the moratorium as untethered to and, indeed, independent of institutional whiteness. Portrayals of Chicanos carrying children, along with Chicanas pushing strollers, and the elderly being pushed in wheelchairs as the community marched, suggested that the collective agency of the movement was life-giving, invigorating, and energized by no one other than Chican@s involved in this demonstration. Characterized by deferral to one another, demonstrators supported and sustained their own political energies. This sampling of images, moreover, resisted claims that Chican@s were part of a "vocal minority" silencing reason, molded by lawlessness, or simply trying to "humiliate" the United States with unsubstantiated dissent. As Nixon claimed, "Let us be united for peace. Let us also be united against defeat. Because let us understand: North Vietnam cannot defeat or humiliate the United States. Only Americans can do that."[72] Just as the women reaching for the Chicanos at the doorway of the café on the cover page demonstrated de/colonial love, Chican@ demonstrators participating in the moratorium were a racial community comprised of individuals uninterested in war yet altogether committed to love and coming alongside one another for community's sake. Whatever antagonism might have been felt and witnessed at the moratorium, it was a product of the LAPD's service to the colonial spirit of the United States—the *polemos* guiding its actions in Viet Nam.[73] The racial character of the Chicano Moratorium was, fundamentally, *not violent*, and these photographs demonstrated that nonviolent political action was the rule, not the exception.

Following Ruiz's article in the middle of the issue, however, images of Chican@ activists in their self-determined positions nearly disappear and, instead, the LAPD features prominently. Chican@ activists show up in photographs, but they are shown to be *responding* to the LAPD and its violent maneuvers. But beyond simply documenting the actions of the LAPD, photographs present the opposing side of the juxtaposition with Chican@ activists. Instead of being guided by any kind of love, photographs of the LAPD exhibit a pervasive and unjustified paranoia. While my use of the term "paranoia" might suggest that I am regarding their actions as lacking rationality, I use the term as a way to capture a sense of overdetermined fear, as in an "excessive sense of fear" motivating (re)actions to threats real or imagined. Racially speaking, paranoia is also a constitutive feature of "white fragility," which hinders reasonable responses to diversifications of political communities.[74] Paranoia, moreover, was the terminology used by Chican@ activists to describe police brutality against Mexican Americans in California. Commenting on the killing of seventeen-year-old Jesse Salcedo in March 1969 by a police officer supposedly attacked by Salcedo, a teen who had a reputation for being a responsible young adult, *La Raza* stated:

> Police paranoia is rampant, it is part and parcel of racism and discrimination. It is triggered off when Mexican youth are seen enjoying themselves; it explodes when Mexican youth let it be known that they know their rights; it shows its ugliness when police see Mexican youth standing on corners as their fathers did before them, as Mexican men have always done as a part of their normal social interaction—or its modern version of weekend car cruising. Police paranoia is fed an [sic] encouraged by the approval of a racist Anglo society, a society that has always exploited Mexicans and murdered them when they've fought against brutality.[75]

Whether or not the LAPD was *authorized* to use force at the moratorium was irrelevant in the special issue. Rather, the issue's photographic representations cast doubt on the *legitimacy* of the LAPD's use of violence by reconfiguring their reactions as a demonstration of fear rather than a result of misapplied "techniques" against actual threats—a claim insisted upon nearly forty years after this moment.[76]

To amplify this question of legitimacy, photographs narrowed in on how the fatal violence ignited at the moratorium would likely have occurred with or without provocation from Chican@ demonstrators. And, given the publicity of Salazar's death, photographs cemented the LAPD's paranoia as a root cause for his killing. One photograph, for example, depicts the impromptu yet cavalier behavior of police officers outside the Silver Dollar Café, where there had been reports of a violent man wielding a weapon (fig. 27). One officer stands with his back toward the door (hardly the actions of someone dealing with a threat inside the café), while another points his weapon at the building, but not at anything in particular. Police officers, though present to engage with a threat inside, appear distracted by those posing no physical threats to them. The officer wielding a weapon lacks a readiness to shoot at the supposed gunman inside as he directs his attention toward the police

Fig. 27. Photographs of police at the Chican@ Moratorium, published in the special issue of *La Raza*, 1970. Permission to reproduce images from *La Raza* granted by Joe Razo. Courtesy of UCLA Chicano Research Center.

officer facing away from the doorway. Neither engages directly with the supposed threat.

While the photograph of the two disengaged officers might have suggested aloofness or justified claims that these officers lacked adequate training, two photographs on the page following this image in the special issue heighten the overdetermined fear consuming the LAPD at the August 29 Moratorium. The images place the doorway of the café at the center of the viewer's field of view, thus providing a "clear" picture of the threat inside the building (fig. 28). These photographs, which re-present police officers with perhaps more poise than what we have seen thus far, nonetheless also portray them as beginning to *militarize* both by adding police bodies and by furnishing vehicular support. In the first photograph, police bodies sprawl, each converging on the doorway either by standing outside pointing a weapon or by moving toward it but never entering. Although each officer appears to act on his own, their collective attention is directed at the doorway, which points to a concerted effort to act together in response to the (pre)supposed threat. In the second photograph, two police officers point their weapons while shielding themselves behind the opened doors of their sheriff's vehicle. The point

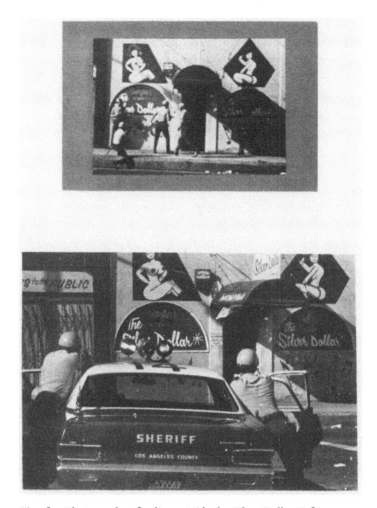

Fig. 28. Photographs of police outside the Silver Dollar Café, published in the special issue of *La Raza*, 1970. Permission to reproduce images from *La Raza* granted by Joe Razo. Courtesy of UCLA Chicano Research Center.

of view represented by the photographs compels viewers to stand behind the officers, forcing us to peer beyond the blackness of the doorway, toward the threat apparently in the shadows.

Although these photographs might depict different moments from that day, juxtaposing these images of the LAPD with those prior of Chican@ demonstrators surfaces the incommensurability between their respective political forms and the racial identity they conjure. Just as with conspiracy theorists, who are compelled to see more than is there,[77] these photographs painted the police officers' violent posture toward the darkness at the doorway of the café where Salazar lay lifeless inside as unwarranted by the "evidence." There was *no* threat inside, nor was there a threat *outside*. Rather, photographs captured a pervasive suspicion, noted by Escobar,[78] that had become prominent in the LAPD in the late 1960s and early 1970s, and through these photographs, the issue demonstrates how an unreasonable fear of someone inside the café had led the LAPD to kill Ruben Salazar. These photographs underscored how the LAPD might not have intended to kill Salazar specifically, but they nonetheless intended to kill *someone*. Focusing on re-presentations of the LAPD in the post-Ruiz article section, the issue displayed the (misguided) intentions of the LAPD to snuff out an unfamiliar not-whiteness from the public sphere.

Photographic depictions of the LAPD's presence outside the empty doorway of the café exhibited a paranoia toward the unfamiliar, and, having been given a (kairotic) opportunity to enact their paranoia, they unleashed fury on Chican@ bodies. After reproducing photographs of the police presence outside the Silver Dollar Café, the issue then featured images of the police brutality at Laguna Park, where the march ended. If the photomontage highlighted the interconnections between the LAPD's behavior and that of the United States in the Viet Nam War, the remaining photographs made the connection emphatic by showcasing the extent to which the United States warred against La Raza with impunity. Thus far, photographs had depicted the LAPD in a posture of war toward Chican@ bodies yet unengaged, resembling militaristic strategies of deterrence characterizing the United States' Cold War posture toward supposed enemies. Deterrence, a military script articulated by John Dulles during the Eisenhower administration, was a communicative act that induced a threat through imagination and visualizations,[79] but while it might appear that deterrence lacked a racial underpinning, namely by science and machine, the nuclear race also relied on othering not-Western nations.[80] These photographs in the final pages, though isolating a local event, highlight the racial motivations undergirding the LAPD's supposed deterrence of Chican@ bodies by showcasing its invasive, terrifying violence(s) against perceived threats. The "balance" created by the images revealed how at the intersection between East LA and Viet Nam was a racial violence perpetrated by whiteness against not-whiteness at all scales. The violence of the moratorium and the judgment of the inquest hearing exemplified, one article claimed, "the abuse of power and the legalized injustice of white supremacy" ("supremacia blanca"). The racially motivated injustice at the moratorium was the same injustice that prevented Chican@s from finding freedom at home even while they fought for democracy in Viet Nam.[81] In East LA, on August 29, 1970, the violence perpetrated by the LAPD put in stark relief the ruthlessness with which whiteness was defended in the United States and around the world. Whiteness politics trumped not-white alternatives anywhere it might be adopted, and, during the moratorium, the LAPD declared war on nonviolent politics with a brutal show of force.

Following a multi-paged commentary on the inquest hearing titled "La Farsa del 'Inquest'" ("The Farce of the 'Inquest'"), photographs pit the invasive violence of the Los Angeles police force against Chican@ nonviolence (fig. 29). Three images, which all share a page, reinforced the issue's linking together of the events in East LA and the Viet Nam War through depictions of the violence perpetrated against Chican@ bodies at the moratorium. Police officers are shown handling not-white protestors aggressively and, in stark ways, putting on a spectacle for spectators forced to watch the violence. And, along with those spectators, readers are compelled to watch the LAPD's show of force as well. Chican@s appear as onlookers throughout, whether men, women, or children, while the issue positions the brutality of the LAPD at the center of readers' fields of view. The third image, however, forwards a stark contrast between Chican@s and the LAPD at the moratorium. The image shows a police officer thrusting his hands inside of a Chicano's mouth. The Chicano man lacks a shirt and is pinned down against a vehicle. He does not resist, and his eyes appear closed, even as the police officer applies pressure to the Chicano's face and torso. The police officer pins the Chicano's body to the car with his forearm and shoves his fingers inside the protestor's mouth while holding his baton in the same hand, which suggests a hastiness and fervor in the police officer's actions. Police in the background observe the encounter between Chicano and police officer, much like Chican@s in the other images do, and, just like them, police officers do not intervene. That Chican@s and police spectate in similar ways suggests that both are acclimated to this kind of treatment.

Chican@ protestors offer no resistance to this invasion, and, in many ways, evince with compelling lucidity the juxtaposition of the issue. In full view of readers, the police officer treats the Chicano's body as a cavity to be searched, an opening to be pried apart. The Chicano man becomes una herida abierta, "an open wound,"[82] personally resolved to endure the officer's violence against him by matching it with nonviolent action. Although these brown bodies are

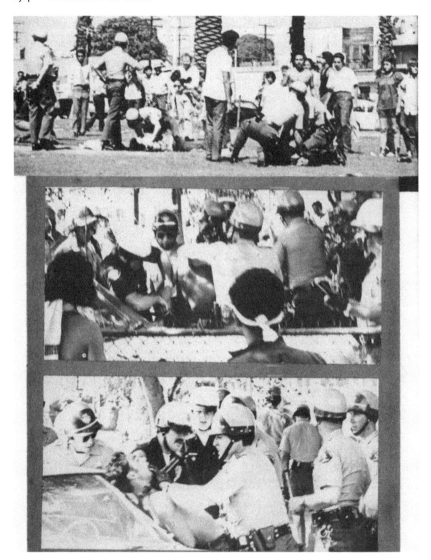

Fig. 29. Photographs of police engaging with Chican@s at Chican@ Moratorium, published in the special issue of *La Raza*, 1970. Permission to reproduce images from *La Raza* granted by Joe Razo. Courtesy of UCLA Chicano Research Center.

treated with ambivalence, with an ambiguity that marks their brownness as other,[83] Chican@ demonstrators directly face the LAPD, who appear as their aggressive colonizers. As Bernadette Calafell has argued, brownness implicates the global and imperial in stark ways in localized moments,[84] and in these photographs the brown bodies of Chican@ demonstrators emerge as a site at which the coloniality exemplified by the LAPD asserts a violent yet fragile control in East Los Angeles on behalf of institutional(ized) whiteness. Chican@ nonviolence contrasts sharply with the demonstration of violence by the LAPD. Yet the significance of Chican@ nonviolent activism shown prior to the Ruiz article and shown here is that this nonviolence is not only mobilizing but also revelatory of the wrath of institutional whiteness. Refusal to act in kind to the violence of the LAPD illuminates the increasing ferocity of institutional whiteness that Chican@s resisted in their moratorium. The LAPD, with its militarized invasion of Laguna Park, was not an objective force keeping "law and order." If anti-war resistance was, as Nixon claimed, a representation of a minority imposing its "point of view" on the rest of the nation, these photographs contended that institutional whiteness was a far more imposing and "humiliating" force in the United States.[85] These photographs displayed a sharp contrast between a nonviolent Chican@ politics and a violent whiteness politics.

One more set of photographs reinforces the violent aggression of whiteness typified by the LAPD. In another pair of photographs spread across two pages, the issue juxtaposes the physical pressures applied by the LAPD on Chican@s otherwise acting nonviolently. This pressure, the photographs suggest, incited a frenzy of Chican@ actions, none of which were directed at police, but which were, nonetheless, induced by the police force at the event (fig. 30). Spliced together, the photos depict an entire scene in chaos. Chican@s are shown running away as they try to escape police following from behind them (on the left side of the image). Some Chican@s appear as if they are about to fall, while others are shown running and looking back at the police right behind them. Foregrounded, too, are police officers appearing as if they are in front of these runners, although these officers are positioned on the right side of the image. Chican@ protestors appear visibly agitated, and with the police officers behind them and in front of them, the cause of their physical movements is implied—they are being hemmed in by the police.

The energies depicted in the photographs could not be any more divergent and, at the same time, the similarities between this moment during the moratorium and the Viet Nam War are the most resonant. With their backs toward the action but still occupying space within it, police in the foreground demonstrate an alarming aloofness, a disarming lack of movement despite standing right in the middle of the action. Their lack of movement contrasts sharply with the frenetic movement of Chican@s in the middle of the photograph. Police bodies invade the space, despite having no apparent

Fig. 30. Double-page spread of a scene at the Chican@ Moratorium, published in a special issue of *La Raza*, 1970. Permission to reproduce images from *La Raza* granted by Joe Razo. Courtesy of UCLA Chicano Research Center.

reason or purpose for being there, and it is Chican@s who carry the brunt of that disinterest. Anti-war demonstrations at the turn of the decade were predicated on a belief that the United States had no legitimate reason to be in Viet Nam and yet was sending troops to Southeast Asia anyway. Similarly, although Mexican Americans believed that they had no compelling "reason" to fight in the war themselves, they were personally subjected into a warring posture on behalf of the US and its coloniality. And, just as the presence of the LAPD at the moratorium ignited the frenzy that ensued and, ultimately, caused the violence that killed Ruben Salazar, Gilberto Diaz, and Lyn Ward, so too were Chican@s subjected to untimely and unprovoked deaths in Viet Nam. This photographic spread, in stark terms, depicts how Chican@s resisting the war did so because they were directly in the line of sight of the United States.

Mexican Americans had little hopes of breaking free, as oppressors pressured them from both sides, imprisoning them domestically and drafting them into international conflict without much recourse for escape. La Raza was in a predicament that could not be escaped except by refusing to play the game in the first place: by throwing away draft notices. Nonviolent activism did not necessarily induce nonviolent responses, nor did a politics of nonviolence mean the accomplishment of objectives. Regrettably, nonviolence, in contexts of violence, proves its ineffectiveness by failing to transform violence directly. The images suggest that a praxis of nonviolent militance is never a "safe" option, particularly for those racialized as other than "white."

Institutional whiteness is always and already violently ambivalent to the nonviolent politics of not-white persons.

Conclusion

Leveraging the death of Ruben Salazar and the opportunity created by the public inquest hearing, photographs circulated in the special issue of *La Raza* magazine (re)racialized Mexican American bodies by demonstrating how La Raza comprised a community under siege in multiple spaces and across scales. Spurred by the immediate violence concluding the moratorium and responding to the racial expectations of non/violence, the special issue linked Ruben Salazar's death, the moratorium, and the Viet Nam War by showing how Mexican Americans were objects of colonial violence in all of them. Although it might be tempting to treat each of these spaces as unrelated, the violence that ensued on August 29, 1970, was an event dedicated to exposing the violence(s) of the Viet Nam War. This cannot be overlooked or dismissed. Salazar himself was opposed to the Viet Nam War and, like other Chican@s, viewed it as a tragedy for the broader Mexican American community.[86] The special issue's photographs, through juxtaposition, put into view the resonances between the violence experienced at home and abroad in the Viet Nam War vis-à-vis institutional whiteness. The LAPD's aggression, paranoia, and invasive militarism were not all that different from the actions of the United States in Southeast Asia. The special issue highlighted these interconnections, even while focusing on non/violence on August 29, 1970, in East LA. The issue made clear that whatever fatal violence might have *included* Chican@s, was not through that association, *induced* by Chican@ activists. On the contrary, Chican@s cultivated love and concern for one another and their communities. Whatever violent actions might have involved Chican@s, whatever physical violations might have been perpetrated against them, and whatever force(s) might have energized their deaths in Southeast Asia, was not due to their own making.

The aesthetics of the issue's photographs, at the same time, were consequences of the racist visual cultures made manifest by the public controversy over who was to blame for the violence. That is, the racial negotiations displayed in the special issue were not simply part of an attempt to "project" a Chican@ identity. Such a view neglects the artistry and resistance with which the Chican@ photographic operates. The photographs were not merely documentations of the August 29 moratorium. Rather, there were discernible aesthetic choices made in the ways in which photographs were arranged, published, and spliced. Each of these aesthetic choices reinforced incommensurability and opposition and, in so doing, made visible what I call here and elsewhere a poetics of deferral. Although the issue issued positive manifestations of identity, the negation of the violence of institutional whiteness emerged as a critical feature of the identity it publicized. From the death of Ruben Salazar to the injuries inflicted on numerous other Chican@ men, women, and children, white police officers as representatives of institutional(ized) whiteness asserted their bodily presence and, in this sense, institutional whiteness induced the aesthetic of Chican@ movement(s) witnessed in *La Raza* magazine. By showcasing how police officers were active in their aggression and passive in their interventions during the moratorium, the special issue's visual rhetoric demonstrated how "objective" accounts of the violence by institutions were racially motivated and far from neutral. As the article titled "Chicanos and the War" argued, "police misreported the death of Ruben Salazar repeatedly, and their story is still confusing and contradictory."[87] Chican@s were not responsible for the violence at the moratorium, nor were they to blame for Salazar's death. The aesthetics of the issue suggested that only an aggressive, paranoid, and invasive whiteness could have produced such destructive upheaval in Los Angeles that ultimately killed someone who was trying to escape it. By juxtaposing Chican@s and the LAPD at the moratorium, the special issue exposed how the racial identity of Chican@ demonstrators was both independent of and dependent on whiteness. Only when the violence of the LAPD was made visible could the nonviolent identity of La Raza come to the fore. Only when seeing the whiteness of that violence could the politics of La Raza come into clear focus.

Viewing the importance of contrast to the issue's (re)racialization of Mexican American bodies, the aesthetics of the special issue exemplify a more profound articulation of the poetics of deferral than Chávez's fast-breaking speech calling explicitly for nonviolent activism. Chávez's speech, which might have approached the issue of non/violence with similar intentions as the editors of *La Raza*, nonetheless chose a means predicated on individuality and isolation. That is, his decision to fast, though rhetorically powerful, was nonetheless an isolating event that split him off from the rest of the community as much as it might have also been a point of mobilization. In the special issue, the poetics of deferral was shot through with communality, and while it might have been more "antagonistic" than Chávez's portrayals, the

Fig. 31. Back cover of a special issue of *La Raza*, 1970. Permission to reproduce images from *La Raza* granted by Joe Razo. Courtesy of UCLA Chicano Research Center.

use of juxtaposition to highlight the power of nonviolent activism generated a more powerful appeal than Chávez's fast or his "Speech Breaking the Fast." Although perhaps not as welcoming as Chávez might have been, the special issue's representation of non/violence, at the least, demonstrated how nonviolent militance constituted the very politics of Chican@ movement activism.

And understanding the racial politics of Chican@ movement(s) was perhaps why Chican@ moratoriums were needed after all. Chican@ moratoriums highlighted how the Viet Nam War represented the tip of the iceberg when it came to physical violences experienced by Mexican Americans in the United States. Unmitigated violence had long been a dominant force with which Mexican Americans grappled, largely in invisible spaces. Now, during the Viet Nam War, Chican@s were showing how public that violence was. Eschewing it was not merely "unpatriotic." Resisting the Viet Nam War was a matter of survival amid unrelenting threats. The back cover reinforced this threat facing Mexican Americans by repeating a photograph of police facing a darkened doorway from behind their vehicle (fig. 31). As if pointing their weapons at the contents of the issue, the image once more evinced how violence from the LAPD was always and already ready to be used against Chican@ bodies, sexualized and gendered, as the full view of the near-naked women on the wall of the building implies. The LAPD, in place to enforce US coloniality, would continue to do so against *all kinds* of perceived foreignness, and it would be up to Chican@s to endure if there was to be a "movement" in the 1970s at all.

CONCLUSION

In 1971, Armando Rendón published *Chicano Manifesto*, a text tracing the politics of La Raza from its indigenous roots in pre-Columbian Mexico to its Chican@ form(s) in the mid- to late 1960s. Forwarding Chican@ movement(s) as, fundamentally, *racial* movements, Chican@ politics, in Rendón's assessment, "strikes at the myths of Anglo supremacy" and, at the same time, "discards the Anglo-or-nothing value system."[1] Publishing an image of the mestiz@ head on the book's cover page, referring to Mexican Americans as La Raza throughout the text, and dedicating the text to the memory of Ruben Salazar, whose death yet lingered after the Chicano Moratorium in 1970 (see chapter 6), Rendón's book reinscribed much of the racial rhetorical work we have traced thus far and even gestured toward its variations (the "Appendix" included multiple Plans such as the Plan de Delano and El Plan Espiritual de Aztlán). By the turn of the decade, Chican@ movement discourse(s) had reached a critical mass of acceptance, and in Rendón's proclamation we witness an effort to solidify Chican@ movement arguments, figures, vocabularies, ideologies, and politics.

Although the publication of *Chicano Manifesto* exhibited an appreciation of and corroboration with Chican@ movement(s), Rendón's reckoning with the violence of the Chicano Moratorium undercut his praise. For, in his view, the violence witnessed at the Los Angeles Moratorium was as damaging to Chican@ politics as it was tragic because Chican@ activists, in part, were to blame. As he described it, the violence at the August 1970 Chicano Moratorium "was not a positive, premeditated effort. It was, essentially, an outburst of anger and frustration, a reaction to a police riot. It was the largest and most destructive of any police-barrio confrontation to date. It was probably the last. But, because of its ultimately self-destructive nature, such an act, however, justified, must be considered outside of constructive, sane Chicano activism."[2] Although Rendón might have viewed the violence at the

Chicano Moratorium as a legitimate response to the "police riot," his attempt to exclude it from "constructive, sane Chicano activism" appeared to absolve the LAPD for their role in inciting the violence. Nodding toward dominant narratives *La Raza*'s special issue contested—namely, that Chican@ movement activists were responsible for the outbreak of violence at Laguna Park—Rendón's comments implied that the death of Salazar occurred as a result of Chican@ activists' "outburst." Voiding the politics stemming from the Chicano Moratorium of any positive content, he effectively silenced the nonviolent postures that movement activists and the special issue in *La Raza* espoused. In doing so, Rendón upheld the LAPD's show of force against Chican@ bodies.

Nevertheless, the publication of Rendón's *Chicano Manifesto* once more underscores the flux constituting the Chican@ movement(s)' racial project that this book has traced between 1965 and 1970. Though affirming pernicious forms of systemic whiteness oppressing Mexican American racial and political formation, Rendón's text typified a negotiation of antecedent Chican@ movement rhetorics and an attempt remake them at the same time. In his own words, Chican@s must "make a conscious assessment of the enemy who very often has used our internal problems to his benefit, as well as devising his own methods to hinder our development as individuals as a group. I speak of the Anglo, of his institutions, of his manipulation of the media and of the minds."[3] Yet, as I conclude this book's rhetorical history, I spotlight Rendón's text to underscore one final poetic taking shape at the start of the 1970s that, once more, underlines both coherence and dissonance in the Chican@ movement racial project even as it appears to concretize in new ways in a new decade. Fueled, in part, by the effectiveness of widespread Latinx activism (including but not limited to that by Mexican Americans) in the 1960s,[4] Chican@ activists also shifted aesthetic gears. In these final pages, I set this poetic turn against the poetics witnessed between 1965 and 1970, since it both elaborated upon them and set in place a distinct trajectory in the decades that followed. Surfacing in Rendón's text but certainly proliferating elsewhere, this aesthetic turn typified a fresh attempt to firm up the outlines of racial identity by what I refer to as a *poetics of mimesis*, a rhetorical "miming" of coloniality's identificational interventions.[5] Keeping in mind how political identities in the Western Hemisphere were and are established and sustained vis-à-vis proactive institutionalization,[6] Mexican American rhetorics in the 1970s invested in formulating a racial identity within arenas typically upholding colonial rule as a mode of survival. As I draw this study of the pivotal years of Chican@ movement(s) to a close, I showcase this particular poetic maneuver in the Chican@ movement racial project to illustrate an ineluctable rhetorical problematic in racial formation(s) involving Latinx communities more broadly. That challenge entails an irresistible pull toward ossification by definition, exposition, and circumscription, and it takes place in institutional arenas of various sorts: publishing houses, universities, political parties, and national organizations. Indeed, attempts to *secure* identity and not simply *form* it is a bulwark of coloniality's tendency to pronounce identity by fiat.[7] This mimetic push, I suggest in these remaining pages, began to permeate Mexican American politics in the 1970s as activists sought not only to participate in racial formation but to secure its production among activists and adherents of Chican@ movement discourse(s). Though these efforts could, in the end, obtain no stable product, aesthetic turns giving form to a poetics of mimesis gave the appearance that it could, and, in turn, drew firm lines where none could exist.

Just a word of clarification before proceeding. There will be some readers who take my final remarks here as not really "conclusive" but, rather, as being like a separate case study. Certainly, this "Conclusion" will read like that at times. However, in structuring my concluding remarks in this way, I hope to introduce some undecidability to the rhetorical history I have proposed thus far. That is, while this book has offered a rhetorical history of a particular time frame, it is simply one way to compose this particular history. The rhetorical history I have provided here is also a *revisable* history. Viewed in this way, the conclusion of this book should be taken to be, in part, a review of this book's chapters, and, in another way, an invitation to consider how a rhetorical history capturing the 1970s might be accomplished.

Institutionalizing Chican@ Movement(s): The Appeal of Mimesis

Rendón's choice of title, *Chicano Manifesto*, illustrates a push toward securing rather than forming a racial identity for Mexican Americans. The singular, gendered terminology ("Chicano") proposed to capture the entire span of Mexican American politics throughout millennia, and from this solitary source, the "Chicano," the text issued a discrete claim to all of *his* political ideologies ("Manifesto"). The book, though recognizing a plethora of political sources constituting Chican@ movement(s) in the 1960s, including the crucial Chicana arm of Chican@ movement(s),[8] nonetheless consolidated all its historical touchstones and voided them of their particularities in an attempt to magnify the politics of La Raza for all time and all places. Distilling an apparent identity *sui generis* for Chican@ politics in and through his text, Rendón crushed its manifold rhetorical impulses in favor of a sweeping metonymy. Rendón's book, in other words, limited what "counted" as Mexican American racial politics by offering a definition of what Chican@ politics is, which, in turn, articulated clearly what it was not.

Of course, it could be argued that Gonzales's "I Am Joaquin," and its poetics of ambivalence (see chapter 3), also proposed the same kind of universal identity for Mexican Americans as Rendón's *Chicano Manifesto*. After all, was not the collective *accumulation* supporting the invention of the "Joaquin" metaphor just as homogenizing as "Chicano Politics," and the "epic" a fabrication of a singular historical narrative intended to represent all Mexican Americans in the United States Southwest?[9] Attending closely to the aesthetics characterizing these texts, however, reveals crucial distinctions between Gonzales's "I Am Joaquin" and the poetics of mimesis guiding texts like Rendón's *Chicano Manifesto* in the 1970s. As I argued in chapter 3, the poetics of ambivalence represented in the aesthetics of Gonzales's poem erupted racial categories imposed by coloniality on Mexican American communities through dividing lines, language codes, and middle-passive verbs. Yet this aesthetic subversion accomplished in and by the publication of "I Am Joaquin" in 1967 surfaces with greater lucidity when we consider that the 1972 publication followed a similar poetics of mimesis. It too compelled a singular history and exemplified an attempt to consolidate Mexican American politics within the singular heading for the purpose of providing a "fine introduction to Chicano culture." Publishers of the 1970s popular text, too, claimed that they had been "deeply moved and impressed by it."[10] Though promising to keep a similar aesthetic for this book form of Gonzales's "I Am Joaquin,"[11] Bantam's final publication spanned at least 122 pages—a tome when compared to the 22-page original—with an appendix detailing "Mexican-American history" and a selection of photographs and illustrations provided not by activists but by Anne Novotny of Research Reports.[12] Promising to keep the cost of the book at about seventy-five cents "so that most young people could afford it," the aesthetics of the 1972 reproduction of Gonzales's text reflected the economics of coloniality and the institutional arrangements supporting the colonial matrix of power that were notably absent from the original publication. Aesthetic differences, in short, distinguish the politics and de/colonial emphasis of publications, which, in turn, means that their *poetics* were also notably, if not drastically, different.

But what of Aztlán? Was not the creation of this synecdoche for all Mexican Americans in the Southwest just as totalizing? Furthermore, was not

Aztlán in need of "queering" on account of its offering a more comprehensive vision than it actually delivered? As a metaphor, yes, "El Plan Espiritual de Aztlán" implied a singular subjectivity for Mexican Americans that coincided with a particular political program in nationalism. However, as I argued in chapters 4 and 5, whether in New Mexico or in California, the reception and proliferation of the myth was not yet quite as exclusive as later applications, nor was it merely reproduced without adjustment. Activists who attended the Chican@ Youth Liberation Conference (CYLC) and departed took to composing a more dappled Aztlán than the nationalist plan that appeared in some reproductions in the Chicano Press Association (CPA). The circulation of El Plan and the aesthetic configurations of publications broadcasting its existence exhibited more incoherence than coherence as activists were split in their decision to publish the prologue and/or reproduce the nationalist plan. As a point of contrast with the way that later movement activists broached republishing the Plan in the 1970s, one can consider the differences between those reproductions published in the CPA and that found in the anthology edited by Stan Steiner and Luis Valdez in 1972.[13] The anthology, titled *Aztlan: An Anthology of Mexican American Literature*, positioned Aztlán as a transcendent label capturing not a "people" *per se* but a literature, a move that elevated "Aztlán" beyond the activism and the rhetoric that birthed it—outside the "scramble," so to speak, and into the stratosphere of intellectual curiosity. Anthologized and published outside of its previous newspaper space, El Plan Espiritual de Aztlán was granted *canonical* status that prior publications did not seem to consider. Infusing Aztlán with a homogenizing power, the anthology shored up the boundaries of the figure and, in so doing, amplified its exclusive potentials. Refusing illustrations with the publication, too, distilled its rhetorical work into verbal, alphabetic rhetoric alone—the epitome of Western communication.[14] Taking the publication of an anthology as its own aesthetic arena, relocating what otherwise existed as a grassroots and malleable text, we can see how crucial aesthetic adjustments are to the politics engendered by a particular text. An anthology sanitizes the text in ways that might not have been possible in the pages of *El Grito del Norte*. To treat them identically is, tragically, to miss their political contributions.

Yet the poetics of mimesis I am proposing for understanding the shifts seen in the 1970s occurred during the "Chicano Renaissance,"[15] a period in which it was claimed that literature stemming from Chican@ movement(s) would contribute a new kind of identity for the "American" experience.[16] The creation of these texts in the 1970s, however, divorced Chican@ movement discourses from the appeal(s) of *movement* activism and in its place substituted institutional arrangements not built for publicizing rhetorics from marginalized communities. Consequently, popular publishing houses Bantam Publishers, Vintage Books, and the MacMillan Company circulated Mexican American political texts like "I Am Joaquin" and El Plan Espiritual de Aztlán without their decisively racial politics. Even Rendón's *Chicano Manifesto*, which positioned Chican@s as an anti-Anglo and anti-Black community, claimed that Chican@s' "racial heritage" equipped them with a unique capacity for developing a flourishing multiculturalism for US life. Rendón added: "Chicanos can approach the crisis of races that torments America as the single group in the nation which represents, with our brother raza, broad racial and cultural integration. Chicanos must explore the multicultural and multiracial wellsprings of la raza Chicana."[17] Rendón's portrayal of Chican@ racial identity, though cast as an alternative to systemic whiteness, also reproduced its priorities without the violence that typically accompanies such explicit revolutionary claims (see chapter 6). Instead of pluriversality, Rendón interposed the "Chicano" as a universal substitution. Chican@ politics offered not an "option" but universality.[18]

The poetics of mimesis engulfing the Chican@ movement(s)' racial project at the turn of the decade, nevertheless, was fueled by the success and spread of institutional arrangements claiming to enact Chican@ movement(s)' goals. The Plan de Santa Barbara, written and published in 1969 as momentum for the birth and proliferation of departments, research centers, and scholarly inquiry into Chican@ experiences gained traction,[19] argued for the installation of the Chican@ "revolution" in higher education. Claiming that the "institutionalization of Chicano programs is the realization of Chican@ power on campus,"[20] the Plan de Santa Barbara *in form* exemplified the rhetorics of prior Plans while yet advocating for Chican@s to have a space at the table of academia. Proponents of Chican@ studies programs leveraged the expansion and proliferation of Chican@ activism to pressure higher education into acceding to their demands for equal and adequate representation in the academy.[21] Moreover, the creation of academic journals such as *Aztlán*, which bolstered the print media boon of the 1960s that also benefited the expansion of the CPA, augmented and legitimized the scholastic contributions of scholar-activists inquiring into Mexican American experiences in the United States.[22] By all accounts the institutional integration witnessed in the 1970s evinced an intellectual realignment that has expanded to include even more Latinx communities in the present day. My intent in rehearsing this academic narrative is not to enter debates about the practical orientations or lack thereof of Chican@ studies programs, as some scholar-activists believed these programs ought to do (and the Plan de Santa Barbara strongly implied). Rather I simply point out that these programs were consequences of Chican@ movement activism and, consequently, intimately tied to it.

Although Chican@ studies scholars have since reckoned with the ways in which integration in higher education impacted Chican@ movement energy and its current forms, the poetics of mimesis witnessed vis-à-vis institutionalization in higher education reinscribed the authorizing power of institutional structures in the attempt to plant Chican@ studies within its soil. Viewed pragmatically, these integrative moves evinced victories; successful pushes against white bureaucracy and systemic violations against Mexican Americans in intellectual circles.[23] Viewed aesthetically, however, these successes can also be attributed to a miming that increased the appeal of Chican@ movement activism according to the style of the white, European academy—a rhetorical move reaching back to scholarly inquiry of "Latin America" after colonization.[24] The attempt to enter the academy instilled a relationship with coloniality's structures that also installed a commitment to upholding it. And, as I have written elsewhere, attempts to secure a Mexican American focused education were met with fierce resistance.[25]

Finally, a poetics of mimesis suffusing Chican@ politics in the 1970s also became manifest in the formation of La Raza Unida Party (LRUP). As I discussed in chapter 5, the success of the CYLC and the invention of "Aztlán" in 1969 spawned visions of decolonization and nation-building among Mexican Americans. Although community organizations like the National Farm Workers Association, the Crusade for Justice, La Alianza, and the Mexican American Youth Organization (MAYO) all had, in some respects, regional if not national aspirations in terms of their reach and scope, those ambitions took a more institutionalizing form after 1969 with attempts to create an official political party that might compete with Democrats and Republicans for Mexican American representation within US electoral politics. The potential for Mexican Americans to vote en bloc and leverage an untapped voting power had been teased in the early 1960s in Crystal City, Texas, after a slate of five Mexican American candidates replaced white incumbents on the city council. Building on the traction of Chican@ movement energies in the late 1960s, the renewed effort to create an official party earned wide appeal as a means of realizing a self-evident political power. The formation of a political party promised to uphold that energy by offering genuine "representation" that Democrats and Republican parties had apparently refused. As literature put out by MAYO described it, the lack of political representation from Democratic and Republican parties required an "alternative to the presently established parties . . . an alternative that recognizes the existence of culturally distinct Peoples and their right to maintain their identity . . . an alternative that advocates for the equal representation of all Peoples."[26] That "alternative" was a party dedicated to La Raza.

The decision to develop an "alternative" political party, however, was fundamentally an aesthetic move that cut in two opposing directions. For, on the one hand, the LRUP affirmed a growing political potency tied to Chican@ movement(s). An "official" party with a corresponding political platform staged the growth of Chican@ movement(s) and their mobilizing potency publicly, and it affirmed in earnest the acceptance of Chican@ movement(s)' political figures (Aztlán) and terminology (La Raza). On the other hand, the promotion of a registered political party, in some ways, represented a return to the originating moment of Chican@ movement(s), coinciding with a "conservative" arm of the movement like the NFWA. From this vantage point, we might view the formation of the LRUP as a *return* to incipient Chican@ movement principles and a *reversal* of a de/colonial trend in Chican@ movement(s). That is to say, the creation of the LRUP, in the name of an "alternative" within established institutional arrangements, retuned de/colonial politics that had begun to push for decolonization. The creation of the LRUP, understood in this sense, was a corrective of sorts, representing a push and a pull in the de/colonial operations energizing the Chican@ movement racial project. Even if the fulfillment of Aztlán was, according to activist José Gutierrez, an inspiration for LRUP and its apparent revolutionary claims, in *form*, the LRUP was not quite as "alternative" as it might have appeared.

The Problematic(s) of a Racial Politics

As a point of comparison and contrast to the poetics guiding Chican@ movement(s) between 1965 and 1970, I have suggested that an aesthetic shift toward mimesis began to take shape after these years and that this shift distinguished the rhetorical features of Chican@ movement(s) from what we saw in the mid- to late 1960s. In analyzing the aesthetics of Chican@ movement rhetorics across space and time, we can see the Chican@ movement racial project was constituted by continuity as well as notable difference(s). What we typically identify as "the" Chican@ movement was a branched and multivalent event with many different parts, and movement rhetorics evolved as activists mobilized, moved across the Southwest, shared their experiences with others, and developed a shared vocabulary promoting political visions of the awakening of La Raza. There were certainly attempts to consolidate movement objectives into concrete, rigid forms, as was the case with the explicit nationalism of El Plan Espiritual de Aztlán and the turn toward institutionalization as movement(s) evolved, but even these programmatic aims were subjected to rhetorical negotiations and not adopted *tout court*. As this book has shown, there was, aesthetically speaking, space for disagreement within Chican@ movement(s), a range of approaches to establishing a political community of and for Mexican Americans. Chican@ movement rhetorics were far from stagnant, nor did they ever seem to ossify. They were multiple; varied; diffuse. Chican@ rhetorics emerging, thus, in the 1970s resonated with their antecedents even as new poetics were developing as well.

This point of contrast between the rhetorical trajectories of the 1970s and Chican@ movement(s)' rhetorics in the 1960s illuminates an inventional problematic sustained throughout Chican@ movement(s). This problematic was not necessarily due to Chican@ movement(s)' rhetorical intervention but, rather, linked to the t(r)opological status of "race" itself. Although it might be tempting to view poetic alterations in Mexican American politics between decades pragmatically, namely, as either a corruption of Chican@ movement politics or a consequence of strategic decisions made by activists, I propose that it might be more appropriate to interrogate how adopting "race" as a central figure affects rhetorical invention from its inception, warping rhetorical work just as much as it might be shaped by it. Viewed as a kind of *topos*, race lacks an elasticity that make it difficult to stretch too far. *Topoi* are, despite their inventional stirring, conservative and linked to community "common sense." These rhetorical "places" ramify social knowledge, rely on established lines of inquiry, and invoke familiar political energies for their persuasive potentials.[27] Despite allowing for or perhaps encouraging aesthetic reconfiguration, race, as a *topos*, carries a proper "locus of enunciation" through which race might be made legible or otherwise appealed to.[28] In a similar way, race's constrained malleability underlines how it also functions as a trope in addition to serving as an argumentative resource. Tropes necessarily invite ossification and immutability. For, without this inflexibility, tropes lose significance, void appeal, or, more crudely, lose "meaning." Race, in operating as a trope, cannot be stretched beyond figural boundaries regardless of how inventive the investment or how persistent the efforts to make it apply differently are. Race, as *topos* and trope, resists such efforts to remake race *in toto*. Race, as a rhetorical construct, might bend, but it does not break.

This resistance from and by "race" inhibits its rhetorical remaking and, for this reason, traps rhetorics participating in racial formation within an inventional circle pulling centripetally toward an aesthetic unyieldingly focused on the "White racial frame," a rhetorical position dedicated to upholding white communities, their perspectives, histories, and views on racialization.[29] Constitutive of coloniality's rhetorical paradigms, race is integral to coloniality's social and political organizations that establish firmly what Jacques Rancière refers to as a "distribution of the sensible."[30] This "distribution" locates certain bodies as colonized, inferior, unfit, and, racially, "other than" white. It is this pull toward whiteness that elucidates how whiteness survives when "racial neutrality" is claimed, or how an unstated category like that of the "honorary white" surfaces as a bulwark against anti-racist policies.[31] The de/colonial rhetorical work I have traced since the start of Chican@ movement(s), which took on various forms and spanned a spectrum ranging from political compatibility to decolonization, inevitably achieved an equilibrium along the axis of race. Construing "La Raza" might have involved appeals to indigeneity, cultural praxis, language, or even autochthony, but, as we have seen, racial rhetorics associated with the Chican@ movement racial project ebbed and flowed vis-à-vis a relationship with whiteness and, even where a focus on "La Raza" prevailed, there was a turn to accommodating the very *structures* set up for the erasure of not-white signs.

Race, consequently, should be understood *primarily* as a colonial construct, and it is this relationship to coloniality that cements race's status in our contemporary moment. Race, as much as the post-structuralist in me struggles to admit, might not qualify strictly as a "floating signifier," but rather might be better understood to be inextricably tethered to colonial structures that have been accreting and churning for hundreds of years. I have argued for how whiteness informed the trajectory of Chican@ movement(s) in the late 1960s elsewhere, but, as I point out there,[32] the ways in which race is imbricated in preexisting structures make it exceedingly difficult to disentangle and remake. Insisting on a consistent, inflexible, stable association between bodies and meanings that are themselves institutionally supported and violently construed, whether self-determined or not, has been and continues to be a colonial *imperative*. For this reason, I suggest, the Chican@ movement racial project, which included attempts to reimagine race, eventually succumbed to a poetics of mimesis that, in the end, made La Raza even more compatible with whiteness—a feature that ultimately gave rise to the problematic yet nearly unavoidable label "Hispanic" in the United States.[33] The rise and persistence of a "Hispanic Serving Institution" is one conspicuous example of the ways in which a racial label seemingly promising more attention also serves as a grounding for increased or, worse, condensed precarity.[34] The Hispanic Serving Institution, for all of its promise, does not and cannot provide an inclusive experience for those identified by it because the *figure* ("Hispanic") essentially institutionalizes exclusions. In the end, race belongs to coloniality, and colonial powers do not relinquish control quite so easily, if at all.

Indeed, so strong is coloniality's hold on race and its t(r)opology that attempts to (re)form or traverse sanctioned racial categories invite the execution of coloniality's strategy par excellence—violence. As we saw in chapter 6, the violence at the Chicano Moratorium was a watershed moment in Chican@ movement politics that left many renegotiating el movimiento and their place within it. So pivotal was this moment that Rendón felt compelled to issue a firm stance with respect to it in his *Chicano Manifesto*. Yet, as I have shown, violence against Mexican American bodies in their various forms, and uniquely so in the late 1960s during the Viet Nam War, applied an unavoidable pressure on the Chican@ movement racial project and the aesthetic formulations witnessed in print spaces. Violence(s) applied by institutions were set in place to uphold whiteness as an aesthetics for political life, eliminate signifiers of not-whiteness from the public sphere, and/or otherwise relegate not-whiteness to private spaces wherein its influence and suasiveness might be rendered inert. The Chican@ movement racial project was shaped, informed, and responsive to broad and public shows of bodily violence. Public violence was an energizing force for Chican@ movement rhetorics in this regard, and this influence becomes most visible when we view it as a response to a CMP working to reduce "Mexican Americans" to a caricature. Targeted physical violence provoked an inventive posture among Mexican Americans, both with respect to whiteness (for example, Californios) and not-whiteness (for example, Aztlán). Chican@ movement activists in the mid- to late 1960s parlayed violence targeting Mexican American bodies and applied to not-white bodies more generally into racial discourse(s) contesting US coloniality.

Consequently, the Viet Nam War, which took an aggressive turn in the middle of the 1960s, cannot be treated simply as circumstantial to Chican@ movement(s). Mexican Americans returned from fighting in Southeast Asia with troubled souls or in body bags, and, in turn, Chican@ movement rhetorics actively disclosed the racist undertones of the war that left Mexican Americans bearing, at least in their eyes, the brunt of a global US imperialism. Of course, there were domestic forms of violence applied on not-white bodies that movement rhetorics also brought to light. Some of these were material and others more symbolic. Yet after the Chicano Moratorium, which epitomized how Chican@ movement(s) matched the intensification of the Viet Nam War with its interweaving of anti-war resistance with the defense of Aztlán, we see corresponding alterations in Chican@ movement politics—the grounds of a poetic of mimesis surfacing in the 1970s. This book's study suggests that the Viet Nam War, which might have appeared to be simply a container for Mexican American activism in the mid- to late 1960s, was constitutive of Chican@ movement(s)' rhetorical forms and their broad appeal(s). The Chican@ movement racial project was globally significant because the violence shaping it was too.

Understanding the significance of the Viet Nam War in shaping the Chican@ movement racial project allows us to see the *global* stakes involved and claimed in racial formation. Certainly, as I pointed out in the Introduction, the Cold War emerged as a context in which racist categories were deployed to perpetuate war abroad and domestically, but even in our present day, the distribution of racial classifications and the apparent "rights" afforded to white communities over not-white persons surfaces clearly in moments where challenges to the racial order appear to surface. To cite a recent example of the global salience of racial categories, in summer 2021 what has since become known as the "Haitian Migrant Whip Controversy" incited shock and horror when US Border Patrol agents were seemingly witnessed (and photographed) whipping Haitian migrants trying to cross the Mexico-Texas border.[35] Images of agents on horseback appeared to show them using reins as makeshift whips to keep migrants from entering the United States. Although an investigation into the event eventually led to the conclusion that whips were not "forcefully" used (strictly defined) against Haitians, the *appearance* of force enacted against not-white bodies attempting to enter a border town highlights the ways in which racial formation is never *only* a local phenomenon or isolated even to national contexts. Rather, in line with the colonial impulse, race exists as a means of organizing the *entire* globe—regions, islands, and seas[36]—and, consequently, race informs and is informed by how the United States as a *global* power engages on an international stage with different bodies. If, as I have suggested in this book, race possesses a global relevance, then understanding how practices of racial formation operate not only in immediate contexts but within a wider international context cannot be ignored.

And, as we continue to unearth and digitize Chican@ texts for public viewing, it seems imperative to continue to interrogate their appeal for our own political moments. After all, contemporary communities, too, deal with racial violence, its legacies and traumas. This negotiation occurs and is made visible in aesthetic (re)formulations. In the mid- to late 1960s, a plethora of prominent and nameless activists came together to throw off fetters of systemic whiteness from Mexican American bodies in "unprecedented" ways. Although these, too, were problematic or were simply too small to have an enduring impact, de/colonial work cannot be judged solely in terms of its effectiveness. Indeed, de/colonial work is necessary because of the ways in which it alters discourse(s) *after* its emergence, as others negotiate it and, in so doing, rewrite it in new ways for new contexts. De/colonial work, after all, simply provides options that might not have existed otherwise. Whiteness was and continues to be an incredible and unbearable weight that calls for total submission, and, as this study suggests, only when many came together to unmask and unmake it in public did the possibility of dissolving its political stronghold materialize, spurred by a diversity of efforts, renegotiations, challenges, and disagreements. Such efforts were, in the end, made possible by a distinct power to see, a *dynamis* energizing different ways of reimagining public life—however much it might have also been tied to an inescapable status quo. Learning how to resist and repel the influence of systemic whiteness in our politics is a lesson with incalculable value in our present day. Learning that lesson from Mexican Americans? Is that not unprecedented?

NOTES

INTRODUCTION

1. Throughout *Becoming La Raza* I make use of terms in the Spanish language. When there are alternative spellings for technical terms (e.g., rasquache versus rascuache), I use spellings that appear frequently in academic literatures. When quoting, I leave "typos" or misspellings alone, but mark these for the reader. Similarly, I leave Spanish terms unitalicized unless found that way in source material. Doing so prevents othering the Spanish language. See Holling and Calafell, "Identities on Stage," 79n2. For the meaning of "presidente" as used here see Valdez's "The Tale of La Raza."
2. Griswold del Castillo and García, *Triumph of Spirit*, 84.
3. Levy, *Cesar Chavez*, 131.
4. Quoted in Torgerson, "Start of a Revolution?"
5. Quoted in Torgerson, "Start of a Revolution?"
6. Dalton, *Moral Vision*; Orosco, *Common Sense of Nonviolence*.
7. Levy, *Cesar Chavez*, 269–71; Izaguirre, "Nonviolence in Context."
8. Bebout, "Hero Making in El Movimiento."
9. Hammerback, Jensen, and Gutierrez, *War of Words*.
10. Mariscal, *Brown-Eyed Children*.
11. Delgado, "Chicano Movement Rhetoric"; McGee, "'Ideograph.'"
12. Ferris and Sandoval, *Fight in the Fields*, 140–41.
13. Minian, "Indiscriminate and Shameless Sex," 64.
14. Yinger, *Rhetoric of Nonviolence*.
15. Alaniz and Cornish, *Viva La Raza*, 155.
16. Until this point, I have been using the terms "Mexican American" and "Chican@" interchangeably. I will continue to do so throughout the book. I am doing this for two reasons. Most book-length monographs discussing the relationship between the Chican@ movement(s) and identity claims tend to follow social scientific stances and try to specify the defining characteristics of each, as well as the generational distinctions that distinguish them according to various degrees of assimilation. I do not find such distinctions to be all that helpful or necessary, particularly since Chican@ movement activists rarely followed such strict distinctions; sometimes, they simply reinvented meanings in accordance with rhetorical sensibilities (see chapter 3). The second reason, however, is that I have cast a wide net for what might "count" as Chican@ discourse. I adopt the perspective of Chican@ literature scholar Bruce-Novoa in this regard, who stated that he identified "Chicana/o" literature based on their association with "the socio-political civil rights struggle begun in the mid-1960s by and on behalf of people of Mexican descent living in the United States." Ultimately, he remarked, "Chicano movement is difficult to define to everyone's satisfaction." Carlos Gallego also argues that "Chicana/o" is a moniker whose circumference is actually much wider if we allow context, rather than nationalist impulses, to inform its construction. Still, Bruce-Novoa's summation captures my approach to Chican@ movement discourse as well, in that it "normally refer[s] to works published since 1965." See Gallego, "Identity to Situatedness"; Bruce-Novoa, *Chicano Authors*, 3.

17. Valdez, "Tale of the Raza."
18. Mariscal, *Brown-Eyed Children*, 178–79.
19. *El Grito Del Norte*, "To Our Readers."
20. Izaguirre, "Nonviolence in Context."
21. Bruce-Novoa, *Chicano Authors*, 3. To start with the farmworkers' movement in California might appear to be a simple adoption of "lore" as this project's starting point. I should note, however, that I am not the first or only scholar to accept this "beginning," nor is this inconsistent with Chican@ movement activists' perceptions of the "beginning" of this moment in the 1960s. My aim here is not to locate an origin, as much as it is to initiate a tracing of the racial underpinnings of Chican@ movement discourse(s). This means that, for the purposes of this rhetorical history, I chose a moment that has been widely recognized as pivotal in Chican@ movement history and has notable threads in later Chican@ movement discourse(s). Beginning with the farmworkers' strike in 1965 satisfies both of these criteria.
22. Mariscal, *Brown-Eyed Children*; Alaniz and Cornish, *Viva La Raza*.
23. Gómez-Quiñones, *Chicano Politics*; Vigil, *Crusade for Justice*; Mario García, *Chicano Generation*.
24. Ruiz, *Out of the Shadows*; Blackwell, *¡Chicana Power!*; Chávez-García, "Genealogy of Chicana History"; Izaguirre, "Movidas after Nationalism."
25. Gómez-Quiñones and Vásquez, *Making Aztlán*.
26. Chakravartty et al., "#CommunicationSoWhite"; Houdek, "Imperative of Race"; Wanzer-Serrano, "Rhetoric's Rac(e/Ist) Problems"; Sowards, "#RhetoricSoEnglishOnly"; Olson, "This Is America."
27. Gabriel and Goldstein, "Debate Over Scope"; Gabriel, "He Fuels Cultural Fires for the Right in Florida."
28. Sharpe, *In the Wake*.
29. Houdek, "In the Aftertimes."
30. "Refusing to Forget," https://refusingtoforget.org, accessed September 26, 2022.
31. Ore, *Lynching*.
32. Ore and Houdek, "Lynching in Times of Suffocation"; Ore, "Lost Cause."
33. Leff, "Interpretation"; Leff and Sachs, "Words the Most Like Things."
34. To highlight the endurance of this thesis, one has only to note that the most recent Sal Castro Memorial Conference in Santa Barbara, California, focused on "long history" as its central theme. See Interdisciplinary Humanities Center UCSB, "Sal Castro Memorial Conference on the Chicano Movement and the Long History of Mexican American Civil Rights Struggles," February 17–18, 2023, https://ihc.ucsb.edu/event/sal-castro-memorial-conference-on-the-chicano-movement-and-the-long-history-of-mexican-american-civil-rights-struggles.
35. Rodriguez, *Rethinking the Chicano Movement*, 23–24.
36. Acuña, *Occupied America*; Chávez, "*¡Mi Raza Primero!*"; Vigil, *Crusade for Justice*; Gómez-Quiñones and Vásquez, *Making Aztlán*.
37. Espinoza, Cotera, and Blackwell, *Chicana Movidas*; Rodriguez, *Rethinking the Chicano Movement*; Sowards, *¡Sí, Ella Puede!*
38. Flores, "Between Abundance and Marginalization," 5.
39. Omi and Winant, *Racial Formation*, 125.
40. Omi and Winant, *Racial Formation*, 109.
41. Cintrón, "Democracy and Its Limitations."
42. Quijano and Wallerstein, "Americanity as a Concept."
43. Quijano, "Coloniality of Power," 533.
44. García and Baca, "Possibility of Decolonial Options."

45. García and Cortez, "Trace of a Mark That Scatters"; Cortez and García, "Absolute Limit of Latinx Writing."
46. Ruiz and Sánchez, *Decolonizing Rhetoric and Composition Studies*.
47. Mignolo, *Darker Side of Western Modernity*.
48. Mignolo and Walsh, "Introduction." I insert a "/" between the prefix de- and coloniality because I find that that decoloniality and coloniality are inextricably linked to one another, as much as they might also exist in opposition. Decoloniality *presumes* coloniality, and coloniality *enables* decoloniality. The "/" signals the intimate interanimation as much as it suggests a distinction.
49. Mignolo, *Darker Side of Western Modernity*, 217.
50. Mignolo and Walsh, "Introduction," 3.
51. Mignolo, *Local Histories / Global Designs*, 85.
52. Mignolo, *Darker Side of Western Modernity*, 10.
53. Feagin and Cobas, *Latinos Facing Racism*; Feagin and Ducey, *Racist America*; Feagin, *White Racial Frame*.
54. Thiong'o, *Decolonising the Mind*, 2–3.
55. Tuhiwai Smith, *Decolonizing Methodologies*, 175.
56. Gallego, "Identity to Situatedness," 136–37.
57. Gallego, "Identity to Situatedness," 130–31.
58. Charland, "Constitutive Rhetoric."
59. Delgado, "Chicano Movement Rhetoric"; Flores and Hasian, "Returning to Aztlán and La Raza."
60. Holling and Calafell, "Introduction," xxii.
61. Flores, "Advancing a Decolonial Rhetoric," 320.
62. Wanzer-Serrano, *New York Young Lords*, 7–8.
63. Wanzer-Serrano, *New York Young Lords*, 86–87.
64. Rancière, *Politics of Aesthetics*.
65. Omi and Winant, *Racial Formation*, 13.
66. Ankersmit, *Aesthetic Politics*, 16.
67. Delgado and Stefancic, "Introduction."
68. Hariman, *Political Style*, 4.
69. I. García, *Chicanismo*, 8.
70. Kirby, "'Great Triangle'"; Kirby, "Aristotle's 'Poetics'"; Walker, *Rhetoric and Poetics*.
71. Rancière and Panagia, "Dissenting Words"; Mignolo, "Epistemic Disobedience."
72. Bruce-Novoa, *Chicano Poetry*; Arteaga, *Chicano Poetics*; Saldívar, "Towards a Chicano Poetics"; Saldívar, *Border Matters*; Izaguirre, "Nonviolence in Context."
73. cárdenas, *Poetic Operations*.
74. Bakhtin, *Problems of Dostoevsky's Poetics*.
75. Burke, *Counter-Statement*; Jasinski, *Sourcebook on Rhetoric*.
76. Mignolo, "Epistemic Disobedience."
77. Clay and Phillips, *Secret Location*.
78. Murphy, *Other Voices*, 86–87.
79. Warner, "Publics and Counterpublics."
80. Limón, "Border Literary Histories."
81. Hammerback and Jensen, "History and Culture as Rhetorical Constraints."
82. Holling, "Retrospective," 298.
83. Trouillot, *Silencing the Past*, 22–30.
84. Zarefsky, "Four Senses of Rhetorical History."
85. Jensen and Hammerback, "From Farmworker to Cultural Icon."

CHAPTER 1

1. Gómez, *Manifest Destinies*, 1, 5.
2. Gómez, *Manifest Destinies*, 4.
3. Feagin, *White Racial Frame*, 88.
4. Feagin, *White Racial Frame*, 11.
5. Hawhee and Olson, "Pan-Historiography," 93.
6. Griswold del Castillo, *Treaty of Guadalupe Hidalgo*, 1–14.
7. Hopkins, *American Empire*, 191.
8. Deopujari, "America's Manifest Destiny and Mexico," 494.
9. James K. Polk, "Special Message to Congress on Mexican Relations," May 11, 1846, https://www.presidency.ucsb.edu/node/200910.
10. "Treaty with the Republic of Mexico," February 2, 1848, https://memory.loc.gov/cgi-bin/ampage?collId=llsl&fileName=009/llsl009.db&recNum=975.
11. Hopkins, *American Empire*, 212–17.
12. Certainly, we might say that Polk used language implicating characteristics for Mexico other than race when discussing the need for the United States' involvement in the Mexican War, as Robert Ivie claims when explaining how Polk characterizes Mexico as "irrational" and US involvement as "rational" ("Progressive Form and Mexican Culpability"). However, after the signing of Treaty of Guadalupe in 1848, on more than one occasion, Polk appeals to Congress to defend white populations from "Indian savages" on the basis that doing so was "reasonable." This appeal to reasonability, suggests a latent yet *public* relationship between rationality and race. See James K. Polk, "Special Message," April 29, 1848. https://www.presidency.ucsb.edu/node/201563.
13. Ivie and Giner, *Hunt the Devil*.
14. Maldonado-Torres, *Against War*, 3.
15. Mignolo, *Local Histories / Global Designs*, 97.
16. Santoni, "Failure of Mobilization"; Stevens, *Origins of Instability*.
17. "Treaty with the Republic of Mexico," 929.
18. Quoted in Griswold del Castillo, *Treaty of Guadalupe*, 3.
19. Quijano, "Coloniality of Power," 533.
20. R. Smith, *Civic Ideals*.
21. Cisneros, "(Re)Bordering the Civic Imaginary." See also Asen, "Discourse Theory of Citizenship."
22. "Treaty with the Republic of Mexico." Article 8 promised Mexican nationals the freedom to choose whether they would join the US citizenry, but that decision could not be delayed. If anyone failed to make their decision known within one year, they would by default have "elected to become citizens of the United States."
23. M. Smith, "Race, Nationality, and Reality."
24. Recall Omi and Winant's statement on the visual nature of race, fully quoted in the Introduction; see *Racial Formation*, 113.
25. Murillo and Silva, "Mine Workers and Weavers"; Acuña, *Occupied America*, 73–74.
26. Gómez, *Manifest Destinies*.
27. Quijano, "Coloniality of Power," 561–64.

28. McClintock, *Imperial Leather*, 352–58; Gamio, *Forjando Patria: Pro-Nacionalismo*. See also Hassan, "Colonialism and Gender," 303.
29. I. López, "Race, Ethnicity, Erasure"; Bonilla-Silva and Dietrich, "New Pigmentocracy."
30. Gómez, *Manifest Destinies*, 87–88.
31. Omi and Winant, *Racial Formation*, 111.
32. Cisneros, *Border Crossed Us*, 32–33.
33. Acuña, *Occupied America*, 136.
34. Cisneros, *Border Crossed Us*, 35–46; Acuña, *Occupied America*, 136; Almaguer, *Racial Fault Lines*, 38.
35. Mignolo, "Loci of Enunciation."
36. See also Feagin, *White Racial Frame*, 11. This same "white racial frame," some have hypothesized, has also influenced the defensive attitude that some later generations of Latin@s take toward being identified as a not-white race; see Rumbaut, "Pigments of Our Imagination," 28.
37. Quijano, "Coloniality and Modernity/Rationality," 169.
38. Guidotti-Hernández, "Embodied Forms of State Domination."
39. Gates, "Introduction," 5.
40. Nakayama and Krizek, "Whiteness."
41. I. López, *White by Law*, 1, 12–14.
42. Cisneros, *Border Crossed Us*, 47.
43. Mignolo, "Delinking," 459.
44. Duany, Feagin, and Cobas, "Introduction," 13.
45. Maldonado-Torres, "On the Coloniality of Being," 243.
46. Mignolo, *Darker Side of Western Modernity*, 8–9.
47. Greene, "Another Materialist Rhetoric."
48. Hardt and Negri, *Empire*.
49. Omi and Winant, *Racial Formation*, 13; Acuña, *Occupied America*, 139–40; Almaguer, *Racial Fault Lines*, 51–53.
50. Quijano and Wallerstein, "Americanity as a Concept," 551. For the ways in which Mexican American women were at the forefront of resistance to the imposition of whiteness in domestic spaces, see Mario García, "Chicana in American History."
51. Ngai, *Impossible Subjects*, 54.
52. Quijano, "Coloniality of Power," 539.
53. Almaguer, *Racial Fault Lines*, 30.
54. Taylor, *Mexican Labor in the United States*, 6.
55. Craig, *Bracero Program*; Gamboa, *Mexican Labor and World War II*; Galarza, *Merchants of Labor*.
56. Crenshaw, "Demarginalizing the Intersection of Race and Sex."
57. Vélez-Ibañez, *Border Visions*, 71.
58. Vélez-Ibañez, *Border Visions*, 80–81.
59. Flores, "Constructing Rhetorical Borders"; Flores, *Deportable and Disposable*.
60. Roediger, *Wages of Whiteness*.
61. Lyndon B. Johnson, "Special Message to the Congress: The American Promise," March 15, 1965, https://www.presidency.ucsb.edu/node/242211.
62. Mirandé, *Chicano Experience*, 19.
63. Romo, *East Los Angeles*, 7–13.
64. Vallejo, *Barrios to Burbs*, 6, 108.
65. Romo, *East Los Angeles*, 148.
66. Althusser, *For Marx*.
67. Acuña, *Occupied America*, 186–87.

68. E. Pérez, *Decolonial Imaginary*, 82.
69. Lira and Stern, "Mexican Americans and Eugenic Sterilization," 31.
70. E. Pérez, *Decolonial Imaginary*, 6.
71. E. Pérez, *Decolonial Imaginary*, 83–98.
72. Gabriela González, "Carolina Munguía and Emma Tenayuca," 205–6.
73. Aguirre, "Mendez v. Westminster School District."
74. D. García, *Strategies of Segregation*.
75. Gilbert Gonzalez, *Chicano Education*, 13.
76. Barrágan Goetz, *Reading, Writing, Revolution*; San Miguel, *Brown Not White*.
77. San Miguel, "Impact of *Brown*."
78. Gilbert Gonzalez, *Chicano Education*, 30–31, 36.
79. Stuart Hall, "Encoding, Decoding."
80. Stuart Hall, "Who Needs 'Identity'?"
81. Stuart Hall, "Whites of Their Eyes," 18.
82. Crenshaw, "Mapping the Margins," 1283.
83. Dávila, "Introduction," 11–12.
84. Dávila, "Introduction," 10; Feagin and Cobas, *Latinos Facing Racism*, 23.
85. Noriega, *Shot in America*, 31–32.
86. García and Castro, *Blowout!*, 137–38.
87. Noriega, *Shot in America*, 38–39.
88. Noriega, *Shot in America*, 29.
89. Corona, "Cultural Location/s," 245.
90. García and Castro, *Blowout!*, 111–12.
91. Rancière, "Politics, Identification, and Subjectivization," 58–59.
92. Mladek, "Introduction," 3–4.
93. Carrigan and Webb, "Repression and Resistance."
94. Mirandé, *Gringo Justice*. See also Mirandé, *Gringo Injustice*.
95. Acuña, *Occupied America*, 72.
96. Paredes, *With His Pistol in His Hand*, 30–31.
97. Ribb, "La Rinchada," 74–75.
98. Anzaldúa, *Borderlands / La Frontera*, 8.
99. J. Gutierrez, *Making of a Chicano Militant*, 62–65.
100. O. Paz, "Labyrinth of Solitude," 12–18.
101. Acuña, *Occupied America*, 251–52.
102. Mazón, *Zoot-Suit Riots*, 2; Escobar, "Unintended Consequences," 175–76.
103. Escobar, "Unintended Consequences," 1492–95. By way of contrast, see also Churchill and Vander Wall, *cointelpro Papers*.
104. Madsen, *American Exceptionalism*.
105. Meléndez, *All Is Not Lost*, 6.
106. Meléndez, *All Is Not Lost*, 7. See also Anderson, *Imagined Communities*.
107. J. Gonzales, "Forgotten Pages," 51.
108. F. Gutierrez, "Reporting for La Raza," 38–41, 65.
109. Meléndez, *All Is Not Lost*, 103–6.
110. Mario García, *Mexican Americans*.
111. Gabriela González, "Carolina Munguía and Emma Tenayuca"; Calderón-Zaks, "Debated Whiteness."
112. Rosales, *Chicano!*, 95–96, 103–8.
113. Lee, *Making a World After Empire*.
114. Duara, "Cold War As a Historical Period"; Parker, "Cold War II."
115. Izaguirre and Cisneros, "Assembling of a March." See also Crick, "From Cosmopolis to Cosmopolitics."

116. Rancière, "Politics, Identification, and Subjectivization," 58–59. See also Rancière and Panagia, "Dissenting Words," 115.
117. Villanueva, "Sobre El Termino 'Chicano,'" 394.
118. Villanueva, "Sobre El Termino 'Chicano,'" 396.
119. Mariscal, "Reading Chicano/a Writing"; Delgado Melgosa, *Neither Eagle nor Serpent*.

CHAPTER 2

1. Minian, "Indiscriminate and Shameless Sex."
2. Minian, *Undocumented Lives*, 186–87; D. Gutiérrez, *Walls and Mirrors*, 186–87.
3. Matt Garcia, *From the Jaws of Victory*.
4. Alaniz and Cornish, *Viva La Raza*, 152.
5. Gonzales, *I Am Joaquín / Yo Soy Joaquín*, 118; Izaguirre, "Social Movement in Fact," 53.
6. Valdez, "Tale of the Raza," 43.
7. *El Malcriado*, "Plan of Delano."
8. Bardacke, *Trampling Out the Vintage*; Muñoz, *Youth, Identity, Power*, 75.
9. Valdez, "Tale of the Raza," 40.
10. Matthiessen, *Sal Si Puedes*, 143.
11. Mariscal, "Left Turns," 59; Mariscal, "Negotiating César."
12. Minian, *Undocumented Lives*, 147.
13. Soto Vega and Chávez, "Latinx Rhetoric and Intersectionality."
14. Flores, *Deportable and Disposable*, 10.
15. Sowards, "Rhetorical Agency."
16. Molina, *How Race Is Made*, 21–25.
17. Gonzales, *I Am Joaquín / Yo Soy Joaquín*, 3.
18. Street, *Everyone Had Cameras*, 11.
19. Street, *Everyone Had Cameras*, 386. See also Jenkins, *Politics of Insurgency*.
20. Pizzolato, "Harvests of Shame."
21. Street, *Everyone Had Cameras*, 405.
22. T. Moore, *Slaves We Rent*.
23. Teague, *Fifty Years a Rancher*, 140–44.
24. Cohen, *Braceros*, 167–68.
25. Creagan, "Public Law 78," 543.
26. *Harvest of Shame* (CBS News Productions, 1960), 22:17–22:39, https://www.youtube.com/watch?v=yJTVF_dya7E.
27. Galarza, *Merchants of Labor*; Cohen, *Braceros*, 141–42.
28. Jenkins, *Politics of Insurgency*, 168. See also A. Perez, "Tu Reata Es Mi Espada."
29. Levy, *Cesar Chavez*, 173.
30. Street, *Everyone Had Cameras*, 408.
31. Street, *Jon Lewis*, 150–54, 166–67.
32. Street, *Everyone Had Cameras*, 421–23; Gunckel, "Building a Movement," 29–30.
33. Johnson, "Birmingham Campaign as Image Event."
34. Gunckel, "Building a Movement," 38.
35. Matthiessen, *Sal Si Puedes*, 40–41.
36. Bender, *One Night in America*, 14–19.
37. Kennedy is quoted in *El Malcriado: The Voice of the Farm Worker*, December 12, 1966, 5.
38. Sandburg, "Prologue."

39. Street, *Everyone Had Cameras*, 405.
40. Street, *Everyone Had Cameras*, 403–4.
41. Bolter and Grusin, *Remediation*, 60–61.
42. Agee and Evans, *Let Us Now Praise Famous Men*, 210.
43. Finnegan, "Studying Visual Modes of Public Address," 256.
44. Blair, Dickenson, and Ott, "Rhetoric/Memory/Place"; Ahmed, *Cultural Politics of Emotion*.
45. Gross, *Secret History of Emotion*, 53.
46. Rivers, "Apathy."
47. Hammerback and Jensen, *Rhetorical Career of César Chávez*.
48. Levy, *Cesar Chavez*, 207–8; see also Bardacke, *Trampling Out the Vintage*, 221.
49. Burke, *Attitudes Toward History*, 179.
50. Hammerback and Jensen, "Ethnic Heritage"; Davis and Virulegio, *Political Plans of Mexico*.
51. Cruz-Malavé, "Testimonio," 270.
52. Pruchnic and Lacey, "Future of Forgetting: Rhetoric, Memory, Affect."
53. Cloud, "Null Persona."
54. Vivian, "Up from Memory."
55. Hawhee, "Kairotic Encounters."
56. Burke, *Rhetoric of Motives*, 23.
57. Bhabha, *Nation and Narration*.
58. Watts, "'Voice' and 'Voicelessness.'"
59. Flores, *Deportable and Disposable*.
60. *El Malcriado*, "Plan of Delano."
61. Burke, *Rhetoric of Motives*, 22.
62. *El Malcriado*, "Plan of Delano." Issue 33 of *El Malcriado*, published and publicized as a "souvenir" of the peregrinación, included English and Spanish versions of the Plan.
63. Kress and van Leeuwen, *Reading Images*, 233.
64. Molina, HoSang, and Gutiérrez, "Toward a Relational Consciousness of Race," 7.
65. Valdez, "Tale of the Raza."
66. Rancière, *Dis-Agreement*.

CHAPTER 3

1. Mariscal, *Brown-Eyed Children*, 142.
2. Chavez, "Organizer's Tale," 50.
3. Fishlow, *Sons of Zapata*.
4. *Austin Statesman*, "March: Spanish Land Grants Demanded."
5. Sutherland Martinez, "Neither Black nor White," 534.
6. Gómez-Quiñones, *Chicano Politics*; Delgado, "Chicano Movement Rhetoric"; Mariscal, *Brown-Eyed Children*; Bardacke, *Trampling Out the Vintage*.
7. Delgado, "Chicano Movement Rhetoric," 449.
8. *La Raza*, "We're Not Agitators," *La Raza*, December 25, 1967, La Raza Publication Records, 1001, Chicano Studies Research Center, University of California, Los Angeles.
9. *La Raza*, "Victory in Delano in 1968," December 25, 1967, La Raza Publication Records, 1001, Chicano Studies Research Center, University of California, Los Angeles.
10. Bruce-Novoa, *Chicano Authors*, 11.
11. Bruce-Novoa, *Chicano Poetry*, 49.
12. Rancière, "Politics, Identification, and Subjectivization."

13. Burke, *Counter-Statement*, 55–56.
14. Moore and Guzman, "New Wind from the Southwest."
15. Nabokov, *Tijerina and the Courthouse Raid*; Cummings, *Grito!*; Oropeza, *King of Adobe*.
16. Hammerback and Jensen, "Rhetorical Worlds."
17. I. García, *Chicanismo*, 33.
18. Bebout, *Mythohistorical Interventions*, 74.
19. Bebout, *Mythohistorical Interventions*, 8.
20. Cisneros, *Border Crossed Us*, 76.
21. Oropeza, "Becoming Indo-Hispano, 195–96.
22. Gurza, "'I am Joaquín.'" This "community," of course, need not be empirically verifiable. See also Anderson, *Imagined Communities*.
23. *El Gallo*, "Viva Tijerina."
24. Bebout, *Mythohistorical Interventions*, 99.
25. Arteaga, *Chicano Poetics*, 10–13.
26. Anzaldúa, *Borderlands / La Frontera*.
27. Saldívar, "Towards a Chicano Poetics"; Saldívar, *Border Matters*; Saldívar, "Border Thinking."
28. Arteaga, *Chicano Poetics*, 146–47.
29. Belgrad, "Performing Lo Chicano," 251–52.
30. Burke, *Counter-Statement*, 153.
31. Muñoz, *Youth, Identity, Power*, 76.
32. Bruce-Novoa, *Chicano Poetry*, 49.
33. R. Gonzales, "Revolutionist," 124–25.
34. Romero, "Wearing the Red, White, and Blue."
35. Izaguirre, "Whiteness of LBJ's Rhetoric."
36. Quoted in Pycior, "From Hope to Frustration," 478.
37. Lyndon B. Johnson, "Remarks at the Swearing in of Vicente T. Ximenes as a Member of the Equal Employment Opportunity Commission," June 9, 1967, https://www.presidency.ucsb.edu/node/238414.
38. Johnson, "Remarks at the Swearing In."
39. Márquez, *LULAC*, 64–67.
40. Kells, *Vicente Ximenes*, 8, 203.
41. Omi and Winant, *Racial Formation*.
42. Muñoz, *Youth, Identity, Power*, 76. Muñoz notes that student organizations such as United Mexican American Students (UMAS), Mexican American Student Confederation (MASC), and Mexican American Youth Organization (MAYO) circulated Gonzales's poem when it was published by La Causa Publications based out of Oakland, CA.
43. Licona, *Zines in Third Space*, 52–53.
44. I. García, *Chicanismo*, 88.
45. "Interagency Committee on Mexican American Affairs."
46. Quoted in Pycior, "From Hope to Frustration," 203.
47. *La Raza*, "Juego Play El Paso Play Juego," October 29, 1967, La Raza Publication Records, 1001, Chicano Studies Research Center, University of California, Los Angeles.
48. *La Raza*, "Which One Do You Know," June 23, 1967, La Raza Publication Records, 1001, Chicano Studies Research Center, University of California, Los Angeles.
49. *La Raza*, "Will El Paso Spark Mexican-American Unity," October 15, 1967, La Raza Publication Records, 1001, Chicano Studies Research Center, University of California, Los Angeles.
50. *La Raza*, "Young Militants Organize," October 29, 1967, La Raza Publication Records, 1001, Chicano Studies Research Center, University of California, Los Angeles.

51. Salazar, "Humphrey Asks Action by Mexican-Americans."

52. *La Raza*, "Plan De La Raza Unida," November 15, 1967, La Raza Publication Records, 1001, Chicano Studies Research Center, University of California, Los Angeles.

53. G. Sánchez, *Becoming Mexican American*, 9.

54. Cisneros, *Border Crossed Us*.

55. Gallego, *Chicana/o Subjectivity*, 45.

56. R. Rodríguez, *Next of Kin*.

57. Scholars generally ignore initial publications of this poem. Prior studies seemingly limit their analyses to a singular reproduction of the poem, mostly the 1972 publication by Bantam Press. Bebout, in his analysis, notes distinctions between the 1967 publication and the 1972 publication. His emphasis, however, is not on analyzing the poem as much as it is on discerning its placement in cultural production (*Mythohistorical Interventions*, 56–57). For his part, Bruce-Novoa's text is unclear about which copy of "I Am Joaquin" he utilizes, although it does appear that he uses the Bantam edition in his analysis (*Chicano Poetry*, 222n1). See also Jensen and Hammerback, "No Revolutions Without Poets," 73n6; Gurza, "I am Joaquín," 94n1; Gallego, *Chicana/o Subjectivity*, 44; Yay, "Capturing the Bronze Power," 35n8.

58. Bruce-Novoa, *Chicano Poetry*, 10. See also, Muñoz, *Youth, Identity, Power*, 76; Bruce-Novoa, *Chicano Authors*, 11; Arteaga, *Chicano Poetics*, 146–47; Jensen and Hammerback, "No Revolutions Without Poets," 73.

59. Limón, *Mexican Ballads*, 125.

60. Steiner, *La Raza*, 378.

61. Jensen and Hammerback, "No Revolutions Without Poets."

62. Document on the rationale for writing the poem, Box 3, Folder 45, The Western History Collection, Rodolfo "Corky" Gonzales Papers, Denver Public Library, Denver, Colorado.

63. Mignolo, "Delinking," 476–77.

64. Toohey, *Reading Epic*; Bakhtin, "Forms of Time."

65. Feagin and Cobas, *Latinos Facing Racism*, 3–6.

66. Adair, "El Malcriado, 1965–66."

67. Rancière, "Politics, Identification, and Subjectivization," 63.

68. Quijano, "Coloniality of Power," 554.

69. Bruce-Novoa, *Chicano Poetry*, 5.

70. Linguist Richard Cureton argues that ellipses constitute an "iconic syntax," appearing as a semblance of the "situation to which the syntax refers" ("Poetic Syntax and Aesthetic Form," 320).

71. Bruce-Novoa, *Chicano Poetry*, 45.

72. "I am Joaquín," 1967, Box 3, Folder 41, The Western History Collection, Rodolfo "Corky" Gonzales Papers, Denver Public Library, Denver, Colorado.

73. Griswold del Castillo and García, *César Chávez*, 38, 154.

74. Gómez-Jiménez, "NearerandnearerandNEARER." See also Heusser, "Visual Rhetoric of e. e. cummings's 'poempictures.'"

75. The English word "my" and the Spanish "mi" are visually similar, and, at least phonetically speaking, could be voiced identically.

76. "Chicano nationalism," n.d., Box 3, Folder 26, The Western History Collection, Rodolfo "Corky" Gonzales Papers, Denver Public Library, Denver, Colorado, 9.

77. Quintilian, *Orator's Education*, 8.4.27.

78. I. Paz, "Introduction," lxv.

79. Eliud Martinez, "'I Am Joaquín,'" 513–14.

80. Mignolo, *Local Histories / Global Designs*, 3.

81. Omi and Winant, *Racial Formation*, 13.

82. Corona, "Cultural Location/s of (U.S.) Latin Rock," 244.

83. Olson and de los Santos, "Expanding the Idea of América"; C. Olson, *American Magnitude*.
84. Acuña, *Occupied America*, 311–12; Barrera, "1968 Edcouch-Elsa High School Walkout"; García and Castro, *Blowout!*, 158.
85. Césaire, *Discourse on Colonialism*.
86. Powell, "Rhetorics of Survivance."
87. Paz, "Introduction," xii. At this point in Gonzales's presentation of "Joaquin" activation, the narrator and figure from whom his name is derived is depicted in the text. However, given the disputed origins, history, and legacies of Joaquin Murrieta, I note that Gonzales's presentation is a re-presentation rather than a factual rehearsal of a "historical" figure.
88. *I Am Joaquín*, 16mm, 1969, https://www.youtube.com/watch?v=2z8Fu4oTh6Y.
89. Hawk, "Sound."
90. Bruce-Novoa, *Chicano Poetry*, 57.
91. Bruce-Novoa, *Chicano Poetry*, 57. See also Candelaria, *Chicano Poetry*, 41.
92. E. Pérez, *Decolonial Imaginary*, 7.
93. Ruiz, *Out of the Shadows*.
94. Alarcón, "Traddutora, Traditora," 72; Alarcón, "Chicana Feminism," 252.
95. Limón, *Mexican Ballads*, 35.
96. Prasch, "Toward a Rhetorical Theory of Deixis."
97. Jensen and Hammerback, "No Revolutions Without Poets," 80.
98. Longeaux y Vasquez, "El Soldado Raso Today."
99. Cotera, Blackwell, and Espinoza, "Introduction."
100. Sowards, "Rhetorical Agency as Haciendo Caras."
101. "La Raza Cosmica," n.d., Box Four, Folder Twelve, The Western History Collection, Rodolfo "Corky" Gonzales Papers, Denver Public Library, Denver, Colorado, 2.
102. Arendt, *On Violence*, 51, 56.
103. Arendt, *On Violence*, 44.
104. Ochieng, "What Cannot Be Done."
105. Charland, "Constitutive Rhetoric."
106. Patil, "Contending Masculinities"; McClintock, *Imperial Leather*.
107. Moraga, "Queer Aztlán."
108. Vasconcelos, *La Raza Cósmica*; M. Miller, *Rise and Fall*. José Vasconcelos's notion of "la raza cosmica" was a racial concept that viewed the emergence of a "mixed" race (mestizo) from existing races (white, Black, etc) as a superior race. Since the "mixed" race was the superior race, all other races were viewed as inferior, and Blackness in particular as particularly subordinate to the others. This perspective on racial divisions also had political implications, which were linked strongly to nationalist programs.
109. Moraga, "Queer Aztlán."
110. Address to the "Stop the War" Rally, August 6, 1966, Box Six, Folder 53, The Western History Collection, Rodolfo "Corky" Gonzales Papers, Denver Public Library, Denver, Colorado, 2.
111. Quijano and Wallerstein, "Americanity," 551–52.
112. 6 Pages on Nationalism, Box Six, Folder 53, The Western History Collection, Rodolfo "Corky" Gonzales Papers, Denver Public Library, Denver, Colorado, 5.

CHAPTER 4

1. *La Raza*, "La Raza Nueva: 13," September 1968, La Raza Publication Records, 1001, Chicano Studies Research Center, University of California, Los Angeles.

2. Valdés, *Barrios Norteños*, 178–79.

3. O'Gorman, "Logic and Rhetoric of Power," 259–302; see also Prasch and Stuckey, "'Empire for Liberty.'"

4. "Main Speech by Premier Chou En-Lai [Zhou Enlai], Head of the Delegation of the People's Republic of China, Distributed at the Plenary Session of the Asian-African Conference," Cold War International History Project (CWIHP), April 19, 1955, 121623, Wilson Center, Digital Archive International History Declassified.

5. Dussel, *Philosophy of Liberation*, 1.

6. Fanon, *Wretched of the Earth*.

7. Westad, *Global Cold War*; Brands, *Latin America's Cold War*.

8. Hallin, "1968: The Year of Media Decision," 3–8.

9. Guzmán, "Mexican American Casualties." The 1969 report updates his 1967 study, which originally covered January 1961–February 1967. See also its book form, *Mexican American Casualties*, published in 1970.

10. Phase I in the Build-Up of U.S. Forces: March–July 1965, IV. C Evolution of the War (26 Vols.), Direction Action: The Johnson Commitments, 1964–1968 (16 Vols.), National Archives, Pentagon Papers, https://www.archives.gov/research/pentagon-papers, accessed April 8, 2020.

11. Mariscal, "Mexican Americans and the Viet Nam War," 350.

12. Vaca et al., "Spanish Surname War Dead Vietnam." Recall that Mexican Americans were *legally* white, although they might have been *experientially* treated as not-white (though not consistently).

13. Molina, HoSang, and Gutiérrez, "Toward a Relational Consciousness of Race," 2; see also Molina, *How Race Is Made*, 3–4.

14. A. Perez, "Tu Reata Es Mi Espada," 258–59; Martínez, *Youngest Revolution*; Oropeza, "Viviendo y Luchando," xxxiii–xxxiv.

15. Oropeza, "Viviendo y Luchando," xxxiv.

16. D. López, "El Grito Del Norte," 540.

17. Espinoza, "Rethinking Cultural Nationalism," 207.

18. Mario T. García, "Chicana in American History."

19. Gabriela González, "Carolina Munguía and Emma Tenayuca."

20. Sowards, "Rhetorical Agency"; Sowards, *¡Sí, Ella Puede!*

21. E. Pérez, *Decolonial Imaginary*, xviii; Izaguirre, "Movidas after Nationalism."

22. Cheng, "Chicana/o Environmentalism"; A. Perez, "Tu Reata Es Mi Espada"; Davis, "Before I Knew Elizabeth Martínez"; Espinoza, "Rethinking Cultural Nationalism."

23. Harlow, *Resistance Literature*.

24. Beverley, "Margin at the Center," 12–13.

25. Yúdice, "Testimonio and Postmodernism"; Beverley, "Introduccion."

26. Yúdice, "Testimonio and Postmodernism," 17.

27. Yúdice, "Testimonio and Postmodernism," 18. It is noteworthy that recent studies of Chican@ student journalism have identified the interconnections between these seemingly "disparate" forms of discourse. See Alemán, "Testimonio as Praxis."

28. Calafell, "Rhetorics of Possibility"; Prieto and Villenas, "Pedagogies from Nepantla"; Reyes and Rodríguez, "Testimonio."

29. Beverley, "Margin at the Center," 12–13. Despite its utility for apprehending both violences against subaltern communities and the contexts in which these violences occur, the testimonio has been subjected to intense scrutiny since the 1980s. See Pratt, "*I Rigoberta Menchú*"; Beverley, *Testimonio*; Stoll, *Rigoberta Menchu*; D'Souza, *Illiberal Education*, 71–73.

30. Quoted in Beverley, *Testimonio*, 13. Others move further back in time than Beverley to locate the testimonio's lineage; see Cruz-Malavé, "Testimonio," 270–71.

31. Mario T. García, *Literature as History*, 4. García's use of the "testimonio" is fascinating, since he does seem to provide an "alternative" history using the "voice" of a marginalized subject. And perhaps he is right to lament that his work has not been critiqued qua "testimonio." Nevertheless, I find it difficult to accept García's work as testimonio per se because he appears to present his work not *only* as *testimonio* but as history too—two generic scholarly forms that are not mutually exclusive but certainly are distinguishable (see Beverley, "On 'Testimonio,'" 14). Beverley argues that the fine line between "oral history" and "testimonio" hinges on *whose* intentionality is represented: that of the recorder or that of the narrator. But what Beverley refers to as "intentionality" I understand to be made visible through an *aesthetic*, and, so, it might be that García's work fails to be recognized as testimonio because of an *aesthetic* deficiency (See also Mario T. García, *Chicano Generation*).

32. Jameson, "On Literary and Cultural Import-Substitution."
33. Harlow, *After Lives*, 93–94.
34. Farr, *Rancheros in Chicagoacán*, 15.
35. Barriga, "Culture of Poverty"; Roybal, "Pushing the Boundaries"; J. Muñoz, *Disidentifications*.
36. Diaz, "Seeing Is Believing."
37. DeRocher, *Transnational Testimonios*, 19; Beverley, "On 'Testimonio,'" 15.
38. Yúdice, "Testimonio and Postmodernism," 15.
39. DeRocher, *Transnational Testimonios*, 16.
40. Gugelberger, "Institutionalization of Transgression," 11.
41. *El Grito del Norte*, "To Our Readers."
42. I. García, *Chicanismo*, 30.
43. Olson and De los Santos, "Expanding the Idea of América."
44. Izaguirre, "Social Movement in Fact."
45. Oropeza, "Viviendo y Luchando," xxix.
46. Oropeza, "Viviendo y Luchando," xxix–xxx.
47. Izaguirre, "Movidas After Nationalism."
48. Oropeza, "Viviendo y Luchando," xxxv.
49. Longeaux y Vasquez, "Despierten! Hermanos," 7.
50. Walsh, "Decoloniality in/as Praxis."
51. Oropeza, *King of Adobe*.
52. A. Garcia, "Development of Chicana Feminist Discourse."
53. Izaguirre, "Movidas after Nationalism."
54. Mignolo, *Darker Side of Western Modernity*.

CHAPTER 5

1. Young, *Soul Power*.
2. Camejo and Rio, "Nat'l Chicano Parley Raised Consciousness."
3. Brands, *Latin America's Cold War*, 3; Gronbeck-Tedesco, "Left in Transition"; Valdez and Rubalcava, "Venceremos!" Mexican American activists, such as Luis Valdez and Enriqueta Longeaux y Vasquez, had already visited Cuba (in 1964 and 1969, respectively). They had been inspired by Cuba's political programs after witnessing it for themselves. See Enriqueta Longeaux y Vasquez, "¡Que Linda Es Cuba!," *El Grito Del Norte*, May 19, 1969.
4. Muñoz, *Youth, Identity, Power*, 91–93.
5. Gonzales and Tijerina, "Social Revolution in the Southwest"; Marín, *Spokesman*; Jensen and Hammerback, "No Revolutions Without Poets."

6. Rossa, "Calif. Brown Beret Leaders Answer L.A. Police Charges."
7. Tuck and Yang, "Decolonization Is Not a Metaphor."
8. By the time of the Denver Conference, Alurista was a published poet; see Alurista, "Poetry of Alurista."
9. Luis Leal, "In Search of Aztlán," 11. An article in *Carta Editorial* explained the origin of Aztlán as part of a piece on Mexican Heritage, and the Chican@ newspaper's *La Verdad* includes a speech by José Gutierrez in which he deploys "Aztlán" as a political term, although his usage is nascent and underdeveloped ("Mexican Heritage").
10. Flores and Hasian, "Returning to Aztlán," 189–90.
11. Delgado, "Chicano Movement Rhetoric," 452. For a variety of perspectives on the nature and scope of Aztlán, see Anaya and Lomelí, *Aztlán*.
12. Burke, *Rhetoric of Motives*, 23.
13. Arteaga, *Chicano Poetics*, 9.
14. Anzaldúa, *Borderlands / La Frontera*.
15. G. Sanchez, *Becoming Mexican American*, 9. Sanchez's definition is perhaps the most "general" while, at the same time, supplying the most "bordered" point of view. Someone that identified or was identified as "Chican@" was "betwixt and between," a person experiencing the social junctures of Mexican and American histories in the United States.
16. Arteaga, *Chicano Poetics*, 10–13; Saldívar, "Towards a Chicano Poetics"; Saldívar, *Border Matters*.
17. Orozco, *No Mexicans, Women, or Dogs Allowed*, 73; Mario T. García, *Latino Generation*.
18. F. Delgado, "Chicano Movement Rhetoric."
19. Alaniz and Cornish, *Viva La Raza*, 158–59; Mariscal, *Brown-Eyed Children*, 163.
20. Belgrad, "Performing Lo Chicano," 251–52.
21. Mario T. García, *Mexican Americans*, 6.
22. Mario T. García, *Mexican Americans*, 17–19, 25, 44–45.
23. Mario T. García, *Chicano Generation*, 14. Despite acknowledging how gender shaped experiences among men and women activists, García nonetheless insists on referring to this entire generation with the masculine designation "Chicano."
24. Mario T. García, *Chicano Generation*, 1.
25. Bhabha, *Location of Culture*, 3.
26. DeChaine, "For Rhetorical Border Studies"; Couture and Wojahn, *Crossing Borders*.
27. Cisneros, "Reclaiming," 566.
28. Mignolo, *Local Histories / Global Designs*, 85.
29. Rancière, *Dis-Agreement*, 9–14.
30. Mignolo, "Cosmopolitanism and the De-Colonial Option," 125.
31. Mignolo, *Local Histories / Global Designs*, 50.
32. Cisneros, "Reclaiming," 566; Flores, "Creating Discursive Space."
33. Flores, "Creating Discursive Space," 152.
34. Mignolo, "Delinking," 459.
35. Finnegan, "Studying Visual Modes of Public Address."
36. Hammerback and Jensen, "Ethnic Heritage."
37. Fahnestock, "Verbal and Visual Parallelism," 131. This point follows nearly all of Fahnestock's categories, namely, parallelism in length, intonation, sound, grammar, semantic, and, perhaps, repetition.
38. Tufte, *Visual Explanations*, 80.
39. Fahnestock, "Verbal and Visual Parallelism," 142.

40. Howard Hollman Newspaper Collection, Special Collections and University Archives, San Diego State University Library.
41. *La Verdad*, "Denver Conference."
42. Alberto, "Nations, Nationalisms, and Indígenas," 110–14.
43. Cortez, "On Disinvention." Cortez's recent essay on notions of mestizaje that continue to pervade scholarship and activism highlights the political *impossibilities* accompanying mestizo constructions of racial identity.
44. *Bronce Magazine*, "Editorial Policy," 29.
45. Flores, "Creating Discursive Space," 151–52.
46. Longeaux y Vasquez, "Preface," 15.
47. Longeaux y Vasquez, "Woman."
48. Gutierrez, "How We Built La Raza Unida Party," 17.
49. Vigil, *Crusade for Justice*, 124.
50. *El Gallo*, "Albert Gurule Seeks Governership."
51. *El Gallo*, "Why Do We Need La Raza Unida Party," 2.
52. *El Gallo*, "Albert Gurule Seeks Governership."

CHAPTER 6

1. Simon Hall, *Rethinking*.
2. Richard Nixon, "Address to the Nation on the War in Vietnam," November 3, 1969, https://www.presidency.ucsb.edu/node/240027.
3. Newman, "Under the Veneer."
4. Oropeza, *¡Raza Sí! ¡Guerra No!*, 114–15, 144.
5. Gómez-Quiñones, *Chicano Politics*, 124–25.
6. Simon Hall, *Rethinking*, 49; Oropeza, *¡Raza Sí! ¡Guerra No!*, 126.
7. Oropeza, *¡Raza Sí! ¡Guerra No!*, 115, 117.
8. *Ruben Salazar: Man in the Middle* (PBS, 2014), https://youtu.be/Ko-Z5Qbjy04. Indeed, so fervent was and still is the commitment to achieving justice for Salazar's untimely and unprovoked death that investigations (and conspiracy theories) surrounding the circumstances of his death have persisted.
9. Mario T. García, "Introduction," 35–37.
10. De Certeau, *Practice of Everyday Life*; Endres and Senda-Cook, "Location Matters."
11. K. Chávez, "Counter-Public Enclaves," 1–18.
12. Crick, "Rhetoric and Events."
13. Izaguirre and Cisneros, "Assembling of a March."
14. K. Chávez, "Body."
15. Escobar, "Dialectics of Repression," 1495–1501.
16. Oropeza, *¡Raza Sí! ¡Guerra No!*, 131–43, 180.
17. Scott and Smith, "Rhetoric of Confrontation."
18. "¡Mi Raza Primero!," 71.
19. Feagin and Cobas, *Latinos Facing Racism*, 134; Feagin, *White Racial Frame*, 112.
20. The issue included articles covering a wide range of topics articulating motives for the Chicano Moratorium, such as "Nuestra Batalla No Esta en Vietnam, Esta Aquí" ("Our Battle Is Not in Vietnam, It Is Here"), "Quien es el Chicano?" ("Who is the Chicano"), and "Marcha Contra La Guerra" ("March Against the War"). There were also articles dedicated to revealing the cause and consequences of Ruben Salazar's death, such as "La Farsa del 'Inquest'" ("The Farce of the 'Inquest'") and a personal testimony from Raul Ruiz, one of the editors of *La Raza* magazine. The issue even included a

personal letter from Ruben Salazar's mother, Sra. Luz Chavez de Salazar, titled "A Mi Hijo lo Eliminaron" ("They Eliminated My Son") that suggested Salazar's death might not have been accidental but intentional.
21. Wanzer-Serrano, "Trashing the System."
22. Gunckel, "Chicano/a Photographic," 385.
23. Ferris and Sandoval, *Fight in the Fields*, 141.
24. "The Nightmare and the Promised Land," n.d., Box 3, Folder 49, The Western History Collection, Rodolfo "Corky" Gonzales Papers, Denver Public Library, Denver, Colorado.
25. *Chicano Moratorium* (Cintec Productions, 1971), https://www.youtube.com/watch?v=famNeiosTVk; *Requiem 29: The Chicano Moratorium*, 2017, https://www.youtube.com/watch?v=Vfa-JfeiIjU. Two video reproductions that detail the events of the August 29 Moratorium can be seen by visiting these links.
26. Ontiveros, *Spirit of New People*, 60.
27. Powers and Perlman, "One Dead, 40 Hurt." The special issue of *La Raza* magazine highlighted the racial tinge of using the word "riot" to describe what happened at the moratorium. See *La Raza*, "Chicanos and the War," September 1970, La Raza Publication Records, 1001, Chicano Studies Research Center, University of California, Los Angeles.
28. Powers and Perlman, "One Dead, 40 Hurt," 18.
29. Powers and Perlman, "One Dead, 40 Hurt."
30. Shaw and Vasquez, "Contradictory Reports"; Wright, "East Los Angeles Calm."
31. Houston, "U.S. Says It Is Probing Reports."
32. Houston, "U.S. Inquiry Urged."
33. Houston, "Jury Splits 4–3." It is important to note briefly the legacies of the terminology "accidental" and "at the hands of another" used for rendering decisions at inquest hearings. Prior to 1970, inquest hearings concluded with one of the following decisions: "accidental homicide," "justifiable homicide," and "criminal homicide." However, the California legislature opted for more ambiguous terminology after a split decision at an inquest hearing involving the death of a Black motorist named Leonard Deadwyler, who was killed by police. With the updated terminology, jurors in Salazar's inquest hearing could at most assert that the death was not "accidental." Yet, apart from a well-defined alternative that might locate responsibility for the death, the more ambiguous label of "at the hands of another" was used to describe Salazar's killing by Deputy Thomas Wilson.
34. Houston and Smith, "Mexican-American Observers Walk Out."
35. Houston, "TV Channels Will Provide Full Coverage."
36. Shaw and Vasquez, "Contradictory Reports."
37. Los Angeles County Office of Independent Review, "Review."
38. Houston and Smith, "Mexican-American Observers Walk Out."
39. Houston and Smith, "Mexican-American Observers Walk Out."
40. Houston and Smith, "Witness at Salazar Hearing Charges Bias."
41. Houston and Smith, "Witness at Salazar Hearing Charges Bias."
42. Ore, *Lynching*.
43. Gunckel, "Chicano/a Photographic," 382.
44. Azoulay, *Civil Imagination*; Raiford, *Imprisoned in a Luminous Glare*; Berger, *For All the World to See*.
45. Gunckel, "Chicano/a Photographic," 378.
46. Gunckel, "Chicano/a Photographic," 378.
47. Gunckel, "Building a Movement," 31.
48. Gunckel, "Chicano/a Photographic," 400–2.

49. Finnegan, "Naturalistic Enthymeme," 133; Olson, Finnegan, and Hope, *Visual Rhetoric*; Hamilton and O'Gorman, "Visualities of Strategic Vision."
50. Foster, "Preface," ix–xiv.
51. Rancière, *Politics of Aesthetics*.
52. Hariman and Lucaites, *No Caption Needed*.
53. Feagin, *White Racial Frame*; Omi and Winant, *Racial Formation*.
54. Molina-Guzmán, *Dangerous Curves*.
55. Ontiveros, *Spirit of a New People*.
56. H. Gonzalez, "Hate Issue."
57. Ore, *Lynching*.
58. Izaguirre, "Nonviolence in Context."
59. Gunckel, "Thinking about La Raza"; Andrade, "History of 'La Raza,'" 36–37.
60. Macfarlane, "Photography and the Western Worker," 197.
61. Aristotle, *Art of Rhetoric*, 1405a; Cicero, *Brutus. Orator*, 166–67.
62. Maldonado-Torres, *Against War*, 1–3.
63. Andrade, "History of 'La Raza,'" 60–61; see also Castro and del Olmo, "Killed in East L.A."
64. Maldonado-Torres, *Against War*, 137–40.
65. Drexler-Dreis, "James Baldwin's Decolonial Love."
66. Conflicting reports led to confusion about what was said between the men in the café and police officers. Chican@s claimed that they were told to go back inside the café. Although unable to confirm what, if any, orders were given to the men at the café, below is an independent review's attempt to unearth what happened during these moments: "One of the men with Mr. Salazar that day reported that he tried to leave the bar to watch the events unfolding outside but was ordered by a deputy with a shotgun to go back in. It would have been completely illogical for Deputy Wilson or any of the other deputies responding to reports of men with guns in the bar to encourage anyone to go into the bar at the same time they were intending to clear it. No deputies admit giving such commands, but none were pressed for an explanation of these reports. It is possible that other deputies, unaware of the account of the men with guns entering the bar, had encouraged people to get into the bar and off of the street as part of a crowd control effort. But no deputies ever came forward to acknowledge having done so, and photographic evidence published by the media shows unarmed men near the doorway of the bar as a deputy who appears to be holding a tear gas gun approaches. The documents we reviewed do not resolve this mystery." See Los Angeles County Office of Independent Review, "Review," 15.
67. Photographs of the outside of the café are reinitiated following the article "Chicano Eyewitness Report" on page 46.
68. For example, *La Raza*, "Chicanos and the War," 13, discusses the racial connections between the violence of the moratorium and Salazar's death.
69. Rodriguez, *Next of Kin*.
70. Rodriguez, "Family," 62; Armas, *La Familia*.
71. Gómez-Quiñones, *Chicano Politics*, 118.
72. Richard Nixon, "Address to the Nation on the War in Vietnam," November 3, 1969, https://www.presidency.ucsb.edu/node/240027.
73. Maldonado-Torres, *Against War*.
74. DiAngelo, "White Fragility," 57–58.
75. *La Raza*, "'Justifiable Homicide' of Jesus Salcedo," March 1969, La Raza Publication Records, 1001, Chicano Studies Research Center, University of California, Los Angeles.
76. Los Angeles County Office of Independent Review, "Review," 15–16.

77. Rice, "Rhetorical Aesthetics of More."
78. Escobar, "Dialectics of Repression."
79. Hamilton and O'Gorman, "Visualities of Strategic Vision," 197.
80. Gusterson, "Nuclear Weapons and the Other," 117–21.
81. *La Raza*, "La Farsa Del 'Inquest,'" September 1970, 58, La Raza Publication Records, 1001, Chicano Studies Research Center, University of California, Los Angeles.
82. Anzaldúa, *Borderlands / La Frontera*, 3.
83. Pérez, *Taste for Brown Bodies*, 103.
84. Calafell, "Brownness, Kissing, and US Imperialism."
85. Nixon, "Address to the Nation."
86. E. Lopez, "Ruben Salazar Death."
87. *La Raza*, "Chicanos and the War," 13.

CONCLUSION

1. Rendón, *Chicano Manifesto*, 4.
2. Rendón, *Chicano Manifesto*, 2.
3. Rendón, *Chicano Manifesto*, 87.
4. Mora, *Making Hispanics*.
5. I have chosen to use the term "mime" here rather than "imitation," a more conventional translation for mimesis. I have done this because, as rhetoricians and classicists have shown, "imitation" is but one way to translate processes related to mimesis. Similarly, given the relationship between this poetic practice and coloniality, I do mean to emphasize the direction of influence here—this turn toward institutionalization derived from a colonial impulse. Another reason for using "mime" instead of "imitation" derives from René Girard's mimetic theory, which, in sum, posits that desires themselves derive from a mediator that induces and influences the acceptance of desires. In rhetorical studies, the interconnections between Girardian mimesis and rhetorical mimesis have yet to receive sustained attention outside of the work of Paul Lynch. In the case of Mexican American politics in the 1970s, it appears that the *desire* for definition stemmed from the inescapable influence of colonial rule among activists. For a history of mimesis in classical traditions, see McKeon, "Literary Criticism"; Givens, "Aristotle's Critique of Mimesis"; Fantham, "Imitation and Evolution." In rhetorical studies, see Clark, "Imitation"; Sullivan, "Attitudes toward Imitation"; Muckelbauer, "Imitation and Invention." For introductory texts in Girardian mimetic theory and rhetorical studies, see Lynch, "Rescuing Rhetoric"; Lynch, "Recovering Rhetoric."
6. Quijano and Wallerstein, "Americanity as a Concept," 549–50.
7. Mignolo, "Epistemic Disobedience," 2–3.
8. Rendón, *Chicano Manifesto*, 183–90.
9. Quijano, "Coloniality of Power," 542.
10. Letter from Bantam Publishers, Box 3, Folder 46, The Western History Collection, Rodolfo "Corky" Gonzales Papers, Denver Public Library, Denver, Colorado.
11. The proposal to Gonzales stated that the "tentative plan would be to reprint both the Spanish and the English versions (side-by-side, as at present), accompanied by photographs and prints to illustrate the historical allusions and the moods of your poem. We might also consider adding a brief chronology of Mexican-American history as an appendix."
12. Chapnick, "Markets and Careers."
13. Valdez and Steiner, "El Plan Espiritual de Aztlan," 402–3.
14. R. Sánchez, "Writing"; Mignolo, *Darker Side of the Renaissance*.

15. Ortego, "Introduction to Chicano Studies."
16. Ortego, "Introduction to Chicano Studies," 332–33.
17. Rendón, *Chicano Manifesto*, 280–81.
18. Mignolo, *Darker Side of Western Modernity*.
19. Muñoz, "Development of Chicano Studies."
20. *El Plan de Santa Bárbara*, 13.
21. I. García, "Juncture in the Road"; Cabán, "Moving from the Margins to Where?"; Pérez-Torres, "Chicana/o Studies's Two Paths"; Soldatenko, *Chicano Studies*; Acuña, *Making of Chicana/o Studies*; D. Lopez, "Cultivating Aztlán."
22. Soldatenko, "Aztlán."
23. Rendón, *Chicano Manifesto*, 282–83.
24. Tenorio-Trillo, *Latin America*.
25. Izaguirre, "Case of El Colegio Jacinto Treviño."
26. "Why Raza Unida Is the Only Alternative for Chicanos," José Angel Gutiérrez Papers, Nettie Lee Benson Latin American Collection, University of Texas Libraries, The University of Texas at Austin.
27. Miller, "Aristotelian Topos."
28. Mignolo, "Loci of Enunciation."
29. Feagin, *White Racial Frame*.
30. Rancière, *Politics of Aesthetics*.
31. Bonilla-Silva and Dietrich, "Latin Americanization"; Alcoff, *Future of Whiteness*; Kendi, *How to Be an Antiracist*.
32. Izaguirre, "Whiteness of LBJ's Rhetoric."
33. Mora, *Making Hispanics*.
34. G. Garcia, "Defined by Outcomes or Culture?"; G. Garcia, *Becoming Hispanic-Serving Institutions*; E. Gonzalez et al., "What Does It Mean?"
35. Sullivan and Kanno-Youngs, "4 Border Patrol Agents."
36. Na'puti, "Oceanic Possibilities."

BIBLIOGRAPHY

Acuña, Rodolfo F. *The Making of Chicana/o Studies: In the Trenches of Academe.* New Brunswick: Rutgers University Press, 2011.
———. *Occupied America: A History of Chicanos.* 8th ed. Boston: Pearson, 2015.
Adair, Doug. "El Malcriado, 1965–66: Bill Esher, Editor." July 12, 2009. Farm Worker Movement Documentation Project. https://libraries.ucsd.edu/farmworkermovement/archives/#sncc.
Agee, James, and Walker Evans. *Let Us Now Praise Famous Men.* Boston: Houghton Mifflin, 1941.
Aguirre, Frederick P. "Mendez v. Westminster School District: How It Affected Brown v. Board of Education." *Journal of Hispanic Higher Education* 4, no. 4 (2005): 321–32. https://doi.org/10.1177/1538192705279406.
Ahmed, Sara. *The Cultural Politics of Emotion.* Edinburgh: Edinburgh University Press, 2014.
Alaniz, Yolanda, and Megan Cornish. *Viva La Raza: A History of Chicano Identity and Resistance.* Seattle: Red Letter Press, 2008.
Alarcón, Norma. "Chicana Feminism: In the Tracks of 'the' Native Woman." *Cultural Studies* 4, no. 3 (1990): 248–56. https://doi.org/10.1080/09502389000490201.
———. "Traddutora, Traditora: A Paradigmatic Figure of Chicana Feminism." *Cultural Critique*, no. 13 (1989): 57–87. https://doi.org/10.2307/1354269.
Alberto, Lourdes. "Nations, Nationalisms, and Indígenas: The 'Indian' in the Chicano Revolutionary Imaginary." *Critical Ethnic Studies* 2, no. 1 (2016): 107–27. https://doi.org/10.5749/jcritethnstud.2.1.0107.
Alcoff, Linda M. *The Future of Whiteness.* Cambridge, UK: Polity Press, 2015.
Alemán, Sonya M. "Testimonio as Praxis for a Reimagined Journalism Model and Pedagogy." *Equity & Excellence in Education* 45, no. 3 (2012): 488–506.
Almaguer, Tomás. *Racial Fault Lines: The Historical Origins of White Supremacy in California.* Berkeley: University of California Press, 1994.
Althusser, Louis. *For Marx.* London: Verso, 1969.
Alurista. "The Poetry of Alurista." *El Grito: A Journal of Contemporary Mexican-American Thought* 2, no. 1 (1968): 5–12.
Anaya, Rudolfo, and Francisco Lomelí, eds. *Aztlán: Essays on the Chicano Homeland.* Albuquerque: University of New Mexico Press, 1991.
Anderson, Benedict R. O'Gorman. *Imagined Communities: Reflections on the Origin and Spread of Nationalism.* Rev. ed. London: Verso, 2006.
Andrade, Francisco Manuel. "The History of 'La Raza' Newspaper and Magazine, and Its Role in the Chicano Community from 1967 to 1977." Master's thesis, California State University, Fullerton, 1979.
Ankersmit, F. R. *Aesthetic Politics: Political Philosophy Beyond Fact and Value.* Stanford: Stanford University Press, 1996.
Anzaldúa, Gloria. *Borderlands / La Frontera: The New Mestiza.* San Francisco: Aunt Lute Books, 1987.
Arendt, Hannah. *On Violence.* Orlando: Houghton Mifflin Harcourt, 1970.

Aristotle. *The Art of Rhetoric*. Translated by J. H. Freese. Loeb Classical Library 193. Cambridge, MA: Harvard University Press, 1926.

Armas, Jose. *La Familia de La Raza*. Albuquerque: Raza Associates, 1972. https://eric.ed.gov/?id=ED091096.

Arteaga, Alfred. *Chicano Poetics: Heterotexts and Hybridities*. Cambridge, UK: Cambridge University Press, 1997.

Asen, Robert. "A Discourse Theory of Citizenship." *Quarterly Journal of Speech* 90, no. 2 (2004): 189–211. https://doi.org/10.1080/0033563042000227436.

The Austin Statesman. "March: Spanish Land Grants Demanded." July 4, 1966.

Azoulay, Ariella Aïsha. *Civil Imagination: A Political Ontology of Photography*. London: Verso, 2015.

Bakhtin, M. M. "Forms of Time and of the Chronotope in the Novel." In *The Dialogic Imagination*, 84–258. Austin: University of Texas Press, 1981.

———. *Problems of Dostoevsky's Poetics*. Edited and translated by Caryl Emerson. Minneapolis: University of Minnesota Press, 1999.

Bardacke, Frank. *Trampling Out the Vintage: Cesar Chavez and the Two Souls of the United Farm Workers*. London: Verso, 2011.

Barragán Goetz, Philis. *Reading, Writing, and Revolution: Escuelitas and the Emergence of a Mexican American Identity in Texas*. Austin: University of Texas Press, 2020.

Barrera, James B. "The 1968 Edcouch-Elsa High School Walkout: Chicano Student Activism in a South Texas Community." *Aztlán: A Journal of Chicano Studies* 29, no. 2 (2004): 93–122.

Barriga, Miguel Diaz. "The Culture of Poverty as Relajo." *Aztlán: A Journal of Chicano Studies* 22, no. 2 (1997): 43–65.

Bebout, Lee. "Hero Making in El Movimiento: Reies López Tijerina and the Chicano Nationalist Imaginary." *Aztlán: A Journal of Chicano Studies* 32, no. 2 (2007): 93–121.

———. *Mythohistorical Interventions: The Chicano Movement and Its Legacies*. Minneapolis: University of Minnesota Press, 2011.

Belgrad, Daniel. "Performing Lo Chicano." *MELUS* 29, no. 2 (2004): 249–64.

Bender, Steven W. *One Night in America: Robert Kennedy, César Chávez, and the Dream of Dignity*. Boulder: Paradigm, 2008.

Berger, Maurice. *For All the World to See: Visual Culture and the Struggle for Civil Rights*. New Haven: Yale University Press, 2010.

Beverley, John. "Introduccion." *Revista de Crítica Literaria Latinoamericana* 18, no. 36 (1992): 7–19. https://doi.org/10.2307/4530620.

———. "The Margin at the Center: On 'Testimonio.'" *Modern Fiction Studies* 35, no. 1 (1989): 11–28.

———. *Testimonio: On the Politics of Truth*. Minneapolis: University of Minnesota Press, 2004.

Bhabha, Homi K., ed. *The Location of Culture*. London: Routledge, 2004.

———. *Nation and Narration*. London: Routledge, 1990.

Blackwell, Maylei. *¡Chicana Power! Contested Histories of Feminism in the Chicano Movement*. Austin: University of Texas Press, 2011.

Blair, Carole, Greg Dickenson, and Brian L. Ott. "Introduction: Rhetoric/Memory/Place." In *Places of Public Memory*, edited by Greg Dickenson, Carole Blaire, and Brian L. Ott, 1–23. Tuscaloosa: University of Alabama Press, 2010.

Bolter, J. David, and Richard Grusin. *Remediation: Understanding New Media*. Cambridge, MA: MIT Press, 1999.

Bonilla-Silva, Eduardo, and David R. Dietrich. "The Latin Americanization of U.S. Race Relations: A New Pigmentocracy." In *Shades of Difference: Why Skin Color Matters*,

edited by Evelyn Nakano Glenn, 40–59. Palo Alto: Stanford University Press, 2009.
Brands, Hal. *Latin America's Cold War*. Cambridge, MA: Harvard University Press, 2010.
Bruce-Novoa. *Chicano Authors: Inquiry by Interviews*. Austin: University of Texas Press, 1980.
———. *Chicano Poetry: A Response to Chaos*. Austin: University of Texas, 1982.
Burke, Kenneth. *Attitudes Toward History*. Berkeley: University of California Press, 1984.
———. *Counter-Statement*. Berkeley: University of California Press, 1968.
———. *A Rhetoric of Motives*. Berkeley: University of California Press, 1969.
Cabán, Pedro A. "Moving from the Margins to Where? Three Decades of Latino/a Studies." *Latino Studies* 1, no. 1 (2003): 5–35.
Calafell, Bernadette M. "Brownness, Kissing, and US Imperialism: Contextualizing the Orlando Massacre." *Communication and Critical / Cultural Studies* 14, no. 2 (2017): 198–202. https://doi.org/10.1080/14791420.2017.1293957.
———. "Rhetorics of Possibility: Challenging the Textual Bias of Rhetoric through the Theory of the Flesh." In *Rhetorica in Motion: Feminist Rhetorical Methods and Methodologies*, edited by Eileen E. Schell and K. J. Rawson, 104–17. Pittsburgh: University of Pittsburgh Press, 2010.
Calderón-Zaks, Michael. "Debated Whiteness amid World Events: Mexican and Mexican American Subjectivity and the U.S.' Relationship with the Americas, 1924–1936." *Mexican Studies / Estudios Mexicanos* 27, no. 2 (August 2011): 325–59. https://doi.org/10.1525/msem.2011.27.2.325.
Camejo, Antonio, and Antonio Rio. "Nat'l Chicano Parley Raised Consciousness." *The Militant*, May 2, 1969.
Candelaria, Cordelia. *Chicano Poetry: A Critical Introduction*. Westport: Greenwood Press, 1986.
cárdenas, micha. *Poetic Operations: Trans of Color Art in Digital Media*. Durham: Duke University Press, 2022.
Carrigan, William D., and Clive Webb. "Repression and Resistance: The Lynching of Persons of Mexican Origins in the United States, 1848–1928." In *How the United States Racializes Latinos: White Hegemony and Its Consequences*, edited by José A. Cobas, Jorge Duany, and Joe R. Feagin, 68–86. London: Routledge, 2015.
Carta Editorial: For the Informed-Interested in Mexican American Affairs. "Mexican Heritage." August 26, 1968.
Castro, Mike, and Frank del Olmo. "Killed in East L.A. Rioting 5 Years Ago: Newsman Salazar Becomes Legend to Some Latins." *Los Angeles Times*, September 1, 1975, sec. Part II.
Certeau, Michel de. *The Practice of Everyday Life*. Translated by Steven Rendall. Berkeley: University of California Press, 1988.
Césaire, Aimé. *Discourse on Colonialism*. Translated by Joan Pinkham. New York: Monthly Review Press, 2000.
Chakravartty, Paula, Rachel Kuo, Victoria Grubbs, and Charlton McIlwain. "#CommunicationSoWhite." *Journal of Communication* 68, no. 2 (2018): 254–66. https://doi.org/10.1093/joc/jqy003.
Chapnick, Howard. "Markets and Careers." *Popular Photography*, March 1981.
Charland, Maurice. "Constitutive Rhetoric: The Case of the Peuple Québécois." *Quarterly Journal of Speech* 73, no. 2 (May 1987): 133–50.
Chávez, César. "The Organizer's Tale." *Ramparts* 5, no. 2 (1966): 43–50.
Chávez, Ernesto. *"¡Mi Raza Primero!" (My People First!): Nationalism, Identity, and Insurgency in the Chicano Movement in Los Angeles, 1966–1978*. Berkeley: University of California Press, 2002.

Chávez, Karma R. "The Body: An Abstract and Actual Rhetorical Concept." *Rhetoric Society Quarterly* 48, no. 3 (2018): 242–50. https://doi.org/10.1080/02773945.2018.1454182.

———. "Counter-Public Enclaves and Understanding the Function of Rhetoric in Social Movement Coalition-Building." *Communication Quarterly* 59, no. 1 (2011): 1–18.

Chávez-García, Miroslava. "A Genealogy of Chicana History, the Chicana Movement, and Chicana Studies." In *Routledge Handbook of Chicana/o Studies*, edited by Francisco A. Lomelí, Denise A. Segura, and Elyette Benjamin-Labarthe, 67–80. London: Routledge, 2018.

Cheng, Emily. "The Vietnam War and Chicana/o Environmentalism in El Grito Del Norte (1968–73)." *American Quarterly* 72, no. 1 (2020): 55–73. https://doi.org/10.1353/aq.2020.0003.

Chicano Moratorium. Cintec Productions, 1971. https://www.youtube.com/watch?v=famNeiosTVk.

Churchill, Ward, and Jim Vander Wall. *The cointelpro Papers: Documents from the FBI's Secret Wars Against Domestic Dissent*. Boston: South End Press, 1990.

Cicero. *Brutus. Orator.* Translated by G. L. Hendrickson and H. M. Hubbell. Loeb Classical Library 342. Cambridge, MA: Harvard University Press, 1939.

Cintron, Ralph. "Democracy and Its Limitations." In *The Public Work of Rhetoric: Citizen-Scholars and Civic Engagement*, edited by John Ackerman and David Coogan, 98–116. Columbia: University of South Carolina Press, 2010.

Cisneros, Josue David. *The Border Crossed Us: Rhetorics of Borders, Citizenship, and Latina/o Identity*. Tuscaloosa: The University of Alabama Press, 2014.

———. "(Re)Bordering the Civic Imaginary: Rhetoric, Hybridity, and Citizenship in La Gran Marcha." *Quarterly Journal of Speech* 97, no. 1 (2011): 26–49.

———. "Reclaiming the Rhetoric of Reies López Tijerina: Border Identity and Agency in 'The Land Grant Question.'" *Communication Quarterly* 60, no. 5 (2012): 561–87.

Clark, Donald Lemen. "Imitation: Theory and Practice in Roman Rhetoric." *Quarterly Journal of Speech* 37, no. 1 (1951): 11. https://doi.org/10.1080/00335635109381613.

Clay, Steven, and Rodney Phillips. *A Secret Location on the Lower East Side: Adventures in Writing, 1960–1980: A Sourcebook of Information*. New York: Granary Books, 1998.

Cloud, Dana L. "The Null Persona: Race and the Rhetoric of Silence in the Uprising of '34." *Rhetoric and Public Affairs* 2, no. 2 (1999): 177–209.

Cohen, Deborah. *Braceros: Migrant Citizens and Transnational Subjects in the Postwar United States and Mexico*. Chapel Hill: University of North Carolina Press, 2011.

Corona, Ignacio. "The Cultural Location/s of (U.S.) Latin Rock." In *The Routledge Companion to Latina/o Media*, edited by María Elena Cepeda and Dolores Inés Casillas, 241–48. New York: Routledge, 2017.

Cortez, José M. "On Disinvention: Dr. Ersula Ore and the Rhetorics of Race at the US–Mexico Border." *Journal for the History of Rhetoric* 24, no. 1 (2021): 87–103. https://doi.org/10.1080/26878003.2021.1881312.

Cortez, José M., and Romeo García. "The Absolute Limit of Latinx Writing." *College Composition and Communication* 71, no. 4 (2020): 566–90.

Cotera, María, Maylei Blackwell, and Dionne Espinoza. "Introduction: Movements, Movimientos, and Movidas." In *Chicana Movidas: New Narratives of Activism and Feminism in the Movement Era*, edited by Dionne Espinoza, María Eugenia Cotera, and Maylei Blackwell, 1–30. Austin: University of Texas Press, 2018.

Couture, Barbara, and Patti Wojahn, eds. *Crossing Borders, Drawing Boundaries: The Rhetoric of Lines across America*. Logan: Utah State University Press, 2016.

Craig, Richard B. *The Bracero Program: Interest Groups and Foreign Policy*. Austin: University of Texas Press, 2015.

Creagan, James F. "Public Law 78: A Tangle of Domestic and International Relations." *Journal of Inter-American Studies* 7, no. 4 (1965): 541–56. https://doi.org/10.2307/165274.
Crenshaw, Kimberlé. "Demarginalizing the Intersection of Race and Sex: A Black Feminist Critique of Antidiscrimination Doctrine, Feminist Theory, and Antiracist Politics." *University of Chicago Legal Forum* 1989, no. 1 (1989): 139–67.
———. "Mapping the Margins: Intersectionality, Identity Politics, and Violence Against Women of Color." *Stanford Law Review* 43, no. 6 (1991): 1241–1300.
Crick, Nathan. "From Cosmopolis to Cosmopolitics: The Rhetorical Study of Social Movements." In *The Rhetoric of Social Movements: Networks, Power, and New Media*, edited by Nathan Crick, 3–29. New York: Routledge, 2020.
———. "Rhetoric and Events." *Philosophy and Rhetoric* 47, no. 3 (August 2014): 251–72.
Cruz-Malavé, Arnaldo. "Testimonio." In *Keywords for Latina/o Studies*, edited by Deborah R. Vargas, Nancy Raquel Mirabal, and Lawrence M. La Fountain-Stokes, 270–73. New York: New York University Press, 2017.
Cummings, Richard. *Grito! Reies Tijerina and the New Mexico Land Grant War of 1967*. Austin: University of Texas Press, 1971.
Cureton, Richard. "Poetic Syntax and Aesthetic Form." *Style* 14, no. 4 (1980): 318–40.
Dalton, Frederick John. *The Moral Vision of César Chávez*. Maryknoll, NY: Orbis Books, 2003.
Dávila, Arlene. "Introduction." In *Contemporary Latina/o Media: Production, Circulation, and Politics*, edited by Arlene Dávila and Yeidy M. Rivero, 1–18. New York: New York University Press, 2014.
Davis, Angela. "Before I Knew Elizabeth Martínez." *Social Justice* 39, no. 2/3 (2012): 96–100.
Davis, Thomas B., and Amado Ricon Virulegio. *The Political Plans of Mexico*. Lanham, MD: University Press of America, 1987.
DeChaine, D. Robert. "Introduction: For Rhetorical Border Studies." In *Border Rhetorics*, edited by D. Robert DeChaine, 1–15. Tuscaloosa: The University of Alabama Press, 2012.
Delgado, Fernando P. "Chicano Movement Rhetoric: An Ideographic Interpretation." *Communication Quarterly* 43, no. 4 (1995): 446–55.
Delgado, Richard, and Jean Stefancic, "Introduction." In *The Latino/a Condition: A Critical Reader*, edited by Richard Delgado and Jean Stefancic, 1–11. 2nd ed. New York: New York University Press, 2011.
Delgado Melgosa, Berta. *Neither Eagle Nor Serpent: La Guerra de Vietnam Como Tema Literario En La Novela Chicana*. Alcalá de Henares, Spain: Universidad de Alcalá, 2012.
Deopujari, M. B. "America's Manifest Destiny and Mexico." *Proceedings of the Indian History Congress* 28 (1966): 489–94.
DeRocher, Patricia. *Transnational Testimonios: The Politics of Collective Knowledge Production*. Seattle: University of Washington Press, 2018.
DiAngelo, Robin. "White Fragility." *International Journal of Critical Pedagogy* 3, no. 3 (2011): 54–70.
Diaz, Ella. "Seeing Is Believing: Visualizing and Performing Testimonio in Chicana/o and Latina/o Art." *Chicana/Latina Studies* 11, no. 1 (2011): 35–83.
Drexler-Dreis, Joseph. "James Baldwin's Decolonial Love as Religious Orientation." *Journal of Africana Religions* 3, no. 3 (2015): 251–78.
D'Souza, Dinesh. *Illiberal Education: The Politics of Race and Sex on Campus*. New York: The Free Press, 1991.

Duany, Jorge, Joe R. Feagin, and José A. Cobas. "Introduction: Racializing Latinos, Historical Background and Current Forms." In *How the United States Racializes Latinos: White Hegemony and its Consequences*, edited by José A. Cobas, Jorge Duany, and Joe R. Feagin, 1–14. London: Routledge, 2015.

Duara, Prasenjit. "The Cold War As a Historical Period: An Interpretive Essay." *Global History* 6, no. 3 (2011): 457–80. https://doi.org/10.1017/S1740022811000416.

Dussel, Enrique. *Philosophy of Liberation*. Translated by Aquilina Martinez and Christine Morkovsky. Maryknoll, NY: Orbis Books, 1985.

Endres, Danielle, and Samantha Senda-Cook. "Location Matters: The Rhetoric of Place in Protest." *Quarterly Journal of Speech* 97, no. 3 (2011): 257–82.

Escobar, Edward J. "The Dialectics of Repression: The Los Angeles Police Department and the Chicano Movement, 1968–1971." *The Journal of American History* 79, no. 4 (1993): 1483–1514. https://doi.org/10.2307/2080213.

———. "The Unintended Consequences of the Carceral State: Chicana/o Political Mobilization in Post–World War II America." *Journal of American History* 102, no. 1 (2015): 174–84.

Espinoza, Dionne. "Rethinking Cultural Nationalism and La Familia through Women's Communities: Enriqueta Vasquez and Chicana Feminist Thought." In *Enriqueta Vasquez and the Chicano Movement: Writing from El Grito Del Norte*, edited by Lorena Oropeza and Dionne Espinoza, 205–31. Houston: Arte Público Press, 2006.

Espinoza, Dionne, María Eugenia Cotera, and Maylei Blackwell, eds. *Chicana Movidas: New Narratives of Activism and Feminism of the Movement Era*. Austin: University of Texas Press, 2018.

Fahnestock, Jeanne. "Verbal and Visual Parallelism." *Written Communication* 20, no. 2 (2003): 123–52. https://doi.org/10.1177/0741088303020002001.

Fanon, Frantz. *The Wretched of the Earth*. Translated by Constance Farrington. New York: Grove Press, 1963.

Fantham, Elaine. "Imitation and Evolution: The Discussion of Rhetorical Imitation in Cicero De Oratore 2. 87–97 and Some Related Problems of Ciceronian Theory." *Classical Philology* 73, no. 1 (1978): 1–16.

Farr, Marcia. *Rancheros in Chicagoacán: Language and Identity in a Transnational Community*. Austin: University of Texas Press, 2010.

Feagin, Joe R. *The White Racial Frame: Centuries of Racial Framing and Counter-Framing*. 3rd ed. New York: Routledge, 2020. https://doi.org/10.4324/9780429353246.

Feagin, Joe R., and José A. Cobas. *Latinos Facing Racism: Discrimination, Resistance, and Endurance*. New York: Routledge, 2015. https://doi.org/10.4324/9781315633749.

Feagin, Joe R., and Kimberley Ducey. *Racist America: Roots, Current Realities, and Future Reparations*. 4th ed. New York: Routledge, 2018.

Ferris, Susan, and Ricardo Sandoval. *The Fight in the Fields: César Chávez and the Farmworkers Movement*. Edited by Diana Hembree. New York: Harcourt Brace, 1997.

Finnegan, Cara A. "The Naturalistic Enthymeme and Visual Argument: Photographic Representation in the 'Skull Controversy.'" *Argumentation and Advocacy* 37, no. 3 (2001): 133. https://doi.org/10.1080/00028533.2001.11951665.

———. "Studying Visual Modes of Public Address: Lewis Hine's Progressive-Era Child Labor Rhetoric." In *The Handbook of Rhetoric and Public Address*, edited by Shawn J. Parry-Giles and J. Michael Hogan, 250–70. Chichester: Wiley-Blackwell, 2010.

Fishlow, David M., ed. *Sons of Zapata: A Brief Photographic History of the Farm Workers Strike in Texas*. Rio Grande City: United Farm Workers Organizing Committee, ALF-CIO, 1967.

Flores, Lisa. "Advancing a Decolonial Rhetoric." *Advances in the History of Rhetoric* 21, no. 3 (2018): 320–22.

———. "Between Abundance and Marginalization: The Imperative of Racial Rhetorical Criticism." *Review of Communication* 16, no. 1 (2016): 4–24.

———. "Constructing Rhetorical Borders: Peons, Illegal Aliens, and Competing Narratives of Immigration." *Critical Studies in Media Communication* 20, no. 4 (2003): 362–87.

———. "Creating Discursive Space through a Rhetoric of Difference: Chicana Feminists Craft a Homeland." *Quarterly Journal of Speech* 82, no. 2 (1996): 142–56.

———. *Deportable and Disposable: Public Rhetoric and the Making of the Illegal Immigrant*. University Park: Pennsylvania State University Press, 2020.

Flores, Lisa A., and Marouf A. Hasian Jr. "Returning to Aztlán and La Raza: Political Communication and the Vernacular Construction of Chicano/a Nationalism." In *Politics, Communication, and Culture*, edited by Alberto González and Dolores V. Tanno, 186–203. Thousand Oaks: Sage, 1997.

Foster, Hal. "Preface." In *Visual and Visuality*, edited by Hal Foster, ix–xiv. Seattle: Bay Press, 1988.

Gabriel, Trip. "He Fuels Cultural Fires for the Right in Florida." *New York Times*, April 24, 2022.

Gabriel, Trip, and Dana Goldstein. "Debate Over Scope of Racism Embroils Schools." *New York Times*, June 2, 2021.

Galarza, Ernesto. *Merchants of Labor: The Mexican Bracero Story*. Santa Barbara: McNally & Loftin, 1964.

Gallego, Carlos. *Chicana/o Subjectivity and the Politics of Identity: Between Recognition and Revolution*. New York: Palgrave Macmillan, 2011.

———. "From Identity to Situatedness: Rodrigo Toscano and the New Chicana/o Poetics." *Aztlán: A Journal of Chicano Studies* 32, no. 2 (2007): 129–38.

El Gallo: La Voz de La Justicia. "Albert Gurule Seeks Governership: La Raza Candidate Concerned with 'Needs of People,'" June 1970. Republished from the *Denver Post*.

———. "Viva Tijerina." June 23, 1967.

———. "Which One Do You Know." June 23, 1967.

———. "Why Do We Need La Raza Unida Party." June 1970.

Gamboa, Erasmo. *Mexican Labor and World War II: Braceros in the Pacific Northwest, 1942–1947*. Seattle: University of Washington Press, 2015.

Gamio, Manuel. *Forjando Patria: Pro-Nacionalismo*. Translated by Fernando Armstrong-Fumero. Boulder: University Press of Colorado, 2010.

Garcia, Alma M. "The Development of Chicana Feminist Discourse, 1970–1980." *Gender and Society* 3, no. 2 (1989): 217–38.

García, David. *Strategies of Segregation: Race, Residence, and the Struggle for Educational Equality*. Oakland: University of California Press, 2018.

Garcia, Gina Ann. *Becoming Hispanic-Serving Institutions: Opportunities for Colleges and Universities*. Baltimore: Johns Hopkins University Press, 2019.

———. "Defined by Outcomes or Culture? Constructing an Organizational Identity for Hispanic-Serving Institutions." *American Educational Research Journal* 54 (2017): 111S–134S.

García, Ignacio M. *Chicanismo: The Forging of a Militant Ethos among Mexican Americans*. Tucson: University of Arizona Press, 1997.

———. "Juncture in the Road: Chicano Studies Since 'El Plan de Santa Barbara.'" In *Chicanas/Chicanos at the Crossroads: Social, Economic, and Political Change*, edited by David R. Maciel and Isidro D. Ortiz, 181–203. Tucson: University of Arizona Press, 1996.

García, Mario T. "The Chicana in American History: The Mexican Women of El Paso, 1880–1920: A Case Study." *Pacific Historical Review* 49, no. 2 (1980): 315–37. https://doi.org/10.2307/3638904.

———. *The Chicano Generation*. Oakland: University of California Press, 2015.

———. "Introduction." In *Border Correspondent: Selected Writings, 1955–1970, Ruben Salazar*, edited by Mario T. García, 1–38. Berkeley: University of California Press, 1998.

———. *The Latino Generation: Voices of the New America*. Chapel Hill: The University of North Carolina Press, 2014.

———. *Literature as History: Autobiography, Testimonio, and the Novel in the Chicano and Latino Experience*. Tucson: The University of Arizona Press, 2016.

———. *Mexican Americans: Leadership, Ideology, and Identity, 1930–1960*. New Haven: Yale University Press, 1989.

García, Mario T., and Sal Castro. *Blowout! Sal Castro and the Chicano Struggle for Educational Justice*. Chapel Hill: University of North Carolina Press, 2011.

Garcia, Matt. *From the Jaws of Victory: The Triumph and Tragedy of Cesar Chavez and the Farm Worker Movement*. Berkeley: University of California Press, 2012.

García, Romeo, and Damián Baca. "Hopes and Visions: The Possibility of Decolonial Options." In *Rhetorics Elsewhere and Otherwise: Contested Modernities, Decolonial Visions*, 1–48. Champaign: National Council of Teachers of English, 2019.

García, Romeo, and José M. Cortez. "The Trace of a Mark That Scatters: The Anthropoi and the Rhetoric of Decoloniality." *Rhetoric Society Quarterly* 50, no. 2 (2020): 93–108. https://doi.org/10.1080/02773945.2020.1714703.

Gates, Henry Louis. "Introduction." In *"Race," Writing, and Difference*, edited by Henry Louis Gates, 1–21. Chicago: University of Chicago Press, 1986.

Givens, Terryl L. "Aristotle's Critique of Mimesis: The Romantic Prelude." *Comparative Literature Studies* 28, no. 2 (1991): 121–36.

Gómez, Laura E. *Manifest Destinies: The Making of the Mexican American Race*. 2nd ed. New York: New York University Press, 2018.

Gómez-Jiménez, Eva María. "'NearerandnearerandNEARER': Foregrounding Effects of the Unconventional Capitalization in the Experimental Poetry of E. E. Cummings." *Journal of Literary Semantics* 46, no. 2 (2017): 109–29. https://doi.org/10.1515/jls-2017-0007.

Gómez-Quiñones, Juan. *Chicano Politics: Reality and Promise, 1940–1990*. Albuquerque: University of New Mexico Press, 1990.

Gómez-Quiñones, Juan, and Irene Vásquez. *Making Aztlán: Ideology and Culture of the Chicana and Chicano Movement, 1966–1977*. Albuquerque: University of New Mexico Press, 2014.

Gonzales, Juan. "Forgotten Pages: Spanish-Language Newspapers in the Southwest." *Journalism History* 4, no. 2 (1977): 50–51.

Gonzales, Rodolfo "Corky." *I Am Joaquín / Yo Soy Joaquín: An Epic Poem, with a Chronology of People and Events in Mexican and Mexican American History*. Toronto: Bantam Pathfinder Editions, 1972.

———. *I am Joaquin: An Epic Poem*. El Gallo Press, 1967.

———. "The Revolutionist." In *Message to Aztlán: Selected Writings of Rodolfo "Corky" Gonzales*, edited by Antonio Esquibel, 96–134. Houston: Arte Público Press, 2001.

Gonzales, Rodolfo "Corky," and Reies Tijerina. "Social Revolution in the Southwest." Auraria Library, Denver, Colorado, November 20, 1967.

Gonzalez, Elsa, Guillermo Ortega, Mauricio Molina, and Gilberto Lizalde. "What Does It Mean to Be a Hispanic-Serving Institution? Listening to the Latina/o/x Voices

of Students." *International Journal of Qualitative Studies in Education* 33, no. 8 (2020): 796–809. https://doi.org/10.1080/09518398.2020.1751896.
González, Gabriela. "Carolina Munguía and Emma Tenayuca: The Politics of Benevolence and Radical Reform." *Frontiers: A Journal of Women Studies* 24, no. 2/3 (2003): 200–29.
Gonzalez, Gilbert G. *Chicano Education in the Era of Segregation*. Denton: University of North Texas Press, 2013 [1990].
Gonzalez, Henry B. "The Hate Issue." *Congressional Record* 115, Pt. 8, April 22, 1969.
Greene, Ronald Walter. "Another Materialist Rhetoric." *Critical Studies in Mass Communication* 15, no. 1 (1998): 21–40.
Griswold del Castillo, Richard. *The Treaty of Guadalupe Hidalgo: A Legacy of Conflict*. Norman: University of Oklahoma Press, 1992.
Griswold del Castillo, Richard, and Richard A. García. *César Chávez: A Triumph of Spirit*. Norman: University of Oklahoma Press, 1995.
El Grito Del Norte. "El Plan Espiritual de Aztlan." July 6, 1969.
———. "To Our Readers." August 24, 1968.
Gronbeck-Tedesco, John A. "The Left in Transition: The Cuban Revolution in US Third World Politics." *Journal of Latin American Studies* 40, no. 4 (2008): 651–73.
Gross, Daniel M. *The Secret History of Emotion: From Aristotle's Rhetoric to Modern Brain Science*. Chicago: University of Chicago Press, 2006.
Gugelberger, Georg M. "Institutionalization of Transgression: Testimonial Discourse and Beyond." In *The Real Thing: Testimonial Discourse and Latin America*, edited by Georg M. Gugelberger, 1–12. Durham: Duke University Press, 1996.
Guidotti-Hernández, Nicole M. "Embodied Forms of State Domination: Gender and the Camp Grant Massacre." *Social Text* 28, no. 3 (2010): 91–117. https://doi.org/10.1215/01642472-2010-005.
Gunckel, Colin. "Building a Movement and Constructing Community: Photography, the United Farm Workers, and El Malcriado." *Social Justice* 42, no. 3/4 (2015): 29–45.
———. "The Chicano/a Photographic: Art as Social Practice in the Chicano Movement." *American Quarterly* 67, no. 2 (2015): 377–412. https://doi.org/10.1353/aq.2015.0030.
———. "Thinking About La Raza: Photography, the Archive, and the Visualization of Protest." *Aztlán: A Journal of Chicano Studies* 43, no. 1 (2018): 177–94.
Gurza, Esperanza. "'I am Joaquín': Speech Act Theory Applied." *Confluencia* 1, no. 2 (1986): 85–97.
Gusterson, Hugh. "Nuclear Weapons and the Other in the Western Imagination." *Cultural Anthropology* 14, no. 1 (1999): 111–43.
Gutiérrez, David G. *Walls and Mirrors: Mexican Americans, Mexican Immigrants, and the Politics of Ethnicity*. Berkeley: University of California Press, 1995.
Gutierrez, Felix. "Reporting for La Raza: The History of Latino Journalism in America." *Agenda* 8, no. 4 (1978): 29–35.
Gutierrez, José Angel. "How We Built La Raza Unida Party." *International Socialist Review* 32, no. 6 (1971): 17–19.
———. *The Making of a Chicano Militant: Lessons from Cristal*. Madison: The University of Wisconsin Press, 1998.
Guzmán, Ralph. "Mexican American Casualties in Vietnam." Merrill College, University of California, 1969.
———. *Mexican American Casualties in Vietnam*. Santa Cruz: University of California, 1970.
Hall, Simon. *Rethinking the American Anti-War Movement*. New York: Routledge, 2012.

Hall, Stuart. "Encoding, Decoding." In *The Cultural Studies Reader*, edited by Simon During, 507–17. 2nd ed. London: Routledge, 1999.

———. "Introduction: Who Needs 'Identity'?" In *Questions of Cultural Identity*, edited by Paul du Gay and Stuart Hall, 1–17. London: Sage, 1996.

———. "The Whites of Their Eyes: Racist Ideologies and the Media." In *Gender, Race and Class in Media: A Text Reader*, edited by Gail Dines and Jean M. Humez, 18–22. Thousand Oaks: Sage, 1995.

Hallin, Daniel. "1968: The Year of Media Decision." In *The Turning Point That Wasn't*, edited by Robert Giles and Robert W. Snyder, 3–8. New York: Routledge, 2017.

Hamilton, Kevin, and Ned O'Gorman. "Visualities of Strategic Vision: Lookout Mountain Laboratory and the Deterrent State from Nuclear Tests to Vietnam." *Visual Studies* 30, no. 2 (June 2015): 195–208. https://doi.org/10.1080/1472586X.2015.1024965.

Hammerback, John C., and Richard J. Jensen. "Ethnic Heritage as Rhetorical Legacy: The Plan of Delano." *Quarterly Journal of Speech* 80, no. 1 (1994): 53–70.

———. "History and Culture as Rhetorical Constraints: Cesar Chavez's Letter from Delano." In *Doing Rhetorical History: Concepts and Cases*, 207–20. Tuscaloosa: University of Alabama Press, 1998.

———. *The Rhetorical Career of César Chávez*. College Station: Texas A&M University Press, 1998.

———. "The Rhetorical Worlds of César Chávez and Reies Tijerina." *Western Journal of Speech Communication* 44, no. 3 (1980): 166–76.

Hammerback, John C., Richard J. Jensen, and Jose Angel Gutierrez. *A War of Words: Chicano Protest in the 1960s and 1970s*. Westport: Greenwood Press, 1985.

Hardt, Michael, and Antonio Negri. *Empire*. Cambridge, MA: Harvard University Press, 2000.

Hariman, Robert. *Political Style: The Artistry of Power*. Chicago: University of Chicago Press, 1995.

Hariman, Robert, and John L. Lucaites. *No Caption Needed: Iconic Photographs, Public Culture, and Liberal Democracy*. Chicago: University of Chicago Press, 2007.

Harlow, Barbara. *After Lives: Legacies of Revolutionary Writing*. London: Verso, 1996.

———. *Resistance Literature*. New York: Methuen, 1987.

Hassan, Narin. "Colonialism and Gender." In *The Wiley Blackwell Encyclopedia of Gender and Sexuality Studies*, edited by Nancy Naples, et al., 303–13. Malden: Wiley-Blackwell, 2016.

Hawhee, Debra. "Kairotic Encounters." In *Perspectives on Rhetorical Invention*, edited by Janet Atwill and Janice M. Lauer, 16–35. Knoxville: University of Tennessee Press, 2002.

Hawhee, Debra, and Christa J. Olson. "Pan-Historiography: The Challenges of Writing History Across Time and Space." In *Theorizing Histories of Rhetoric*, edited by Michelle Ballif, 90–105. Carbondale: Southern Illinois University Press, 2013.

Hawk, Byron. "Sound: Resonance as Rhetorical." *Rhetoric Society Quarterly* 48, no. 3 (2018): 315–23.

Heusser, Martin. "The Visual Rhetoric of e. e. cummings's 'poempictures.'" *Word and Image* 11, no. 1 (1995): 16–30. https://doi.org/10.1080/02666286.1995.10435894.

Holling, Michelle A. "Retrospective on Latin@ Rhetorical-Performance Scholarship: From 'Chicano Communication' to 'Latina/o Communication?'" *Communication Review* 11, no. 4 (2008): 293–322.

Holling, Michelle A., and Bernadette Marie Calafell. "Identities on Stage and Staging Identities: ChicanoBrujo Performances as Emancipatory Practices." *Text and Performance Quarterly* 27, no. 1 (2007): 58–83.

———. "Introduction." In *Latina/o Discourse in Vernacular Spaces: Somos de Una Voz?*, edited by Michelle A. Holling and Bernadette Marie Calafell, xv–xxv. Lanham: Lexington Books, 2011.

Hopkins, A. G. *American Empire: A Global History*. Princeton: Princeton University Press, 2018.

Houdek, Matthew. "The Imperative of Race for Rhetorical Studies: Toward Divesting from Disciplinary and Institutionalized Whiteness." *Communication and Critical/Cultural Studies* 15, no. 4 (2018): 292–99. https://doi.org/10.1080/14791420.2018.1534253.

———. "In the Aftertimes, Breathe: Rhetorical Technologies of Suffocation and an Abolitionist Praxis of (Breathing in) Relation." *Quarterly Journal of Speech* 108, no. 1 (2022): 1–27. https://doi.org/10.1080/00335630.2021.2019301.

Houdek, Matthew, and Kendall R. Phillips. "Rhetoric and the Temporal Turn: Race, Gender, Temporalities." *Women's Studies in Communication* 43, no. 4 (2020): 369–83. https://doi.org/10.1080/07491409.2020.1824501.

Houston, Paul. "Jury Splits 4–3 on Salazar Death; DA Will Review Case." *Los Angeles Times*, October 6, 1970, sec. Part I.

———. "TV Channels Will Provide Full Coverage of Salazar Inquest: In Unprecedented Move, Stations Agree to Pool Service and Rotate Live Color Telecasts of Entire Proceedings." *Los Angeles Times*, September 9, 1970, sec. Part II.

———. "U.S. Inquiry Urged in Salazar's Death: Bradley, KMEX Officials, Latin Leaders Join in Call for Probe." *Los Angeles Times*, September 1, 1970, sec. Part I.

———. "U.S. Says It Is Probing Reports That Outsiders Fomented Riot: Investigation Centers on Allegations Dissidents Violated Federal Law by Crossing State Lines to Create Trouble." *Los Angeles Times*, September 2, 1970, sec. Part I.

Houston, Paul, and Dave Smith. "Mexican-American Observers Walk Out of Salazar Inquest: Protesting Testimony as Irrelevant, Group Leaves Twice, Last Time During Showing of Sheriff's Riot Videotape." *Los Angeles Times*, September 11, 1970, sec. Part I.

———. "Witness at Salazar Hearing Charges Bias in Questions." *Los Angeles Times*, September 18, 1970, sec. Part I.

"Interagency Committee on Mexican American Affairs: News Briefing by Chairman Vicente T. Ximenes Announcing a Hearing to Be Held in El Paso on October 27 and 28. September 12, 1967." *Weekly Compilation of Presidential Documents* 3, no. 37 (September 18, 1967): 1281–82.

Ivie, Robert L. "Progressive Form and Mexican Culpability in Polk's Justification for War." *Central States Speech Journal* 30, no. 4 (Winter 1979): 311–20.

Ivie, Robert L., and Oscar Giner. *Hunt the Devil: A Demonology of US War Culture*. Tuscaloosa: University of Alabama Press, 2015.

Izaguirre, José G., III. "Chicana/o Movement Politics, the Cold War, and the White Racial Frame: The Case of El Colegio Jacinto Treviño." *Journal for the History of Rhetoric*. Forthcoming.

———. "Movidas After Nationalism: Enriqueta Longeaux y Vasquez and Chicana Aesthetics." *Rhetoric Society Quarterly* 53, no. 4 (2023): 538–52.

———. "Nonviolence in Context: César Chávez, the Chican@ Movement, and a Poetics of Deferral." *Journal for the History of Rhetoric* 23, no. 1 (2020): 54–83. https://doi.org/10.1080/15362426.2019.1685415.

———. "'A Social Movement in Fact': La Raza and El Plan de Delano." *Rhetoric Society Quarterly* 50, no. 1 (2020): 53–68. https://doi.org/10.1080/02773945.2019.1685125.

———. "The Whiteness of LBJ's Rhetoric: The Appointment of Vicente T. Ximenes to the Equal Employment Opportunity Commission." *Quarterly Journal of Speech* 109, no. 2 (2023): 154–78. https://doi.org/10.1080/00335630.2022.2149846.

Izaguirre, José G., III and Josue David Cisneros. "The Assembling of a March: Rhetorics of the Farm Workers' 1966 Pilgrimage." In *The Rhetoric of Social Movements: Networks, Power, and New Media*, edited by Nathan Crick, 33–49. New York: Routledge, 2020.
Jameson, Fredric. "On Literary and Cultural Import-Substitution in the Third World." In *The Real Thing: Testimonial Discourse and Latin America*, edited by Georg M. Gugelberger, 170–91. Durham: Duke University Press, 1996.
Jasinski, James. *Sourcebook on Rhetoric: Key Concepts in Contemporary Rhetorical Studies*. Thousand Oaks: Sage, 2001.
Jenkins, J. Craig. *The Politics of Insurgency: The Farm Worker Movement and the Politics of the 1960s*. New York: Columbia University Press, 1985.
Jensen, Richard J., and John C. Hammerback. "From Farmworker to Cultural Icon: Cesar Chavez's Rhetorical Crusade." In *Social Controversy and Public Address in the 1960s and Early 1970s: A Rhetorical History of the United States*, edited by Richard J. Jensen, 9:83–118. Lansing: Michigan State University Press, 2017.
——. "'No Revolutions Without Poets': The Rhetoric of Rodolfo 'Corky' Gonzáles." *Western Journal of Speech Communication* 46, no. 1 (1982): 72–91.
Johnson, Davi. "Martin Luther King Jr.'s 1963 Birmingham Campaign as Image Event." *Rhetoric and Public Affairs* 10, no. 1 (2007): 1–25.
Kells, Michelle Hall. *Vicente Ximenes, LBJ's Great Society, and Mexican American Civil Rights Rhetoric*. Carbondale: Southern Illinois University Press, 2018.
Kendi, Ibram X. *How to Be an Antiracist*. New York: One World, 2019.
Kirby, John T. "Aristotle's 'Poetics': The Rhetorical Principle." *Arethusa* 24, no. 2 (1991): 197–217.
——. "The 'Great Triangle' in Early Greek Rhetoric and Poetics." *Rhetorica: A Journal of the History of Rhetoric* 8, no. 3 (1990): 213–28. https://doi.org/10.1525/rh.1990.8.3.213.
Kress, Gunther, and Theo van Leeuwen. *Reading Images: The Grammar of Visual Design*. London: Routledge, 2006.
Leal, Luis. "In Search of Aztlán." In *Aztlán: Essays on the Chicano Homeland*, edited by Rudolfo Anaya and Francisco Lomelí, 6–13. Albuquerque: University of New Mexico Press, 1991.
Lee, Christopher J. *Making a World After Empire: The Bandung Moment and Its Political Afterlives*. Athens: Ohio University Press, 2010.
Leff, Michael C. "Interpretation and the Art of the Rhetorical Critic." *The Western Journal of Speech Communication* 44 (1980): 337–49.
Leff, Michael, and Andrew Sachs. "Words the Most Like Things: Iconicity and the Rhetorical Text." *Western Journal of Communication* 54 (1990): 252–73.
Levy, Jacques E. *Cesar Chavez: Autobiography of La Causa*. New York: W. W. Norton, 1975.
Licona, Adela C. *Zines in Third Space: Radical Cooperation and Borderlands Rhetoric*. Albany: State University of New York Press, 2012.
Limón, José E. "Border Literary Histories, Globalization, and Critical Regionalism." *American Literary History* 20, nos. 1–2 (2008): 160–82.
——. *Mexican Ballads, Chicano Poems: History and Influence in Mexican-American Social Poetry*. Berkeley: University of California Press, 1992.
Lira, Natalie, and Alexandra Minna Stern. "Mexican Americans and Eugenic Sterilization: Resisting Reproductive Injustice in California, 1920–1950." *Aztlán: A Journal of Chicano Studies* 39, no. 2 (2014): 9–34.
Longeaux y Vasquez, Enriqueta. "Despierten! Hermanos." *El Grito Del Norte*, November 1968.

———. "Preface." In *Enriqueta Vasquez and the Chicano Movement: Writing from El Grito Del Norte*, edited by Lorena Oropeza and Dionne Espinoza, ix–xvi. Houston: Arte Público Press, 2006.
———. "¡Que Linda Es Cuba!" *El Grito Del Norte*, May 19, 1969.
———. "El Soldado Raso Today." *El Grito Del Norte*, August 29, 1970.
———. "The Woman." *El Grito Del Norte*, July 6, 1969.
López, Dennis. "Cultivating Aztlán: Chicano (Counter)Cultural Politics and the Postwar American University." *American Studies* 58, no. 1 (2019): 73–111. https://doi.org/10.1353/ams.2019.0013.
———. "*El Grito Del Norte*, Chicana/o Print Culture, and the Politics of Anti-Imperialism." *Science and Society* 79, no. 4 (2015): 527–54.
Lopez, Enrique Hank. "Ruben Salazar Death Silences a Leading Voice of Reason." *Los Angeles Times*, September 6, 1970, sec. C.
López, Ian F. Haney. "Race, Ethnicity, Erasure: The Salience of Race to LatCrit Theory." *California Law Review* 85, no. 5 (1997): 1143–211.
———. *White by Law: The Legal Construction of Race*. Tenth anniversary ed. New York: New York University Press, 2006.
Los Angeles County Office of Independent Review. "Review of the Los Angeles County Sheriff's Department's Investigation into the Homicide of Ruben Salazar." February 22, 2011. http://shq.lasdnews.net/shq/LASD_Oversight/Report%20on%20the%20Sheriff's%20Department's%20Investigation%20into%20the%20Homicide%20of%20Ruben%20Salazar.pdf.
Lynch, Paul L. "Recovering Rhetoric: René Girard as Theorhetor." *Contagion: Journal of Violence, Mimesis, and Culture* 27, no. 1 (2020): 101–22.
———. "Rescuing Rhetoric: Kenneth Burke, René Girard, and Forms of Conversion." *Contagion: Journal of Violence, Mimesis, and Culture* 24, no. 1 (2017): 139–58.
Macfarlane, Ellen. "Photography and the Western Worker: Organizing Farm Labor in Early 1930s California." *Southern California Quarterly* 100, no. 2 (2018): 183–215.
Madsen, Deborah L. *American Exceptionalism*. Edinburgh: Edinburgh University Press, 1998.
El Malcriado: La Voz del Campesino. "The Plan of Delano." March 17, 1966.
———. "The Plan of Delano." April 10, 1966.
Maldonado-Torres, Nelson. *Against War: Views from the Underside of Modernity*. Durham: Duke University Press, 2008.
———. "On the Coloniality of Being: Contributions to the Development of a Concept." *Cultural Studies (London, United Kingdom)* 21, nos. 2–3 (2007): 240–70.
Marín, Christine. *A Spokesman of the Mexican American Movement: Rodolfo "Corky" Gonzales and the Fight for Chicano Liberation, 1966–1972*. San Francisco: R and E Research Associates, 1977.
Mariscal, Jorge. *Brown-Eyed Children of the Sun: Lessons from the Chicano Movement*. Albuquerque: University of New Mexico Press, 2005.
———. "Left Turns in the Chicano Movement, 1965–1975." *Monthly Review: An Independent Socialist Magazine* 54, no. 3 (2002): 59–69.
———. "Mexican Americans and the Viet Nam War." In *A Companion to the Vietnam War*, edited by Marilyn B. Young and Robert Buzzanco, 348–66. Malden, MA: Blackwell, 2002.
———. "Negotiating César: César Chávez in the Chicano Movement." *Aztlán: A Journal of Chicano Studies* 29, no. 1 (2004): 21–56.
———. "Reading Chicano/a Writing About the American War in Viet Nam." *Aztlan: A Journal of Chicano Studies* 25, no. 2 (2000): 11–49.

Márquez, Benjamin. *LULAC: The Evolution of a Mexican American Political Organization.* Austin: The University of Texas Press, 1993.
Martinez, Eliud. "'I Am Joaquín' as Poem and Film: Two Modes of Chicano Expression." *Journal of Popular Culture* 13, no. 3 (1980): 505–15.
Martínez, Elizabeth (Betita). *The Youngest Revolution: A Personal Report on Cuba.* New York: Dial Press, 1969.
Matthiessen, Peter. *Sal Si Puedes (Escape If You Can): Cesar Chavez and the New American Revolution.* Berkeley: University of California Press, 2014.
Mazón, Mauricio. *The Zoot-Suit Riots: The Psychology of Symbolic Annihilation.* Austin: University of Texas Press, 2010.
McClintock, Anne. *Imperial Leather: Race, Gender and Sexuality in the Colonial Contest.* New York: Routledge, 1995.
McGee, Michael Calvin. "The 'Ideograph': A Link Between Rhetoric and Ideology." *Quarterly Journal of Speech* 66, no. 1 (1980): 1–16.
McKeon, Richard. "Literary Criticism and the Concept of Imitation in Antiquity." *Modern Philology* 34, no. 1 (1936): 1–35.
Meléndez, A. Gabriel. *So All Is Not Lost: The Poetics of Print in Nuevomexicano Communities, 1834–1958.* Albuquerque: University of New Mexico Press, 1997.
Mignolo, Walter. "Cosmopolitanism and the De-Colonial Option." *Studies in Philosophy and Education* 29, no. 2 (2010): 111–27. https://doi.org/10.1007/s11217-009-9163-1.
———. *The Darker Side of the Renaissance: Literacy, Territoriality, and Colonization.* 2nd ed. Ann Arbor: University of Michigan Press, 2003.
———. *The Darker Side of Western Modernity: Global Futures, Decolonial Options.* Durham: Duke University Press, 2011.
———. "Delinking: The Rhetoric of Modernity, the Logic of Coloniality and the Grammar of De-Coloniality." *Cultural Studies* 21, nos. 2–3 (2007): 449–514.
———. "Epistemic Disobedience, Independent Thought and De-Colonial Freedom." *Theory, Culture, and Society* 26, nos. 7–8 (2009): 1–23.
———. *Local Histories / Global Designs: Coloniality, Subaltern Knowledges, and Border Thinking.* Princeton: Princeton University Press, 2012.
———. "Loci of Enunciation and Imaginary Constructions: The Case of (Latin) America, I." *Poetics Today* 15, no. 4 (1994): 505–21.
Mignolo, Walter D., and Catherine E. Walsh. "Introduction." In *On Decoloniality: Concepts, Analytics, Praxis*, 1–12. Durham: Duke University Press, 2018.
Miller, Carolyn R. "The Aristotelian Topos: Hunting for Novelty." In *Rereading Aristotle's Rhetoric*, edited by Alan G. Gross and Arthur E. Walzer, 130–46. Carbondale: Southern Illinois University Press, 2000.
Miller, Marilyn Grace. *Rise and Fall of the Cosmic Race: The Cult of Mestizaje in Latin America.* Austin: University of Texas Press, 2009.
Minian, Ana Raquel. "'Indiscriminate and Shameless Sex': The Strategic Use of Sexuality by the United Farm Workers." *American Quarterly* 65, no. 1 (2013): 63–90.
———. *Undocumented Lives: The Untold Story of Mexican Migration.* Cambridge, MA: Harvard University Press, 2018.
Mirandé, Alfredo, ed. *The Chicano Experience: An Alternative Perspective.* Notre Dame: University of Notre Dame Press, 1994.
———. *Gringo Injustice: Insider Perspectives on Police, Gangs, and Law.* New York: Routledge, 2019.
———. *Gringo Justice: Catholicism in American Culture.* Notre Dame: University of Notre Dame Press, 1994.
Mladek, Klaus. "Introduction." In *Police Forces: A Cultural History of an Institution*, edited by Klaus Mladek, 1–9. New York: Palgrave Macmillan, 2007.

Molina, Natalia. *How Race Is Made in America: Immigration, Citizenship, and the Historical Power of Racial Scripts.* Berkeley: University of California Press, 2014.
Molina, Natalia, Daniel Martinez HoSang, and Ramón A. Gutiérrez. "Introduction: Toward a Relational Consciousness of Race." In *Relational Formations of Race: Theory, Method, and Practice,* edited by Natalia Molina, Daniel Martinez HoSang, and Ramón A. Gutiérrez, 1–18. Oakland: University of California Press, 2019.
Molina-Guzmán, Isabel. *Dangerous Curves: Latina Bodies in the Media.* New York: New York University Press, 2010.
Moore, Joan W., and Ralph Guzman. "New Wind from the Southwest." *The Nation,* May 30, 1966.
Moore, Truman. *The Slaves We Rent.* New York: Random House, 1965.
Mora, G. Cristina. *Making Hispanics: How Activists, Bureaucrats, and Media Constructed a New American.* Chicago: University of Chicago Press, 2014.
Moraga, Cherríe L. "Queer Aztlán: The Re-Formation of Chicano Tribe." In *The Last Generation: Prose and Poetry,* 145–74. Boston, MA: South End Press, 1993.
Muckelbauer, John. "Imitation and Invention in Antiquity: An Historical-Theoretical Revision." *Rhetorica* 21, no. 2 (May 1, 2003): 61–88. https://doi.org/10.1525/rh.2003.21.2.61.
Muñoz, Carlos, Jr. "The Development of Chicano Studies, 1968–1981." In *Chicano Studies: A Multidisciplinary Approach,* 5–18. New York: Teacher's College, Columbia University, 1984.
———. *Youth, Identity, Power: The Chicano Identity.* Rev. ed. London: Verso, 2007.
Muñoz, José Esteban. *Disidentifications: Queers of Color and the Performance of Politics.* Minneapolis: University of Minnesota Press, 2013.
Murillo, Dana Velasco, and Pablo Miguel Silva. "Mine Workers and Weavers: Afro-Indigenous Labor Arrangements and Interactions in Puebla and Zacatecas, 1600–1700." In *City Indians in Spain's American Empire: Urban Indigenous Society in Colonial Mesoamerica and Andean South America, 1530–1810,* edited by Dana Velasco Murillo, Mark Lentz, and Margarita R. Ochoa, 104–27. Chicago: Sussex Academic Press, 2014.
Murphy, Sharon, ed. *Other Voices: Black, Chicano, and American Indian Press.* Dayton: Pflaum/Standard, 1974.
Nabokov, Peter. *Tijerina and the Courthouse Raid.* Berkeley: Ramparts Press, 1970.
Nakayama, Thomas K., and Robert L. Krizek. "Whiteness: A Strategic Rhetoric." *Quarterly Journal of Speech* 81, no. 3 (1995): 291–309.
Na'puti, Tiara R. "Oceanic Possibilities for Communication Studies." *Communication and Critical/Cultural Studies* 17, no. 1 (2020): 95–103. https://doi.org/10.1080/14791420.2020.1723802.
Newman, Robert P. "Under the Veneer: Nixon's Vietnam Speech of November 3, 1969." *Quarterly Journal of Speech* 56 (1970): 168–78.
Ngai, Mae M. *Impossible Subjects: Illegal Aliens and the Making of Modern America.* Princeton: Princeton University Press, 2014.
Noriega, Chon A. *Shot in America: Television, the State, and the Rise of Chicano Cinema.* University of Minnesota Press, 2000.
Ochieng, Omedi. "What Cannot Be Done." *Philosophy & Rhetoric* 55, no. 1 (2022): 53–59.
O'Gorman, Ned. "'The Logic and Rhetoric of Power': George F. Kennan, Paul H. Nitze, and Planning for Cold War." In *World War II and the Cold War: The Rhetoric of Hearts and Minds,* edited by Martin J. Medhurst, 8:259–302. East Lansing: Michigan State University Press, 2018.
Olson, Christa J. *American Magnitude: Hemispheric Vision and Public Feeling in the United States.* Columbus: Ohio State University Press, 2021.

———. "Introduction: This Is America." *Journal for the History of Rhetoric* 24, no. 1 (2021): 1–6. https://doi.org/10.1080/26878003.2021.1881306.

Olson, Christa J., and René Agustín De los Santos. "Expanding the Idea of América." *Rhetoric Society Quarterly* 45, no. 3 (2015): 193–98.

Olson, Lester C., Cara A. Finnegan, and Diane S. Hope, eds. *Visual Rhetoric: A Reader in Communication and American Culture*. Los Angeles: Sage, 2008.

Omi, Michael, and Howard Winant. *Racial Formation in the United States*. 3rd ed. New York: Routledge, 2015.

Ontiveros, Randy J. *In the Spirit of New People: The Cultural Politics of the Chicano Movement*. New York: New York University Press, 2014.

Ore, Ersula. "The Lost Cause, Trump Time, and the Necessity of Impatience." *Rhetoric Society Quarterly* 51, no. 3 (2021): 237–39. https://doi.org/10.1080/02773945.2021.1918516.

———. *Lynching: Violence, Rhetoric, and American Identity*. Jackson: University Press of Mississippi, 2019.

Ore, Ersula, and Matthew Houdek. "Lynching in Times of Suffocation: Toward a Spatiotemporal Politics of Breathing." *Women's Studies in Communication* 43, no. 4 (2020): 443–58. https://doi.org/10.1080/07491409.2020.1828709.

Oropeza, Lorena. "Becoming Indo-Hispano: Reies López Tijerina and the New Mexican Land Grant Movement." In *Formations of United States Colonialism*, edited by Alyosha Goldstein, 180–206. Durham: Duke University Press, 2014.

———. *The King of Adobe: Reies López Tijerina, Lost Prophet of the Chicano Movement*. Chapel Hill: University of North Carolina Press, 2019.

———. *¡Raza Si! ¡Guerra No! Chicano Protest and Patriotism During the Viet Nam War Era*. Berkeley: University of California Press, 2005.

———. "Viviendo y Luchando: The Life and Times of Enriqueta Vasquez." In *Enriqueta Vasquez and the Chicano Movement: Writing from El Grito Del Norte*, edited by Lorena Oropeza and Dionne Espinoza, xix–liii. Houston: Arte Público Press, 2006.

Orosco, José-Antonio. *Cesar Chavez and the Common Sense of Nonviolence*. Albuquerque: University of New Mexico Press, 2008.

Orozco, Cynthia. *No Mexicans, Women, or Dogs Allowed*. Austin: University of Texas Press, 2009.

Ortego, Philip D. "Introduction to Chicano Studies." In *The Chicano Renaissance*, edited by Livie Isauro Duran and H. Russell Bernard, 331–50. New York: The MacMillan, 1973.

Paredes, Américo. *With His Pistol in His Hand: A Border Ballad and Its Hero*. Austin: University of Texas Press, 1958.

Parker, Jason. "Cold War II: The Eisenhower Administration, the Bandung Conference, and the Reperiodization of the Postwar Era." *Diplomatic History* 30, no. 5 (2006): 867–92.

Patil, Vrushali. "Contending Masculinities: The Gendered (Re) Negotiation of Colonial Hierarchy in the United Nations Debates on Decolonization." *Theory and Society* 38, no. 2 (2009): 195–215.

Paz, Ireneo. "Introduction." In *Life and Adventures of the Celebrated Bandit: Joaquin Murrieta, His Exploits in the State of California*, ix–cxiii. Houston: Arte Público Press, 2001.

Paz, Octavio. "The Labyrinth of Solitude." In *The Labyrinth of Solitude and The Other Mexico, Return to the Labyrinth of Solitude, Mexico and the United States, The Philanthropic Ogre*, translated by Lysander Kemp, 9–212. New York: Grove Press, 1985.

Perez, Annemarie. "'Tu Reata Es Mi Espada': Elizabeth Sutherland's Chicana Formation." In *Chicana Movidas: New Narratives of Activism and Feminism in the Movement*

Era, edited by Dionne Espinoza, Maylei Blackwell, and Dionne Espinoza, 245–60. Austin: University of Texas Press, 2018.
Pérez, Emma. *The Decolonial Imaginary: Writing Chicanas into History*. Bloomington: Indiana University Press, 1999.
Pérez, Hiram. *A Taste for Brown Bodies: Gay Modernity and Cosmopolitan Desire*. New York: New York University Press, 2015.
Pérez-Torres, Rafael. "Chicana/o Studies's Two Paths." Review of *The Making of Chicana/o Studies: In the Trenches of Academe* by Rodolfo F. Acuña and *Chicano Studies: The Genesis of a Discipline* by Michael Soldatenko, *American Literary History* 25, no. 3 (2013): 683–92.
Pizzolato, Nicola. "Harvests of Shame: Enduring Unfree Labour in the Twentieth-Century United States, 1933–1964." *Labor History* 59, no. 4 (2018): 472–90. https://doi.org/10.1080/0023656X.2018.1467259.
El Plan de Santa Bárbara: A Chicano Plan for Higher Education. Oakland: La Causa, 1969.
Powell, Malea. "Rhetorics of Survivance: How American Indians Use Writing." *College Composition and Communication* 53, no. 3 (2002): 396–434. https://doi.org/10.2307/1512132.
Powers, Charles T., and Jeff Perlman. "One Dead, 40 Hurt in East L.A. Riot: Times Columnist Ruben Salazar Killed by Bullet." *Los Angeles Times*, August 30, 1970, sec. A.
Prasch, Allison M. "Toward a Rhetorical Theory of Deixis." *Quarterly Journal of Speech* 102, no. 2 (2016): 166–93.
Prasch, Allison M., and Mary E. Stuckey. "'An Empire for Liberty': Reassessing US Presidential Foreign Policy Rhetoric." *Quarterly Journal of Speech* 108, no. 4 (2022): 357–81. https://doi.org/10.1080/00335630.2022.2128202.
Pratt, Mary Louise. "'I Rigoberta Menchú and the 'Culture Wars.'" In *The Rigoberta Menchú Controversy*, edited by Arturo Arias, 29–48. Minneapolis: University of Minnesota Press, 2001.
Prieto, Linda, and Sofia A. Villenas. "Pedagogies from Nepantla: Testimonio, Chicana/Latina Feminisms and Teacher Education Classrooms." *Equity and Excellence in Education* 45, no. 3 (2012): 411–29. https://doi.org/10.1080/10665684.2012.698197.
Pruchnic, Jeff, and Kim Lacey. "The Future of Forgetting: Rhetoric, Memory, Affect." *Rhetoric Society Quarterly* 41, no. 5 (2011): 472–94. https://doi.org/10.1080/02773945.2011.597818.
Pycior, Julie Leininger. "From Hope to Frustration: Mexican Americans and Lyndon Johnson in 1967." *The Western Historical Quarterly* 24, no. 4 (1993): 469–94.
Quijano, Aníbal. "Coloniality and Modernity/Rationality." *Cultural Studies* 21, nos. 2–3 (2007): 168–78. https://doi.org/10.1080/09502380601164353.
———. "Coloniality of Power, Eurocentrism, and Latin America." *Nepantla: Views from South* 1, no. 3 (2000): 533–80.
Quijano, Aníbal, and Immanuel Wallerstein. "Americanity as a Concept, or the Americas in the Modern World-System." *International Social Science Journal* 44, no. 134 (1992): 549–57.
Quintilian. *The Orator's Education*. Edited and translated by Donald A. Russell. Vol. 3: *Books 6–8*. 5 vols. Loeb Classical Library 124. Cambridge, MA: Harvard University Press, 2002.
Raiford, Leigh. *Imprisoned in a Luminous Glare: Photography and the African American Freedom Struggle*. Durham: University of North Carolina Press, 2011.
Rancière, Jacques. *Dis-Agreement*. Translated by Julie Rose. Minneapolis: University of Minnesota Press, 1999.

———. "Politics, Identification, and Subjectivization." *October* 61 (1992): 58–64. https://doi.org/10.2307/778785.
———. *The Politics of Aesthetics: The Distribution of the Sensible*. New York: Continuum, 2004.
Rancière, Jacques, and Davide Panagia. "Dissenting Words: A Conversation with Jacques Rancière." *Diacritics* 30, no. 2 (2000): 113–26.
Rendón, Armando B. *Chicano Manifesto*. New York: Collier-Macmillan, 1971.
Reyes, Kathryn Blackmer, and Julia E. Curry Rodríguez. "Testimonio: Origins, Terms, and Resources." *Equity and Excellence in Education* 45, no. 3 (2012): 525–38. https://doi.org/10.1080/10665684.2012.698571.
Ribb, Richard. "La Rinchada: Revolution, Revenge, and the Rangers, 1910–1920." In *War Along the Border: The Mexican Revolution and Tejano Communities*, edited by Arnoldo De León, 56–106. College Station: Texas A&M University Press, 2011.
Rice, Jenny. "The Rhetorical Aesthetics of More: On Archival Magnitude." *Philosophy and Rhetoric* 50, no. 1 (2017): 26–49.
Rivers, Nathaniel A. "Apathy." In *A New Handbook of Rhetoric: Inverting Classical Vocabulary*, edited by Michele Kennerly, 139–54. University Park: Pennsylvania State University Press, 2021.
Rodriguez, Marc S. *Rethinking the Chicano Movement*. New York: Routledge, 2015.
Rodriguez, Richard T. "Family." In *Keywords for Latina/o Studies*, edited by Deborah R. Vargas, Nancy Raquel Mirabal, and Lawrence M. La Fountain-Stokes, 61–64. New York: New York University Press, 2017.
———. *Next of Kin: The Family in Chicano/a Cultural Politics*. Durham, NC: Duke University Press, 2009.
Roediger, David R. *The Wages of Whiteness: Race and the Making of the American Working Class*. London: Verso, 1999.
Romero, Tom, II. "Wearing the Red, White, and Blue Trunks of Aztlán: Rodolfo 'Corky' Gonzales and the Convergence of American and Chicano Nationalism." *Aztlán: A Journal of Chicano Studies* 29, no. 1 (2004): 83–117.
Romo, Richardo. *East Los Angeles: History of a Barrio*. Austin: University of Texas Press, 2010.
Rosales, F. Arturo. *Chicano! The History of the Mexican American Civil Rights*. Houston: Arte Público Press, 1996.
Rossa, Della. "Calif. Brown Beret Leaders Answer L.A. Police Charges." *The Militant*, April 8, 1968.
Roybal, Karen. "Pushing the Boundaries of Border Subjectivity, Autobiography, and Camp-Rasquachismo." *Aztlán: A Journal of Chicano Studies* 38, no. 2 (2013): 71–93.
Ruiz, Iris D., and Raúl Sánchez, eds. *Decolonizing Rhetoric and Composition Studies: New Latinx Keywords for Theory and Pedagogy*. New York: Palgrave MacMillan, 2016.
Ruiz, Vicki L. *From Out of the Shadows: Mexican Women in Twentieth-Century America*. 10th anniversary ed. Oxford: Oxford University Press, 2008.
Rumbaut, Rubén. "Pigments of Our Imagination: On the Racialization and Racial Identities of 'Hispanics' and 'Latinos.'" In *How the United States Racializes Latinos: White Hegemony and Its Consequences*, edited by José A. Cobas, Jorge Duany, and Joe R. Feagin, 15–36. London: Routledge, 2015. https://doi.org/10.4324/9781315634104.
Salazar, Ruben. "Humphrey Asks Action by Mexican-Americans: Vice President Addresses El Paso Parley, Tells Latins to 'Speak Up' About Problems." *Los Angeles Times*, October 28, 1967, sec. Part One.
Saldívar, José David. *Border Matters: Remapping American Cultural Studies*. Berkeley: University of California Press, 1997.

———. "Border Thinking, Minoritized Studies, and Realist Interpellations: The Coloniality of Power from Gloria Anzaldúa to Arundhati Roy." In *Identity Politics Reconsidered*, edited by Linda Martín Alcoff, Michael Hames-García, Satya P. Mohanty, and Paula M. L. Moya, 152–70. New York: Palgrave Macmillan US, 2006.

———. "Towards a Chicano Poetics: The Making of the Chicano Subject, 1969–1982." *Confluencia* 1, no. 2 (1986): 10–17.

Sánchez, George J. *Becoming Mexican American: Ethnicity, Culture, and Identity in Chicano Los Angeles, 1900–1945*. New York: Oxford University Press, 1993.

Sánchez, Raúl. "Writing." In *Decolonizing Rhetoric and Composition Studies: New Latinx Keywords for Theory and Pedagogy*, edited by Iris D. Ruiz and Raúl Sánchez, 77–89. New York: Palgrave MacMillan, 2016.

Sandburg, Carl. "Prologue." In *The Family of Man*. New York: Maco, 1955.

San Miguel, Guadalupe. *Brown, Not White: School Integration and the Chicano Movement in Houston*. College Station: Texas A&M University Press, 2005.

———. "The Impact of *Brown* on Mexican American Desegregation Litigation, 1950s to 1980s." *Journal of Latinos and Education* 4, no. 4 (2005): 221–36. https://doi.org/10.1207/s1532771xjle0404_2.

Santoni, Pedro. "The Failure of Mobilization: The Civic Militia of Mexico in 1846." *Mexican Studies / Estudios Mexicanos* 12, no. 2 (1996): 169–94. https://doi.org/10.2307/1051843.

Scott, Robert L., and Donald K. Smith. "The Rhetoric of Confrontation." *Quarterly Journal of Speech* 55, no. 1 (1969): 1–8.

Sharpe, Christina. *In the Wake: On Blackness and Being*. Durham: Duke University Press, 2016.

Shaw, David, and Richard Vasquez. "Contradictory Reports Given in Slaying of Columnist Salazar." *Los Angeles Times*, August 30, 1970, sec. A.

Smith, Marian L. "Race, Nationality, and Reality." *Prologue Magazine* 34, no. 2 (2002). https://www.archives.gov/publications/prologue/2002/summer/immigration-law-1.html.

Smith, Rogers M. *Civic Ideals: Conflicting Visions of Citizenship in U.S. History*. New Haven: Yale University Press, 1999.

Soldatenko, Michael. "Aztlán: How a Journal Built a Discipline." *Diálogo* 20, no. 2 (2017): 7–18. https://doi.org/10.1353/dlg.2017.0028.

———. *Chicano Studies: The Genesis of a Discipline*. Tucson: University of Arizona Press, 2009.

Soto Vega, Karrieann, and Karma R. Chávez. "Latinx Rhetoric and Intersectionality in Racial Rhetorical Criticism." *Communication and Critical/Cultural Studies* 15, no. 4 (2018): 319–25. https://doi.org/10.1080/14791420.2018.1533642.

Sowards, Stacey K. "Rhetorical Agency as Haciendo Caras and Differential Consciousness Through Lens of Gender, Race, Ethnicity, and Class: An Examination of Dolores Huerta's Rhetoric." *Communication Theory* 20, no. 2 (2010): 223–47. https://doi.org/10.1111/j.1468-2885.2010.01361.x.

———. "#RhetoricSoEnglishOnly: Decolonizing Rhetorical Studies through Multilingualism." *Quarterly Journal of Speech* 105, no. 4 (2019): 477–83. https://doi.org/10.1080/00335630.2019.1669891.

———. *¡Sí, Ella Puede! The Rhetorical Legacy of Dolores Huerta and the United Farm Workers*. Austin: University of Texas Press, 2019.

Steiner, Stan. *La Raza: The Mexican Americans*. New York: Harper & Row, 1970.

Stevens, Donald Fithian. *Origins of Instability in Early Republican Mexico*. Durham: Duke University Press, 1991.

Stoll, David. *Rigoberta Menchu and the Story of All Poor Guatemalans.* London: Routledge, 2018.
Street, Richard Steven. *Everyone Had Cameras: Photography and Farmworkers in California 1850–2000.* Minneapolis: University of Minnesota Press, 2008.
———. *Jon Lewis: Photographs of the California Grape Strike.* Lincoln: University of Nebraska Press, 2013.
Sullivan, Dale L. "Attitudes Toward Imitation: Classical Culture and the Modern Temper." *Rhetoric Review* 8, no. 1 (1989): 5–21.
Sullivan, Eileen, and Zolan Kanno-Youngs. "4 Border Patrol Agents Face Disciplinary Action." *New York Times,* July 9, 2022, sec. National.
Sutherland Martinez, Elizabeth (Betita). "Neither Black nor White in a Black-White World." In *Hands on the Freedom Plow: Personal Accounts by Women in SNCC,* 531–40. Urbana-Champaign: University of Illinois Press, 2010.
Taylor, Paul S. *Mexican Labor in the United States.* 2 vols. Berkeley: University of California Press, 1930.
Teague, Charles Collins. *Fifty Years a Rancher; The Recollections of Half a Century Devoted to the Citrus and Walnut Industries of California and to Furthering the Cooperative Movement in Agriculture.* Los Angeles: The Ward Ritchie Press, 1944.
Tenorio-Trillo, Mauricio. *Latin America: The Allure and Power of an Idea.* Chicago: University of Chicago Press, 2017.
Thiong'o, Ngũgĩ wa. *Decolonising the Mind: The Politics of Language in African Literature.* Nairobi: East African Publishers, 1992.
Toohey, Peter. *Reading Epic: An Introduction to the Ancient Narratives.* London: Routledge, 1992.
Torgerson, Dial. "Start of a Revolution? 'Brown Power' Unity Seen Behind School Disorders." *Los Angeles Times,* March 17, 1968.
Trouillot, Michel-Rolph. *Silencing the Past: Power and the Production of History.* Boston: Beacon Press, 2015.
Tuck, Eve, and K. Wayne Yang. "Decolonization Is Not a Metaphor." *Decolonization: Indigeneity, Education and Society* 1, no. 1 (2012): 1–40.
Tufte, Edward R. *Visual Explanations: Images and Quantities, Evidence and Narrative.* Cheshire, CT: Graphics Press, 1997.
Tuhiwai Smith, Linda. *Decolonizing Methodologies: Research and Indigenous Peoples.* London: Zed Books, 2012.
Vaca, Nick C., Octavio Romano-V., Andres Ybarra, and Gustavo Segade. "Spanish Surname War Dead Vietnam." *El Grito: A Journal of Contemporary Mexican-American Thought* 3, no. 1 (1969). https://opendoor.northwestern.edu/archive/items/show/363.
Valdés, Dennis Nodín. *Barrios Norteños: St. Paul and Midwestern Mexican Communities in the Twentieth Century.* Austin: University of Texas Press, 2000.
Valdez, Luis. "The Tale of the Raza." *Ramparts* 5, no. 2 (1966): 40–43.
Valdez, Luis, and Roberto Rubalcava. "Venceremos! Mexican-American Statement on Travel to Cuba." In *Aztlan: An Anthology of Mexican American Literature,* edited by Luis Valdez and Stan Steiner, 214–18. New York: Knopf, 1972.
Valdez, Luis, and Stan Steiner, eds. "El Plan Espiritual de Aztlan." In *Aztlan: An Anthology of Mexican American Literature,* edited by Luis Valdez and Stan Steiner, 402–3. New York: Vintage Books, 1972.
Vallejo, Jody Agus. *Barrios to Burbs: The Making of the Mexican American Middle Class.* Stanford: Stanford University Press, 2012.
Vasconcelos, José. *La Raza Cósmica: Misión de La Raza Iberoamericana.* Paris: Agencia Mundial de Librería, 1948.

Vélez-Ibañez, Carlos G. *Border Visions: Mexican Cultures of the Southwest United States.* Tuscon: University of Arizona Press, 1996.
La Verdad. "Denver Conference." April 1969.
Vigil, Ernesto. *The Crusade for Justice: Chicano Militancy and the Government's War on Dissent.* Madison: University of Wisconsin Press, 1999.
Villanueva, Tino. "Sobre El Termino 'Chicano.'" *Cuadernos Hispanoamericanos* 336 (1978): 387–410.
Vivian, Bradford J. "Up from Memory: Epideictic Forgetting in Booker T. Washington's Cotton States Exposition Address." *Philosophy and Rhetoric* 45, no. 2 (2012): 189–212.
Walsh, Catherine E. "Decoloniality in/as Praxis." In *On Decoloniality: Concepts, Analytics, Praxis.* Durham: Duke University Press, 2018.
Wanzer-Serrano, Darrel. *The New York Young Lords and the Struggle for Liberation.* Philadelphia: Temple University Press, 2015.
———. "Rhetoric's Rac(e/ist) Problems." *Quarterly Journal of Speech* 105, no. 4 (2019): 465–76. https://doi.org/10.1080/00335630.2019.1669068.
———. (As Darrel Enck-Wanzer). "Trashing the System: Social Movement, Intersectional Rhetoric, and Collective Agency in the Young Lords Organization's Garbage Offensive." *Quarterly Journal of Speech* 92, no. 2 (2006): 174–201. https://doi.org/10.1080/00335630600816920.
Warner, Michael. "Publics and Counterpublics." *Public Culture* 14, no. 1 (2002): 49–90.
Watts, Eric King. "'Voice' and 'Voicelessness' in Rhetorical Studies." *Quarterly Journal of Speech* 87, no. 2 (2001): 179–96.
Westad, Odd Arne. *The Global Cold War: Third World Interventions and the Making of Our Times.* Cambridge, UK: Cambridge University Press, 2005.
Wright, Robert A. "East Los Angeles Calm After Riot: Police Patrol Area Where 1 Died and 53 Were Hurt." *New York Times,* August 31, 1970.
Yay, İrfan Cenk. "Capturing the Bronze Power on the Silver Screen: An Epic Journey in Twenty Minutes." *Studies in Latin American Popular Culture* 30 (2012): 17–37.
Yinger, Winthrop. *Cesar Chavez: The Rhetoric of Nonviolence.* Hicksville, NY: Exposition Press, 1975.
Young, Cynthia A. *Soul Power: Culture, Radicalism, and the Making of a U.S. Third World Left.* Durham: Duke University Press, 2006.
Yúdice, George. "Testimonio and Postmodernism." *Latin American Perspectives* 18, no. 3 (1991): 15–31.
Zarefsky, David. "Four Senses of Rhetorical History." In *Doing Rhetorical History: Concepts and Cases,* edited by Kathleen J. Turner, 19–32. Tuscaloosa: University of Alabama Press, 1998.

INDEX

Page numbers in italics denote figures, and endnotes are indicated by "n" followed by the endnote number.

accumulation, as rhetorical figure, 90–95, 97, 100, 102
Acuña, Rodolfo, 8, 148
aesthetics
   aesthetic fragmentation, 59–65, 60–64
   aesthetic interventions, 72
   of border rhetorics, 127–28, 143–44
   Chican@ movement aesthetics, 13–18
   contesting colonial aesthetics, 39–41
   de/colonial aesthetic, characterized, 25
   in (re)figurations of non/violence, 150, 151, 159, 162
   ideological vs. aesthetic approaches, 3–5
   of juxtaposition, 150–52, 160, 161–62, 177–80, 179
   reflecting divergent politics, 184
   shift toward mimesis, 182–83, 188
   of testimonio, 108–13
   whiteness as public aesthetic, 27–31
   See also *Basta! La Historia de Nuestra Lucha* (photobook); de/colonial aesthetic; *El Grito del Norte* newspaper; El Plan Espiritual de Aztlán; "I Am Joaquin: An Epic Poem" (Gonzales); *La Raza* magazine
Agee, James, 49
agency, curtailing of, 54–59, 55–56, 59
Agricultural Workers Organizing Committee (AWOC), 46, 47
Alaniz, Yolanda, 3, 42
Alberto, Lourdes, 134, 136
Alurista (poet), 123, 130, 132, 134, 135, 137, 143
ambivalence. *See* poetics of ambivalence
American Exodus, An (Lange and Taylor), 45
"Americanization," 35, 84
anti-war resistance, 38, 147–48
   See also Chicano Moratorium (1970)
Anzaldúa, Gloria, 38, 73, 109, 125
apathy. *See* poetics of apathy

Arendt, Hannah, 101
Arteaga, Alfred, 73
Axelrod, Beverly, 107, 108–9
   See also *El Grito del Norte* newspaper
Azoulay, Ariella, 156
Aztlan (Valdez and Steiner), 66, 185
Aztlán (nation-state), (re)invention of, 19, 123–24, 128, 145, 187–88
   See also El Plan Espiritual de Aztlán

Bakhtin, Mikhail, 17
Ballis, George, 46, 47, 49
   See also *Basta! La Historia de Nuestra Lucha* (photobook)
Bandung Conference (1955), 106
"barrioization," 33
Basta! La Historia de Nuestra Lucha (photobook)
   aesthetic fragmentation, 59–65, 60–64
   curtailing of agency, 54–59, 55–56, 59
   as de/colonial construction, 67
   injecting apathy into racialization, 48–51
   as memory vs. history, 51–54, 52
   redefining racial identity, 44–45, 66
Bebout, Lee, 71, 204n57
Belgrad, Daniel, 73, 125
Beverley, John, 109–10, 207n31
Bhabha, Homi, 54, 126
bilingualism, appeal to, 79, 81, 82, 85, 161
Blackwell, Maylei, 8
Borderlands / La Frontera (Anzaldúa), 125
border rhetoric, 72, 124, 125–28, 143–44
border thinking, 11, 126–27
bracero program, 33, 47
Bradley, Thomas C., 153
Bronce magazine, 136–40, 138–39
Brown Berets, 38, 122
Bruce-Novoa, 82, 88, 95, 195n16, 204n57
Burgos, Elizabeth, 109
Burke, Kenneth, 53, 73

238 INDEX

Calafell, Bernadette, 174
capitalism, race-induced poverty and, 32–34
cárdenas, micha, 17
Casa de las Americas, 110
Castro, Vicky, 6
Césaire, Aimé, 93
Charland, Maurice, 14
Chávez, César
   1967 El Paso Conference and, 78
   as "assimilationist," 125
   exemplifying politics of deferral, 159
   farmworkers' movement decline and, 42
   on influence of farmworkers' movement, 68
   as nonviolence advocate, 1, 2, 5, 159, 168, 178–79
   public image, 43, 158
   in writing Plan de Delano, 53
Chávez, Ernesto, 8, 148
Chávez, Ignacio, 150
Chávez, Richard, 48
"Chicana/o" term, 41, 41, 125, 208n15
Chican@ moratoriums, formation of, 147–48
   See also Chicano Moratorium (1970)
Chican@ movement(s)
   author's methodology, 18–24, 195n1, 195n16, 196n21
   borders, in extant scholarship, 125
   Chican@ movement aesthetics, 13–18
   emergence of Chican@ underground press, 105
   extended geography of, 105–8, 109, 113–18, 119–20
   ideological vs. aesthetic approaches, 3–5
   institutionalization of, 183–88, 212n5
   inventing rhetorical histories of, 8–13
   marked by hybridity, 73
   as multivalent, 10, 188–89
   nationalism as political program of, 123
   non/violence, question of, 1–3
   print spaces enabling formation of, 40–41
   significance of race in, 5–7, 69, 109
   See also de/colonial aesthetic; poetics of ambivalence; poetics of apathy; poetics of deferral; poetics of mimesis; poetics of relationality; poetics otherwise
"Chicano generation," 125–26
Chicano Manifesto (Rendón), 181–82, 183–84, 186
Chicano Moratorium (1970)
   Chican@ photographic and, 156–62, 160
   de/colonial love, 162–68, 163, 165–67
   formation of Chican@ moratoriums, 147–48
   police paranoia, 168–72, 170–71
   racially forming power of non/violence, 149–52
   Ruben Salazar and (in)visible violence, 152–56
   as "unconstructive," 181–82
   violence of institutional whiteness, 172–77, 174, 176, 179–80
"Chicano Power," 105
Chicano Press Association (CPA), 18, 105, 124, 128, 151, 186
"Chicano Renaissance," 185
Chicano Youth Liberation Conference (1969)
   ambitions of, 122–23
   criticisms of discourse following, 158
   El Plan Espiritual de Aztlán and, 129, 137, 138, 138, 140, 144
   nationalist energy of, 107, 121
Chican@ photographic, 151, 156–62, 160
"Chican@ poetics," 17
Cisneros, Josue David, 31, 72, 81, 126, 127
citizenship, racial classification and, 28–31, 198n22
Civil Rights Movement, 40, 47
Cleofes (poet), 119
Cloud, Dana, 54
Cobas, José A., 31
Cold War
   "Americanization" and, 35
   conflation of race with criminality and, 38
   decolonization as political project, 13
   impact on non-white people, 9, 105–6, 192
colonialism
   contesting colonial aesthetics, 39–41
   establishment of whiteness as aesthetic, 27–31
   Iberian colonialism, 29, 91, 93
   institutionalizing Chican@ movement(s), 183–88, 212n5
   institutionalizing whiteness, 31–38
   "paradigm of war" and, 161–62
   race as construct of, 10–11, 100–101, 190–91
   racially inspired love and, 164
   subversion of colonial narratives, 90–93
   See also de/coloniality
coloniality vs. colonization, 31–32

"Colonial Matrix of Power" (CMP), 11, 191
"commodity identities," 33
Community Service Organization (CSO), 108
Conferencia de las Mujeres (1971), 6
Congress of Industrial Organizations, 46
"constitutive rhetoric," 14
Cornish, Megan, 3, 42
Cortez, José, 11
"cosmic race," 101, 102, 205n108
Crenshaw, Kimberlé, 33, 36
criminality, racial prejudice and, 37–38
Crusade for Justice, 73, 82, 121, 122

Dávila, Arlene, 36
De Anda, Joe, 154–55
Death of the Valley (Lange and Pirkle), 45
de/colonial aesthetic
　Basta! as de/colonial construction, 67
　characterized, 25
　contesting colonial aesthetics through print, 39–41
　institutionalizing whiteness through violence, 31–38
　whiteness as public aesthetic, 27–31
　"white racial frame," 12, 26, 157, 190, 199n36
"decolonial imaginary," 35
de/coloniality
　author's use of, 197n48
　decentering whiteness from activism, 51
　de/colonial love, 162–68, *163*, *165*–67
　de/colonial mode, characterized, 11–12, 25
　de/colonial praxis, 13–18, 103
　El Grito del Norte as de/colonial, 120–21
　racial rhetorical criticism and, 8–13
decolonization
　de/coloniality vs., 12–13
　pushing toward, 23, 143–46
　turn to nationalism and, 123
deferral. *See* poetics of deferral
Delgado, Fernando, 14, 69, 123, 125
Denver Youth Conference (1969).
　See Chicano Youth Liberation Conference (1969)
Diaz, Gilberto, 149
DiGiorgio Corporation, 46
Discourse on Colonialism (Césaire), 93
"distribution of the sensible," 157, 190
Duany, Jorge, 31
Dulles, John, 172
Dussel, Enrique, 106

East LA Blowouts
　feminist contributions and, 6
　"I Am Joaquin" and, 92
　responding to media misrepresentations, 36
　See also Chicano Moratorium (1970)
El Ciudadano newspaper, 39
El Clamor Público newspaper, 39
El Gallo newspaper
　advertising Chicano Youth Liberation Conference, 122
　advertising "I Am Joaquin" poem, 75
　author's approach and, 21
　publication of El Plan Espiritual de Aztlán, *130*, *131*, *132*, *134*, *135*, *137*
Elgin Company, 36
El Grito del Norte newspaper
　author's approach and, 21
　founding of, 107
　poetics of relationality in, 113–18
　publishing El Plan Espiritual de Aztlán, 136–37, 140–43, *141*–*42*
　racial emphasis of, 5
　re-presenting Latinx experiences, 108–13
　toward nationalist project, 119–21
ellipses, as stylistic intervention, 88–90
El Malcriado newspaper, 48–49, 62, 85, 157
El Mosquito newspaper, 39
El Paso Conference (1967), 23
El Plan de Delano
　fragmentation of, 59–65, *60*–*64*
　as memory, 51–54, *52*
　nonviolent activism and, 1
　racial significance of, 42–44
　redefining racial identity, 44–45, 66
　remaking of, 48–51
　representative gap between farmworkers and, 54–59, *55*–*56*, *59*
　underlying conservatism, 22, 43–44
　Luis Valdez as coauthor of, 2
El Plan de La Raza Unida, 42, 79–81, *80*
El Plan de Santa Barbara (1969), 42, 186, 187
El Plan Espiritual de Aztlán
　author's approach and, 19, 21
　as decolonizing "program," 13, 143–46
　otherwising Mexican American politics, 23, 129–43, *130*, *133*, *135*, *138*–*39*, *141*–*42*
　as rhetorical achievement, 123–24, 128
　rhetorical bordering and, 125–28
　variances between publications, 184–85
embodiment, 49, 111, 149

Equal Employment Opportunity
    Commission (EEOC), 74
Escobar, Edward J., 149, 172
Esher, Bill, 49
Espinoza, Dionne, 8
"ethos" and "praxis," 16

Fahnestock, Jeanne, 131
familia, ideal of, 165–66, 165–67
Family of Man (Steichen), 49
Fanon, Frantz, 164
Farm Worker Press, 48
farmworkers' movement
    aesthetic fragmentation, 59–65, 60–64
    curtailing of agency, 54–59, 55–56, 59
    influence on subsequent activism, 68–70
    injecting apathy into racialization, 48–51
    memory vs. history, 51–54, 52
    (re)racializing farmworkers, 45–48
    reinventing racial claims, 66–67
    underlying conservatism, 22, 42–45, 159
Farr, Marcia, 110
Feagin, Joe R., 12, 26, 31
feminism
    constructs of difference, 127, 137–40, 138–39
    in extant scholarship, 6
    relational notion of La Raza and, 109
    See also gender; poetics of relationality; women
Finnegan, Cara, 157
Fisher, M.F.K., 45
Flores, Francisca, 6
Flores, Lisa
    feminist constructs of difference, 127, 137–40, 138–39
    ideologically-based approach, 14
    "imperatives" of racial rhetorical criticism, 9, 10
    on racialization of Mexican Americans, 44
Food and Justice magazine, 85
fragmentation, aesthetic, 59–65, 60–64
"Frito Bandito" campaign, 36

Galarza, Ernesto, 78
Gallego, Carlos, 13–14, 81–82, 195n16
García, Ignacio, 71
García, Mario, 110, 125–26, 207n31
Garcia, Matt, 42
García, Romeo, 11, 16
Gates, Henry Louis, 30

gender
    El Plan Espiritual de Aztlán and, 132, 136–40, 138, 139, 143, 144
    in "I Am Joaquin," 95, 96, 98–99, 102
    See also women
generation, as ideograph, 125–26
Girardian mimesis, 212n5
Giumarra Vineyard Corporations, 1
Gómez, Laura, 26, 29
Gómez-Quiñones, Juan, 8, 123, 143, 148
Gonzales, Henry, 158
Gonzales, Rodolfo "Corky"
    on achieving liberation, 103–4
    appeal of ambivalence and, 71–83, 76–77, 80
    on August 29 moratorium, 152
    emphasis on nationalism, 123
    as La Raza Unida Party leader, 145
    tensions between activists, 5
    See also "I Am Joaquin: An Epic Poem" (Gonzales)
Great Society initiatives, 74–75
"Gringo Justice," 37
Gross, Alan, 50
Gunckel, Colin, 48, 151, 156
Gutierrez, José Angel, 5–6, 145, 188
Guzman, Ralph, 71, 106–7

Hall, Stuart, 36
Hamilton, Kevin, 157
Hammerback, John C., 19–20, 53, 71
Hariman, Robert, 16, 157
Harvest of Shame (CBS), 45–46, 47
Hasian, Marouf, 14
Hawhee, Debra, 21, 26
Hijas de Cuauhtémoc newspaper, 6
Hillstrom, Joseph, 63, 65
Hispanic Serving Institution, 190–91
history vs. memory, 51–54, 52
Holling, Michelle, 19
homophobia, 82
Houdek, Matthew, 7
Huelga (Nelson), 48
Huerta, Dolores, 2, 44, 108

I, Rigoberta Menchú (Menchú and Burgos), 209
"I Am Joaquin: An Epic Poem" (Gonzales)
    aesthetic investments, 68–71
    ambivalent past, 90–96
    ambivalent present, 87–90, 96–102
    appeal of ambivalence and, 71–83, 76–77, 80
    as de/colonial praxis, 103

INDEX 241

publications of, 184, 204n57
spatio-temporal ambivalence, 96–102
temporal and linguistic ambivalence, 83–86, *84*, *86*
universal identity and, 184
Iberian colonialism, 29, 91, 92
icons, formation of, 157
identity
 "Américan" identity, 114
 "commodity identities," 33
 indigenous aesthetics in "I Am Joaquin," 90–95
 "La Raza" as communal identity, 101–2
 mediated images of, 36
 posited in and through texts, 13–14
 racial identities as colonial constructs, 10–11, 100–101, 190–91
 (re)racialization through contrast, 149–52, 156–62, *160*, 177–80, *179*
 redefining racial identity, 44–45, 66
 securing vs. forming of, 183–84, 186
"ideographs," 3, 125–26
indigeneity
 as feature of La Raza, 136, 140, 143
 Iberian colonialism and, 29
 indigenous aesthetics in "I Am Joaquin," 78, 90–95
(in)visible violence, 152–56
Inter-Agency Committee on Mexican American Affairs (IACMAA), 74
intersectional poverty, 33
Ivie, Robert, 27, 198n12

Jensen, Richard J., 19–20, 53, 71
Johnson, Lyndon B. (LBJ administration), 74–75, 83
Jones, Pirkle, 45
juxtaposition, aesthetics of, 150–52, *160*, 161–62, 177–80, *179*

Kennedy, Robert F., 49
Kerner Report, 37

La Alianza Federal de Mercedes, 68, 71–74
labor
 nativist sentiments, 42
 photography as farmworker activism, 45–48
 violence through, 32–34
 See also farmworkers' movement
Laguna Park (Ruben Salazar Park), 152, 172, 175, 182
Lange, Dorothea, 33, 45, 47
language and language codes

author's approach, 16–17, 195n1, 195n16
bilingualism, appeal to, 79, 81, 82, 85, 161
"Chicana/o" term, 41, 125, 208n15
 in *El Grito del Norte* newspaper, 111–12, 114–15, 117–18
 in El Plan Espiritual de Aztlán reproductions, 129, 131, 140, 143, 144
 in "I Am Joaquin," 71, 78, 83–85, *84*, 91
"ideographs," 3, 125–26
"La Raza," term usage, 10, 23, 105, 122–23, 128
rationality, rhetorical use of, 27–28, 198n12
singular use of Spanish, 134
See also rhetoric
La Raza community
 as communal identity, 101–2
 de/colonial love, 162–68, *163*, *165–67*
 emergence of La Raza Unida Party, 145–46
 inventing an inclusive raza, 113–18
 "Plan de La Raza Unida," 42, 79–81, *80*
 (re)racializing Chican@ politics, 9–10, 149–52, 156–62, 177–80
 relational notion of, 109
 term usage, 10, 23, 105, 122–23, 128
 visual parallelism and, 131–32
 See also de/colonial aesthetic; poetics of ambivalence; poetics of apathy; poetics of deferral; poetics of mimesis; poetics of relationality; poetics otherwise
"la raza cosmica," 101, 102, 205n108
La Raza magazine
 aesthetics of juxtaposition, 150–52, *160*, 161–62, 177–80, *179*
 Chican@ photographic, 156–62, *160*
 de/colonial love, 162–68, *163*, *165–67*
 exemplifying racial tensions, 69
 police paranoia, 168–72, *170–71*
 printing of "I Am Joaquin" poem, 75–78, *76–77*
 printing of "Plan de La Raza Unida," 80
 violence of institutional whiteness, 172–77, *174*, *176*, 177–80
 "Yearbook" publication (1968), 105
"La Raza Unida Conference" (1967), 79, 85
La Raza Unida Party (LRUP), 145–46, 187–88
Latin American Defense Organization (LADO), 122
Latin American Student Organization (LASO), 122

242 INDEX

Latin@ Vernacular Discourse (LVD), 14–15
"Latinx"
   as colonial construct, 11
   re-presenting Latinx experiences, 108–13
La Verdad newspaper, 132, *133*, 134
La Voz newspaper, 21
League of United Latin American Citizens (LULAC), 40
Lechuga, Michael, 11
LeGerrette, Carlos, 132
Le Monde magazine, 119
Lewis, Jon, 47
Limón, José E., 41, 82
Longeaux y Vasquez, Enriqueta, 6, 109, 116–17, 120, 132, 140
López, Dennis, 108
Los Angeles Police Department (LAPD)
   aggression of whiteness typified by, 172–77, *174*, *176*, 179–80
   and death of Ruben Salazar, 149, 154–56, 164, 167
   in *La Raza* photomontage, 159–62, *160*, *164*
   paranoia and unwarranted violence, 168–72, *170–71*
   Armando Rendón on, 181–82
   systemic discrimination, post-WWII, 38
Los Angeles Times, 152–53
love, de/colonial, 162–68, *163*, *165–67*
Lucaites, John L., 157

Macfarlane, Ellen, 159
Maldonado-Torres, Nelson, 28, 31–32, 161, 164
Mannheim, Karl, 126
March Against Death (1969), 147
Mariscal, Jorge, 3, 68, 106, 148
Martínez, Elizabeth Sutherland "Betita," 69, 107, 108–9
   See also *El Grito del Norte* newspaper
media
   contesting colonial aesthetics through, 39–41
   coverage of Viet Nam War, 106
   emergence of Chican@ underground press, 105
   re-presentational violence, 36–37
   representations of whiteness and violence, 156
   See also *individual publications*
Meléndez, Gabriel, 39
Melville, Arthur, 116
Melville, Marjorie, 116
memory vs. history, 51–54, *52*
Menchú, Rigoberta, 109
Mendez v. Westminster, 35
mestizaje (racial or cultural mixing), 73, 81, 102, 103, 136, 205n108
Mexican American politics
   coloniality and violence, 31–32
   de/colonial aesthetic, characterized, 25
   epistemic violence, 34–36
   extra-legal violence, 37–38
   labor of violence, 32–34
   Mexican American media and print, 39–41
   otherwising of, 129–43, *130*, *133*, *135*, *138–39*, *141–42*
   (re)racializing Chican@ politics, 9–10, 149–52, 156–62, 177–80
   re-presentational violence, 36–37
   whiteness as public aesthetic, 27–31
   "white racial frame," 12, 26, 157, 190, 199n36
   See also de/colonial aesthetic; poetics of ambivalence; poetics of apathy; poetics of deferral; poetics of mimesis; poetics of relationality; poetics otherwise
Mexican American Student Confederation (MASC), 122
Mexican American War
   enabling "white racial frame," 26
   and whiteness as public aesthetic, 27–31
Mexican American Youth Organization (MAYO), 122, 145
Mignolo, Walter D.
   on "border thinking," 11–12, 126–27
   on "Colonial Matrix of Power," 32
   de/coloniality vs. decolonization, 12–13
   on Mexican American War, 28
   politics of poetic processes, 16–17, 30
"mimeograph revolution," 18
mimesis. *See* poetics of mimesis
Minian, Ana Raquel, 3, 42, 43–44
Mirandé, Alfredo, 33
Molina, Natalia, 44, 64–65
Moore, Joan W., 71
Moraga, Cherríe, 102, 109
Moreno, Lucy, 6
Mount, Julia Luna, 6
Munguía, Carolina, 35, 108
Muñoz, Carlos, 148
Muñoz, José Esteban, 73
Muñoz, Rosalio, 147
Murrow, Edward R., 46

narrative(s)
  gap between sign and signified, 54–55
  process(es) of history vs., 20
  racial formation through, 91
  testimonio, characterized, 109–10, 207n31
National Advisory Committee on Farm Labor, 48
National Farm Labor Union, 46
National Farm Workers Association (NFWA)
  in 1965 wage strike, 47
  bilingual publications, 85
  featured in *Basta!*, 63, 63–64, 64
  ideology of nonviolence, 3
  impact of Dolores Huerta, 108
  nonviolent activism, successes of, 1
  partnerships with other organizations, 68
  underlying conservatism, 42
  See also farmworkers' movement
nationalism
  border rhetoric, 125–28, 143–44
  decolonization and, 143–46
  El Grito del Norte newspaper and, 119–21
  ideal of familia, 165
  nativist sentiments, 42
  otherwising Mexican American politics, 129–43, 130, 133, 135, 138–39, 141–42
  as point of contention, 148
  rhetorical turn to, 123–24
  and separatism, in "I Am Joaquin," 72, 73, 82, 102, 103
  See also poetics otherwise
Nelson, Eugene, 48
newspapers, as expressions of opposition, 39–40
  See also individual publications
Nieto-Gomez, Anna, 6
Nixon, Richard, 147, 168, 175
Noguchi, Thomas T., 153
non/violence
  de/colonial love, 162–68, 163, 165–67
  formation of Chican@ moratoriums, 147–48
  police paranoia vs., 168–72, 170–71
  promotion of nonviolence, 1, 2, 5, 159, 168, 178–79
  question of, 1–3, 150
  (re)racializing Chican@ politics, 149–52, 156–62, 160, 177–80, 179
  racially forming power of, 149–52
  Ruben Salazar and (in)visible violence, 152–56
  violence of institutional whiteness vs., 172–77, 174, 176
Noriega, Chon, 36, 37

O'Gorman, Ned, 157
Olson, Christa, 21, 26
Olson, Lester, 157
Omi, Michael, 9, 10, 15–16, 91
Ontiveros, Randy, 152
Orden Hijos de America ("The Order of Sons of America"), 125
Ore, Ersula, 7, 158
Oropeza, Lorena, 117, 148–49
otherwising. *See* poetics otherwise

pachuco style, 38
"pan-historiography," 21, 26
"paradigm of war," 28, 161–62
parallelism, 129, 131–32, 134, 139, 144
Paz, Octavio, v, 8, 38
Pérez, Emma, 35, 109
photography
  "Chican@ photographic," 151, 156–62, 160
  as farmworker activism, 45–48
  injecting apathy into racialization, 48–51
  rhetorical energy of, 155–56
  See also Basta! La Historia de Nuestra Lucha (photobook)
Pitchess, Peter J., 153
Pittluck, Norman, 153, 155
place-making, 149
Plan de Delano. *See* El Plan de Delano
"Plan de La Raza Unida," 42, 79–81, 80
Plan de Santa Barbara (1969), 42, 186, 187
Plan Espiritual de Aztlán. *See* El Plan Espiritual de Aztlán
poetics
  "Chican@ poetics," 17
  of de/colonial praxis, 13–18
  terminology of, 16–17
poetics of ambivalence
  ambivalent past, 90–96
  ambivalent present, 87–90, 96–102
  appeal of ambivalence, 22, 71–83, 76–77, 80
  characterized, 70–71
  influence of farmworkers' movement, 68–71
  racial solidarity, 103–4
  spatio-temporal ambivalence, 96–102
  temporal and linguistic ambivalence, 83–86, 84, 86

poetics of apathy
  aesthetic fragmentation, 59–65, 60–64
  curtailing of agency, 54–59, 55–56, 59
  injecting apathy into racialization, 48–51
  memory vs. history, 51–54, 52
  (re)racializing farmworkers, 45–48
  reinventing racial claims, 66–67
  underlying conservatism, 22, 42–45
poetics of deferral
  de/colonial love, 162–68, 163, 165–67
  defined, 151
  formation of Chican@ moratoriums, 147–48
  police paranoia, 168–72, 170–71
  (re)racializing Chican@ politics, 149–52, 156–62, 160, 177–80, 179
  racially forming power of non/violence, 149–52
  Ruben Salazar and (in)visible violence, 152–56
  violence of institutional whiteness, 172–77, 174, 176
poetics of mimesis
  Chican@ movement discourse(s), 181–82
  institutionalizing Chican@ movement(s), 183–88, 212n5
  problematic(s) of racial politics, 182–83, 188–93
poetics of relationality
  aesthetic(s) of testimonio, 23, 108–13
  domestic and international concerns, 105–8
  inventing an inclusive raza, 113–18
  toward nationalist project, 119–21
poetics otherwise
  border rhetorics, 125–28
  Chicano Youth Liberation Conference, 122
  otherwising Mexican American politics, 129–43, 130, 133, 135, 138–39, 141–42
  pushing toward decolonization, 23, 143–46
  rhetorical turn to nationalism, 123–24
poetry, 13–14
police paranoia, 168–72, 170–71
Polk, James K., 27, 198n12
Por Que magazine, 119
Powell, Malea, 93
power, violence and, 101
"praxis" and "ethos," 16
print media, contesting colonial aesthetics, 39–41
  See also *individual publications*
process(es) vs. narrative(s) of history, 20

public controversy, 149, 158–59
Public Law 78 (PL 78), 46–47

Quijano, Aníbal, 10–11, 28, 30, 32

race
  centrality in Chican@ movement, 5–7, 69
  Chican@ movement aesthetics and, 13–18
  injecting apathy into racialization, 48–51
  institutionalizing whiteness through violence, 31–38
  nativist sentiments, 42
  non/violence as racially forming, 147–52
  photography activism and, 45–48
  problematic(s) of racial politics, 24, 182–83, 188–93
  (re)racializing Chican@ politics, 9–10, 149–52, 156–62, 177–80
  racially inspired love, 164
  rhetorical criticism in de/colonial mode, 8–13
  as tropic, 30, 189
  visual cultures and, 157–58
  whiteness as public aesthetic, 27–31
  See also de/colonial aesthetic; poetics of ambivalence; poetics of apathy; poetics of deferral; poetics of mimesis; poetics of relationality; poetics otherwise
"racial project," defined, 9–10
Rancière, Jacques, 16, 37, 157, 190
rationality, rhetorical use of, 27–28, 198n12
Razo, Joe, 155, 159
reduplication, 143
relationality. *See* poetics of relationality
Rendón, Armando, 181–82, 183–84, 186
representational intersectionality, 36
Revolutionist, The (Gonzales), 73–74
rhetoric
  accumulation as rhetorical figure, 90–95, 97, 100, 102
  border rhetoric, 125–28, 143–44
  Chican@ photographic, 151, 156–62, 160
  in choosing violence or nonviolence, 150
  "constitutive rhetoric," 14
  criticism in de/colonial mode, 8–13
  establishment of whiteness through, 29–31, 39
  memories as rhetorical constructions, 51–54
  rationality, rhetorical use of, 27–28, 198n12

rhetorical violence, 39
testimonio, characterized, 109–10, 207n31
visual rhetoric, 44–45, 48–51, 70, 79, 131, 151, 157
See also *Basta! La Historia de Nuestra Lucha* (photobook); *El Grito del Norte* newspaper; El Plan Espiritual de Aztlán; "I Am Joaquin: An Epic Poem" (Gonzales); language and language codes; *La Raza* magazine
Rivers, Nathaniel, 50
Rodriguez, Marc, 8
Roosevelt, Eleanor, 38
Ruíz, Iris, 11
Ruiz, Raul, 155, 159, 165
Ruiz, Vicki, 95

Saiz, Richard, 132
Salazar, Ruben, 149, 152–56, 162–65, 169–72, 177–78, 210n33, 211n66
Salcedo, Jesse, 169
Sánchez, George I., 78–79
Sánchez, Raúl, 11
second-person pronouns, 111, 114, 117–18
sexism, 82
sexual liberation, 42
social mobility, 34
social movement rhetoric, 149
solidarity, racial, 103–4, 116, 119–20
Sowards, Stacey, 8, 44
spatio-temporal ambivalence, 96–102
Steichen, Edward, 49
Steiner, Stan, 66, 82, 185
Stoll, David, 110
Story of Wine in California, The (Fisher and Yavno), 45
Street, Richard, 47
Street, Steven, 45
Sutherland Martínez, Elizabeth "Betita," 69, 107, 108–9
See also *El Grito del Norte* newspaper
syntactic parallelism, 131

Taylor, Paul, 33, 45
Teatro Campesino, 2
temporal and linguistic ambivalence, 83–86, *84, 86*, 96–102
Tenayuca, Emma, 108
tercermundismo ("Third-Worldism"), 123
terminology. See language and language codes
testimonio, characterized, 109–10, 207n31
Tet Offensive (1968), 106

Texas Rangers (law enforcement agency), 37–38
textual phenomena, 18
"Third World Left," 122
Third-World Liberation Front, 122
Tierra Amarilla, New Mexico, 1, 71–74, 81
Tijerina, Reies López
1967 El Paso Conference and, 78
1967 Tierra Amarilla takeover, 1, 71–74, 81
in *El Grito del Norte*, 113, 120
influence on other activists, 108
on shifting rhetorical landscape, 68
tensions between activists, 5
on violent protest, 1–2
Tlatelolco Massacre (1968), 119
transcendence, 53–54, 159
Treaty of Guadalupe (1848), 21, 27, 28
tropes, racial, 30, 189
Trouillot, Michel-Rolph, 20
Tufte, Edward, 131

United Farm Workers (UFW), 44, 159
See also National Farm Workers Association (NFWA)
United Fruit Co., 116
United Mexican American Students (UMAS), 122
United States
aggressive stance in Viet Nam, 41
annexation of Mexican territory, 27–28
border violence, 192
imperialism, 108, 115–16, 121
opposition to military interventions, 106
See also Mexican American politics

Valdés, Juán Sebastián, 114
Valdez, Luis
Aztlan, 66, 185
on need for political revolution, 2
pictured in *Basta!*, 55, *55–57*
on race in Chican@ movement activism, 5, 43
in writing Plan de Delano, 53
Valdez, Valentina, 109
Vallejo, Jody, 34
Valley Labor Citizen, 47
Varela, Maria, 137, 138
Vasconcelos, José, 205n108
Vásquez, Genaro, 115
Vasquez, Irene, 8
Vasquez, Yermo, 91
verbal performances, 110
Viet Nam Moratorium Committee, 147

Viet Nam War
  author's approach and, 21
  contributions to Chican@ movement, 41, 120, 191–92
  disproportionate impact on Mexican Americans, 9, 106–7, 117–18
  El Plan Espiritual de Aztlán and, 124
  "I Am Joaquin" and, 96–98, 103–4
  La Raza Unida Party and, 38, 145–46
  Enriqueta Longeaux y Vasquez on, 117
  moratorium violence and, 172–73, 175–76, 176, 177, 179
  opposition to, 38, 147–48
  Tet Offensive campaign, 106
  violence and power, 101
  See also Chicano Moratorium (1970)
Vigil, Ernesto, 8
violence
  coloniality and, 31–32
  de/colonial love vs., 162–68, 163, 165–67
  in either/or choices, 87–88
  epistemic, 34–36
  extra-legal, 37–38
  of institutional whiteness, 172–77, 174, 176
  labor of, 32–34
  masking of gender-based violence, 95, 98–99
  police paranoia, 168–72, 170–71
  power and, 101
  racial classification and, 192
  racial solidarity and, 103–4, 116, 119–20
  re-presentational, 36–37
  (in)visible, 152–56
  See also non/violence
visual parallelism, 131–32, 134

Wanzer-Serrano, Darrel, 15
Ward, Lyn, 149
war language, 27–28
Western Frontier, 36
"white fragility," 169

whiteness
  alignments with, 22, 42–45, 159
  decentering of, from farmworker activism, 51
  "distribution of the sensible," 157, 190
  institutionalized through violence, 31–38
  La Raza nationalism and, 127, 136, 144
  media representations of violence and, 156
  paranoia and violence of, 168–77, 170–71, 174, 176
  political possibilities of nationalism and, 123
  as public aesthetic, 27–31, 74–75, 87
  in rhetorical studies, 6–7
  "white racial frame," 12, 26, 157, 190, 199n36
  See also race
"white racial frame," 12, 26, 157, 190, 199n36
Wilson, Thomas, 154, 158, 210n33, 211n66
Winant, Howard, 9, 10, 15–16, 91
women
  contributions to Chican@ movement(s), 108–9, 140
  de/colonial love and, 163, 164
  epistemic discrimination, 35
  in "I Am Joaquin," 95–96, 98–99, 102
  intersectional oppression, 33
  representational intersectionality and, 36
  See also gender; poetics of relationality

Ximenes, Vicente T., 74–75, 78

Yavno, Max, 45
Ybarra, Lea, 137
Young Lords Organization (YLO), 15, 122

Zapata, Emiliano, 36
Zaragosa, Jorge, 51–53, 52, 56
Zoot Suit Riots, 38

Other books in the series:

Karen Tracy, *Challenges of Ordinary Democracy: A Case Study in Deliberation and Dissent* / Volume 1

Samuel McCormick, *Letters to Power: Public Advocacy Without Public Intellectuals* / Volume 2

Christian Kock and Lisa S. Villadsen, eds., *Rhetorical Citizenship and Public Deliberation* / Volume 3

Jay P. Childers, *The Evolving Citizen: American Youth and the Changing Norms of Democratic Engagement* / Volume 4

Dave Tell, *Confessional Crises and Cultural Politics in Twentieth-Century America* / Volume 5

David Boromisza-Habashi, *Speaking Hatefully: Culture, Communication, and Political Action in Hungary* / Volume 6

Arabella Lyon, *Deliberative Acts: Democracy, Rhetoric, and Rights* / Volume 7

Lyn Carson, John Gastil, Janette Hartz-Karp, and Ron Lubensky, eds., *The Australian Citizens' Parliament and the Future of Deliberative Democracy* / Volume 8

Christa J. Olson, *Constitutive Visions: Indigeneity and Commonplaces of National Identity in Republican Ecuador* / Volume 9

Damien Smith Pfister, *Networked Media, Networked Rhetorics: Attention and Deliberation in the Early Blogosphere* / Volume 10

Katherine Elizabeth Mack, *From Apartheid to Democracy: Deliberating Truth and Reconciliation in South Africa* / Volume 11

Mary E. Stuckey, *Voting Deliberatively: FDR and the 1936 Presidential Campaign* / Volume 12

Robert Asen, *Democracy, Deliberation, and Education* / Volume 13

Shawn J. Parry-Giles and David S. Kaufer, *Memories of Lincoln and the Splintering of American Political Thought* / Volume 14

J. Michael Hogan, Jessica A. Kurr, Michael J. Bergmaier, and Jeremy D. Johnson, eds., *Speech and Debate as Civic Education* / Volume 15

Angela G. Ray and Paul Stob, eds., *Thinking Together: Lecturing, Learning, and Difference in the Long Nineteenth Century* / Volume 16

Sharon E. Jarvis and Soo-Hye Han, *Votes That Count and Voters Who Don't: How Journalists Sideline Electoral Participation (Without Even Knowing It)* / Volume 17

Belinda Stillion Southard, *How to Belong: Women's Agency in a Transnational World* / Volume 18

Melanie Loehwing, *Homeless Advocacy and the Rhetorical Construction of the Civic Home* / Volume 19

Kristy Maddux, *Practicing Citizenship: Women's Rhetoric at the 1893 Chicago World's Fair* / Volume 20

Craig Rood, *After Gun Violence: Deliberation and Memory in an Age of Political Gridlock* / Volume 21

Nathan Crick, *Dewey for a New Age of Fascism: Teaching Democratic Habits* / Volume 22

William Keith and Robert Danisch, *Beyond Civility: The Competing Obligations of Citizenship* / Volume 23

Lisa A. Flores, *Deportable and Disposable: Public Rhetoric and the Making of the "Illegal" Immigrant* / Volume 24

Adriana Angel, Michael L. Butterworth, and Nancy R. Gómez, eds., *Rhetorics of Democracy in the Americas* / Volume 25

Robert Asen, *School Choice and the Betrayal of Democracy: How Market-Based Education Reform Fails Our Communities* / Volume 26

Stephanie R. Larson, *What It Feels Like: Visceral Rhetoric and the Politics of Rape Culture* / Volume 27

Billie Murray, *Combating Hate: A Framework for Direct Action* / Volume 28

David A. Frank and Franics J. Mootz III, eds., *The Rhetoric of Judging Well: The Conflicted Legacy of Justice Anthony M. Kennedy* / Volume 29

Kristian Bjørkdahl, ed., *The Problematic Public: Lippman, Dewey, and Democracy in the Twenty-First Century* / Volume 30

Ekaterina V. Haskins, *Remembering the War, Forgetting the Terror: Appeal to the Family Memories of World War II in Putin's Russia* / Volume 31

Carolyn D. Commer, *Championing a Public Good: A Call to Advocate for Higher Education* / Volume 32

Derek G. Handley, *Struggle for the City: Citizenship and Resistance in the Black Freedom Movement* / Volume 33

Milton Keynes UK
Ingram Content Group UK Ltd.
UKHW041313021224
3319UKWH00006B/90